HITLER'S NAVY

HITLER'S NAVY

A REFERENCE GUIDE TO THE KRIEGSMARINE 1935–1945

Jak P Mallmann Showell

With a section on uniforms by Gordon Williamson

Naval Institute Press

ANNAPOLIS, MARYLAND

Copyright © Jak P Mallmann Showell 2009

First published in Great Britain in 2009 by
Seaforth Publishing,
Pen & Sword Books Ltd,
47 Church Street,
Barnsley S70 2AS

Published and distributed in the
United States of America and Canada by the
Naval Institute Press,
291 Wood Road, Annapolis,
Maryland 21402-5034

Library of Congress Control Number: 2008943073

ISBN 978 1 59114 369 7

Printed and bound in Malaysia for Imago

TITLE PAGE The long sleek bows of a Type VIIC with jumping wire running from near the camera
to the top of the conning-tower. This served as an aerial and was also intended to help the boat
slide under nets, but very few submarines of the Second World War came into contact with such
obstructions. It could also be used for attaching personal safety harnesses.

CONTENTS

The first ships of the new generation of post-First World War destroyers were fitted with 150mm guns, but these proved to be too heavy and too slow and the idea was abandoned again long before 1939. At first the navy fell back on a smaller, 127mm, calibre, but quickly developed a double 128mm turret for destroyers. The photo shows such a turret being installed on *Z32* between 1939 and 1941 at the Deschimag AG Weser works in Bremen.

INTRODUCTION

Almost thirty years have passed since the first edition was written and now I would like to add the many people who got in touch to correct mistakes or elucidate events about which they have special knowledge. I am most grateful to everybody who has helped and many have not only provided additional information, but also become good friends.

Most of what was written some thirty years ago still applies, despite so much new material having come to light. Naval history is exciting inasmuch as both sides kept diaries, which were written the moment events unfolded and therefore it is possible to reconstruct what actually went on. The younger generations must be urged most strongly to study this material, for it shows that much of what the media bombards us with is terribly one-sided, not really true and many eyewitness accounts are figments of the imagination. I hope this book will inspire younger generations to study original papers of those events and one day write accurate accounts of our most turbulent history.

I am most grateful to Horst Bredow of the German U-boat Museum (formerly the U-boat Archive) for allowing me access to documents, books and photographs from his magnificent collection. Many of the photos for this new edition have come from the museum. I should also like to thank the staff of Bletchley Park, especially John Gallehawk, for allowing me access to their archive.

The following have kindly sent corrections, made positive suggestions, verified facts or provided encouragement during difficult times: Professor Heinfried Ahl (Pilot Officer of *Kormoran*); Margaret Bidmead (Royal Navy Submarine Museum); Jan Bos; 'Professor' Gus Britton (at one time Deputy Director of the Royal Navy Submarine Museum); Bundesarchiv in Freiburg; Commander Richard Compton-Hall (one time director of the Royal Navy Submarine Museum); Ernst-August Gerke (U-boat commander); Captain Otto Giese (officer aboard liner *Columbus*, blockade breaker *Anneliese Essberger* and U-boats); Ursula von Friedeburg; Hans-Karl Hemmer (*Pinguin* and *Adjutant*); Wolfgang Hirschfeld (Radio Operator in U-boats, author and historian); George Högel; Peter Huckstepp; Harry Hutson; Karl Keller; Wes Loney (ex RAAF pilot); Christopher Lowe; Edward McLaughlin; Ian Miller (sons and daughters of US merchant mariners); Heinrich Mueller; Dr Timothy Mulligan; Lionel Leventhal (publisher of the first edition of this book, who provided a great deal of encouragement); Edward Rumpf; Klaus Schäle (S-boats); Torsten Schwenk; Heinz Tischer (photographer aboard *Thor*); Charles Walker (British merchant seaman). Many of these people are now dead, but I am most grateful for their support and should like to apologize to those who have been missed out of this list.

Unless otherwise stated, photographs have come from the author's collection or from Deutsches U-Boot-Museum.

JAK P MALLMANN SHOWELL
Folkestone, England, April 2008

ACKNOWLEDGMENTS TO THE FIRST EDITION, 1979

Gordon Willamson has been responsible for writing the sections on ranks, uniforms, badges and flags, which he has illustrated with his own drawings. I would like to thank him for all the other help he has given me.

Special thanks must go to Kpt.z.S. a.D. Otto Köhler (U-boat Commander and later Commander of the Acoustic Torpedo School) for devoting many hours to sorting out information, verifying facts and checking the manuscript; it would have been most difficult to have completed this project without his help. Also many thanks to his wife, Erika, for putting up with the untidy piles of paper in their lovely flat and for looking after me so well while I was working with Otto in Munich.

I am most grateful to 'Ajax' Bleichrodt (U-boat Commander and Knight of the Iron Cross with Oakleaves) for talking with me about his wartime experiences; and I wish to thank his son, Dr Wolf-Heinrich Bleichrodt, for kindly helping me after Ajax's tragic death.

Heinrich Böhm (who served aboard *Admiral Graf Spee* and later became the first torpedo mechanic of *U377*) has been a most willing helper by clarifying details, providing some excellent photographs and a fair volume of new information – all of which has been greatly appreciated.

Thanks also to the Deutscher Marinebund e.V.; especially to Kurt Reimers and the staff of *U995* for making it possible for me to have two special tours of the boat. Their explanations have been a great help. *U995* is now a museum next to the Naval Memorial at Laboe near Kiel and is well worth a visit.

Old photographs have been identified with help from Peter Cremer, Walter Lüdde-Neurath, Bernhard Rogge, Walter Richter, Professor Friedrich Ruge and Adalbert Schnee.

Jack and Hanni Fletcher, Klaus and Anneliese Mallmann, Karl and Adele Prawitt and Heidi Prawitt have helped with numerous administrative problems, which has been a tremendous help. Neville Button and Imke Showell read through the manuscript before it went to press.

I am also indebted to many people and institutions that have kindly helped me in the past. It would be difficult to mention everybody by name, but all support has been deeply appreciated, and I should like to thank everyone who has taken an interest in my project. Each of the following has made a direct contribution: Ing. Franz Albert; Rudolf Bahr; Patrick Beesly, RN; Henry Birkenbagen; Wilhelm Brauel, Bundesarchiv, Koblenz, especially Dr Haupt and his staff; Buchhändler Vereinigung, particularly Waltraut Schütte; Michael Cooper; Kpt.z.S. a.D. Hans Dehnert; Roel Diepeveen; Commodore J F van Dulm of the Royal Netherlands Navy; Trevor Dart; Admiral Kurt Freiwald; Professor Ulrich Gabler; Kpt.z.S. a.D. Helmuth Giessler; Konteradmiral Eberhard Godt; Kpt.z.S. a.D. Rolf Güth; Korvkpt. a.D. Jan Hansen-Nootbaar; Günther Heinrich; Geoffrey Jones; Fritz Köhl; Flottillenadmiral a.D. Otto Kretschmer; David Lees; Heinrich Lehmann-Willenbrock; David Littlejohn; Kpt.z.S. a.D. Hans Meckel; Peter Nops; Commander F C van Oosten of the Royal Netherlands Navy; Arthur Pitt, RN; Richard Reskey; Donald Ream; Konteradmiral Hans Rösing; Professor Dr. Jürgen Rohwer; Daniel Rose; Helmut Schmoeckel; Kpt.z.S. a.D. Herbert Schultze; Flottillenadmiral Dr. Werner Schünemann; Franz Selinger; M. R B Squires of the Imperial War Museum; Tom Stafford; Hans Staus; Frederick J Stephens; Wrekin Photo Services; Commander Craig Walter, RN; Captain J J Wichers of the Royal Netherlands Navy; and Garry York.

MAJOR ASPECTS OF GERMAN NAVAL HISTORY

THE BIRTH OF THE NAVY

Before the unification of Germany, each of the small states paid for its defence alone. Among the poorest of these states were the coastal regions, which could not afford to build fleets on the scale of the larger powers. Instead, they maintained small ships intended to combat piracy rather than fend off organized, armed aggression. Indeed, the first real German navy was not created until almost fifty years after the Battle of Trafalgar, so it is a relatively young force.

The decision to found a navy was taken at Frankfurt-am-Main in 1848 – during the war against Denmark – after the Danes had declared their intention of blockading German sea ports. This first German Navy was but a modest affair, although there were a few individual efforts of note, such as the construction of Germany's first submarine – *Brandtaucher*. Designed by Wilhelm Bauer, a Bavarian artillery warrant officer, she was launched at Kiel on 18 December 1850 – an event that caused the blockading

Danish ships to leave the bay and anchor farther out in the Baltic. But, on balance, the maritime force, or Bundesmarine (Federal Navy) achieved very little and was disbanded again in 1852. The ships were handed over to the Royal Prussian Navy – also founded in 1848 – and Germany's first great admiral, Rudolf Brommy (original spelling Bromme), who had been the driving force behind the fleet's development, was dismissed (without even a pension).

The first autonomous naval command, or admiralty, of the Royal Prussian Navy was founded during 1853. A year later it came under the command of Prince Adalbert of Prussia, who held the title 'Admiral of the Prussian Coast'. There was still no battle fleet, and the main function of the Navy was still seen as a transport vehicle for the Army. The next major change came in 1866, after Austria's withdrawal from the German Alliance and Prussia had founded the North-German Federation. This resulted in the Navy being renamed Nord-Deutsche Bundesmarine (North-German Federal Navy) during October 1867. But, although this move

The Kaiser Wilhelm Bridge in Wilhelmshaven at the beginning of the twenty-first century. Wilhelmshaven was once a bustling military harbour and the huge bollard in the foreground is a reminder that, at one time, this was the home for massive ships. The bridge, too, reminds present generations of Germany's affluence under the Kaiser. It was the biggest swing bridge in the world when it was built and it still functions today. After reparations at the end of the First World War, all the basins of this harbour looked even emptier than they do today.

Deschimag AG Weser, Germany's biggest shipyard on the river Weser in Bremen, looking forlorn and empty. Determining the exact date of this picture is difficult without local knowledge, but this gives a good impression of how shipyards looked shortly after the First World War, when the Allies had removed equipment and facilities.

After the First World War Germany lost control of the Kiel Canal, which was then administered by an International Commission. This shows the old Imperial Coat of Arms by the locks in Brunsbüttel, at the Elbe estuary side. Locks are necessary on both ends of the canal because the water in it is kept one metre higher than the normal average of the Baltic while the Brunsbüttel locks permit all-tide access into the estuary of the Elbe. This monument was erected in such a way that the Royal Eagle looks out to sea, on the left. The Eagle on the ceiling of the Grand Hall at the Naval Officers' School in Mürwik looks to the right – the wrong way – because the Kaiser felt it was important to emphasize the connection with the sea rather than face the land.

Large ships of the Kaiser's High Seas Fleet in the Wilhelmshaven Naval Base before the end of the First World War. This purpose-built, non-tidal harbour was some five kilometres long. (Measuring from the biggest locks to its far end). It had numerous basins for all manner of specialist purposes, a canal connection to Emden and some impressive innovations such as the biggest rotating bridge of the time. Despite its huge size, many ships had to moor side by side because there was not enough quay space to accommodate all who were seeking berths. This hive of activity came to a sudden end in 1918 at the end of the First World War. (WZ Bilddienst, Wilhelmshaven)

was a step in the right direction, the basic problem remained: the Federation's membership still comprised small, independent kingdoms and principalities between which there was little love lost. Indeed, the twenty-five Germanic states had a long history of conflict, not only between themselves but also with neighbouring nations.

The unification of Germany came about quite unexpectedly in 1870, after France had declared war on the largest of these Germanic kingdoms, Prussia. The French hoped that the Catholic princes in the south would help them suppress the Protestant economic development in the north. But this did not happen. Surprisingly, Bavaria, Baden and Württemberg took up arms in support of Prussia, and soon the three armies were heading west, singing as one 'Lieb Vaterland magst ruhig sein, fest und treu steht die Wacht am Rhein' ('Dear fatherland, be peaceful, the guard is standing firm and faithful at the Rhine'). They did not stop at the Rhine, but fought their way to Paris, surrounded the city and crushed all opposition.

The dramatic success of this campaign created a deep feeling of unity among the German people, with even the Catholics of the south calling for King Wilhelm I of Prussia to become emperor of all the German states. For the first time

in Germany's history the majority of those who held the reins of government wanted a united nation. Their wish was granted on 18 January 1871, when the German Empire was born in the Galerie des Glaces in Versailles. The Navy was then appropriately renamed Kaiserliche Marine (Imperial Navy).

The creation of a unified Germany sparked off a chain reaction of reforms, and developments in science and technology were especially rapid. The accession in 1888 of Kaiser Wilhelm II, who had a special interest in ships, brought about a new approach to the Navy. During his reign, it graduated from being a mediocre collection of coastal craft to a powerful battle fleet capable of challenging that of any other nation. The fleet was constructed along the same lines as the British Navy, with powerfully-armed battleships forming the backbone of the force. One of the basic problems of this set-up was that officers and men were trained to come to terms with the rapid technological developments, without too much thought going into how best the monstrous weapons might be used. It was this sort of thing that prompted Grand Admiral Alfred von Tirpitz – the architect of the German Navy – to make the justifiable comment: 'Germany does not understand the sea.'

KAISERLICHE MARINE, REICHSMARINE AND KRIEGSMARINE

Battleships, the Kaiser's greatest symbols of power, played no decisive role in the First World War. Instead, the main burden of the fighting was carried by torpedo-boats, minesweepers, submarines and similar vessels – many of which were developed and built under harsh war conditions. Most of the hard fighting was conducted by young men, not by the admirals, and the fact that many of these sailors were at odds with their High Command was made quite clear by a breakdown of discipline, especially in the larger units. The peak of human obedience to authority had been reached during the early part of the war, when thousands of men, on both sides, faced certain death without questioning the orders of their superiors. But as the war drew to a close, attitudes in the German armed forces changed to such a degree that, rather than face more futile bloodbaths, many men preferred to mutiny.

The Navy found itself in a strange situation after the war, for it had not really suffered a great defeat, but neither had it scored any decisive victory. In addition, many of the ships were still afloat and in fighting condition, although by the terms of the Treaty of Versailles these had to be handed over to the Allies. Despite the ill-feeling against authority, several young officers found this clause humiliating, and wanted to sail into the British surrender ports with guns ablaze and fight to the death. However, this extreme element must have been a small minority, for the Fleet entered the Royal Navy anchorage at Scapa Flow peacefully. It was not until later, while lying at anchor in deep water, that the war flags fluttered once more from the mast heads – an indication that the ships were being scuttled and were on their way to the sea bed. German morale may have been at an extremely low ebb, but the Imperial Navy's old tradition of sinking one's ship before surrendering it was still alive. So, with nearly all ships lost, 1919 saw the end of the Kaiser's Navy. Those not sunk at Scapa Flow were either sunk elsewhere or handed over to the Allies, and the few remaining in German hands were already obsolete.

The foundation day of the new Navy (Reichsmarine) is considered to be 1 January 1921, for by that time Germany had reduced her strength sufficiently to meet the requirements of the peace treaty. The Kaiser's flag was officially hauled down for the last time on 31 December 1921 – some two years after the end of the war. However, new laws relating to the Navy were not finalized until later. The new Reichsmarine flag was hoisted for the first time on 11 April 1921. It consisted of black, white and red horizontal stripes with a large iron cross in the middle, and had a small canton of black, red and gold horizontal stripes in the top left-hand corner. (Later, on 14 March 1933, the canton was removed by order of President Paul von Hindenburg – shortly after Hitler's elevation to chancellor. Unfortunately, this useful aid for determining dates of photographs was rather small; occupying only a minute part of the upper black stripe, and it is often not distinguishable.) The Reichsmarine was renamed Kriegsmarine on 21 May 1935, its new identity being underlined five months later, on 9 November, by the introduction of a new flag bearing a large swastika. This flag was used until it was finally torn down in May 1945.

The old imperial flag was used to commission at least one ship in the war years. During *M18*'s commissioning ceremony, a rolled up flag bearing the printed name 'war flag' was attached to the flag staff. The commander then gave the order to hoist the flag, whereupon the royal eagle and cross unfurled itself to flutter in the light breeze! After the initial panic had died down, a correct flag was hurriedly found and the ceremony continued. Luckily, *M18* had sufficient drinks on board to help make the press and publicity men forget the incident, but the German High Command did eventually learn of the slip-up when it was reported, in depth, by a Swedish newspaper.

A prefix, like HMS, was also used for ships during the emperor's time: SMS for Seine Majestäts Schiff. In later years, warships were distinguished from merchant vessels by the words Reichsmarine Schiff or Kriegsmarine Schiff. However, the abbreviations RMS and KMS were rarely, if ever, used by the Navy. In the Kriegsmarine it was far more common to prefix warships with their class, for example: Panzerschiff *Deutschland*, Schlachtschiff *Tirpitz* or Torpedo-boot *Möwe*.

THE TREATY OF VERSAILLES

The end of the First World War and the imposition of harsh peace terms forced drastic changes upon the German Navy; perhaps hardest of all was coming to terms with the Treaty of Versailles, the conditions of which were dictated by the Allies. It was a hefty political document with far-reaching effects on the German economy and armed forces. The Navy was affected as follows:

1. a. National conscription had to be abolished.
   b. The armed forces were restricted to volunteers. The Navy was to be restricted to a total of 15,000 men, including 1,500 officers. This figure included crews for

In 1918 Germany lost more than the war and its head of state; it was also left floundering without an identity. The coat of arms and standards that had represented the young country for less than fifty years suddenly turned sour and something new had to be devised. This was not easy because Germany was without a depth of tradition or longstanding institutions. The old Imperial Standard on the right was replaced by a new one representing the Weimar Republic. The main colours (black on the top, white and red) were taken over by the new Republic and a small canton with a black, red and yellow stripe was added to the top left corner. These colours go back further than the Kaiser, to when a small band of soldiers, wearing black uniforms with red edging and golden buttons resisted Napoleon's onslaught through Europe. Despite being old, safe colours, without modern political connections, they did not last long and the canton was removed around the time Hitler came to power, as can be seen on the second flag from the left. The trouble with these new standards was that they also represented defeat and the dishonour associated with the Treaty of Versailles. So the majority of people were pleased when the National Socialists introduced a new flag in 1935; one with a swastika, an ancient symbol representing eternity and success. It gave Germany a new national identity.

These photos were taken at the beginning of the twentieth century at Howaldtswerke in Kiel. They show one of the world's leading shipyards when it was at the cutting edge of technological development. (Photos: HDW, Kiel)

all ships, coastal defence forces and staff for shore stations.

c. There was to be no naval reserve force.

d. Volunteers had to sign on for at least twenty-five years in the case of officers and twelve years for other ranks.

e. Personnel leaving the Navy were not permitted to serve in any capacity in any armed force. Those remaining had to commit themselves to serve until the age of forty-five.

f. Members of the merchant navy were not allowed to receive military training.

2. a. The number of ships had to be limited to:
6 Battleships plus 2 in reserve
6 Cruisers plus 2 in reserve
12 Destroyers plus 4 in reserve
12 Torpedo-boats plus 4 in reserve
Additional small craft were also limited.

b. Germany was not permitted to build or own submarines (including merchant submarines), aircraft carriers, heavy artillery or military aircraft.

3. Displacements of replacement ships were limited to:

Battleships	10,000 tons
Small cruisers	6,000 tons
Destroyers	800 tons
Torpedo-boats	200 tons

Ships sunk or destroyed could be replaced, but otherwise, ships had to be between fifteen and twenty years old before a new ship could be built as a replacement. (Neither was Germany permitted to sell a fairly new warship and then build another in its place.) All armament was limited and determined by the Allies.

4. Germany had to maintain ships for clearing mines.

5. All German warships not in German ports ceased to belong to Germany and all rights to them had to be renounced.

6. a. No fortifications could be erected near the Baltic shipping lanes. Existing defence installations had to be

The situation for the average German citizen was dire immediately after the First World War. People were not only faced with rapidly escalating inflation, but also a shortage of almost everything, with many living on starvation diets. Here people search through cinders from factory slag heaps, hoping to find some partly unburned coal.

Weapons after the First World War had to be scrapped, and the mountains of waste grew quickly, the Allies ensuring that weapons were rendered useless and that war reparations were paid.

removed. All information about these fortifications, including hydrographic details, had to be made available to the Allies.

b. All fortifications and naval installations (except Heligoland) within 50km (approximately 30 miles) of the German coast or from the German islands were allowed to remain in their end-of-war condition. New fortifications were not permitted within that zone. Armament, both total number of guns and calibre, could not be increased from their 1918 state.

7. The German government had to hand over documents and information to the Allied Naval Control Commission. These included plans, specifications and other details of armaments and of radio communication equipment.

8. Germany had to agree that Germany and her Allies were responsible for all war losses and all war damage.

The main aim of the Treaty was to limit the power of the German nation, whose meagre obsolete fleet was only permitted to meet a possible attack from the East, where the revolution in Russia was still showing signs of political unrest. But, whilst the Treaty severely limited the material aspects, it was a complete failure on the psychological side. Indeed, these harsh terms sowed the seeds of their own undoing, and were a major factor in the events that led to the Second World War. The German Emperor was forced to abdicate, leaving his position of Head of State free for anyone to climb into. And the Treaty of Versailles provided the National Socialists with the ideal ladder. The hatred for authority shown by

German soldiers at the end of the war, the general unrest and the strikes were quickly given direction. Both the Allies and the German government became objects at which the masses could vent their anger and frustration; the former were loathed as suppressors, while the latter were despised for agreeing to the terms of the Treaty.

The sailors' main grudges were not against the material impositions, but the order to hand over the Fleet to the Allied navies, not being permitted a free German defence constitution, and having national defence controlled by an international commission. The majority also disagreed with the clause whereby German soldiers had to face Allied military tribunals; and there was total rejection of the clause by which the men had to consider themselves guilty of all war damage. The Navy did not, as the Allies might have expected, sit down on its wilted laurels and devote the following years to polishing the remains of the Fleet. Germans work well under pressure, and the Treaty of Versailles presented a suitable stimulus to get together and work hard.

Selection for the German Navy was rigorous, with only the best men from the old Imperial Navy accepted. In the 1920s there were thirty to forty applicants for every post, so it was possible to pick and choose. Only candidates with the highest qualifications were admitted to the ranks, making the Navy into an elite fighting force and a special school for warrant officers was established near Kiel. This pool of concentrated talent was put to work finding ways around the restrictions imposed by the Treaty, and a very great deal was achieved. For example, submarines were not permitted, so in 1922 a 'Submarine Development Bureau' – employing the cream of German submarine designers – was set up in Holland, where it concealed its true purpose by posing as an ordinary Dutch shipbuilding firm. Although guns were limited in size, the problem was neatly side-stepped with the perfection of quick-firing guns and the development of rockets. Radar was invented as a radio direction-finder, in order to make heavy artillery more effective. Germany had working radar sets before Britain started work on the project, yet the idea was never developed to its full potential. As battleships were restricted to 10,000 tons, it was probably expected that Germany would build smaller dreadnoughts, but she went one better and developed the pocket battleship – a new concept in naval warfare. The first product of this idea, Panzerschiff *Deutschland*, was much admired by foreign navies, with some naval commentators heralding her as the warship of the future.

So, step by step, the small naval force of the Reichsmarine slowly and unobtrusively made its limited power much more effective. And some measure of its success can be gauged if one considers that this modestly-sized navy, often with only a handful of operational units in the Atlantic per month, was to keep the world's most powerful fleet on the defensive for some four years. Apart from enjoying a numerical advantage, the British were also in the enviable position of being able to decipher a fair proportion of German secret radio signals. Add to this the support they received from the rapidly expanding United States Navy, and one can see that the small German navy's efforts were no mean achievements.

The Naval Officers' School – the Red Palace by the Sea – at Mürwik (Eckernförde) as seen from the water's edge. This impressive building was opened just a few years before the beginning of the First World War because the Naval Academy in Kiel, now occupied by administration for Schleswig-Holstein, could be expanded no further.

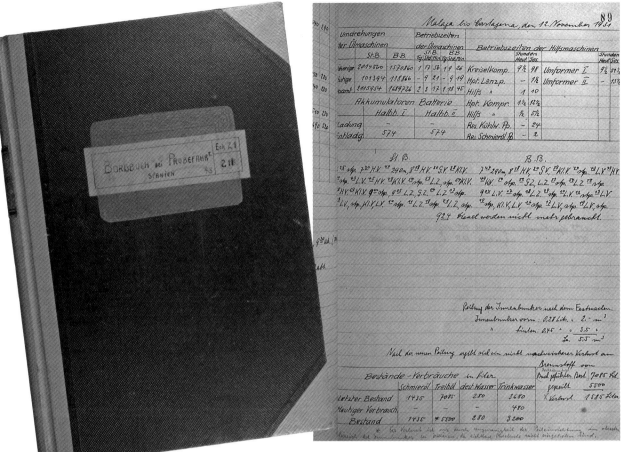

This is the log book for one of the first U-boats built by German staff in Spain and is now in the German Submarine Museum; it is a significant document. The sample page shows an entry for 12 November 1931. Trying to understand the code in this log is not easy, but it is a record from the dawn of modern submarine development.

THE WASHINGTON NAVAL TREATY

There was very little naval development of significance in Germany during the 1920s. However, meetings of the major maritime powers, on 12 August 1921 and during the following winter, saw the formation of a new international treaty, which indirectly affected the German Navy. This Washington Treaty, signed on 6 February 1922, limited armaments at sea. It was agreed that battleships should have their guns restricted to 16 inch calibre and that cruisers should be no larger than 10,000 tons with 8 inch guns.

The tonnage under this treaty was measured with the United States ton, which is slightly smaller than the British or Imperial ton, used in the Treaty of Versailles. (A British or long ton is equal to 2240 pounds and the US or short ton 2000 pounds.) In Germany, people became quite enthusiastic about these developments because they saw the possibility of sidestepping the restrictions of their peace treaty and make their new ships slightly bigger than anything other nations were likely to build. Although the limitations of Versailles meant that battleships with 16in guns were completely out of the question, the cruiser figures were very interesting: the international limitation on the displacement of cruisers coincided with the maximum tonnage laid down for German battleships. So the German designers came up with the idea of building a ship that would be too fast for any enemy battleship and much superior to a cruiser. This concept, the so-called 'pocket battleship', was by no means easy to develop, One of the biggest problems was that of propulsion and, in the end, it was decided to use powerful diesel engines. It was essential to test the design before it was installed in a

Germany's secret submarine development bureau was based in Holland under the name inscribed on this cover. The strange thing is that the records in the folder are in French, not German nor Dutch.

Generalfeldmarschall Paul von Hindenburg visiting the Navy some time before the National Socialists came to power. Born in Posen in 1847, he was elected as Reichspresident in 1932, and in 1933, he appointed Hitler as Chancellor. On the left, wearing the uniform of a Vice Admiral, is Erich Raeder who became Supreme Commander-in-Chief of the Navy.

repudiated the Treaty of Versailles and re-introduced national conscription on 16 March 1935. The words he used, however, were not his own. Parts of this famous speech were word for word those of one written seven years earlier by Defence Minister Groener – Hitler appears to have been the first front line politician prepared to stand up and present it. He certainly expected some repercussions from the Allies, but they were too busy with their own internal affairs and took no notice. It is curious that the Versailles Treaty, which was meant to effectively clip the wings of German power, was allowed to be thrown out by the very people it was designed to control. So, with no trouble at all, Hitler was left free to lay the foundation stone of his mighty war machine. At the same time, he made every effort to maintain good relations with Britain, partly because he expected her to present the biggest problems should difficulties arise. This consideration led to the next major milestone in the development of the German Navy: The Anglo-German Naval Agreement, which was signed on 18 June 1935 by Sir Samuel Hoare for Britain and by Special Envoy Joachim Ribbentrop for Germany. With this agreement, Hitler hoped to show that he had no desire to conduct a war against Britain. Germany volunteered to restrict her naval strength to thirty-five per cent of the Royal Navy; however, submarines were considered as a sepa-

major warship, so the prototypes were eventually fitted into the artillery training ship *Bremse*, which was launched in January 1931. The first pocket battleship, Panzerschiff *Deutschland*, splashed into the water on 19 May 1931 and was completed two years later, to be commissioned on 1 April 1933. Her powerful diesel engines gave her a top speed of 26 knots, a range of 10,000 nautical miles, and she carried six 11 inch guns. The designers cheated with her displacement figures, making her a little heavier than she should have been: when empty she displaced 11,700 tons and when fully loaded almost 16,000. Her high top speed enabled her to run away from an enemy battleship; but she could blast a cruiser out of the water from outside the range of the cruiser's guns. It has been suggested that the development of this ship pointed clearly to future merchant raiding but this is far from the mark. It was very much the case of the new ship propulsion systems making merchant raiding a viable proposition. Incidentally, although marine diesel engines have strong roots in Germany, the first diesel-propelled, ocean-going merchant ship, MS *Selandia*, was launched by Burmeister and Wain of Copenhagen (Denmark) before the First World War, in November 1911.

HITLER AND THE ANGLO-GERMAN NAVAL AGREEMENT

In the early 1930s, the naval leadership was still labouring under extreme difficulties and could not finance all the schemes it would have liked. Many of their clandestine projects were paid for by overcharging on permitted developments and then filtering off the excess to pay for the illicit plans. The first real boost came after Hitler had been appointed chancellor, for he was not only in favour of rearmament, but strongly encouraged it.

Adolf Hitler made his famous proclamation in which he

rate case, and a forty-five per cent ratio was agreed. Parity in submarines was also agreed in principle, but in that event Germany would have to sacrifice tonnage in other categories, and Britain would have to approve the move.

Although the political intrigues and manoeuvrings that took place at this time are beyond the scope of this book, a few observations should be made. There were several reasons for Britain's apparent capitulation to German demands. For various domestic reasons, the British government of the day was not prepared to take a hawkish stance, and the Admiralty were convinced that the British fleet would not be strong enough to take on both Japan and the foremost European naval power simultaneously. Therefore, until terms with Japan could be agreed, they were keen to reach an agreement with Germany that would preclude the possibility of another arms race. Reactions to the agreement were like signs of relief. Earl Beatty, the British Fleet Commander during the latter part of the First World War stated that Britain had at least one country with which they need not conduct an armaments race. And Hitler told Admiral Erich Raeder, Commander-in-Chief of the German Navy, the day the agreement was signed was the happiest of his life – quite understandably, since he had thrown out the Versailles Treaty and had now received international approval for doing so!

LEFT Minesweepers were permitted under treaty provisions, and many of the older, smaller ships were converted to burn oil rather than coal. At the beginning of the Second World War, however, they were converted back again because the valuable oil was more difficult to obtain than home-produced coal. The smoke issuing forth from this flotilla suggests the boats were running on poor-quality coal.

ABOVE Torpedo boat 158 was built in Stettin before 1909 and remained as a unit of the German Navy until the end of the Second World War, to be broken up as late as 1950. This shows the starboard view flying the flag with swastika, which suggests it was taken after 1935. These solid workhorses served along the European coasts under the severest of conditions.

BELOW The battleship Elsass, launched at F. Schichau in Danzig in 1903 and broken up in 1936. After the First World War it served as training ship and, as can be seen here, as an ice breaker. Although slow and with a limited range of just over 5000 nautical miles at ten knots, these were seaworthy vessels. The flag flying at the stern is the old one from the Weimar Republic with the canton in the top left-hand corner.

Raeder himself told his officers they could not have hoped for better conditions for the coming decade. He went on to say that the agreement ruled out the possibility of Germany having to fight another war against Britain. Later, he prohibited any theoretical studies of a conflict with Britain. And the next set of routine battle orders circulated by the High Command on 27 May 1936 made no mention of Britain – France and Russia were considered as potential enemies.

The Anglo-German Naval Agreement permitted Germany to build and own previously prohibited ship groups, such as submarines and aircraft carriers. The first aircraft carrier, Hull 'A' (*Graf Zeppelin*), was launched on 8 December 1938, but never completed. Hull 'B' was laid down at Germania Works in Kiel and later scrapped at an early stage of construction. The third one, not due to be launched until about 1940, was never started.

THE NAVAL AIR ARM

In 1935, aircraft – also prohibited under the Versailles Treaty – were no longer considered to be auxiliary weapons, but fully integrated tools for naval warfare. Thoughts of engaging aeroplanes had been in the minds of the higher commanders since the First World War, and plans for building a naval air arm were considered long before 1935. A 'private' flying club, with aeroplanes capable of landing on water, had been in existence for some years before Germany was permitted to own military aircraft.

The Naval Air Arm, Luftkreis IV, which was later renamed Luftwaffenkommando See, was founded by the Luftwaffe to work in cooperation with the Navy for coastal defence. In the event of a war, one of its branches, the Marineluftstreitkräfte (later Seeluftstreitkräfte), under the command of Generalmajor Geissler (Führer der Marineluftstreitkräfte or FdL) was to come under the direct command of the Fleet Commander.

ABOVE The creation of a naval air arm was high on the list of priorities for the Reichsmarine, despite the Treaty of Versailles prohibiting Germany from building or owning military aircraft. Plans were made to leave space on the bigger warships for the installation of catapults. However, at the same time as Hitler repudiated the Treaty of Versailles, Göring (later Supreme Commander-in-Chief of the Luftwaffe), declared that everything that flew came under his control. So the Navy was stifled in the developing of the aircraft it needed, though a certain amount of research did go ahead. One major problem was to find ways of launching aircraft and this was one field where civilian authorities were just as much involved as the Navy. An airmail service to South America was in operation long before the start of the war and this long flight involved a mid-ocean refuelling stop, where aircraft landed next to a depot ship, were hauled on board and re-launched with a catapult. This photograph depicts a single-engine Heinkel He 60, which was used as a general-purpose reconnaissance plane with a range of just over 400 miles.

RIGHT Landing aircraft on water can be relatively simple as long as it is calm, but the majority of warships operated out at sea. At first ships dragged a huge, heavy rubber mat while moving at a fair speed to help flatten waves, then an area of calm water inside the 'U', created if a ship turns in a tight circle at speed, was employed. This two-engined Heinkel He 59 was used for training and general reconnaissance, but it was adaptable enough to fly during the Spanish Civil War as a bomber and all-purpose dogsbody. It had a crew of four and carried a radio direction finder, the circular aerial which is just visible on the body between the engine and the '60'.

It was considered important to have good naval minds commanding aircraft at sea, so personnel were selected exclusively from the Navy. The training was rigorous, and only a fraction of the men who embarked upon it were accepted for flying duties. The majority returned to ship-based work. In 1935 it was planned to create some 25 squadrons with a grand total of about 300 aircraft.

These squadrons were planned to be equipped with various types of aircraft:

a. Land-based aircraft – long-range, short-range, multi-purpose and fighters.
b. Carrier-based: fighters, dive-bombers and general purpose aircraft.
c. Ship-based reconnaissance aircraft.

The Luftwaffe became more interested in ships, docks and other naval targets as time progressed, and a true naval air arm never materialized. Hermann Göring, Commander-in-Chief of the Luftwaffe and, early on in the war, a close friend of Adolf Hitler, always maintained 'Everything which flies belongs to me!' Nevertheless, small naval air groups did exist, but there were too few in number to have any significant impact on the overall war picture.

SUBMARINES

Germany was able to build submarines much faster than cruisers because she had kept abreast of modern technological trends through her 'Development Bureau' in Holland. This 'private' enterprise had built several submarines for foreign countries, whose new vessels were taken on long sea

After 1935, when Germany was allowed to build military aircraft again, a number of strange objects were seen in the skies, many of them in out-of-the-way locations. This gyrocopter was photographed during a naval week in Kiel. Helicopters also featured in the naval armoury because the Navy desperately wanted something capable of hovering. The reason for this was that airships played a major role during the First World War in locating mines and the Navy was keen on finding a vehicle that could move slowly to search the sea lanes for obstructions such as newly moored mines. However, despite the urgency, only a few helicopters flew before the end of the Second World War.

In the end, the Arado Ar 95 was given priority over the earlier Heinkel models and it was this type that saw much of the service onboard German warships during the Second World War. This type was almost 60mph faster than the Heinkel, while its range was only marginally less. In addition, it could reach altitudes of 26,000 feet, which was almost 10,000 feet higher. The crew would have had problems breathing at that altitude unless oxygen was carried.

After the First World War, permanent, land-based command centres were phased out and flotillas were supplied with a tender or mother ship. The Royal Navy went one better by providing such vessels with workshop facilities for carrying out repairs as well, but this was not done in Germany, where the surface ship acted only as floating headquarters. This shows the depot ship *Donau* with the 1st U-boat Flotilla. The boats were small, Type IIB coastal versions numbered from *U7* upwards. The Type IIA boats, from *U1* to *U6* went to the Submarine School Flotilla, which came under the jurisdiction of the Torpedo Inspectorate, not the U-boat Commander.

trials by German submarine experts before being handed over. So, by 1935, Germany not only had the technology to construct modern submarines, but the necessary core of trained men to operate them. Despite this technological development many of the characteristics of the U-boats were quite primitive and the boats that emerged after 1935 were lacking even the basic essentials. Among other things, there were no efficient ventilation systems, no food storage facilities and no adequate lavatories.

Several submarines had been partly constructed during 1934, put into a top secret store in Kiel, and were only waiting to be assembled. This advanced state of readiness enabled the first new submarine, *U1*, to be launched two days before the signing of the Anglo-German Naval Agreement. *U1* was commissioned a fortnight later, after which she joined the submarine school's flotilla. Her commander was Kptlt. Klaus Ewerth. The first new 'Front' (operational) U-boat, *U7*, was commanded by Kptlt. Kurt Freiwald and commissioned on 8 August. All operational submarines were grouped together in one flotilla – named 'Weddigen', after the First World War submarine hero – and were commanded by Kapitän zur See Karl Dönitz.

Dönitz has often been described as a 'successful First World War U-boat commander', which is most misleading since he had many strings to his bow and was successful at most jobs he tackled. Destiny must have given him a glimpse

Hitler chose Karl Dönitz as Raeder's successor. Raeder's predecessors (Admirals Paul Behnke and Hans Zenker) had been in office for about four years each and Raeder had served for some fourteen years by the time he resigned in January 1943, but he did not have a strong deputy who could easily step into his position. Dönitz was hardly acquainted with the intricacies of the Supreme Naval Command and lacked experience for taking on such a demanding job. The photo shows Dönitz as Rear Admiral, shortly after having been awarded the Knight's Cross, which can be seen around his neck.

Karl Dönitz wearing the uniform of a Vice Admiral presenting an award. Dönitz was the type who led from the front and made a point of meeting as many in-coming U-boats as possible. Being with his men was of utmost importance to him and he had an excellent memory for people. When interviewing ex-U-boat men the author has listened to criticism of Dönitz's command, but never heard anyone question his loyalty to his men and leadership qualities.

The light cruiser *Emden*, the first cruiser built after the First World War, in the third sea lock in Wilhelmshaven. These led from the tidal waters of the North Sea into Germany's largest non-tidal military harbour. One of the main reasons for building this ship in the naval dockyard was to test whether the infrastructure was capable of tackling such a complicated task. The armament of single gun turrets indicated that performance was not high on the list of priorities. The ensign, flying at the stern, has the small canton in the upper right-hand corner, so this picture was taken shortly after commissioning. The pair of locks in this picture were the biggest at the time when this photo was taken, but another set was added later to accommodate large battleships. The small locks have now been walled up and only the big ones remain.

The band practising on *Emden*'s forecastle. Behind them is the single gun turret while a large range finder is just visible above the small bridge.

Emden was used mainly as a training ship and for many flag-waving voyages to distant waters. There was plenty for new recruits to learn such as how to roll hammocks correctly. The Navy had rules and regulations for everything and storing hammocks was no exception. Here a group of new recruits are having their handiwork inspected before the hammocks are stowed away for the day. Space was always at a premium, even in the bigger ships, where many men lived, ate, slept and worked all together. Men who slept in hammocks said that they provided more comfort in a storm than a fixed bed.

of what his future held, for he was given the nickname 'diva' (meaning star or prima donna) by his fellow cadets at training school. By 1935 Dönitz had spent most of his 25 years' service in the surface Navy – his experience as a submariner only amounting to two and a half years. So, on that score, there were certainly many others better qualified for the position of Flag Officer for Submarines. When asked after the war why Dönitz had been chosen Grand Admiral Raeder replied that there had been no prime reason, but, looking back, he was convinced he had done the right thing.

At first Raeder had thought Hitler would be unsuccessful with the Anglo-German Naval Agreement, and therefore made no plans to develop a special submarine arm. In 1934, when Germany started to think seriously about building underwater craft, Raeder thought the Navy might be permitted a handful of submarines, but these would be attached to some existing unit. Then, out of the blue, he was faced with the prospect of creating an autonomous submarine arm, for which there was no obvious leader. It was at about this time that Karl Dönitz – who was returning from a successful tour 'showing the flag' in the Far East aboard the light cruiser *Emden* – sailed into the reckoning. This small, energetic commander had served in submarines, albeit briefly, and had twice before successfully commissioned brand new units: first, the 4. Torpedoboots Halbflottille, and secondly *Emden* – which had been de-commissioned for a lengthy refit and then re-commissioned with a new crew.

That Dönitz's appointment as Flag Officer for Submarines was a hasty and temporary move on Raeder's part is indicated by several factors. First, before docking at Wilhelmshaven at the end of her tour of the Far East, *Emden* had called in at Vigo, where the German naval representative had given Dönitz several documents including orders from

Although not allowed to build or own U-boats, it is now well known that Germany kept abreast of rapidly changing submarine development by maintaining technical bureaux in foreign countries. One aspect of the work involved the design of the internal layout and this photograph shows a life-size wooden model of a submarine, built before the prototype of a new design was laid down. It gave the designers an ideal opportunity to correct any mistakes that might not have been noticed on paper plans.

Hitler with his SS Adjutant aboard the battleship *Gneisenau*. Many of the naval officers who met him were impressed by his deep knowledge of naval matters.

the Supreme Naval Command instructing him to go ahead with plans for another cruise to the Far East in the autumn. So Raeder had not yet made his decision, although it was only a short time after this that *Emden* reached Wilhelmshaven and Dönitz was informed of his new post. Secondly, in 1936 it was planned that Dönitz would return to cruisers as a flotilla commander and take a squadron on a world tour. As a result, his successor, Hans-Georg von Friedeburg, was appointed a few years later in the autumn of 1938 to start the necessary training. But the war came too soon, and it was decided to keep Dönitz as head of U-boats and give von Friedeburg command of the large and complex Organisation Department.

SURFACE SHIPS

After the Anglo-German Naval Agreement, there was no similar expansion in the construction of surface ships as there had been in the field of submarines. Germany still had several design problems to overcome, the largest of which was, without doubt, the propulsion question. One school of thought argued for diesel engines, used in the pocket battle-

The launch of battleship *Gneisenau* at Deutsche Werke in Kiel on 8 December 1936. The hull on the extreme left is what was to become the heavy cruiser *Prinz Eugen*. The aircraft carrier *Graf Zeppelin* was built by the same yard, but, when comparing this with other photographs in this book, the reader will notice that both *Gneisenau* and *Graf Zeppelin* were launched from a 'right-hand' slip, facing the water. So, the other ship in this picture (on a left-hand slip) must be *Prinz Eugen*.

ships, and the other was favour of superheated high-pressure steam turbines. In the end, the German Navy decided to use the latter in battleships and heavy cruisers – a move considered by many to have been 'the' catastrophe in battleship construction. The main disadvantage with superheated high-pressure steam turbines was their limited range. Pocket battleships could be employed in the South Atlantic or even in the Indian Ocean, but the large battleships could only operate in the North Atlantic near their German bases. However, at that time there were no great thoughts about conducting a battleship war in the Atlantic. Equally out of the question was a blockade of either French or British ports by German surface ships. The prime function of battleships was considered to be the prevention of a blockade of German ports by enemy warships. So their limited range was not thought to be critical, as they would only be required to operate at relatively short distance from home.

The construction programme of June 1936, therefore, only met the requirements for the immediate future, and there were no plans to build up to the limits of the Anglo-German Naval Agreement. The following proposed launching dates were circulated to departments of the Supreme Naval Command during June 1936:

Dec 1937	Pocket battleship 'E'
June 1938	Pocket battleship 'D'
July 1938	Cruiser 'H'
Sept 1938	Cruiser 'G'
April 1939	Aircraft carrier 'A'
May 1939	Cruiser 'I'
Nov 1939	Aircraft carrier 'B'
Dec 1939	Cruiser 'K'
March 1940	Pocket battleship 'F'
April 1940	Pocket battleship 'G'
End of 1940	Cruiser 'L'
May 1941	Pocket battleship 'H'
Dec 1936 to Oct 1938	Destroyers *Z1* to *Z22*
Aug 1936 to May 1938	U-boats *U21* to *U44*
Nov 1937 to Feb 1938	Torpedo-boats *1* to *8*
Aug 1938 to Dec 1939	Minesweepers *1* to *9*
Oct 1936 to Jan 1937	Fleet Escorts *F7* to *F10*
Oct 1937 to the end of that year at the earliest	Submarine escorts *1* and *2*

PLAN 'Z'

Thus far, construction plans had been conceived in an atmosphere of 'no war with Britain'. Raeder informed Hitler on several occasions that Germany's naval development was not sufficient to cope with a war against a major sea power, but each time the Führer replied by saying there would be no war against Britain because such an act would signal the end of the Reich. Not until early 1938 did Hitler tell Raeder that the Kriegsmarine might have to consider meeting the Royal Navy on a war footing. Even then, he stressed that it would not be before 1948 at the earliest.

By 1937, warship development had progressed sufficiently for the first long-term planning policy to be effected. The plan was intended to remain in force for the years from 1938 until 1948, and would see the fleet develop to the lim-

its of the Anglo-German Naval Agreement. All the original demands and suggestions for new warships were evaluated by Kpt.z.S. Werner Fuchs, and put down on paper as Plan 'X'. (X being the 'unknown' from algebraic equations.) This was an immense document and could not be considered under the terms of the Naval Agreement, so he modified the details and reduced the plan to a practical size. His tailored version was designated as 'Plan Y' and was laid before the Supreme Naval Command, who modified the ideas still further. The final version then became known as 'Plan Z'. It has been suggested that the 'Z' stood for 'Ziel' or 'goal' but the sequence simply progressed from the letter 'X' – often used for an unknown quantity in algebra – and just happened to end with 'Z'.)

Plan 'Z' had been conceived under the ideal of 'no war with Britain', but matters had to be reconsidered after Hitler

The three-gun 'Hitler Turret' on the bows of pocket battleship *Deutschland*, with the black, white and red stripes as national identification mark during the Spanish Civil War. This picture may show the dramatic moment shortly after the *Deutschland* was attacked by Republican aircraft on 29 May 1937, which killed a number of her crew. Although these 11-inch (280mm) guns were more powerful than in any comparable enemy cruiser, they had the disadvantage of being mounted in a single turret, preventing the division of the main armament when confronted with two targets.

told Raeder that there were voices in Britain who were clamouring for another war and Germany might have to fight the Royal Navy after all. However, there were no alternative options and plans went ahead the way they had been formulated.

When the 'Z' Plan was being formulated, there were two distinct opinions on naval warfare in the German Navy. One idea, which received the backing of the Supreme Naval Command, was to build a powerful surface fleet consisting of mainly battleships and cruisers. The other idea was to

develop a navy centred on submarines and small craft such as torpedo-boats.

Plan 'Z' was strongly opposed by Kpt.z.S. Karl Dönitz, who could only muster a long list of foul adjectives to describe the decision. Another opponent of Plan 'Z' was Fregkpt. Hellmuth Heye who, acting on an instruction from Raeder, produced a thesis on the subject of war with Britain. He concluded that it would not be possible to defeat Britain by pitting German battleships against her merchant shipping. But it appears that nobody took much notice of Heye during

Kiel with Germaniawerft towards the right. This site is now occupied by a new Scandinavian ferry terminal. The railway lines, running through the cobblestones on the left, have vanished and this area is now ruled by pedestrians and cars. The glass hangars, visible on the right, were built before the First World War for constructing new generations of surface ships, but necessity dictated that the slips should be used mainly for the production of U-boats.

Plan 'Z' – ship construction for 1938–1948

Type of ship	Total number to be built by 1948	Ultimate total to be built	Under construction at the start of the war	Completed or almost completed at the start of the war
Aircraft carrier	4	4	Design 'B'	1 (*Graf Zeppelin*)
Battleship	4	4	–	4 (*Gneisenau, Scharnhorst, Bismarck, Tirpitz*)
Battleship, Type 'H'	6	6	–	–
Pocket battleship early type[1]	3	6	–	3 (*Deutschland, Admiral Scheer, Admiral Graf Spee*)
Pocket battleship later type	10	12	–	–
Heavy cruiser	5	5	–	3 (*Admiral Hipper, Blücher, Prinz Eugen* plus *Seydlitz,*[2] *Lützow*[3])
Light cruiser	12	24	M, N, O, Q and R designs	6 (*Emden, Königsberg, Karlsruhe, Köln, Leipzig, Nürnberg*)
Scout cruiser[4]	20	36	–	–
Destroyer	58	70	Several	22
Torpedo boat[5]	90	90	About 15	About 20
Submarine	241[6]	241	Several	57

1. Pocket battleships were based on the *Deutschland* design. It was planned to build different versions later.
2. *Seydlitz* was launched at Deschimag AG Weser in Bremen on 19 January 1939 and about three quarters complete when work was stopped and the hull converted to aircraft carrier. This plan was cancelled in 1943 and the uncompleted hull towed to Königsberg during the spring of 1944. It was scuttled towards the end of the war.
3. The cruiser hull named *Lützow* was sold to Russia and the pocket battleship *Deutschland* was re-named *Lützow*.
4. Scout cruisers were about half way between destroyers and cruisers in size.
5. Torpedo boats were not what the British called 'E-boat' but they looked more like small destroyers.
6. This number may appear to be impressive, especially when one considers Dönitz's request for 300, but these boats represented only a small fraction of the total expenditure; roughly the same cost as four battleships and amounting to approximately ten per cent of the total force. This total included all types from small training units to huge submarine cruisers, carrying heavy artillery.

the summer of 1938. Perhaps this was because he was an individualist with unconventional and 'quite mad ideas' – which he fully demonstrated towards the end of the war by building up the Midget Weapons Unit to a fantastically high standard, against terrific odds and in an incredibly short time. In addition to Heye, there were several other submarine supporters in the Supreme Naval Command: Hermann Boehm, Fleet Commander, and Hermann Densch, Commander-in-Chief of Reconnaissance Forces, were both in favour of U-boats. In fact, Densch had a pet-saying: 'We must build submarines on every meadow, in every shed and on every stream – it is our only hope of winning.'

But theirs were only faint cries in the wilderness, for the majority were in favour of a battleship navy. Many in the Supreme Naval Command kept repeating their stereotype views that there would be no war with Britain, and that, under war conditions, Dönitz's submarine tactics would be found wanting. Several powerful men in the High Command maintained their belief that only the mightiest and heaviest battleships would penetrate the shipping lanes of the Atlantic. They considered submarines to be outdated and obsolete weapons.

The High Command also had some knowledge of Britain's asdic, which, it was thought, might prevent a successful submarine war. Similarly, they pointed to the Prize

Ordinance Regulations (pages 41 and 201), which imposed numerous operational limitations on submarines and further restricted their effectiveness.

The final decision on the type of construction policy to adopt was made by Hitler. The Naval High Command gave him two alternatives: either a battleship fleet or a U-boat dominated navy. Hitler chose the surface fleet outlined in the 'Z' Plan and, on 27 January 1939, gave the programme top priority – just over six months before the outbreak of the Second World War. So, it is safe to say that the 'Z' Plan had little influence on the outcome of the war.

The new capital ships were to be equipped with eight 406mm (16 inch) and twelve 150mm (6 inch) guns; they would carry four aeroplanes, have a top speed of thirty knots, and a range of over 12,000 nautical miles at a cruising speed of just under twenty knots. (Construction of *Bismarck* and *Tirpitz* had, of course, already started before the 'Z' Plan was formulated.) The Chiefs of Staff also examined what had been Germany's main weakness during the First World War – that of trying to operate far out in the Atlantic from bases in the German Bight. This problem was solved by planning to put the new long-range battleships based on the *Deutschland* into the South Atlantic where they would be serviced by supply and repair ships seeking out remote spots in the Southern Ocean for the more lengthy repairs.

Scharnhorst, easily identified by the coat of arms on the bows. The Germans classed this and her sister, *Gneisenau*, as battleships; although other seafaring nations tended to refer to the 'Elusive Sisters' as battlecruisers. *Scharnhorst* was the first major battleship to be launched after the First World War. She took to the water at the Naval Dockyard in Wilhelmshaven on 3 October 1936, while *Gneisenau* was launched just over two months later at Deutsche Werke in Kiel.

The launching of the aircraft carrier *Graf Zeppelin* at Deutsche Werke in Kiel on 8 December 1938. The ship was never completed and vanished in mysterious circumstances after the war, while under tow to Russia. The most likely explanation is that it ran into a mine, though conspiracy theories abound. The wreck was found at the beginning of the twenty-first century, but details are still sketchy.

THE END OF THE TREATIES

In 1939 came the final break. First, on 27 January 1939, Germany informed the British government that they wished to increase their submarine strength to equal that of the Royal Navy. And then, on 28 April during a speech to the German government, Hitler denounced the Anglo-German Naval Treaty after the British guarantee of Poland.

The German Navy had been on full war alert since early August 1939, and many ships had been sent to their war stations. But this in itself was nothing new, because full war alert had been ordered on several previous occasions, such as the re-occupation of the demilitarized Rhineland, the Austrian Anschluss and the crisis in the Sudetenland. Even at this late stage, few people in the German High Command seriously thought there would be a war with Britain – least of all Admiral Raeder, who was still telling his officers that the German Navy did not have sufficient ships for such a conflict, and that, in the event of a war, all they could show was how to die with dignity.

During the morning of 3 September 1939, Raeder was handed a note informing him of Britain's declaration of war on Germany. Raeder then faced his High Command and sent them into battle with these words: 'Meine Herren, wir haben keine Wahl. Voller Einsatz. Mit Anstand sterben' ('Gentlemen, we have no choice. Total engagement. Die with dignity!').

EARLY WARTIME SURFACE VESSELS

The pre-war ship construction plan was abandoned shortly after the war started; ships nearing completion were finished, others were scrapped, and there was no further significant development of large surface warships during the war years. All of the ships launched henceforth had been designed long before the start of the conflict, and the naval designers concentrated on building small surface boats capable of operating in coastal waters under air protection.

Some of the boats built during the war were created in quite astonishing circumstances. Probably one of the wildest projects was the construction, in Norway, of the Navy's smallest minesweepers. These Zwerge (Dwarfs) were the brainchild of Kptlt. Hans Bartels, who commanded the minesweeper *M1* at the start of the war. After taking part in the invasion of Norway, *M1* developed mysterious engine trouble and was unable to return to Germany with the rest of the flotilla. By the time the fault had been traced and repaired, the other ships were too far away for her to catch up, so Bartels reported to the senior German naval commander, who was only too pleased to use *M1*'s services.

Bartels distinguished himself by carrying out several extraordinary feats: he managed to capture a destroyer, together with an entire torpedo-boat flotilla; and, later, he even captured an Allied convoy and took it into a German-held port. The men of *M1* also 'defended' several small Norwegian ports from possible enemy attacks from the sea, by making mock mines – ingeniously devised by welding spikes onto empty petrol cans – and then mooring them in the harbour approaches. This charade was given an air of reality when the British laid a few mines of their own! Unfortunately for Bartels, these were rather inconveniently placed – right in the German shipping lanes. Undaunted, Bartels and *M1*, together with several modified fishing boats, tried to clear them. Three of the fishing boats were lost in quick succession making it quite clear that existing craft were unsuitable for sweeping mines in shallow fjord waters. It was apparent to Bartels that he needed an easily manoeuvrable craft with a shallow draught, capable of passing over the mines without detonating them. Such boats did not exist, so Bartels decided to build his own. While looking for suitable designs, he found a Norwegian fishing vessel with all the necessary requirements. Unfortunately, the engines (which were almost certainly purchased from Sweden) did not fit, until someone struck on the idea of turning the plans around and putting the propeller in the bows. It worked. The bows were flattened, a new point added at the stern and, in the end, everything fitted together quite well.

Twelve such Zwerge were constructed, and the Supreme Commander-in-Chief of the German Navy was invited to the commissioning ceremony – and to pay the necessary bills. But Grand Admiral Raeder did not take up this offer and, in the end, Bartels moved one of them to Berlin, moored it in the canal outside Naval Headquarters and Raeder inspected it there. Raeder took a dim view of Bartels' independence, however, and promoted him to the rank of First Officer of the destroyer *Z34*, in the hope that he might re-learn some naval discipline. Later in the war, Bartels returned to his unorthodox way of life when he worked under the equally unconventional Admiral Hellmuth Heye in the Midget Weapons Unit.

MAGNETIC MINES

Accounts of events at the start of the war tend to highlight the sinking of the aircraft carrier HMS *Courageous*; the sinking of the battleship HMS *Royal Oak* in Scapa Flow; the Battle of the River Plate, when the pocket battleship *Admiral Graf Spee* was scuttled; and the Norwegian Campaign of spring 1940. But these famous actions give a slightly false picture of the war, because the majority of German ships were not sent out to hunt British warships. The main burden of the fighting at sea was carried by small vessels, such as U-boats, destroyers, torpedo-boats and minesweepers, which conducted numerous successful mining operations in British sea lanes. Mines, especially the magnetic variety, were certainly the most important weapon in the German naval armoury during the winter of 1939/40.

The magnetic mine was not a German invention for Britain had developed it before the end of the First World War – although with little success. By 1939, the German Navy had perfected the weapon which Raeder, certain there would be no war with Britain until 1948 at the earliest, carefully locked away in a top-secret store. With this ace up their sleeve, the Germans sat back, convinced that the Royal Navy were unaware of the mine's presence in Hitler's arsenal. But, in the event, it was they who were caught out: for, when war broke out, the few existing models were still lying in cold storage and, until mass production of the magnetic type could be organized, the Navy had to make do with old percussion mines.

The German Naval Command was well aware that, once they realized magnetic mines were being used, the British would quickly find the means to neutralize their effect. To do this, it would be necessary to find out how the detonation system worked. After that it would be a simple matter of generating strong magnetic fields that would cause the mines to explode short of their target. The de-magnetizing of merchant ships would also be possible. In a way, the German Navy was helped by having so few magnetic mines: ordinary mines were cleared by minesweepers, after which the channel was declared open to merchant shipping, while magnetic mines were not cleared during such sweeps. They remained on the sea bed, only rising as the first large iron ship passed over. The German Navy took great care to deposit these mines in areas where they would have maximum effect and where they were not likely to be washed ashore. Ironically, it was an aircraft of the Luftwaffe that finally rendered this most deadly weapon ineffectual, by dropping one on the mud flats near Shoeburyness (Southend, Essex) late in November 1939. The pilot could not have chosen a better place for presenting this valuable trophy to the Royal Navy, for it landed in soft mud without damage and without the safety destruct mechanism for shallow water switched on and only a short distance from a fully-equipped military workshop. A British naval specialist, Lt.Cdr. J. G. D. Ouvry, simply walked out to it during the hours of darkness, took rubbings of the screw and nut heads, and then returned in daylight with specially made tools for opening the mine. He thus defused one of the war's most valuable prizes.

THE TORPEDO CRISIS OF 1939/40

During the early days of the war, it was realized that U-boats could get close to British harbours and ships without being detected, and that they were usually only discovered when their torpedoes failed to explode at the target. When this happened, the 'eels' (German slang for torpedoes) either detonated early or passed underneath the target, blowing up harmlessly on the other side. This often resulted in serious consequences for the firer, because the old G7a torpedoes – which were still being used – left a noticeable wake of small bubbles as they passed through the water, thus pointing to the U-boat's position. The ' G' was derived from an earlier name before the word 'torpedo' became widespread, and the Germans used the code name Geradelaufapparat (running in straight line apparatus). The '7' refers to the length in metres and 'a' to it being the first variation of this type).

The G7a torpedo worked quite simply by compressed air helping to burn fuel in a four-cylinder combustion engine, which was fed with a mixture of fuel, hot air and steam. The later G7e torpedoes were fully electric, with batteries and motor. Although these did not leave a wake, they had the disadvantage of requiring much more maintenance and had to be withdrawn from the tubes for battery charging about once every three days. Their performance was also inferior to the 'air' type.

Initially, most of the torpedo failures were attributed to war nerves on the part of the U-boat crews. It was thought that the men acted too hastily and did not complete the fir-

A torpedo mine being loaded aboard *U561*. There were two basic types: TMB and TMC, both of which had been developed from TMA. (Torpedo Mine Type A, B or C.) Type TMB was one third and Type TMC half as long as a standard torpedo. Thus two or three could be placed into one tube at a time, but special modifications were required to the tubes and not all commanders were trained in using mines. Yet, they formed a most important part of Germany's armoury during the first winter of the war, when a large number of U-boats, torpedo boats and destroyers were sent out to mine British ports. Of course, surface ships used ordinary, standard mines instead of the special TM variety.

Firing torpedoes was a highly skilled undertaking. This shows torpedoes being released from a surface ship. Early torpedoes fired from underwater gave away their presence by the bubbles from released air; by the time the Second World War started torpedoes left their tubes without releasing any air.

ing procedure. But the facts pointed to quite a different reason: only about one-third of the total of torpedoes fired detonated on target. By the end of October 1939, Karl Dönitz, head of the U-boat arm, was certain the fault did not lie with his men. Indeed, he was constantly being inundated with complaints from his commanders, of which the following are but a few examples.

Kptlt. Herbert Schultze had come into port with *U48* and reported that half of the ten torpedoes he had fired had been duds. Less than a week later, Kptlt. Wilhelm Zahn had had several battleships lined up in front of *U56*'s three tubes – it was a Type IIC U-boat – and had fired a salvo at HMS *Rodney*. The crew had heard the torpedoes strike her hull, but there had been no detonation. After stopping a merchant ship, Kptlt. Viktor Schütze decided to sink it with a torpedo, but found that four had to be fired from very close range before one detonated. Shortly afterwards, Kptlt. Herbert Sohler 'flew off the handle' at his debriefing, telling Dönitz that on three occasions he had managed to get within point-blank range of a convoy: each time, it was like shooting at a solid wall of ships, yet his torpedoes achieved nothing. All he heard were two premature explosions.

Stories like these abounded throughout 1939 and well into the following year before the reasons for the failures were discovered. The situation during the Norwegian Campaign of spring 1940 was appalling: out of a total of forty-eight U-boats, forty-two engaged the enemy, but over thirty of these attacks failed because the torpedoes did not work. At least

twenty-five Allied warships were attacked but only one submarine was sunk.

However, the first two U-boats sunk by enemy action were lost as a result of premature explosions alerting the escorts. The first casualty, *U39*, commanded by Korvkpt. Gerhard Glattes, went down on 14 September 1939 after attacking the aircraft carrier HMS *Ark Royal. U39*'s torpedoes were of the old-fashioned compressed air variety that left a tell-tale wake. Escorts were alerted and some men in HMS *Foxhound* actually spotted the U-boat's dark shadow beneath the surface of the water. *Foxhound* raced over to the spot and dropped several well placed depth charges. *U27*, commanded by Korvkpt. Hans Franz, was the second boat to go down. Again a salvo of three torpedoes detonated short of their target and two escorts, HMS *Forester* and HMS *Fortune*, darted over to the suspected position. And again, well placed depth charges brought the boat to the surface. Some of the crew managed to get out before it sank and, through letters sent back to Germany from prisoner-of-war camps, at least the details of *U27*'s fate reached Dönitz's desk. (Such information was written in code and sent to close relatives, who had instructions to forward mail to the Naval High Command.)

During November 1939, Dönitz recorded in his diary: 'The Torpedo Inspectorate has perpetrated a real blunder.' Fortunately, Grand Admiral Raeder had reached the same conclusion and hastily appointed Professor E A Cornelius to find out what had gone wrong and to eliminate the fault. Cornelius had worked as torpedo specialist at Eckernförde

Although not terribly clear, this shows a G7e torpedo being loaded into a submarine. Note that the bars running from the body to rudders at the rear of the propeller are missing. This type contained a number of high-performance batteries and an electric motor, which did not leave a trail of oil and bubbles as it sped through the water; but it required more maintenance because the batteries needed regular recharging. Firing adjustments could be made while torpedoes were lying in their tubes, but they had to be partly withdrawn for recharging. There appears to have been no standard method for attaching torpedoes to cranes, as there are photos showing a variety of fittings as well as a multitude of makeshift methods using rope.

before the war, and his knowledge in this field spanned some twenty years. However, it was not until about mid-1940 that the fault was run to earth and the sordid details were brought to light at a court martial.

There were three major faults which, to make matters more complex, did not affect every torpedo. Some of these problems were not recognized until the end of the war. This, understandably, clouded the problem, for as one fault was isolated and rectified another would crop up. The three major faults were:

1. Peacetime experiments had not accurately simulated the rigours of war. Torpedoes had simply been put on board a ship and, a few hours later, fired at a target – hardly an adequate test when one considers that under war conditions torpedoes were tossed about by rough seas for days, sometimes even weeks, before being used. This was especially detrimental to torpedoes used by submarines. Air pressure inside a submarine was most variable, and would usually increase slightly the longer the boat remained submerged. Torpedoes were expelled from the tubes by compressed air, which would then escape from the machinery into the interior of the boat. (A special free-running piston would be fitted behind the torpedo and, when the order to fire was given, compressed air would be released into the space behind the piston. This worked in a similar way to an air gun: the piston was pushed forward along the torpedo tube, pushing the torpedo in front of it. The piston would stop at the end of the tube and the compressed air was

allowed to escape into the interior of the boat, thus preventing it from sending tell-tale bubbles to the surface.) Such increases in pressure affected the controls of the torpedoes and made them run erratically. The depth mechanism, especially, was affected.

2. The explosive could be detonated by two different methods, the necessary adjustment for whichever detonation was required having to be made before the torpedo was fired. This was no great problem because it could be carried out while the torpedo was in the tube, waiting to be fired. The commander had the choice of either exploding the torpedo on impact, using the so-called contact pistol, or the detonation could take place magnetically. By the latter method, the torpedo would swim deep under the target and blow up beneath it. This had far greater impact than a torpedo exploding at the side, for such an explosion could easily break a merchant ship in two. The problem with the magnetic detonator was that too little was known about the earth's magnetic fields. This was especially evident during the Norwegian Campaign, where it was thought the proximity of the North Pole and the abundance of iron ore (magnetic magnetite) could affect the torpedo mechanism. After the Norwegian Campaign the torpedoes were mainly used with the contact pistol.

3. Torpedoes had a safety mechanism to prevent them from exploding too close to the firer. This device worked quite simply with the aid of a small propeller at the front of the torpedo. The propeller would spin around when the tor-

Torpedoes were usually supplied without detonators, which were delivered separately inside watertight tins. This shows the tin and the business end of a torpedo as they were displayed at the Warship Preservation Trust in Birkenhead.

A German G7a torpedo on display at the Naval Museum in Wilhelmshaven. Training torpedoes could be distinguished from the real thing by their red and white striped heads. Many of them also contained a powerful lamp so that progress could be observed at night.

pedo travelled through the water, and this turned a screw that pushed the two contacts of the detonator together so that, if activated, they could touch. This safety mechanism made it impossible for the torpedo to explode accidentally until it had travelled at least 300m (a little over 320 yards) through the water. The blades of this propeller also acted as a trigger for the contact pistol and this was where the major fault lay, for each blade was marginally shorter than the radius of the torpedo. As a result, the explosives were detonated when the torpedo hit a flat target, such as those used for practice or when the torpedo hit the side of a merchant ship with a deep draught; but it was also possible for the torpedo to hit a curved hull without the triggers being pushed back to activate the contact pistol. In those instances, the torpedo would bounce off, slide under the target and often carry on swimming. The contact pistol worked quite well against merchant ships, but the same problem cropped up in later years when U-boats started attacking small warships escorting convoys.

Experiments with new magnetic pistols had started in 1927, as a result of irregularities discovered during the First World War. These tests had been carried out using the very old G7v torpedoes, which were an earlier type to the G7a compressed air variety. The new pistol, consisting of a modified magnetic pistol, had been tested during the autumn of 1928 by firing torpedoes at an iron plate suspended in water. The torpedoes missed their target, and hit the framework instead, but the detonators went off, suggesting that the pistols were functioning.

At that time, there was no independent body for testing new torpedo developments, and all the work – designing, building, testing and evaluating – was carried out by the Torpedoversuchsanstalt (TVA). This arrangement was not changed until almost the end of the Spanish Civil War, when Admiral Raeder ordered the establishment of an independent testing command to find out why torpedoes used off the Spanish coast were not functioning properly. This body, called the Torpedoerprobungskommando (TEK), subsequently appeared, and was considered by many people to be in direct competition with the TVA. Consequently, there was considerable friction between the two.

The TEK carried out several tests, including firing torpedoes at the raised hull of the old sailing ship Niobe, and discovered several irregularities. But their findings were channelled back to the Supreme Naval Command through the TVA where some people were of the opinion that torpedoes were functioning perfectly and anyone could make them fail if they tried hard enough. Apparently, some of the test results were not passed on to the Supreme Naval Command, and it was not until after the war had started that one of the TVA's junior officers took matters into his own hands and complained directly to the admiral about the nature of some of his duties. He felt he could no longer tolerate the irregularities in the administration. After this, Raeder dismissed several top officials and, in the summer of 1940 ordered a full inquiry – by which time the Norwegian Campaign was over.

At a court martial held later, it was revealed that the trouble had been caused by the TVA, which had been responsible for what was described as 'criminal negligence'. But, apparently, they were not solely to blame, for several of their engineers were turned down when they requested ships for torpedo-testing in rough weather. Unfortunately, they had received little support, and often had to make do with small boats not capable of going far out to sea.

FIRING A TORPEDO

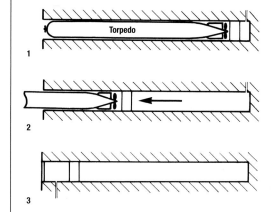

1. Torpedo in tube, ready to fire.
2. Compressed air, acting on the piston, expels the torpedo from the tube. The torpedo motor then starts and the torpedo adjusts to its pre-set running depth.
3. The outer doors are closed and the water trapped between the doors and the piston is drained out. The breech end of the tube is then opened, draining the compressed air in the tube back into the submarine (thus preventing tell-tale bubbles of air escaping to the surface). The piston can now be retrieved and the tube is ready to be re-loaded.

TORPEDO SAFETY MECHANISM

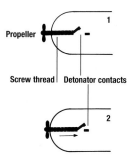

1. As it leaves the submarine, the detonator cannot be activated.
2. As the passage through the water causes the nose propeller to rotate, the screw thread brings the detonator into such a position that it can be activated.

THE MAGNETIC PISTOL

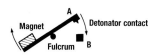

This was far more complicated than this diagram would suggest, but the basic principle was simple. As the torpedo passed beneath the target, the magnetic field of the target would attract the magnet and thus close contacts A and B, detonating the torpedo.

THE CONTACT PISTOL

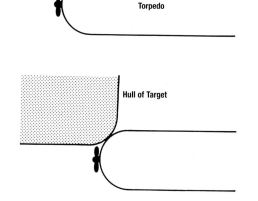

The contact pistol detonated the torpedo by the blades of the nose propeller being bent back at they hit the target. However, the curvature of the target's hull and the short radius of the torpedo nose propeller could fail to detonate the torpedo.

SUBMARINE TACTICS

In 1935, there existed three important but diverse schools of thought on submarine warfare: the views of the Admiralty in London, those of the Oberkommando der Marine in Berlin and the ideas of Karl Dönitz.

Powerful battleships and fast cruisers formed the backbone of the Royal Navy's fleet. Submarines, on the other hand, had no place in this pattern. They were too slow to operate alongside battleships and cruisers, and were more easily affected by bad weather. Some people at the Admiralty saw uses for submarines in theatres of war where the Royal Navy was numerically inferior, but on the whole they were considered unimportant weapons. This attitude is borne out by looking at the total number of ships in the British Navy at the start of the Second World War: it was the largest fleet afloat, yet it only had fifty-seven submarines.

After the First World War, Britain had perfected an ultrasonic detection device for finding submerged submarines. As a submerged submarine was totally blind and fairly immobile, it was easy to destroy once it had been detected. Experiments with this device, called 'asdic' (now known as sonar) together with new submarine defence methods led the British Shipping Defence Advisory Committee to state in 1937 that the submarine would never again present the problems faced in the Great War, when Britain's supply routes had been almost cut off by U-boats. This statement helped confirm the opinion that submarines were obsolescent.

Such negative ideas were also fairly widespread in Berlin, although they did not cut any ice with Karl Dönitz. On the contrary, he could see a terrific future for underwater weapons and was convinced the sceptics were wrong. In 1935, he started to revolutionize the submarine's role by introducing four new basic ideas.

1 SHORT-RANGE ATTACK

U-boat officers receiving secret training at the Submarine Defence School in Kiel before 1935 had been instructed to keep at least three kilometres (one and three quarter miles) away from their target; otherwise they risked detection by the 'secret weapon' (asdic). The British Advisory Committee probably also assumed that submarines would attack from similar ranges. In practice, it meant that a submarine would have to fire a salvo of torpedoes; even then, there was a good chance of missing because of the difficulty in judging speed, range and direction at such distances.

Dönitz changed these conventional tactics by instructing his commanders to attack from half a kilometre (550 yards). From such a short distance, he could almost guarantee a hit with one torpedo. Dönitz told his men to adopt the short-range method of attack until the exact performance of the 'secret weapon' was known. He added that the German Navy was not even certain it existed, but that, if it did, the device would be affected by wave action, salinity and noise from the vessel in which it was fitted, and so would offer the hunter no significant advantage.

The short-range method of attack was far more effective than might at first be imagined. It was not just a case of making every torpedo a possible hit – the submarine's role was changed from one of mere nuisance value to a most deadly weapon capable of tearing a convoy to pieces. Take the following example. Type VII, the most important U-boat class, had one stern and four bow torpedo tubes, carrying twelve torpedoes. It took at least twenty minutes to reload one tube, and that had to be done away from wave action. In the Atlantic, this meant that the boat would have to dive, slow down to a few knots and remain there for well over an hour: by the time the boat resurfaced, it would have lost sight of the convoy. And the time required for reloading was not the only problem, for sometimes the amount of manoeuvring needed to get into an attacking position further reduced the chances of getting even one hit in a convoy. But at short range there would be five potential sinkings. Research carried out after the publication of the first edition of this book suggests that this short-range attack plan was devised by U-boat commanders, rather than by Dönitz. The first person to try it was Kptlt. Erich Topp in *U57* on 24 August 1940, when he shot all three torpedoes of this tiny Type IIC in a few minutes and obtained a hit with every one. The targets were three British ships, *Saint Dunstan*, *Cumberland* and *Havildar*.

2 SURFACE ATTACKS AT NIGHT

Submariners from many countries had been looking for ways of perfecting submerged attacks. Obviously, the early submarines still spent a great deal of time on the surface, either recharging batteries and air cylinders or travelling to their war stations. On the whole, however, commanders avoided surfacing in daylight or during attacks.

Karl Dönitz changed such views by purposely putting his U-boats on the surface. They were to live and fight on the surface and only dive to avoid the enemy or heavy seas. This way, submarine performance could be improved considerably. Top speed, for example, could be increased from eight knots to seventeen. The cruising speed while submerged was four knots or less, but on the surface the boats could easily manage about ten knots. A surfaced submarine had a minute silhouette, and Dönitz felt certain he could find successful night-time methods of attack, when surface ships would stand out well on the horizon and the submarine would be barely visible to enemy lookouts.

3 TIRPITZ'S DREAM

Dönitz also realized that submarines were the ideal tools for implementing the ideas of Grand Admiral Alfred von Tirpitz. During the 1880s, Tirpitz had forecast a revolution in naval warfare, and he had predicted that the big guns of the battleships would be replaced by torpedoes. He had also advocated the use of small, fast torpedo-boats for night attacks. During Tirpitz's lifetime, designers lacked the necessary technology to build such craft and, when the idea became more feasible, they lacked the necessary imagination, which resulted in the concept being modified to increase armament, action radius and to carry greater loads. When the boats were eventually finished, they looked like small destroyers, and did not bear even a vague resemblance to Tirpitz's original idea!

Now, in 1935, Dönitz knew he had the answer: an easily manoeuvrable torpedo-carrier, almost undetectable at night and capable of operating in the Atlantic. The word 'torpedo' is most important: Dönitz saw it as the most effective weapon so far devised for submarines. He regarded artillery as a secondary armament, to be used on targets that could not retaliate. One puncture in the delicate hull of a submarine would render it helpless. A surface ship, on the other hand, could take numerous hits without affecting its firepower. (This fact was not appreciated by some influential members of the Supreme Naval Command, who laid plans to build huge 2,000-ton cruisers, capable of engaging destroyers in artillery combat. These Type XI U-cruisers never progressed beyond the drawing-board stage. Plans were made to build four at Deschimag Works in Bremen, but the war came too soon and they were never laid down.)

4 WOLF PACKS

It has often been said that Wolf Pack, Patrol Line or Rudel tactics, were dreamed up by Dönitz while in a prison camp during the First World War, but this is not so. The idea had been suggested by Kommodore und Kpt.z.S. Hermann Bauer, Flag Officer for Submarines of the High Seas Fleet, back in 1917 – about the time that Dönitz first went into submarines. Indeed several wolf packs were organized during the First World War, but they lacked efficient radio to bring them together for battle. Dönitz was the first to put the theory into successful practice. The plan evolved slowly. By 1939, the technique called for a group of U-boats to spread out across the path of the anticipated convoy. During daylight, all boats would sail at an economical speed (roughly 10 knots) towards the expected ships. At dusk, they would turn and sail in the convoy's direction, to make it more difficult for the enemy to slip through the net during the night. The first boat to spot the convoy would report to headquarters (see page 106), send out homing signals and continue shad-

owing the merchant ships until the pack was assembled for a mass attack. Each commander was usually free to decide the best way of intercepting the convoy. Those nearby had an easy task, for they only needed to head towards the homing signals, But boats farther away had the more difficult task of anticipating where the merchant ships would be in a few days time and heading for that spot.

The combination of close range attack and wolf pack tactics raises the question of collisions. Although these operations resulted in several U-boats milling about in relatively confined areas, there were surprisingly few accidents. The first one did not occur until 8 December 1942, when *U221*, commanded by Kptlt. Hans Trojer, ran into the stern of *U254*, commanded by Kptlt. Hans Gilardone. *U221* managed to return to France, but the other boat, unable to dive, was later sunk by aircraft from 120 Squadron of the RAF. The U-boat Command realized it had been impossible for Trojer's lookouts to spot *U254* in the bad conditions prevailing at the time, and the incident was dismissed as an unfortunate accident.

SUBMARINE CONSTRUCTION

Several publications have either given the impression or stated that Karl Dönitz was responsible for building submarines before the war, but this is a misconception. In reality, Dönitz did not manage to influence U-boat construction until long after the war had begun. The U-Bootsamt, a department in the Supreme Naval Command with no direct link with the U-boat arm, had been responsible for construction policies before the war. Because of this organizational division, Dönitz was totally unaware of the large quantities of material compiled by this department; nor did he realize that the plans he submitted between 1936 and 1939 had been largely disregarded. Before the end of 1939, Dönitz was unable to make any real impression on U-boat construction policies.

Dönitz laid his first emergency war plans before Grand Admiral Raeder on 8 September 1939. This memorandum, outlining the requirements for a battle in the Atlantic, made the following recommendations:

- To build torpedo-carrying U-boats, concentrating on Types VII and IX.
- To build large minelaying U-boats with longer range than existing submarine types.
- To build large, long-distance supply submarines. Speed would not be important, as long as they could remain at sea for long periods and cover vast distances.
- For the long term also, to build long-range torpedo-carrying submarines.

This eventually resulted in the construction of Types VIIC and IXC, Type XB, Type XIV supply submarines and Type IXD2.

The British declaration of war caught the German Navy by surprise, and some of its higher officials suddenly realized that their previous priority of having sufficient deck space for parades was no longer of any use. Drastic new measures had to be taken. Existing plans were scrapped and, during that

THE PRINCIPLE OF THE 'WOLF PACK' ATTACK

1. During daylight hours, all boats of the group would sail at an economical cruising speed towards the anticipated convoy.

2. During the hours of darkness, the U-boats reverse direction to sail slowly in the same direction as the convoy.

3. At daybreak, the U-boats resumed cruising towards the oncoming convoy.

4. When shadowing convoys, U-boat would try to sail in front of the merchant ships, rather than following on behind them.

Convoy

Maximum visibility

Wolf Pack line abreast   U-boat

The ink description is misleading. The original owner of the photograph may have joined the U-boat Arm on 1 August 1942, but this photo must have been taken a long time before then. Before the war, virtually every U-boat carried two red and white striped rescue buoys, which could be released from the inside in an emergency. These contained a bright light as well as a telephone and can be seen as white marks towards the rear of each boat. The white blobs nearer the conning towers are the insides of open hatches. The other reason for dating the photograph before 1942 is because the mooring of boats in 'packs', as here, was prohibited with the outbreak of war to prevent them becoming easy targets for bombers. This photograph shows the famous Tirpitz Pier in the naval harbour in Kiel.

This looks like tender *Saar*, lying with Type II boats in Kiel. Note that the school boats of Type IIA, *U1, U2* and *U4* have black numbers, and the 'operational' Type IIB, *U9*, has a white number. Net cutters can be seen on these bows. They were of little use and were later phased out.

A Type VII with an early conning tower design. The armament consisted of one 88mm quick-firing deck gun forward of the conning tower and a single 20mm anti-aircraft gun on the platform by the rear of the tower. The entire tower was made mainly from non-magnetic, phosphorous bronze, which prevented interference with the magnetic compass, housed in a bulge at its base. This was viewed by the helmsman in the central control room through an illuminated periscope. The jumping wires, running from the top of the tower to the bows and the stern served as radio aerials, hence the thick, ball-like insulators to prevent them 'shortening' to the boat. The wires were also thought to have been useful in helping boats pass under nets, but very few came into contact with such obstacles and their alternative main use was for attaching safety harnesses when men worked on the upper deck in rough weather. The thin rod sticking up above the top of the tower is a periscopic rod radio aerial, which could be raised and lowered from inside the boat. The other is the attack periscope with small head lens. The absence of lookouts suggests that the boat is in safe waters where surprise attacks were unlikely.

Commissioning *U869*, a Type IXC/40 with improved anti-aircraft armament at Deschimag AG Weser in Bremen. The 20mm quadruple gun is clearly visible and the upper platform would have had two double 20mm weapons that were fired from the shoulder, like huge rifles. These guns were perfectly balanced on their mounts, making them easier to aim at fast-moving aircraft than having to coordinate the two hand wheels of the bigger gun. Circular, pressure-tight ammunition containers are also visible and so is the lid of a hatch leading down into the interior. This gun platform was not pressure resistant and the space under the deck would have filled with water when the boat dived, so a ladder led down from this high level to the pressure-resistant hatch cover on the pressure hull down below. Adding such anti-aircraft armament made it more difficult when it came to loading supplies.

first autumn, new policies were devised. The Navy's first wartime construction plans stated: 'Future U-boat types will be decided by the Flag Officer for Submarines.' (At the start of the war, the head of the U-boat arm held the status of Flag Officer. Dönitz was not made Commander-in-Chief until October 1939.)

This new programme was laid before Hitler on 10 September 1939. He agreed to it, but, because at that time Hitler did not want a war with Britain, he did not give authorization for the necessary raw materials to be delivered to naval dockyards until 8 December 1939.

The general situation regarding submarine construction was quite astonishing. On average, there were sixteen U-boats in the Atlantic during each month of 1939. The number fell to thirteen during the winter of 1939/40, and it remained at that low ebb until mid-1941, when the average increased to about thirty-five. This means that a maximum of only about sixteen boats were in the Atlantic at any one time during the U-boats' 'First Happy Time' – when they all but defeated the world's most powerful maritime nation. One wonders what might have happened if Germany had more submarines during that fateful period.

Quoting numbers and averages, as has been done here, is a favourite occupation of many historians, but it can be most misleading and sometimes does not show the true picture at all. When one examines the details behind the statistics, one can find quite chaotic situations. Take January of 1942 as an example. Dönitz's war diary gives the following situation:

There were 91 operational submarines. 23 were in the Mediterranean and the Supreme Command had issued orders to send another 2, bringing the total to 25; 6 boats

were stationed just west of Gibraltar, and 4 more were in Norwegian waters. This left a total of 56 boats for the important convoy battles in the North Atlantic. Some historians have quoted a total of 85 boats in the Atlantic, but such figures are misleading. About half of the operational boats were in dock because the U-boat arm was lacking the materials, tools and skilled men to repair them.

This earlier conning-tower design, with the upper lip (wind deflector) on the conning tower curving upwards, was changed shortly after the beginning of the war; later, it curved downwards. The aperture above the spray deflector, about halfway up the tower, was an inlet for the radio aerial and the outlet of a horn is just visible below it. The gun is an 88mm quick-firing deck gun for use against surface targets. It could be aimed upwards, but was too cumbersome to cope with even slow-flying aircraft. Maintaining this weapon at sea was a major problem as there were about eighty greasing points and even if these could be regularly maintained, the gun was hard to operate. Carrying ammunition from below the radio room via the top of the conning tower and then over slippery decks was an added hazard.

This photograph shows very well how difficult it was to spot a submarine on the surface. Add a dark night and it was almost impossible. Observers in aircraft had the advantage that they did not need to look for the submarine, but for the imposing bow waves it created.

THE PHASES OF THE BATTLE OF THE ATLANTIC

Column A	Front U-boats lost to enemy action outside home waters. Figures based on Axel Niestlé's *German U-boat Losses during World War Two*, (see Bibliography)
Column B	The number of ships sunk by U-boats
Column C	The average number of U-boats at sea
Column D	The number of ships sunk per U-boat at sea
Column E	Comments (*see also further notes opposite*)

Month	A	B	C	D	E
1939					
Sep	3	41	23	1.8	1. U-boats were tied by Prize Ordinance Regulations
Oct	4	27	10	2.7	
Nov	1	21	16	1.3	
Dec	1	25	8	3.1	2. Some restrictions were relaxed
1940					
Jan	2	40	11	3.6	
Feb	5	45	15	3.0	3. Major restrictions lifted
Mar	3	23	13	1.8	4. U-boats recalled for Norway and Denmark invasion
Apr	4	7	24	0.3	
May	1	13	8	1.6	5. Unrestricted warfare around France and Britain started.
Jun	1	58	18	3.2	
Jul	2	38	11	3.5	
Aug	2	56	13	4.3	6. Unrestricted warfare area enlarged
Sep	1	59	13	4.5	
Oct	1	63	12	5.3	
Nov	2	33	11	3.0	
Dec	0	37	10	3.7	
1941					
Jan	0	21	8	2.6	
Feb	0	39	12	3.3	
Mar	5	41	13	3.2	7. Three U-boat aces lost. Radar's first success
Apr	2	43	19	2.3	
May	1	58	24	2.4	8. Decline in ships sunk by U-boats
Jun	4	61	32	1.9	
Jul	0	22	27	0.8	9. High Frequency Direction Finders started sea trials.
Aug	4	23	36	0.6	
Sep	2	53	36	1.5	
Oct	2	32	36	0.9	
Nov	3	13	38	0.3	
Dec	10	26	25	1.0	
1942					
Jan	3	62	42	1.5	10. America joined the war
Feb	2	85	50	1.7	11. U-boats used new code machine
Mar	6	95	48	2.0	
Apr	3	74	49	1.5	
May	4	125	61	2.0	
Jun	3	144	59	2.4	
Jul	11	96	70	1.4	12. Dramatic increase in number of U-boats at sea
Aug	9	108	86	1.3	
Sep	9	98	100	1.0	13. First fast-moving U-boat patrol line
Oct	16	94	105	0.9	
Nov	12	119	95	1.3	
Dec	5	60	97	0.6	14. Britain captured new U-boat code machine
1943					
Jan	7	37	92	0.4	
Feb	17	63	116	0.5	
Mar	14	108	116	0.9	15. Biggest convoy battles – HX229 & SC122 crossed unscathed
Apr	16	56	111	0.5	16. Crisis Convoy – almost all of HX231 got through
May	40	50	118	0.4	17. Black May – dramatic increase in U-boat losses
Jun	17	20	86	0.2	
Jul	38	46	84	0.5	
Aug	23	16	59	0.3	
Sep	8	20	60	0.3	18. Wolf pack operations were re-launched
Oct	26	20	86	0.2	
Nov	17	14	78	0.2	
Dec	8	13	67	0.2	
1944					
Jan	14	13	66	0.2	
Feb	17	18	68	0.3	
Mar	23	23	68	0.3	
Apr	19	9	57	0.2	
May	21	4	43	0.1	
Jun	26	11	47	0.2	19. D-Day – Allied invasion of Normandy
Jul	20	12	34	0.4	
Aug	33	18	50	0.4	
Sep	20	7	68	0.1	
Oct	11	1	45	0.0	
Nov	7	7	41	0.2	
Dec	13	9	51	0.2	
1945					
Jan	7	11	39	0.3	
Feb	18	15	47	0.3	
Mar	22	13	56	0.2	
Apr	39	13	54	0.2	
May	22	3	45	0.1	

1. U-boat activities were governed by Prize Ordinance Regulations, which prohibited surprise attacks against merchant ships unless they were engaged in warring activities. Ships had to be stopped and their papers inspected. They could only be sunk if they were carrying contraband. Permission to commence operations against enemy shipping transmitted to *Admiral Graf Spee* and *Deutschland* on 26 September.

Prize Ordinance Regulations did not place too many restrictions on the laying of mines and this, together with an embarrassing shortage of torpedoes, resulted in U-boats and other small surface ships being used as minelayers during the first winter of war. U-boats alone sailed on well over thirty mine mine-laying missions. Surface ship activities in British coastal waters have been only scantily documented.

2. Some Prize Ordinance Regulations were slowly relaxed in December 1939.

3 and 4. Some of the waters around the British Isles, mainly the east coast and Welsh and Cornish coasts, were declared to be a warzone where U-boats were allowed to attack without warning. A build-up of British and French forces in Norway gave the Germans the impetus to invade that country and Denmark. As a result U-boats were withdrawn from the shipping lanes. The Norwegian Campaign resulted in long queues at German repair yards and it was summer before U-boats reappeared on the high seas in significant numbers. In the meantime, the first auxiliary cruisers were leaving Germany with the main objective of remaining at sea for the longest possible period to draw British and French warships away from European waters.

5 and 6. Shortly after Germany occupied the French Atlantic coast, U-boats were given a freer hand by having Prize Ordinance Regulations lifted in all areas around Britain and France. These waters were declared to be a warzone where shipping could be sunk without warning. However, full unrestricted warfare did not start until August 1940. The lifting of regulations and the declaration of an unrestricted warfare zone around Britain and France resulted in a dramatic increase in the number of ships sunk. The British Naval War Staff stated that the high loss of personnel was due to merchant ships not being supplied with sufficient life-saving aids. U-boat successes peaked in October 1940 and from then on the number of ships sunk per U-boat at sea dropped steadily.

7 and 8. British ship-based radar was installed during this period and had its first major success in March 1941, when five U-boats, including three famous aces, were sunk. This was an incredible increase on previous months. A noteworthy and steady decline in U-boat successes continued until America joined in the war.

9. For several months the Americans continued sacrificing their tankers and other merchant ships without taking precautions against U-boats.

10–16. In February 1942, Germany introduced a new four-wheel Enigma machine for U-boats in the Atlantic, meaning that British code breakers were locked out until the end of the year, when one of these devices was captured from *U559*. The high tonnage being sunk by U-boats during 1942, reflected the number of U-boats at sea. For much of the year, there were around one hundred U-boats at sea, but despite the Allies not being able to read the secret U-boat code, the majority of merchant ships avoided U-boats. This high number of U-boats at sea remained around the one hundred mark for about six months before a large convoy battle took place. This happened in March 1943 when the fast convoy, HX229, ran into the back of the slow convoy, SC122; almost one hundred merchant ships were faced with one of the biggest U-boat groups and the largest convoy battle of all time took place. However, the number of merchant ships sunk per U-boat at sea remained low. Only a few weeks later, convoy HX231 crossed the Atlantic with hardly any losses.

17. U-boat fortunes took a drastic downward turn in May 1943 when forty were lost at sea – a dramatic increase from previous months. Dönitz withdrew some of his forces from the danger area, but he also asked his flotilla commanders to conduct a secret ballot among all the crews, asking the men whether they wanted to give up or continue with the struggle. The result was an overwhelming vote in support of continuing, despite the heavy losses.

18. Wolf pack operations were re-launched in September 1943 with the Leuthen and Rossbach Groups leading the way into the Atlantic. They had several new weapons to make this possible: warning devices that told them when Allied radar was being used in their vicinity; new improved anti-aircraft guns, which were thought capable of dealing with modern, fast-flying and front-armoured aircraft; new sound-sensitive, anti-destroyer (T5 – Zaunkönig) torpedoes and improved anti-convoy torpedoes. Unknown to the U-boat Command at the time, none of these had any significant impact.

19. Accounts of U-boat operations around D-Day need to be up-dated because much of the immediate post-war assessment appears to be inaccurate. Research by the diver Innes McCartney has shown that more U-boats than had previously been thought managed to make their way into the Channel. Originally, most of these boats were thought to have been sunk by the Royal Air Force in Operation Cork, the sealing off of the English Channel, but divers have found a significant number of wrecks close to the invasion beaches. Maps showing Allied losses towards the end of the war include significant numbers of sinkings around the British Isles, yet there appears to be little evidence of these losses in the statistics, and a further assessment would be valuable.

Lookouts on top of the conning tower. Each watch usually consisted of four men and one officer. The man looking towards the camera can be identified as an officer by the braid on the peak of his cap. It is difficult to distinguish the cap's peak of the man behind him; he could be either a commissioned or a warrant officer. In the middle are the binoculars of the torpedo aimer. These were usually only clipped in position when taking aim or when using the device for taking bearings. These binoculars did not have a grid inside and simply provided magnification. The angle settings from the stand below them were automatically transmitted down into the boat. The light machine-gun on the right did little more than provide the crew with a confidence boost. It had to be dismantled every time the boat dived and was not powerful enough to inflict any significant damage on aircraft.

THE WALTER U-BOAT

U-boats commissioned up to 1942 were not submarines in the true sense of the word. It would be more correct to call them submersibles. (Today they are often referred to as 'conventional' submarines.) They operated mostly on the surface and only dived to evade the enemy or rough seas. Occasionally, should the enemy be in the right position, it was possible to deliver a deadly attack while submerged, but such action required great skill and, more important, a lot of luck, because their submerged speed was nowhere near that of a surface ship. Once submerged, the submarines were more or less stationary, only able to move at the equivalent of a moderate walking pace, for their top speed of about eight knots could not be maintained for long periods.

The story of the Walter U-boat starts in 1934, a year after Hitler came to power and a year before the Anglo-German Naval Treaty – in other words, at a time when Germany was not allowed to build submarines. Hellmuth Walter, an unknown and minor employee at the Germania Works in Kiel, approached the Supreme Naval Command with plans for a new type of submarine. Like many inventors who offered their services, he was given a file reference number and his documents were carefully locked in a safe. Walter was just one of many. But about a year later, when Germany started to build submarines again, Walter returned to the Supreme Command and reminded them of his project. Finding them uninterested and realizing that he was making no progress, he turned to Dönitz, who was a flotilla commander at the time. Walter told Dönitz that his design would be capable of maintaining a submerged speed of about twenty-five knots for quite considerable periods. (This speed was faster than most surface submarine-hunters.) He went on to explain how he had met blank apathy at the Supreme Naval Command and how no one seemed interested in his idea. As Dönitz sardonically remarked later, 'Of course it's of no use to the Supreme Command – you can't parade a band on the upper deck!'

Walter's plans were eventually accepted and a small boat was built, although it had to be partly financed by the Germania Works. Resources were somewhat limited and, as a result, it took a long time to develop the project and the boat was not launched until 1940. However, it proved quite successful; being something of an impressive achievement, especially when one considers that Walter was no submariner and that he had no experienced full-time submarine engineers to help him; and, despite the difficulties, two naval advisers eventually suggested that the boat should be mass produced. Initially, this recommendation was rejected by the Supreme Naval Command, who gave Dönitz a dose of his own medicine by telling him that he had asked for Type VIIC; now, when he had got his way, was he changing his mind and asking for something completely different? Eventually, Grand Admiral Raeder personally gave the go-ahead for the new project. He also agreed to enlarge research facilities, so that more fast underwater boats could be built.

Many sceptics were still not convinced of the new wonder boat's superior performance, even after it had completed trials. For the benefit of several high-ranking officials, it was planned for *U792*, one of the experimental boats, to cruise submerged at various speeds over a measured mile. A powerful searchlight, like that used on trial torpedoes, was fitted to the front of the boat, enabling observers in a fast launch to watch the progress below the surface of the water. The first run at ten knots was completely satisfactory. Unfortunately, no one appeared to have taken into account that the U-boat could turn in under 200 yards, which was about half the distance required for the launch's tightest turn. Consequently, the observers lost sight of *U792* and the day ended with suggestions of the trials having been rigged. The group from the Supreme Naval Command returned to Berlin with an indifferent impression. The leaders of the U-boat arm were the next to see *U792* in action, and, this time, there was no formality, speedboats or fancy lights. Admiral Dönitz collared the leaders of the testing team, took them into a quiet corner, away from other ears, and asked them point-blank: 'Is that thing of any use?' 'Use! Herr Admiral, it's not only useful, it's a revolution.' Dönitz came away from the trials with his characteristic enthusiasm fired by the project. The next step was to get approval from the Supreme Naval Command to mass-produce the boats. But time was running out and Germany had lost many valuable weeks.

THE ELECTRO-BOAT

The Walter project gave birth to another new idea in 1942, when it became clear that the old methods of submarine attack were becoming less effective. Dönitz, wanting the Walter boat at the front and not as an additional novelty in the Baltic, called a meeting during November 1942 in Paris, to discuss the project's future. Walter could offer no prospect of the new boats being ready in the immediate future for, as he explained, everything about them was new and untried – everything from the engines and the fuel they needed to the tanks in which it was stored. (The highly dangerous hydrogen peroxide fuel was stored inside a special pressure hull,

Sections for the new electro boats of Type XXI were built inland and transported aboard barges to assembly yards near deeper water. This speeded up operations, but time was against Germany and only two left for operational voyages. Some were scuttled by the Germans towards the end of the war and many more were destroyed by the Allies some time after the ceasefire.

situated under the hull, in a figure of eight pattern.) Two submarine construction officers suggested that it might be quicker to build a Walter U-boat as a conventional submarine and use the lower hull to accommodate additional batteries, which should produce a much faster underwater speed. Initially, Dönitz liked this suggestion, but he came to the conclusion that the boat would still have to surface to charge the batteries with its diesel engines, and it would have to remain on the surface even longer than existing boats because there would be more batteries to charge. Dönitz emphasized that the submarines should spend as little time as possible on the surface, at which point Walter came up with the idea of fitting a flexible air-pipe to a small float and tow-

ing it behind the submerged submarine. Such a float could be made so small as to be hardly visible at night.

All these ideas were made 'off the cuff' at the meeting, so it was necessary to consider them in detail and calculate whether they were feasible. The resulting work on the electric submarine was most encouraging. A top speed of about twenty knots, or even more, was foreseen. Walter's assistants also considered the flexible breathing pipe, but Dipl. Ing. Heep thought a rigid air pipe might be better. Ulrich Gabler (after the war a professor and a leading ship designer) further modified the idea by drawing on knowledge gained from Dutch boats captured earlier in the war. He wanted to build the pipe in such a way that it could also be used in rough

A Type XXI that had been sunk and raised again. The men on the hull give some idea of the huge size of these new ocean-going boats. Although they represented a major technological advance on earlier models, they still retained some older features. The 20mm anti-aircraft guns, for example, were already obsolete by 1943, when Germany learned to their cost that they lacked the necessary punch to bring down fast-flying and front-armoured aircraft.

This is a rare photograph of *V80*, the high-speed research boat at the Germaniawerft in Kiel. 'V' stands for Versuchsboot – experimental boat. The '80' refers to its displacement of eighty tons when submerged. The boat had a crew of five men and no armament, but could get up to some twenty-eight knots while remaining fully submerged. These days, submarines are capable of cruising faster when submerged than when on the surface, but this was a highly revolutionary concept in 1938/39, when this boat was designed.

weather, when waves would frequently wash over the top.

The results of these calculations were laid before Dönitz shortly after he took overall command of the Navy during January 1943, and he suggested that the electro-submarine be built immediately, while research continued on the Walter turbine project. The Construction Bureau at the Supreme Naval Command was approached, and they calculated that it would be 1946 before the first operational boats could be completed. Apparently, the Bureau did not agree to their immediate mass-production, saying they could not take responsibility for building a new and untried craft in such large numbers. It was emphasized that the date '1946' could only be a rough estimate, since Hitler's support had to be gained and the calculation did not allow for any possible disruption by air raids. But, for the U-boat Command, 1946 was too late, and they approached Dr Albert Speer who was head of the Military Armaments Department in the government. Negotiations paid off and, shortly afterwards, Speer's department came back to U-boat Command with new suggestions.

One of the directors suggested pre-fabricating the new boats; if they could be built in sections and assembled at a river-side shipyard, production time could be halved, and the first boats would be ready by 1944. Furthermore, the engineers saw no difficulty in starting mass-production without first building a prototype. These plans were laid before Hitler on 8 July 1943, and it was agreed that Speer should build forty new boats per month. Such expectations were never achieved, although the boats were constructed at an incredibly fast rate – especially when one considers the valuable labour lost with the continuing production of the obsolete Type VIIC U-boats. Autumn 1943 saw a marked increase in Allied air raids and, as a direct consequence of the Allied leaders' decision at the Yalta Conference to make the defeat of the U-boats one of their main aims, U-boat bases and building yards were singled out for heavy bombing. Yet, despite this, no great success seems to have been achieved and the United States' Strategic Bombing Survey of the German U-boat Industry states, 'No damage from air attack was caused to any of the submarines built by ordinary methods.'

The few electro-boats that were used on operational missions before the end of the war proved enough to make their crews realize they were the weapons of the future – weapons that could have turned the tide of war in the Atlantic, had they arrived in time. It is interesting to speculate what might have happened in the Battle of the Atlantic if the boats had been ready in the summer of 1942 or even 1943, for the Allied navies would have had no countermeasures ready. The Allies were certainly surprised when they unearthed this new design in the German building yards at the end of the war. Yet, Britain knew these boats were on their way and had already carried out trials with a hastily improvised Royal Navy submarine, which achieved high underwater speeds by having much of its internal space filled with batteries.

U-BOAT CONSTRUCTION AND DR ALBERT SPEER

Until 1943, the absence of a central office for submarine armament meant that construction was an uncommonly long-winded procedure. The initial ideas usually started at the Marinekommandoamt I (Naval Command Office I), which considered the strategic requirements for new projects. Then, the military and technical aspects were considered by the Marinekonstruktionsamt (Naval Construction Office) and also by the Marinekommandoamt A IV a. The latter employed numerous experts in the major technical fields. These two departments then decided on the details of the new ship, and their resulting plans only had to be approved by the Supreme Naval Command before construction could begin. The Naval Construction Office was also responsible for all stages of ship construction, including submarines. There was an additional specialist office for U-boats within the Supreme Naval Command which dealt with the problems unique to submarines.

At that time the Navy was also responsible for building its own ships. Dönitz considered that it would be far better if this responsibility could be handed over to industry, thus allowing the Navy to concentrate on fighting the war. So, towards the end of 1942, he approached the Armaments Minister, Dr Albert Speer, with a view to his ministry taking over U-boat construction. (Speer had already done something similar for the Army.) Speer agreed, and the office for submarine construction at the Supreme Command (U-Bootsamt) was disbanded and replaced by the Shipbuilding Commission, under the leadership of Konteradmiral Karl Topp. This body comprised naval construction experts and industrialists, with an admiral at their head to ensure that they actually built ships that the Navy wanted.

Hitler agreed to this new construction arrangement on 31 March 1943 and, as a result, a new fleet building programme went ahead. It proved most successful, for the industrial representatives, with their knowledge of modern techniques, often cut corners that the Navy alone could not.

THE HEINKEL 177

The story behind the development of the Heinkel He 177 (Greif) is most interesting and highlights the lack of co-oper-ation between the various branches of the German armed forces. The aeroplane was originally proposed in 1934 as a long distance bomber. Two prototypes were built: the Dornier Do 19 and the Junkers Ju 89. Neither proved successful and the designs were abandoned until 1938, when they were re-considered under the name of the Heinkel He 177 (Greif). The Navy became interested in the He 177 because of its suitability to provide long-range reconnaissance support for U-boats, but only a few unsuccessful prototypes were built. Numerous changes to the specifications were required and progress was rather slow. In 1938 the U-boat arm was still in its infancy and was not at that time concerned with air support. The Navy did not push the project, and the idea was dropped.

Dönitz finally asked for the He 177 in 1942. But, instead of producing it, the Luftwaffe informed him that the aircraft would not be available for the U-boat arm. According to Hermann Göring, anything that flew automatically belonged to the Luftwaffe; and the new long-range aeroplane was no exception. It too was considered an exclusive development of the Luftwaffe, who were determined that other interested parties would have to wait their turn. (Relations were so deplorable at one stage that when Raeder asked for urgent air support, he was told that the Navy would get such support when Göring considered the time right!) In the end, research for a very long-range submarine-support aircraft was abandoned in favour of an aeroplane to fill the heavy bomber role, and the few aeroplanes that were built were required by the Air Force for their own bombing projects. So, the weapon that the Navy thought was being kept for a rainy day never materialized.

U-BOAT POLICY, SEPTEMBER 1942

It has often been stated that the U-boat offensive collapsed suddenly during the summer of 1943. This may be borne out by the statistics if one looks at them quickly, but not by the facts supporting them. What remained of the offensive certainly collapsed during the fateful May of 1943, but it had started to crumble as early as the end of 1940. A significant cause of this decline took place in March 1941 when several U-boat aces were lost and radar began to play a significant role in the war at sea.

The year 1941 was looked upon as having been a difficult one for U-boats, but relatively few U-boats were sunk while their successes were over estimated. So the setbacks were looked upon more as temporary setbacks, rather than indica-tors of a major turn of events. In late spring 1942, however, the new trends in the Atlantic alarmed the U-boat Command sufficiently to prompt a discussion of the changes in the war pattern early that summer. A detailed list of modifications necessary to keep pace with developments was drawn up and laid before Raeder on 28 September 1942. Being so impor-tant, it was discussed with Hitler in the Reich's Chancellery, Dönitz outlining the recent trends in the Battle of the Atlantic, and pointing out that the main battle had moved from American waters back into the middle of the ocean, where U-boats were facing much better-protected convoys. The Allies were tending to guard merchant ships with two rings of defence: there was a tight ring of escorts around the convoy, with some warships in the convoy's ranks; and there were also more escorts spread around this net at much greater distances from the core, making it difficult for U-boats to get close-in for their attacks. High Frequency Direction Finders (H/F D/F) started coming into service during the autumn of 1941. These made it possible to determine the direction of even short radio signals. Once installed aboard escorts and some merchant ships, this invention made it possible to determine the time of an attack when U-boats broke radio silence to start their run in. At the same time, it indicated the direction the attack was coming from and escorts with radar could intercept to force the U-boat under and locate it with asdic.

Aeroplanes presented one of the biggest problems. The 'air gap' (the area in the middle of the Atlantic that could not be reached by land-based aircraft) was decreasing, and Dönitz predicted it would not be long before it closed completely. He emphasized the importance of aircraft operating in conjunction with U-boats, to reconnoitre and find enemy convoys, and he suggested the new Heinkel 177 be put into production to meet this demand. Dönitz also asked for the performances of U-boats and their armament to be improved. He especially made the following recommendations, with all of which Hitler agreed:

• To increase the underwater speed by building the new Walter U-boats (see below).
• To increase the maximum diving depth. (The effectiveness of depth charges and asdic decreases as depth is increased.)
• To develop new weapons for U-boats.
• To increase anti-aircraft armament.

NEW WEAPONS FOR OLD U-BOATS

This section deals with new weapons discussed with Hitler during September 1942, although they were somewhat different to those actually installed less than a year later.

During the summer of 1942, it became apparent to the U-boat Command that attacks from both aircraft and small surface warships were preventing some U-boats from getting close enough to convoys. Although very often the warships did not find the submarines, they did prevent the U-boat commanders from pressing home their attacks. Torpedoes had virtually no effect against small surface escorts, which had such shallow draughts that the 'eels' passed harmlessly beneath them. In addition, the escorts travelled too fast for the submarines to take accurate aim, and they often faced the U-boats head-on, making themselves small, difficult targets.

The German Navy had a weapon to combat this problem, and Dönitz asked for it to be put into mass-production. It was a special torpedo, just like an ordinary G7e, but with a sound-detection head at the front which enabled it to find its way to the target by homing in on propeller noise. However, this Zaunkönig (acoustic torpedo), or T5, did not produce the expected results, although the Naval High Command had high hopes of it (see page 52).

Torpedoes for use against merchant ships were also modified, to make it possible for U-boats to fire from greater distances without first taking careful aim. These torpedoes travelled in a straight line for a predetermined distance and then looped. Fired amongst a convoy, there was a good chance of them hitting a ship. Torpedo-firing mechanisms in U-boats were improved by fitting angle deflectors. As a result,

it was no longer necessary to point the whole boat at the target, and torpedoes could be fired at angles of up to ninety degrees to the boat's course.

It is important to emphasize that the German torpedoes still had a minor fault – one that had not been eliminated after the torpedo crisis of 1939/40. Although they detonated, they often failed to sink their targets. The battles of 1943 were plagued by far too many stragglers from the convoys, ships that had either been slowed down or stopped by one U-boat and then had to be sunk by another. This situation was so bad that Dönitz was prompted to note in his diary: 'The torpedoes are having less effect than in 1918.' Merchant ships produced during the war were built with several watertight compartments to prevent them sinking if the hull was holed. Even so, the torpedoes should have had more effect.

In 1942, 'bees' (German slang for aeroplanes) only presented U-boats with a few problems, and it was still possible to avoid conflict. At that time the RAF did not have any long-range aircraft available, so the U-boats were only threatened when they were close to the coast. The U-boat Command anticipated the closing of the 'air gap' in the Atlantic, and they were planning ahead to meet a situation that would require them to fight off aircraft while attacking convoys. Konteradmiral Werner Lange, Commander-in-Chief of Amtsgruppe U-Bootswesen at OKM/SKL (a department in the Supreme Naval Command dealing with U-boat matters), showed how the conning-towers could be modified to accommodate 15mm machine-guns. 20mm anti-aircraft guns, it was suggested, should be fitted in addition to 37mm and 50mm automatic guns. Hitler showed little interest in the 50mm gun – with which the Luftwaffe had experienced many problems – but Raeder emphasized to the Führer the importance of continuing research. He also reported on the discoveries with the so-called 'N-Stoff', an explosive for igniting heavy oil, which it was hoped would help sink more enemy ships. Several other ideas were discussed at the September meeting. It was suggested that U-boats should be fitted with 10-metre high (33ft.) lookout masts. These were attached to a few U-boats, but they did not become operational on a large scale. It was also thought possible to cover U-boats with a rubber-like skin to absorb asdic impulses. Such covering, known as 'Alberich Skin', was used later in 1944/45, but it also had a limited practical use because it was difficult to attach to the outside of the boat.

'THROW THE SURFACE FLEET INTO THE DUSTBIN'

The question of how to employ the surface fleet came to a head shortly after Christmas 1942, when Erich Raeder resigned as Supreme Commander-in-Chief of the Navy, to be replaced by the head of the U-boat arm, Karl Dönitz. The conflict between Raeder and Hitler had entered its final round during those last days of 1942, when part of the North Norway Naval Squadron arrived in the Arctic Seas to intercept convoy JW51B. (This was similar to the famous PQ series, running from Britain to North Russia.) Vizeadmiral Oskar Kummetz moved out to attack with the heavy cruisers *Hipper* and *Lützow* plus six destroyers; but he was forced to approach the operation with virtually one hand tied behind his back, since all commanders had been given strict instruc-

The after deck of one of either *Schlesien* or *Schleswig-Holstein* with a large number of cadets on board. Some of the boilers were removed before the beginning of the Second World War to provide more accommodation in the cramped interior.

tions not to put their ships at risk. This order had been issued shortly after the sinking of the *Bismarck*, whose loss had dealt a stunning blow to German prestige particularly Hitler's – even though he appears to have been the only person to have predicted this dramatic end, as early as the day on which the ship was launched. So, excessive caution, bad weather and good escorts (including the cruisers *Sheffield* and *Jamaica*) were pitched against the German squadron. Shortly after starting the action, Kummetz received a signal by way of a reminder: 'No unnecessary risks'. Then, *Hipper* received a hit in her boiler room, and the destroyer *Eckholdt* was sunk. By this time the light was failing and visibility was bad, making ideal conditions for Allied destroyers to creep in close for a torpedo attack, so Kummetz decided to break off the action, and limped back to Altenfjord.

Meanwhile, over Hitler's headquarters there hung an air of gloom, dispelled for a brief time by the New Year celebrations and by expectations of an impending victory in the Arctic. But Germany had suffered severe setbacks on the Eastern Front: the Army in Russia was in a deplorable state, and the great defeat at Stalingrad was looming large on the horizon. Germany, and Hitler in particular, desperately needed a victory. So, when he received the signal from Kummetz stating 'Am engaging convoy', Hitler literally jumped for joy. A short time later, *U354*, commanded by Kptlt. Karl-Heinz Herbschleb, reported that the battle appeared to have reached its climax: the men in the U-boat could see the fireworks, but they could not give any details of how the battle was progressing. After this, the lines to the north of Norway went dead and nothing more was heard. Despite this ominous occurrence, Hitler bounced around his

headquarters like an excited child, telling newcomers they would soon hear some good news, and taking every opportunity to seek out Vizeadmiral Theodor Krancke, the Navy's permanent representative at the Führer's headquarters, to ask for news. But none came. In the end, Hitler was informed by a BBC announcement that an Allied convoy had successfully beaten off a much stronger German cruiser force in the Arctic Seas. This really activated his adrenalin, and he threatened to make U-boats out of the whole surface fleet.

To make matters worse, the lines to the north of Norway remained dead; Kummetz could not be contacted by radio, telephone or telex. When Krancke telephoned Raeder, requesting him to come and see Hitler at once, Raeder, guessed what was afoot, waited for news and planned his 'offensive' before setting out. Hitler had cooled down a little by the time the two men eventually met, but he was not fully composed. Raeder was subjected to a rude and insulting tirade for over an hour, during which he was told that the surface fleet was useless and that the whole capital fleet should be thrown into the dustbin. Instead of losing his temper, however, Raeder played a trump card that he had been contemplating for some time: he asked to be relieved of his post. (The relationship between Hitler and Raeder had started to deteriorate before the start of the war. This situation, plus his dislike of the Führer had led Raeder to contemplate resigning and making way for another person.) Hitler was thrown off balance by this unexpected broadside, and he immediately changed tack, saying it had not been a personal attack but that the capital ships were no good. Raeder remained adamant and maintained that he could not continue with his duties. He went on to suggest that the whole matter could be

When Grand Admiral Raeder, seen here on the left, resigned as Supreme Commander-in-Chief of the Kriegsmarine he suggested that Admiral Rolf Carls (on the extreme right) might be his best successor, but he also suggested that Hitler might prefer Admiral Karl Dönitz, if the Führer wished to emphasize and promote the U-boat war.

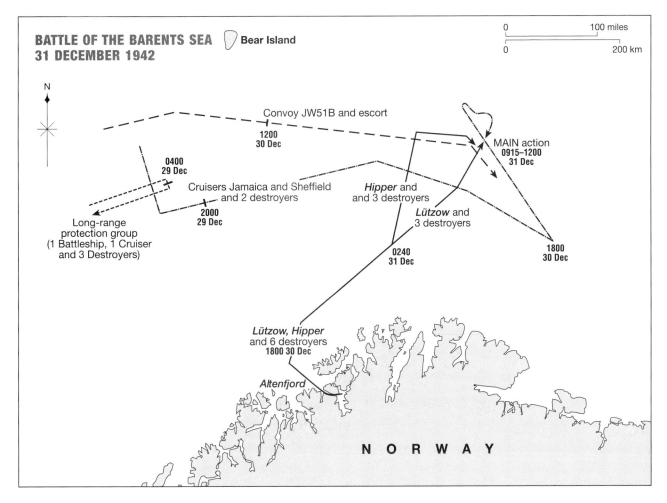

BATTLE OF THE BARENTS SEA
31 DECEMBER 1942   Bear Island

0   100 miles
0   200 km

N

Convoy JW51B and escort

1200
30 Dec

0400
29 Dec

MAIN action
0915–1200
31 Dec

Cruisers Jamaica and Sheffield
and 2 destroyers

Hipper and
and 3 destroyers

2000
29 Dec

Lützow and
3 destroyers

Long-range
protection group
(1 Battleship, 1 Cruiser
and 3 Destroyers)

0240
31 Dec

1800
30 Dec

Lützow, Hipper
and 6 destroyers
1800 30 Dec

Altenfjord

N O R W A Y

solved quietly, without embarrassment to Hitler: the resignation could coincide with the tenth anniversary of the
NSDAP's (National Socialist Workers' Party) coming to
power and it could appear quite natural. This Hitler
accepted, but he asked Raeder to consider the matter carefully and to nominate two successors. Raeder suggested
Admiral Rolf Carls (Commander-in-Chief of the Naval
Group Command North) and Admiral Karl Dönitz. He considered Carls more suitable, because of his experience and, as
he would not be 'stepping over' anybody, his appointment
would not cause any bad feeling. Hitler might prefer Dönitz,
however, if he wished to stress the U-boat war.

Dönitz was called to Hitler's headquarters on 25 January
1943, was officially informed of Raeder's resignation, and was
then asked to become his successor. He was requested to take
office on 30 January (the tenth anniversary of Hitler's coming to power and the end of the Battle of Stalingrad, which
marked one of the great turning points in the Second World
War). Dönitz was also told of Hitler's decision to scrap the
capital ships in favour of U-boats and, ironically, this important issue was the subject of the first battle between the two
men. One would have expected Dönitz to be pleased that
Hitler had fully recognized the paramount importance of the
U-boat arm, but in fact he took the opposite view. He told
Hitler that the surface fleet was tying up vast enemy resources
which, once Britain realized the large ships were out of
action, would be unleashed against U-boats and German
towns. Characteristically, Hitler continued to argue his case
against the battleships, saying they were useless, but Dönitz

stood firm and, in the end, Hitler acquiesced, maintaining
nevertheless that it would not be long before Dönitz realized
the mistake he was making.

DÖNITZ AS SUPREME COMMANDER-IN-CHIEF

Another disagreement between Hitler and the new Grand
Admiral occurred when Hitler received news of a German
ship being sunk by a British submarine in the eastern
Mediterranean. Hitler commented acidly: 'The English can
do it! We have our submarines sitting all around Gibraltar
and they cannot sink a thing!' At this, much to the astonish-
ment of those present, Dönitz retorted 'Our best boats are
around Gibraltar, where they are fighting the strongest maritime power in the world. They could also sink ships if they
were put into an area totally devoid of submarine-hunters. I
have put our best men around Gibraltar and, let me tell you,
they are a darn sight better than the English!' Hitler went red
in the face at this outburst, but did not reply and, afterwards,
Dönitz thought his days as Supreme Commander-in-Chief
were numbered. In fact, however, the confrontation marked
a turning-point in the relationship between the two men.
Hitler never again lost his temper with Dönitz, and he never
again murmured disparaging comments about the Navy –
not even after the submarine offensive totally collapsed. The
Führer was always correct and polite towards the Grand
Admiral. He seemed to appreciate Dönitz's advice and always
referred to Dönitz as 'Herr Grossadmiral'. Later, Hitler

would often telephone Dönitz's headquarters during air raids to make sure he was safely in his bunker. Hitler also supplied Dönitz with an armoured Mercedes, and requested him not fly, in case the aircraft was shot down.

The gulf between Hitler and the naval leadership started to close after January 1943, and this has led to several assertions that Dönitz's promotion was a political manoeuvre. His appointment was followed by a certain amount of reorganization that necessitated the sacking of several admirals, and this too has been interpreted as another step towards bringing the Navy in line with party politics. Actually, there was no political motive for Dönitz's appointment. Although in sympathy with the Party, he was never Hitler's puppet, and party politics never permeated the Navy as much as they did the other armed forces. Dönitz remained neutral throughout any political moves; he did not meddle with Party officials, and neither did he allow them to interfere with the Navy. They tried to infiltrate on several occasions, but got no farther than the Grand Admiral, who presented a solid wall of Prussian principles. Dönitz politely told people he was Supreme Commander and would therefore decide what went on. On one occasion, several naval officials were due to be tried by the People's Court in Berlin for offending Party ideals. Dönitz sent word to have them released, and informed the presiding judge that the Navy's judicial system was quite capable of dealing with breaches of discipline.

It is true that National Socialist Guidance Officers were attached to several ships, as well as naval land units, to spread the gospel of the Party. However, these men had a great deal less power in naval establishments than in the Army or Luftwaffe. Some U-boat commanders even exercised their right of 'instant dismissal' to get rid of such people. (Every man serving in U-boats had the right to leave his boat, without giving a reason, as soon as a replacement could be found. Similarly, a commander could remove any member of his crew. There was no red tape and, usually, such requests were complied with instantly.) But it would be wrong to give the impression of naval justice having been correct at all times. One U-boat commander was recalled from holiday for what his colleagues thought would be a presentation of the Knight's Cross – instead, he was executed. Apparently, he had tuned the ward-room radio to the BBC wavelength. His other misdemeanours included making sour remarks about German leaders and removing a photograph of Adolf Hitler.

The suggestion that the sacking of various admirals in early 1943 was a move to dispose of opposition to the NSDAP in the Navy is somewhat absurd when one considers that several of the retiring admirals were Party sympathisers, while many of those that remained did not support the National Socialists. Neither of the two famous admirals directly under Dönitz, Eberhard Godt and Hans-Georg von Friedeburg, were renowned for their support of the Party.

In order to understand how Dönitz and his generation saw the National Socialists' rise to power, it is necessary to turn back the pages of history to the beginning of the century. Dönitz's upbringing – like that of his contemporaries – placed little value on individuality, but had instilled in him a deep sense of obedience and service to the State. So, when Dönitz and his contemporaries saw the tremendous strides made by Hitler and the NSDAP to pull Germany from the abyss of depression after the First World War, they could not help but be impressed. Many influential visitors to Germany were impressed by what they saw, and returned to their homelands singing the praises of the new order. So, if Hitler was held in such high esteem by foreigners, why should the German people not be proud of their leader and their new national status?

THE DEFEAT OF THE CONVENTIONAL SUBMARINE

The war in the Atlantic took a dramatic turn during April and May of 1943. In April, convoy HX231 managed to drive off almost all attacking U-boats; in May, submarine losses rose to forty-two from only fifteen in the previous month. Losses rocketed to levels the U-boat Command had not thought possible, not even in their worst nightmares. Dönitz recorded in his diary that he was used to disappointments and setbacks, but never in such proportions. On 24 May, he admitted defeat and ordered all U-boats out of the North Atlantic. Boats with little fuel were instructed to return home, and the rest were directed to different areas. The fantastic losses made it quite clear that the conventional submarine was obsolete. But, as the new underwater boats would not be ready for some while, the U-boat Command considered it vital to maintain pressure in the Atlantic by sending in the old boats again, and also by implementing several new ideas straightaway.

- A scientific branch within the Navy must breach the gap between research and the front-line of the battle, and ensure that the new technology become operational as soon as possible. The development of radar detection apparatus was considered of paramount importance.
- Anti-aircraft armament must be increased to keep aeroplanes away from submarines, and better protection provided for the men on top of the conning-tower.
- The acoustic torpedo must be made operational at once.
- Fast underwater boats must be brought into service as soon as possible.

IMPROVED ANTI-AIRCRAFT ARMAMENT

The strengthening of anti-aircraft armament was the easiest to implement of the four points listed above. The large gun in front of the conning-tower was removed, and the existing gun platform behind the tower enlarged to carry two twin 20mm guns. Another platform was also added to the rear of operational boats – to hold either one quadruple 20mm or a single 37mm AA gun. (There were slight variations in the exact armament; as a result, several interesting and unusual experimental designs can still be seen in photographs.) The first boat with the modified armament, *U758* (a Type VIIC boat) under command of Kptlt. Helmut Manseck, left Brest on 8 June 1943. An aircraft attacked early that evening, and the new guns were given their first operational test. The aircraft, not expecting the extra sting, received hits, whereupon it dropped a smoke buoy, jettisoned its bombs and disappeared from view. Shortly afterwards, two more aircraft appeared, and began circling out of range of the boat's guns. Finally, a third aeroplane came on the scene and attacked: it dropped depth-charges, but was hit and crashed into the sea. *U758* kept the other aircraft at a distance of about two miles, but at least eleven of the submarine's crew had been injured, and Manseck decided it was time to 'go down into the cellar'. (This incident taught him that the additional conning-tower armour was only sufficient to protect the men from direct hits, for numerous minor injuries had been caused by flying metal.) Despite the injuries, the event was thought quite encouraging and, although the men did not consider the new armament ideal, they felt that the problem could be overcome with more experience and training.

During 1942, the idea of building special submarines as 'submersible AA batteries' had been considered. When Kptlt. Odo Loewe returned to base with *U256*, badly damaged, and the engineers declared her unfit for further rigorous convoy action, someone came up with the bright idea of keeping her on the surface in the Bay of Biscay as a special anti-aircraft submarine. However, at that time there was no necessity for such craft and, although a suitable deck layout design was completed, nothing else was done. Eventually, it was decided to fit a single 37mm, one quadruple 20mm and two twin 20mm AA guns. It was planned to mount one platform in front of the conning-tower to enable the 'trap' to shoot forwards. (Normally, AA guns mounted on U-boats could only fire backwards or sideways.)

The first boat to sail with these modifications was *U441*, commanded by Kptlt. Götz von Hartmann, which left Brest on 22 May 1943. Next day, their first action against an enemy aeroplane produced mixed fortunes. The gunners only managed to shoot the Sunderland down after it had dropped its depth-charges, and these caused such heavy damage that *U441* was forced to return for repairs. July 1943 found *U441* back in the 'Black Pit of Biscay', where she saw further action on the 11th. Again, her gunners shot down their attacker, but not before it had killed ten crewmen and wounded a further dozen, including the commander. After patching up the men, the medical officer, Dr Pfaffinger, took control and sailed the boat back to port. The wounded had hardly been removed to hospital before the news spread like wildfire around the base, and numerous people volunteered to take the not-too-badly-damaged boat back to sea.

About another half a dozen boats were converted to aircraft traps, but their limited success merely illustrated the RAF's superiority. Consequently, they were converted back to the ordinary conning-tower design shortly after the anti-aircraft operations started, which helps to explain why there are so few photographs of them. Most of these aircraft traps operated in the Bay of Biscay, but recently some photographs were donated to the German U-boat Museum that showed at least one of these boats in a Norwegian port.

Operational U-boats crossing the Bay of Biscay also tried a new technique to overcome the aircraft problem. They travelled through the most dangerous area, near the coast, in small groups – the idea being that, once enemy aircraft had been spotted, the boats would be brought into a fairly tight formation, and their combined fire used with telling effect. However, the RAF very soon became wary of the boats' extra sting and changed their methods of attack. Instead of coming in straightaway, the aircraft would circle out of reach of

A schnorkel head valve. A variety of different types were tried out, but the majority worked on the same simple principle as the system that cuts off water inside lavatory cisterns. The modern, newly-built electro boats were fitted with periscopic schnorkels, but on older boats they hinged at deck level. The hinged contraption was raised hydraulically until the pipe clipped into a bracket on the top of the tower. This worked reasonably well, but schnorkeling was uncomfortable for the crew and did little other than provide a meagre difference between life and death. The top speed was limited to a maximum of five knots when wave conditions were perfect, otherwise the schnorkel was liable to break off, this was a long way short of the speed needed to chase convoys.

the anti-aircraft guns, and call for help. Then, either a number of aircraft would attack simultaneously from different directions, or the Royal Navy would appear on the horizon. This increased the odds against the U-boats and they gave up fighting in this way. Instead they returned to an earlier technique of crossing the danger zone in the Bay of Biscay submerged.

SCHNORKELS

The events of summer 1943 made it clear that U-boats would either have to be removed from the surface completely or give up the battle in the Atlantic. The new electro-submarines were not due to be operational until the summer of the following year, so a stop-gap had to be found. It was decided to fit existing boats with breathing pipes, making it possible for them to run their diesel engines while submerged. Such an idea was not new – indeed, it had been committed to paper long before man had the technology to build submarines, and ventilation masts had also been used by several navies to provide fresh air for the crews of submarines. But it was Commander J. J. Wichers of the Royal Netherlands Navy who developed the first practical pipe to supply air to the diesel engines as well, and thus he made it possible for submarines to use these engines without breaking the surface. Wichers' idea was only partly exploited, as the Dutch principle could only be used in relatively good conditions; if the seas were rough, the boats still had to come to the surface. Wichers had conceived his idea as a means of keeping submarines just below the surface of the water to avoid overheating in hotter tropical climates.

This early Dutch ventilation mast had several advantages that were not unappreciated by submarine crews. When, for example, the Dutch commander, Commodore J F van Dulm (who served under the British flag in *O21* during the war), was informed of an Admiralty committee's decision to remove *021*'s ventilation mast, he expressed his sorrow. It made life much more comfortable because it could still be raised to draw air into the boat, but at the same time it prevented waves from washing in, and kept the boat's interior much drier.

Some of these Dutch masts were captured when the German forces invaded Holland, but at that time there was no need for such structures, and they were removed from the boats taken over by the German Navy. In 1942, Ulrich Gabler, together with Engineer Heinrich Heep, modified the principle to make it possible to use the air mast under all sea conditions, even if the water washed over the top of the duct. Unfortunately, this was most uncomfortable for the crew, because the men had difficulties adjusting to the great variations in pressure created. The invention only provided the difference between death from enemy action and an unpleasant and most difficult existence. Schnorkels presented far more problems than they solved, and they certainly did not change the U-boats' role from the defensive back to the offensive.

Constructing and fitting the devices presented no great problem, however, and the work went ahead during the spring of 1944. The Dragoner Group was the first U-boat pack to have all its boats fitted with schnorkels. This pack of five boats was at sea from 20 May 1944 until the end of that month, and their operation proved quite unsuccessful. *U247*, commanded by Oblt.z.S. Gerhard Matschulat, managed to sink the 200-ton trawler *Norneen* on 5 July 1944, but that was hardly the sort of success needed to keep pace with the battle. Not that the U-boat men failed to make the effort; they worked, fought and died harder than ever before. It is really astonishing that so many of them survived those last months, when the odds were weighted so heavily against them.

THE TORPEDO CATASTROPHE

The acoustic torpedo, known as T5 or Zaunkönig (wren), and other special torpedoes used later during the war, were basically the same electric Type G7e as made in 1940. The propulsion and detonation systems were similar, but additional equipment was added to the nose.

The T5 had been developed long before the war, but, as the weapon was not required and the Navy wanted to preserve its secrecy, it was not put into general service. It is difficult to pinpoint exactly when the project started, and appears to have roots going back to the First World War, but we do know that working models were available for experiments as early as 1936. This can be determined by an incident involving the torpedo-boat *Möwe*. One of her officers, Freiherr W. Nikolaus von Lyncker, recalled how *Möwe* was passing the firing ranges near Eckernförde, when a torpedo ran off course, followed the torpedo-boat and ended up in the propeller. A loud clatter alerted all who had not seen the 'eel' approach, and they watched while the apologetic owners of the stray torpedo collected the somewhat battered specimen. After this, the acoustic torpedo appears to have vanished into obscurity and did not reappear until the middle of the war. A special school, under the command of Korvkpt. Otto Köhler, was established in Gotenhafen

(Gdynia) during the summer of 1943 to instruct U-boat officers in the operational use of this anti-destroyer weapon. The T5 was introduced exclusively for U-boats, and it was not issued to motor torpedo-boats until the late autumn of 1944. Instruction facilities were later also founded in other parts of Europe, and Köhler commuted with his staff from one end of the Continent to the other, working wherever required.

This acoustic torpedo was no longer a simple device designed to run into a target's propeller. The idea of rendering it useless by the target towing a noise-maker some distance astern was appreciated early in its development, and the T5 had a special programme to avoid such 'foxers'. When it came close to the noise source, an automatic steering control would turn the rudder and make it swim in a circle. The sound-detection head was situated at the end of a small cone-shaped structure, which funnelled noise from about thirty degrees either side of its path and shielded the detector from side noises. Therefore, the torpedo would not respond to the 'foxer' while it was swimming in a small circle. At some point, however, the front would be directed towards the real propeller, and the 'eel' would head for this louder sound source. Again, the automatic steering control would take effect to guide the torpedo around the noise; but this time the ship would be too long to avoid the 'eel's' small circular deviation, and the torpedo would collide with or pass under the hull, triggering off a contact pistol or activating a magnetic detonator.

Faults in German torpedoes (page 33) were not fully recognized in 1940, and some of these irregularities kept cropping up later with disastrous results. In fact, these faults – and not the Royal Navy's 'foxers' – were responsible for saving so many British ships. German wartime records show that acoustic torpedoes had but a 50 per cent success rate. Half of the failures were attributed to recognized mistakes, about 14 per cent to unexplained errors and only about 10 per cent to misfires. But an entirely different picture emerged after the war, when British wartime records were made available for the first time. Prof Dr Jürgen Rohwer calculated that just over 700 acoustic torpedoes were fired during the war, and only 77 of these were definite hits. His figures boil down to a success rate of just over 16 per cent.

Most of the torpedoes ran erratically and exploded some distance behind the target, making the Allies think the 'foxers' were successful. The U-boat crew, on the other hand, would have regarded the explosion as a sinking because they would have been unable to observe the result; commanders were ordered to dive to sixty metres (about 200 feet) after firing, to prevent the T5 from turning around and homing-in on the noise from the U-boat.

German acoustic torpedoes were also responsible for sinking at least two German U-boats. Both *U377* and *U972* were recorded as 'Lost by unknown cause. No survivors', and the facts surrounding these two sinkings have only recently come to light with the release to the general public of various formerly secret British documents. Each boat sent an SOS call after her last recorded radio contact, stating that she had been torpedoed and was sinking. There is no reference to these signals in the record of losses kept by the U-boat Command, but they were picked up and deciphered by Admiralty Intelligence in London. The Royal Navy knew that the Germans were using new torpedoes, and were keeping an ear

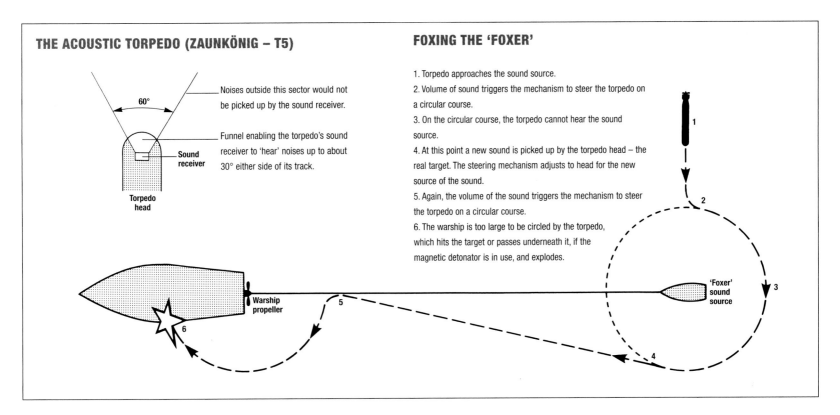

THE ACOUSTIC TORPEDO (ZAUNKÖNIG – T5)

60°

Noises outside this sector would not be picked up by the sound receiver.

Funnel enabling the torpedo's sound receiver to 'hear' noises up to about 30° either side of its track.

Sound receiver

Torpedo head

Warship propeller

FOXING THE 'FOXER'

1. Torpedo approaches the sound source.
2. Volume of sound triggers the mechanism to steer the torpedo on a circular course.
3. On the circular course, the torpedo cannot hear the sound source.
4. At this point a new sound is picked up by the torpedo head – the real target. The steering mechanism adjusts to head for the new source of the sound.
5. Again, the volume of the sound triggers the mechanism to steer the torpedo on a circular course.
6. The warship is too large to be circled by the torpedo, which hits the target or passes underneath it, if the magnetic detonator is in use, and explodes.

'Foxer' sound source

cocked for any useful information. When they received the news, the Admiralty made a thorough check of all their operations in the Atlantic and found there had been no Allied torpedo attacks. Both torpedoes must therefore have been fired from German ships. Interestingly enough though, the Royal Navy was most casual when it came to recording facts and recent research by Axel Niestlé shows that the data for *U377* and *U305* had been mixed up; the published details for *U305* actually apply to *U377* and vice versa. In addition to this, the team led by John Chatterton found *U869* off New York, which almost certainly was sunk by its own acoustic torpedo while aiming at some target which never noticed the attack.

Acoustic torpedoes were used for the first time in large-scale combat between 18 and 23 September 1943, when the Leuthen Group of U-boats were operating in the shipping lanes of the eastern Atlantic. Several T5s were fired, but without any success. These boats were also fitted with the new anti-aircraft armament, so it was decided to try a new method of attack: as U-boats were disadvantaged by Allied radar at night, they assembled on the surface in broad daylight and approached a convoy. Their guns were ready to keep enemy aircraft at bay, and the acoustic torpedoes were ready to deal with any approaching escorts. Despite their forward planning, however, the U-boats were distinctly worsted. On 20 September an Allied aeroplane dropped an acoustic torpedo out of the guns' range and managed to sink *U338*, commanded by Kptlt. Manfred Kinzel.

U-boats were not the only branch of the German Navy with such incredibly misinterpreted torpedo results attributed to them. Motor torpedo-boats (Schnellboote) also failed to sink many of the ships they recorded as sunk. The present-day figures for early 1945 show that in some 350 torpedo-boat operations mines sank 25 ships and damaged 7; torpedoes only sank 6 ships and damaged 1. So, during early

1945, the torpedo-boat arm had far greater success with mines than with their specifically designated weapon. The German records also show that, during a torpedo attack in February/March 1945, a small number of MTBs sank 11 ships and, at roughly the same time, a further 7 ships were sunk by 8 torpedoes fired from 4 MTBs. According to the British records, however, during each operation only 2 ships had actually been sunk. Such disastrous results were almost certainly due to torpedo failures.

It would appear, then, that the German torpedoes brought into production during the war failed to achieve the expected results, although the Navy did have some noteworthy successes with the Ingolin torpedoes. These revolutionary weapons were put into production just before the end of the war, but none was completed in time to see operational service. Research into the possibilities of a high-performance torpedo that would leave no bubble or oil trail was started at about the same time as the Walter U-boat project. The highly-concentrated hydrogen-peroxide fuel (called 'Ingolin' after Professor Walter's son, Ingo) was mixed with other chemicals in the combustion chamber to drive a variety of power units. One of the simplest forms, Type G7ut, was similar in principle to that used in the early piston engine of Type G7a. It was thought that exhaust gases would dissolve in sea-water before they reached the surface, but oil mixed with the fuel left a telltale wake as it rose to the surface. This problem was eventually overcome and a hundred such torpedoes were put into production during early 1945. These were probably also fitted with a Zaunkönig type of sound-detection head.

Several different Ingolin torpedo projects were conducted simultaneously, and Korvkpt. Hans-Heinrich Giessler was appointed in the summer of 1944 to find out whether any of them could be made for immediate operational use. He found the performances to be most impressive. Goldfisch of Type G5ut reached a speed of forty-five knots for a range of about three and a half kilometres (two miles). The main problem for operational ships was the nature of the fuel, for it would explode if even the smallest particle of impurity found its way into the system. This applied to small dust particles left during the construction of the engine as well as dirt. In submarines, this explosion problem was overcome by storing the fuel on the outside of the pressure hull, where it could mix with seawater and dissolve in the event of an accident. The insides of operational ships, especially U-boats, were not as clean as laboratories, and torpedoes stored there were bound to be a potential danger. Yet the problems were partly overcome and, if the war had lasted longer, the torpedoes might have seen service.

THE END OF THE WAR

After the fateful month of March 1943, when the largest ever convoy battle took place, the conflict in the Atlantic never regained its momentum. Another battle, this time concentrated in European coastal waters, started during the summer of 1944. Non-German literature tends to give the impression that these were but the death throes of a desperate and badly-beaten navy, vainly trying to make an impact before dying. In fact, it was the German Navy's biggest – and one of its most successful – campaigns. It started late in 1944, when, in a spirit similar to that displayed by the British at Dunkirk, the German Navy sent every available seaworthy ship into the Baltic and started the mammoth task of evacuating those in the eastern provinces and ferrying them to the west, out of reach of the advancing Russian Army. The undertaking was the largest evacuation ever, and was a combined operation between the Kriegsmarine and the merchant navy. Between January and 8 May 1945, over two million refugees were transported in some 800 ships. The total number of evacuees was considerably higher, but the exact number may never be determined because of the chaos at the time. The rescue ships took on as many people as possible, often under heavy attack, and the main concern was to save as many lives as possible.

The evacuation operations started during the autumn of 1944, when Dönitz gave permission for civilian refugees to be carried, together with wounded, aboard naval transports. Some 6,000 members of the Hitler Youth, who had been digging defensive ditches around Memel, Germany's most easterly port, were also evacuated from there during the autumn of 1944, bringing the total to almost 47,000 by the end of the year. The most important evacuations started during January 1945, and the approximate number of refugees transported by sea was as shown below.

Roughly 20,000 refugees were killed by enemy action during the whole operation; less than 1 per cent of the total. In comparison, 18 per cent of those who attempted to escape overland were lost. This story of immense suffering, deep deprivation and large-scale mistreatment of civilians is really only now coming to light.

The losses at sea were attributed to three main causes:
- The rescue transports were overcrowded.
- Air temperatures dropped down to minus 24 degrees Celsius, which meant that if the ship went down there was no hope of survival in the water.
- The transports and hospital ships were easy targets for enemy aircraft and submarines.

The largest losses were as shown opposite.

One of the conditions of the terms of surrender was that German naval units should hand over their equipment undamaged, and ships should not be scuttled. At the same time, German forces were not permitted to transmit radio messages in code. Dönitz agreed to these conditions and appointed two liaison officers, Fregkpt. Heinrich Liebe and Oblt.z.S. Martin Duppel, to ensure that no ship was sunk by German soldiers. But, because neither of the two officers would believe this instruction until they had heard it from Dönitz's own lips, most U-boats in German ports were scuttled before the Allies could reach them. On their way to see Dönitz, the two men met the Supreme Commander's adjutant, Walter Lüdde-Neurath, who refused them access, saying Dönitz was too busy to see them. Lüdde-Neurath knew full well that Dönitz would not go against the agreement made with the Allies, and he would order the boats to be preserved. Equally, he knew that Dönitz loathed the idea of giving such an order and he wanted to follow the tradition of the Navy and sink the ships. Lüdde-Neurath handled the issue with great skill, telling the two men that as naval commanders they should know their duty – if he were in their shoes, he would know what to do. Both men understood what he was driving at, and, as radio could not be used, the vital code word 'Regenbogen' ('scuttle all ships') was passed by telephone and word of mouth to many German ports.

The Navy did not come to an abrupt end in May 1945, but disbanded slowly. At first, the men carried on as before, (although they were not permitted to wear swastikas on their uniforms). Some German officers, fearing a rebellion from the younger faction, took to wearing pistols. Later, the men were screened in prisoner-of-war camps, and the hard-line National Socialists and war criminals were weeded out. The vast majority of Germans in Western hands were soon released to start rebuilding their shattered homeland.

Numerous ships not scuttled were distributed among the Allied navies, and the vast majority of the U-boats were sunk in the Atlantic by the Royal Navy in 1945/46 (Operation Deadlight). Only a limited number of small ships, suitable for minesweeping, remained in German hands.

REFUGEES TRANSPORTED BY SEA FROM GERMANY'S EASTERN PROVINCES

From Danzig, Gotenhafen and Hela[1] between January and 8 May 1945: 1,047,000 refugees plus 300,000 soldiers and wounded.

From Libau, between January and 8 May 1945: 75,000 wounded plus 25,000 soldiers.

From Königsberg and Pillau, between 25 January and 25 April 1945: 451,000 refugees plus 141,000 soldiers and wounded.

From Kolberg, during mid-March 1945: 70,000 refugees plus 7,500 soldiers and wounded.

Total: At least 2,116,500

1. Bernd Schlummer, working in the German Submarine Museum, made a rather interesting discovery that officialdom found time to produce a special stamp on the isolated Hela peninsula for post carried west by submarine during this hectic period. Conditions were so desperate that at one stage the only foods available were beans and sugar, which were cooked in bath tubs ripped from houses and heated in the open by lighting a fire underneath.

U805, a later version of a Type IXC, with the specially incised bows for quicker diving, seen here having surrendered to United States Forces. The 20mm anti-aircraft guns are visible on the upper gun platform. The circular hatches at deck level are the tops of ammunition containers.

All German armed forces were disbanded during May 1945 after the arrest of the Dönitz government. However, an active branch of the Navy was re-founded on 1 August 1945 in the form of the German Minesweeping Administration, which used ex-Kriegsmarine personnel to help clear mines from European waters. Ironically, under the Geneva Convention these men were technically prisoners-of-war, and could not be employed for tasks that would put their lives at risk, but in Germany they had the status of 'free men' under the control of Allied Forces.

The German Minesweeping Administration operated with two commands – one based in Kiel serving the Baltic, the other based in Cuxhaven for the North Sea – and later with six. At its peak, there were just fewer than 28,000 men and over 20 flotillas of approximately 400 floating units. They were eventually disbanded in 1948 and replaced by another minesweeping unit of a more civilian character. This in turn was dissolved in June 1951, and the ships passed over to other existing organizations. Interestingly enough, however, at least two Kriegsmarine flotillas were never put out of action: 13th and 16th Räumbootsflottille (13th and 16th Motor Minesweeper Flotillas). They continued to serve under the Minesweeping Administration and were later incorporated in the new Federal Navy.

PRINCIPAL LOSSES IN SEABORNE EVACUATIONS FROM GERMANY'S EASTERN PROVINCES IN 1945

Date	Name of Ship	Size GRT	Number saved	Number killed
30/31 Jan	*Wilhelm Gustloff*	25,484	900	4–6,000
9/10 Feb	*General von Steuben*	14,660	300	3,000
17 Feb	*Eifel*	1,429	?	680
12 March	*Andross*	3,000	2,000	550
9 April	*Albert Jensen*	5,500	not loaded	
10 April	*Neuwerk*	803	?	800
11 April	*Moltkefels*	7,862	3,500	1,000
11 April	*Posen*	1,062		1,000
13 April	*Karlsruhe*	897	150	800
16/17 April	*Goya*	5,230	100?	6,000
25 April	*Emily Sauber*	2,475	2,000	50

Other ship losses with considerable numbers of prisoners or refugees on board:

3 May	*Deutschland*	21,046
3 May	*Cap Arkona*	27,561
3 May	*Vega*	7,388
3 May	*Bolkoburg*	3,436

The figures in 'Numbers Killed' column are those available in 1978. Modern research would suggest that those with losses over one thousand are twice as high as was then indicated.

THE ORGANIZATION OF THE KRIEGSMARINE

THE NAVY IN 1922

The reorganization programme begun after the First World War was not completed until a year after the new Reichsmarine flag was introduced in April 1921 (page 11), and the first Navy List was not published until 5 March 1922. Published annually, until 1937 this list gave details of all units; the 1938 edition only had a list of personnel. During the war years, it is doubtful whether the exact details of naval organization were committed to paper, or, at least, as a bound volume.

In 1922, the Navy was divided into two operational sections covering the Baltic and the North Sea areas. There were also several additional educational units and some inspectorates. The structure of the Navy in 1922 was as follows:

SUPREME NAVAL COMMAND (MARINELEITUNG)
Chef der Marineleitung (Chief of the Navy): Admiral Paul Behncke.
Under the Emperor (Kaiser), the Supreme Naval Command was known as the Admiralität (Admiralty); it was later called Oberkommando der Marine (OKM).

NAVAL COMMAND BALTIC
Commander: Ernst Freiherr von Gagern.
    Headquarters: Kiel.
Naval Forces Baltic.
    Battleship: *Hannover*.
    Cruisers: *Berlin, Medusa, Thetis*.
    Survey ship: *Panther*.
    Smaller ships: 1st Flotilla, 5th Half Flotilla.
Land Forces Baltic.
    Coastal Defence Departments I, III and IV.
    Communication Departments with training establishment.
    Schiffsstammdivision der Ostsee (Training Division for New Recruits).

NAVAL COMMAND NORTH SEA
Commander: Hans Zenker.

The majority of German flotillas were administrative units and only rarely operated at sea as a group. Instead, individual ships were sent to various commanders for use in prescribed operations. This shows the officers of the 12th U-boat Flotilla in Bordeaux under Klaus Scholtz. He is the taller of the two Korvettenkapitäne, with the Knight's Cross around his neck. U-boat flotillas were responsible for repairs, replenishments and looking after the men in port, but they only exercised operational control while the boats were in their immediate coastal waters. This flotilla specialized in large, long-distance boats and also accommodated some of the Japanese boats that made voyages to Europe. In addition to this, there was also a contingent of Italian boats in Bordeaux, but these were looked after by their own staff, headed by a Flag Officer for the Atlantic.

The landward side of naval barracks in Kiel, showing the type of accommodation provided for men in port. These buildings also contained a number of offices. This complex was built at the beginning of the twentieth century and was much too small to cope with the demands made by the Second World War. As a result, passenger ships had to be moored in the harbour to make up the shortfall.

The large notice over the door says, 'Precinct 5th U-Flotilla Base' and the smaller signs tell us that this building was also occupied by the Camouflage Staff, the departmental doctor and the base's security patrols.

Germany had only one purpose-built submarine base, and that was at Bant in Wilhelmshaven, which can be seen here. In Kiel U-boats had to share accommodation with surface units in or near the naval harbour at Wik. The Bant barracks contained virtually everything that was required by U-boats, including a diving tower to practise escaping from submerged submarines. The building on the right is the 'casino' (now demolished), which translates as bar or mess.

Headquarters: Wilhelmshaven.
Naval Forces North Sea.
 Battleship: *Braunschweig*.
 Cruisers: *Arcona, Hamburg*.
 Smaller ships: 2nd Flotilla, 11th Half Flotilla.
Land Forces North Sea.
 Coastal Defence Departments II, IV and VI.
 Schiffsstammdivision der Nordsee (Training Division for New Recruits).

OTHER MAIN UNITS
Artillery Inspectorate.
Torpedo and Mine Inspectorate.
Naval Schools: Flensburg (Mürwik) and Kiel (Wik).
Naval Archive.
Naval Shipyards: Wilhelmshaven and Kiel.
Main Naval Depots with Command Posts: Cuxhaven, Emden, Kiel, Pillau, Swinemünde, Wilhelmshaven.
Ports with smaller naval offices: Bremen, Hamburg, Königsberg, Lübeck, Stettin.

THE FLEET IN 1932

With the appearance of several new ships during the 1920s, the naval administration adapted to meet the additional demands put upon it. As a result, coastal sections – the Naval Commands for the Baltic and North Sea – were enlarged, and the Fleet itself underwent several changes. The following is a rough outline of its organization during October 1932 – a few months before Hitler was appointed Chancellor. Ships not listed here were either temporarily out of commission or were under the command of other establishments.

THE FLEET COMMAND (FLOTTENKOMMANDO)
Flottenchef (Fleet Commander): Walter Gladisch.
Stabschef (Chief of Staff): Hermann Boehm.

BATTLESHIPS (LINIENSCHIFFE)
Befehlshaber der Linienschiffe or B.d.L.
 (Commander-in-Chief Battleships): Kpt.z.S. und Kommodore Max Bastian,
Hessen: Kpt.z.S. Friedrich Götting.
Schlesien: Kpt.z.S. Wilhelm Canaris.
Schleswig-Holstein: Kpt.z.S. Rolf Carls.
Meteor (survey ship): Korvkpt. Friedrich-Wilhelm Kurze.

RECONNAISSANCE FORCES (AUFKLÄRUNGSSTREITKRÄFTE)
Befehlshaber der Aufklärungsstreitkräfte or B.d.A.
 (Commander-in-Chief Reconnaissance Forces): Konteradmiral Carl Kolbe.

Cruisers
 Emden: Fregkpt. Werner Grassmann.
 Königsberg: Fregkpt. Otto von Schrader.
 Leipzig: Kpt.z.S. Hans-Herbert Strobwasser.

1st Torpedo-Boat Flotilla: Korvkpt. Kurt Fricke.
 1st Torpedo-Boat Half Flotilla: Kptlt. Hans Bültow (Training),
 G7: Kptlt. Hans Geisse.
 G8: Oblt.z.S. Rolf Johannesen.
 G10: Oblt.z.S. Eberhard Godt.
 G11: Oblt.z.S. Hans Henigst.
 2nd Torpedo-Boat Half Flotilla: Korvkpt. Wilhelm Meisel,

The naval buildings in Wilhelmshaven were virtually impossible to hide because of their position on the water's edge and some suffered from the full force of the Allied bombing campaign. This shows the main gate and office block for the naval dockyard, which survived the war and still guards the modern Navy's harbour installations.

T151: Oblt.z.S. Georg Waue.
T153: Oblt.z.S. Heinrich Bassenge.
T156: Kptlt. Heinz-Dietrich von Conrady.
T158: Kptlt. Claus Trampedach.

2nd Torpedo-Boat Flotilla: Fregkpt. Hermann Mootz.
  3rd Torpedo-Boat Half Flotilla: Korvkpt. Leopold Bürkner.
  Iltis: Kptlt. Hans Gloeckner.
  Jaguar: Kptlt. Gottfried Pönitz.
  Tiger: Oblt.z.S. Herbert Friedrichs.
  Wolf: Kptlt. Hans Michahelles.

3rd Torpedo-Boat Half Flotilla (Training): Kptlt. Hellmuth Heye.
  Albatros: Oblt.z.S. Alfred Schemmel.
  Falke: Oblt.z.S. Ernst Thienemann.
  Kondor: Oblt.z.S. Heinz Bonatz.
  Möwe: Oblt.z.S. Hermann Jordan.

1st Minesweeper Half Flotilla: Kptlt. Friedrich Ruge.
  M66: Oblt.z.S. Alfred Wolf.
  M98: Kptlt. Heinrich Bramesfeld.
  M109: Oblt.z.S. (?) Kobel.
  M111: Oblt.z.S. Jürgen Wattenberg.
  M126: Kptlt. Johannes Isenlar.
  M129: Kptlt. Axel von Blessingh.
  M132: Oblt.z.S. Kurt Thoma.
  M146: Kptlt. Max Freymadl.

1st Motor Torpedo-Boat Half Flotilla: Kptlt. Erich Bey.
  S2: Oblt.z.S. Hans Eckermann.
  S3: Oblt.z.S. Hans-Rudolf Rösing.
  S4: Oblt.z.S. Manfred Fuhrke.[1]
  S5: Oblt.z.S. Karl Stockmann.
  Nordsee (tender): Oblt.z.S. Zimmermann.

THE FLEET IN 1935

In 1935, two years after Hitler's appointment as Chancellor, new defence laws were passed. These included the repudiation of the Treaty of Versailles and the re-introduction of national conscription. In addition, some previously banned branches of the Navy were re-established, thus opening the way for the Third Reich to embark upon its objective of rapid military development.

The Fleet Command (Flottenkommando)
Flottenchef (Fleet Commander): Vizeadmiral Richard Foerster.
Stabschef (Chief of Staff): Kpt.z.S. Otto Schniewind.
Flagship: *Admiral Scheer*.
  Main port for flagship: Kiel.
  Fleet tender: *Hela*.

Battleships and Pocket Battleships (Linienschiffe)
Befehlshaber der Linienschiffe or B.d.L. (Commander-in-Chief Battleships): Konteradmiral Rolf Carls.
Flagship: *Deutschland*.
  Main port: Wilhelmshaven.
Admiral Graf Spee: Kpt.z.S. Conrad Patzig.
  Main base: Wilhelmshaven. Still training; to be commissioned during January 1936, will then become flagship for Fleet Commander.
Admiral Scheer: Kpt.z.S. Wilhelm Marschall.
  Main base: Kiel.
Deutschland: Kpt.z.S. Paul Fanger.
  Main base: Wilhelmshaven.
Schleswig-Holstein: Kpt.z.S. Günther Krause.
  Main base: Wilhelmshaven.

Reconnaissance Forces (Aufklärungsstreitkräfte)
Befehlshaber der Aufklärungsstreitkräfte or B.d.A. (Commander-in-Chief for Reconnaissance Forces): Konteradmiral Hermann Boehm.

The pocket battleship *Admiral Scheer* with the three rectangular windows of the admiral's bridge clearly visible. This massive command tower was removed shortly after the beginning of the war and replaced by a slimmer structure.

1. Fuhrke was killed in an air crash while flying from Spain to Germany in 1938 and, therefore, is not mentioned in wartime records.

Flagship: *Königsberg*, later *Leipzig*, later *Nürnberg*.
Main port: Kiel.

Cruisers

Köln: Fregkpt. Otto Backenköhler. Main base:
Wilhelmshaven.
Königsberg: Fregkpt. Oswald Paul. Main base: Kiel.
Leipzig: Fregkpt. Otto Schenk. Main base:
Wilhelmshaven. (Still undergoing trials).
Nürnberg: Kpt.z.S. Hubert Schmundt. Main base: Kiel
(To be commissioned during November 1938).

Torpedo Boats

Führer der Torpedoboote or F.d.T. (Flag Officer for
Torpedo Boats): Fregkpt. Oskar Kummetz.
Flag Officer's boat: *Leopard*: Kptlt. Hans von Davidson.
Base: Swinemünde.
Tender: *Jagd*: No commissioned officer in charge during
October 1935.

1st Torpedo-Boat Flotilla: Korvkpt. Carl Gutjahr. Base:
Swinemünde.
G7: Kptlt. Franz Frerichs.
G8: Kptlt. Moritz Schmidt (Flagship).
G10: Kptlt. Gerhardt Böhmig.
G11: Kptlt. Theodor Detmers.

2nd Torpedo-Boat Flotilla (Training): Korvkpt. Kurt
Weyher.
Base: Kiel.
Albatros: Kptlt. Hubert Freiherr von Wangenheim
Leopard:
Luchs: Kptlt. Richard Rothe-Roth.
Seeadler: Kptlt. Georg Langenfeld.

Torpedo-boats on exercise.

3rd Torpedo-Boat Flotilla (Training): Korvkpt. Günther
Gumprich.
Base: Wilhemshaven.
Iltis: Kptlt. Arthur Wenninger.
Jaguar: Kptlt. Karl Schmidt.
Tiger: Kptlt. Hugo Förster.
Wolf: Kptlt. Hans Erdmenger.

4th Torpedo-Boat Flotilla: Korvkpt. Hans Henning
Base: Wilhelmshaven.
Falke: Kptlt. Alwin Albrecht.

Early S-boats moored up. The word was derived from Schnellboot, meaning fast boat, and were known as E-boat (enemy boat) in England. Both the bridge housing and the torpedo tubes give the impression of having been added rather as an afterthought with little effort made to integrate them into the design. Later boats appeared to be more streamlined, with some of the tubes merging with the hull.

The waters of the German North Sea coast are shallow and the shipping channels only a couple of hundred metres wide in places; strong tides are another feature. On this coast large warships could not be built with such deep draughts as their French, British and American counterparts, and even ordinary minesweepers found the depth limiting. These 'Räumboote', or 'clearance boats', were mini-minesweepers that were specially built to cope with shallow harbour approaches. The guns are semi-automatic 37mm for anti-aircraft use.

Greif: Kptlt. Manfred Fuhrke.
Kondor: Kptlt. Conrad Engelhardt.
Möwe: Kptlt. Hansjürgen Reinicke.

Motor Torpedo Boats
(Called Schnellboote in Germany and E-boats (Enemy boats) in Britain.)

1st Motor Torpedo-Boat Flotilla: Korvkpt. Paul Schubert.
  Base: Kiel.
  Tender: *Tsingtau*: Kptlt. Anton Ruhland.
  Base: Swinemünde.
  S7: Kptlt. Kurt Sturm.
  S8: Kptlt. Eberhard von Bogen (Killed in a sailing boat accident in 1936).
  S9: Kptlt. Rudolf Petersen.
  S10: Oblt.z.S. Hans-Henning von Salisch.
  S11: Kptlt. Fro Harmsen.
  S12: Oblt.z.S. Günther Hosemann.

Minesweepers and Escorts
  Minesweepers and Escorts: Kpt.z.S. Kurt Ramien.
  Base: Kiel.
  Commander's boat: *T196*: Oblt.z.S. Hagen Küster.

1st Minesweeper Flotilla: Korvkpt. Ernst-Felix Krüder.
  Base: Pillau.

M75: Kptlt. Karl Neitzel.
M89: Kptlt. Archibald MacLean.
M111: Kptlt. Heinz-Ehler Beucke.
M132: Kptlt. Gerhard von Kampst.
M146: Kptlt. Walter Rauff.
M151: Kptlt. Hans Sönnichsen.

1st Escort Flotilla (Training): Korvkpt. Siegfried Weiss.
  Base: Kiel.
  M133: (F1) Kptlt. Siegfried Flister.
  M117: (F2) Kptlt. Bernhard Busse.
  M104: (F5) Kptlt. Hans John.
  T157: (F6) Kptlt. Alfred Schumann.
  F9: Kptlt. Paul Morgenstern.
  F10: Kptlt. Hermann Knuth.

2nd Escort Flotilla (Training): Korvkpt. Ernst Lucht.
  Base; Kiel.
  M89 (F3): Kptlt. Rüdolf Lell.
  M50 (F4): Kptlt. Werner Musenberg.
  F7: Oblt.z.S. Hans-Werner Neumann.
  F8: Kptlt. Peter Reichmann.

1st Motor Minesweeper Flotilla: Kptlt. Hugo Pahl.
  Base: Kiel.
  Tender: *Zieten*: Oblt.z.S. Hans Stubbendorff.
  R11, R12, R13, R14, R18, R19. (These boats were

The sail training ship *Gorch Fock* running into Hamburg. A station, where harbour and river pilots were exchanged, can be seen in the background.

probably not commanded by commissioned officers; so their names would not have been recorded in the Navy Lists.)

Submarine Flotilla Weddigen

Submarine Flotilla Weddigen: Kpt.z.S. Karl Dönitz.
  Base: Kiel.
  Escort ship: *T23*: Kptlt. Heinz Fischer.
  Tender: *Saar*: Korvkpt. Rudolf Wiegner.
  U7: Kptlt. Kurt Freiwald.
  U8: Kptlt. Harald Grosse.
  U9: Kptlt. Hans-Günther Looff.
  U10: Oblt.z.S. Heinz Scheringer.
  U11: Kptlt. Hans-Rudolf Rösing.
  U12: Oblt.z.S. Werner von Schmidt.
  (*U1–U6* were attached to the Submarine School, which was under the jurisdiction of the Torpedo Inspectorate, not the U-boat Flotilla.)

MAJOR SHIPS NOT UNDER COMMAND OF THE FLEET COMMANDER

The list below gives the ship's name, year launched and main port. Wilhelmshaven came under the command of the North Sea Naval Station and Kiel under the Baltic Station.

Arkona (M115) 1918 Kiel
Bremse 1931 Kiel
Brummer 1935 Wilhelmshaven
Delphin 1919 –
Drache 1908 Kiel
Elbe 1931 Wilhelmshaven
Emden 1925 Training ship
Frauenlob (M134) 1919 Wilhelmshaven
Fuchs 1919 Kiel
Gorch Fock 1933 Kiel
Grille 1934 Kiel
Hannover 1905 Wilhelmshaven
Hela 1919 Kiel
Karlsruhe 1927 Training ship
Meteor 1915 Wilhelmshaven
Nautilus (M81) Kiel
Nire 1914 Kiel
Nordsee 1914 Kiel
Peilboot II 1911 Wilhelmshaven
Peilboot V 1912 Wilhelmshaven
Pelikan 1917 Kiel
Schlesien 1906 Training ship
Taucher 1934 Kiel
T23 1912 Kiel
T151 1907 Pillau
T153 1907 Kiel
T156 1907 Kiel
T157 1907 Kiel
T158 1907 Kiel

Learning the ropes.

Naval Bases

Main Naval Bases with deep-water anchorage: Kiel, Wilhelmshaven.

Other Naval Bases: Berlin, Bremen,* Borkum, Cuxhaven, Eckernförde,* Emden, Flensburg (Mürwik), Grauerort near Stade,* Hamburg,* List on island of Sylt,* Malente, Neumünster,* Norderney, Pillau, Stettin,* Stopmühle,* Stralsund, Swinemünde, Wangerooge, Wesermünde (Bremerhaven).

* These towns had only one or two small offices.

LEFT Pillau in the eastern Baltic. While western towns went on full alert with total blackout around the time as war was declared, many of the eastern areas remained free from restrictions and carried on the way they had before the war. Much of the eastern Baltic freezes solid for several weeks or even months during the winter. Pillau is situated on a narrow spit of land between the Baltic and a massive freshwater lagoon, the Frisches Haff, at the mouth of a deep ship canal leading to Königsberg. The small port was often used by training units of the German Navy and came into the limelight towards the end of the war, when refugees were evacuated from there before the town was cut off by advancing Russian armies.

Kiel harbour in November 1940 with a passenger ship being used for accommodation with its prominent white superstructure. The U-boats are probably Type VIICs.

ABOVE The Garrison Church in Wilhelmshaven which contains some fascinating memorabilia of Germany's painful history. This photo was probably taken before the war, but anyone entering this sanctuary will find a place of poignant remembrance. With the absence of swastikas in Germany, except for educational purposes, the visitor must look carefully to find the names of those that lost their lives during the Second World War era.

ORGANIZATION OF THE KRIEGSMARINE, NOVEMBER 1938

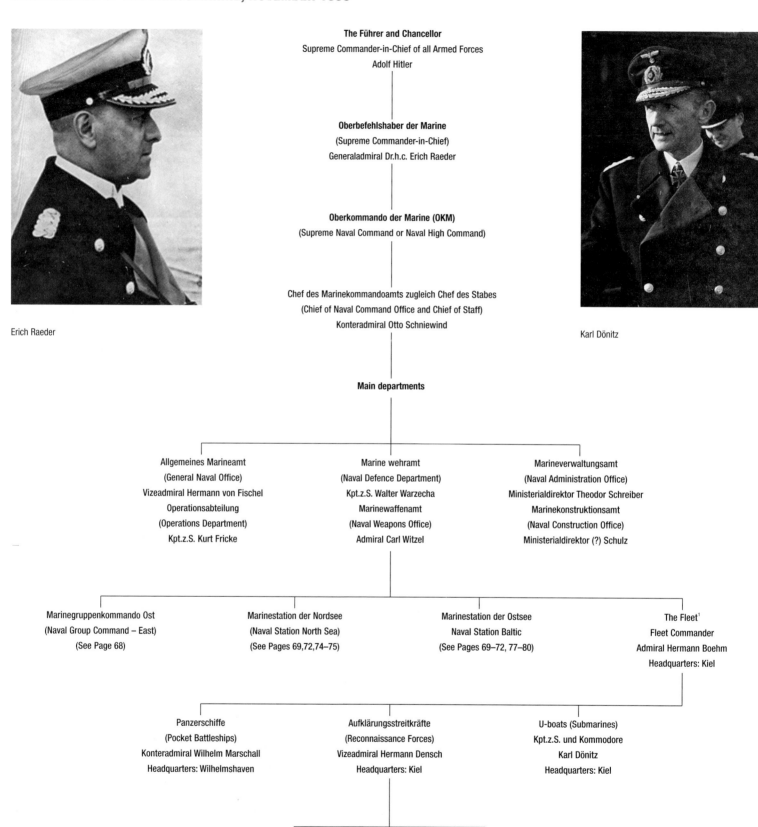

Erich Raeder

Karl Dönitz

The Führer and Chancellor
Supreme Commander-in-Chief of all Armed Forces
Adolf Hitler

Oberbefehlshaber der Marine
(Supreme Commander-in-Chief)
Generaladmiral Dr.h.c. Erich Raeder

Oberkommando der Marine (OKM)
(Supreme Naval Command or Naval High Command)

Chef des Marinekommandoamts zugleich Chef des Stabes
(Chief of Naval Command Office and Chief of Staff)
Konteradmiral Otto Schniewind

Main departments

Allgemeines Marineamt	Marine wehramt	Marineverwaltungsamt
(General Naval Office)	(Naval Defence Department)	(Naval Administration Office)
Vizeadmiral Hermann von Fischel	Kpt.z.S. Walter Warzecha	Ministerialdirektor Theodor Schreiber
Operationsabteilung	Marinewaffenamt	Marinekonstruktionsamt
(Operations Department)	(Naval Weapons Office)	(Naval Construction Office)
Kpt.z.S. Kurt Fricke	Admiral Carl Witzel	Ministerialdirektor (?) Schulz

Marinegruppenkommando Ost	Marinestation der Nordsee	Marinestation der Ostsee	The Fleet[1]
(Naval Group Command – East)	(Naval Station North Sea)	Naval Station Baltic	Fleet Commander
(See Page 68)	(See Pages 69,72,74–75)	(See Pages 69–72, 77–80)	Admiral Hermann Boehm
			Headquarters: Kiel

Panzerschiffe	Aufklärungsstreitkräfte	U-boats (Submarines)
(Pocket Battleships)	(Reconnaissance Forces)	Kpt.z.S. und Kommodore
Konteradmiral Wilhelm Marschall	Vizeadmiral Hermann Densch	Karl Dönitz
Headquarters: Wilhelmshaven	Headquarters: Kiel	Headquarters: Kiel

Torpedo Boats	Minesweepers
Konteradmiral Günther Lütjens	Fregkpt. Friedrich Ruge
Headquarters: Kiel	Headquarters: Cuxhaven

1. There was also a small flotilla
(Donauflottille) on the River Danube

ORGANIZATION STRUCTURE IN 1938

Hitler appointed himself Supreme Commander-in-Chief of the German armed forces on 4 February 1938 and, during that year, all men in the Navy took an oath swearing obedience to him. Technically, this gave Hitler direct command, but in reality there was little interference from him or the NSDAP. The Navy clung fiercely to the traditions it had forged under the Emperor, and all the Führer's orders were filtered through the Naval High Command (which, on occasion, saw fit to refuse his instructions). Although Erich Raeder did not like Hitler, on balance he probably followed the Führer's wishes more closely than did his successor, Karl Dönitz. Dönitz was one of the few with the courage and character to voice his opinions, even if they contradicted those of the Führer.

THE FLEET AT THE START OF THE WAR

Ships not mentioned in this section were either temporarily out of service, in dock or still undergoing trials.

Battleships, Pocket Battleships and Cruisers

The following list gives the commander of each ship and its location at the beginning of the war.

Admiral Graf Spee: KS Hans Langsdorff. Left Wilhelmshaven on 21 August to operate in the South Atlantic.
Admiral Scheer: KS Hans-Heinrich Wurmbach. Lying at anchor in the Schillig Roads, outside Wilhelmshaven. Machinery was being dismantled for a major refit.
Deutschland: KS Paul Wenneker. North Atlantic.
Emden: KS Werner Lange. At anchor off Wilhelmshaven.
Köln: KS Theodor Burchardi. The Baltic.
Königsberg: KS Kurt Caesar Hoffmann. She was in the Baltic on the last day of August, patrolling off Poland. From there she sailed via the Kiel Canal into the North Sea.

Hitler visiting *Tirpitz*, 1 April 1939.

Looking astern on the pocket battleship *Deutschland*, which was stationed in the North Atlantic at the start of the war. The aft rangefinder, pointing at a target, is clearly visible in the foreground, supporting the mast from which the ensign is flying. Explosives produced plenty of smoke and additional radar-controlled rangefinders really came into their own after a few rounds had been fired.

Leipzig: KS Heinz Nordmann. With *Admiral Graf Spee* off the coast of Mexico.

Nürnberg: KS Otto Klüber. The Baltic.

Schlesien: KS Kurt Utke. The Baltic.

Schleswig-Holstein: KS Gustav Kleikamp. In the Baltic off Danzig. She fired the first shots of the war at sea.

U-boats

The following lists the boats in commission on 1 September 1939, the commander, type and operational status (O = Operational, T = Training, Tr = Operational but still on trials):

U1: KL Jürgen Deecke	IIA – T	
U2: KL Helmuth Rosenbaum	IIA – T	
U3: KL Joachim Schepke	IIA – T	
U4: KL Harro von Klot-Heydenfeldt	IIA – T	
U5: KL Günter Kutschmann	IIA – T	
U6: KL Joachim Matz	IIA – T	
U7: OL Otto Salmann	IIB – T	
U8: KL Georg Peters	IIB – T	
U9: KL Ludwig Mathes or Max Schulte	IIB – O	
U10: KL Wilhelm Schulz	IIB – T	
U11: KL Viktor Schütze	IIB – T	
U12: KL Dietrich von der Ropp	IIB – O	
U13: KL Karl Daublebsky von Eichhain	IIB – O	
U14: KL Horst Wellner	IIB – O	
U15: KL Peter Frahm	IIB – O	
U16: KL Hannes Weingaertner	IIB – O	
U17: KL Heinz von Reiche	IIB – O	
U18: KL Max Hermann Bauer	IIB – O	
U19: KL Hans Meckel	IIB – O	
U20: KL KarI-Heinz Moehle	IIB – O	
U21: KL Fritz Frauenheim	IIB – O	
U22: KL Werner Winter	IIB – O	
U23: KL Otto Kretschmer	IIB – O	
U24: KL Udo Behrens	IIB – O	
U25: OL Georg-Heinz Michel	IA – O	
U26: FL Oskar Schomburg	IA – O	
U27: KL Johannes Franz	VIIA – O	
U28: KL Günter Kuhnke	VIIA – O	
U29: KL Otto Schuhart	VIIA – O	
U30: KL Fritz-Julius Lemp	VIIA – O	
U31: KL Johannes Habekost	VIIA – O	
U32: OL Hans Jenisch	VIIA – O	
U33: KL Hans-Wilhelm von Dresky	VIIA – O	
U34: KL Wilhelm Rollmann	VIIA – O	
U35: KL Werner Lott	VIIA – O	
U36: KL Wilhelm Fröhlich	VIIA – Tr?	
U37: KL Heinrich Schuch	IXA – O	
U38: KL Heinrich Liebe	IXA – O	
U39: KL Gerhard Glattes	IXA – O	
U40: EL Werner von Schmidt	IXA – O	
U41: KL Gustav-Adolf Mugler	IXA – O	

U4, one of the early Type IIA coastal boats. Life in them was not only cramped, but also uncomfortable as they rolled and pitched badly. This photo must have been taken shortly after commissioning because the flag indicates it was before the introduction of the swastika. The spike-like object forward of the conning-tower is a mount for a 20mm, but without the gun in position.

U42: KL Rolf Dau	IXA – Tr
U43: KL Wilhelm Ambrosius	IXA – Tr
U44: Commissioned 4 Nov 1939	IXA
U45: KL Alexander Gelbaar	VIIB – O
U46: KL Herbert Sohler	VIIB – O
U47: KL Günther Prien	VIIB – O
U48: KL Herbert Schultze	VIIB – O
U49: KL Curt von Gossler	VIIB – Tr
U50: Commissioned 12 Dec 1939	VIIB
U51: KL Dietrich Knorr	VIIB – Tr
U52: KL Wolfgang Barten	VIIB – O
U53: KL Ernst-Günther Heinicke	VIIB – Tr
U54: Commissioned 23 Sept 1939	VIIB
U55: Commissioned 21 Nov 1939	VIIB
U56: KL Wilhelm Zahn	IIC – O
U57: KL Claus Korth	IIC – O
U58: KL Herbert Kuppisch	IIC – O
U59: KL Harald Jürst	IIC – O
U60: KL Georg Schewe	IIC – Tr
U61: KL Jürgen Oesten	IIC – Tr

Destroyers

Destroyers' numbers were prefixed by the letter 'Z', which stood for Zerstörer. In addition to a number, some of them were also given a name. (Details on page 94)

Z1: KK Fritz Bassenge (Flagship for Commander-in-Chief Torpedo-Boats)
Z2: KK Max-Eckart Wolff
Z3: KK Claus Trampedach
Z4: KK Moritz Schmidt
Z5: KK Hans Zimmer (Flagship, 2nd Flotilla)
Z6: KK Gerhardt Böhmig
Z7: KK Theodor Detmers
Z8: KK Fritz Berger
Z9: KK Gottfried Pönitz
Z10: KK Karl-Jesko von Puttkamer
Z11: KK Kurt Rechel
Z12: KK Karl Smidt
Z13: KK Alfred Schulze-Hinrichs
Z14: KK Rudolf von Pufendorf
Z15: KK Rolf Johannesson
Z16: KK Alfred Schemmel
Z17: KK Erich Holtorf
Z18: KK Herbert Friedrichs
Z19: KK Friedrich Kothe
Z20: KK Theodor Bechtolsheim Freiherr von Mauchenheim
Z21: KK Hans Erdmenger (Ship still undergoing trials at the start of the war.)

Torpedo-Boats

Albatros: KL Herbert-Max Schultz
Falke: KL Günther Hessler
Greif: KL Wilhelm Verlohr
Iltis: KL Heinz Schuur
Jaguar: KL Franz Kohlauf
Kondor: KL Hans Wilcke
Leopard: KL Karl Kassbaum
Luchs: KL Eckart Prölss
Möwe: KL Konrad Edler von Rennenkampff
Seeadler: KL Werner Hartenstein

Tiger: KL Helmut Neuss (Boat sunk after a collision on 25 August 1939.)
Wolf: KL Lutz Gerstung

Motor Torpedo-Boats (Schnellboote)

These numbers were prefixed by the letter 'S'. The following were operational at the start of the war:
S6, S7, S8, S9, S10, S11, S12, S13, S14, S15, S16, S17, S18, S19, S20, S21, S22.

Minesweepers (Minensuchboote)

These numbers were prefixed by the letter 'M'. The following were operational at the start of the war:
M1, M2, M3, M4, M5, M6, M7, M8, M9, M10, M11, M12, M13, M14, M15, M16, M17, M18, M19, M20, M21, M22.

THE SUPREME NAVAL COMMAND (Oberkommando der Marine, or OKM)

The Supreme Naval Command comprised of the Supreme Commander-in-Chief's staff and the main departments mentioned in the diagram on page 64. This organization became somewhat complicated as the war progressed; the armaments section alone mushroomed to nine main departments and over fifty sub-departments. (For detailed information on these and other departments, please consult *Die deutsche Kriegsmarine, 1939–1945*, Volume I, by W Lohmann and H H Hildebrand.) There was one major change during the reorganization of October/November 1939: the General Naval Office (Allgemeines Marineamt) was disbanded and replaced by the Seekriegsleitung or SKL (Chief of Naval War Staff). This was not a completely new innovation, for the title had first appeared during the 1930s when it was used synonymously with OKM.

The Supreme Naval Command's headquarters were in Berlin – at Tirpitzufer (now called Reichpietschufer) next to the Landwehr Canal – until November 1943 when the building was bombed. Then the staff moved to new quarters in Eberswalde, code named 'Bismarck'. A small core of men remained in the city, where alternative accommodation was under construction, but this was never occupied by the Navy. In addition to 'Bismarck', two other quarters were erected, but only one of them was used. Code-named 'Koralle' it was situated in the small, isolated village of Bernau, about nineteen miles north-east of the Reich's Chancellery. It was there that Dönitz moved with his staff in the summer of 1943.

In 1944 it became clear that the Supreme Naval Command would have to move out of reach of the advancing Russian Army and vacate its offices in the Berlin region. Dönitz decided to split the High Command and, early in 1945, the core of the staff from 'Bismarck' was ordered to move west. Dönitz considered it to be his duty, as Supreme Commander-in-Chief, to remain near Hitler's headquarters in order to keep in touch with the rapidly moving front. He did this by commuting between 'Koralle' and Hitler's command bunker.

Dönitz and his Naval War Staff evacuated the thick concrete bunkers at 'Koralle' during early April 1945, and took up residence in the command train 'Auerhahn'.

Unfortunately, this proved to be a case of 'out of the frying pan and into the fire'. Shortly after their arrival, a shunting operation put paid to all electrical power; then, to cap it all, enemy aircraft were reported overhead and the emergency lights went out too. When this happened, Dönitz acted on a suggestion from his adjutant and ordered everybody back to 'Koralle'.

Although Berlin's defences deteriorated rapidly under the new Russian bombardment begun on 16 April, the decision to move from 'Koralle' was not made until the 19th. Even so, it came as a surprise to Dönitz's adjutant, Walter Lüdde-Neurath, for he had just gone to bed that night when the telephone rang and he was told to be ready to move within the hour. It was not a moment too soon. Just half an hour after Dönitz's armoured Mercedes, staff cars, vans and the important mobile radio transmitter – which could reach most ships at sea via several huge fixed radio stations – rolled out of the compound, the first of the Russian troops arrived. The German Naval War Staff remained at Dönitz's flat in the heart of Berlin for a few days before finally moving west to Plön in Schleswig-Holstein. Meanwhile, other branches of the Naval High Command had been staying at Varel, near Wilhelmshaven, since February 1945, and now they too moved north of the Elbe to occupy a small camp near Eutin in Schleswig-Holstein.

Time was fast running out. The situation in Plön became quite hectic after Lüdde-Neurath telephoned the Dräger Works in Lübeck – which was about half an hour's drive from

Plön – only to be told that there were enemy tanks driving past. He lost no time in collecting the Grand Admiral and beating a hasty retreat to Flensburg, where the German Naval War Staff remained until disbanded by the Allies.

NAVAL GROUP COMMANDS

The pre-war administration pattern changed on 18 August 1939, when the previously planned 'Three Front War Programme' came into effect as an emergency measure to cover possible conflict in the Baltic, North Sea and the Atlantic. These three areas were to be controlled by Naval Group Command East, Naval Group Command West and by the Naval War Staff (SKL). Naval Group Command East had been in existence since November 1938 – the date of its foundation in Kiel – with the aim of defending the Baltic. (See diagram, page 64) A similar department for the west was then founded in Sengwarden, near Wilhelmshaven, during August 1939. At first, it was only concerned with the defence of the German Bight and the North Sea, but later it also took control of Norwegian waters. Eventually its headquarters were moved to France, where the Command restricted its operations to French Atlantic waters. The German Bight, the North Sea, Norwegian waters and other parts previously controlled by the Naval Group Command East were taken over by a new unit called Naval Group Command North. A further division was created during 1941 to cover the waters

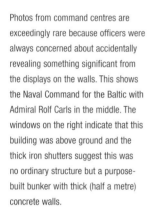

Photos from command centres are exceedingly rare because officers were always concerned about accidentally revealing something significant from the displays on the walls. This shows the Naval Command for the Baltic with Admiral Rolf Carls in the middle. The windows on the right indicate that this building was above ground and the thick iron shutters suggest this was no ordinary structure but a purpose-built bunker with thick (half a metre) concrete walls.

Admiral Rolf Carls in one of the rooms for the Baltic Naval Command. The windows suggest that this was taken inside an ordinary building, rather than a bunker.

of northern Norway. This was called Admiral Polar Seas (Admiral Nordmeer), and its headquarters were in Kirkenes, aboard the depot ship *Tanga*. During May 1942 the staff moved aboard the yacht *Grille* moored at Narvik, where they remained until the Command was disbanded in June 1944.

Naval Commands Baltic and North Sea

After the First World War these two Commands were called Stationskommando Ostsee and Stationskommando Nordsee (Station Command Baltic and Station Command North Sea). Later, they were known as Marinestation der Ostsee or Nordsee (Naval Station for Baltic or North Sea). Both Commands were upgraded to Marineoberkommando and their commanding officers promoted from Commanders-in-Chief to Supreme Commanders-in-Chief during February 1943. The two Commands operated as separate, autonomous divisions under their own leaders (see diagram on page 64) and were responsible for coastal defence, the training of new recruits and other general training. (In this book they will be dealt with as one unit, because it will save duplicating information and should be easier to understand.)

Naval Command Baltic and Operation Barbarossa

As soon as the office of Naval Commander-in-Chief 'C' was created in May 1941, the staff was positioned in Memel to await the start of the attack on Russia. Several naval forces moved from there to support the Army, and a few were engaged in battles of their own – especially during the storming of Libau. In November 1941, the post was disbanded and all existing forces were placed under the command of Naval Commander-in-Chief 'D' – a position that had also been

While the German Navy was responsible for creating huge towns such as Wilhelmshaven, it also maintained some small, out of the way outposts. This shows the radio station at Stolpmünde on the Baltic coast, some 100 kilometres west of Danzig. This photo is most interesting because when one compares it with other pictures in this book one will see that the set-up is identical to the communications centre in Wilhelmshaven. The large building accommodated men and offices; officers lived in a small house with gable roof and there were two bunkers: a large one on the left and a small one on the right. The small one in Wilhelmshaven is still standing. The keeping of a multitude of log books was a major task in some of these more remote locations and helped to prevent the staff from drifting away or going fishing when they should be working. Quite a number provided idyllic locations, far from the ravages of the war and sometimes there was very little to do, yet the men on duty were not allowed to remove headsets from their ears and even gulped down hurried meals with earphones still on while remaining at their post.

established in May. From then on C-in-C 'D' was responsible for the entire coastal defences of the far-eastern Baltic. (For a list of the forces under his command, see 'Coastal Commander East Baltic' on page 78) Later, in May 1944, he was given the title Commanding Admiral East Baltic. Originally, the forces under Naval Commander-in-Chief 'C' were known as Marinestosstruppabteilung (Naval Assault Detachment). Two special units were later founded and known by their commanders' names – Special Command Bigler and Special Command Gläser. Although the important forces under Naval Commander-in-Chief 'D' have been listed, there were also several other AA and artillery divisions.

Proper Nouns

It is difficult, if not impossible, to provide direct translations of certain German proper nouns. On the other hand, keeping some of the original German names would only help to confuse readers who do not understand German. The following translations may lend a guiding hand.[1]

Training Regiment: Schiffsstammregiment
Training Detachment: Schiffsstammabteilung
NCO Training Detachment: Marinelehrabteilung
Naval Reserve Detachment: Marineersatzabteilung
Naval Artillery Regiment: Marineartillerieregiment
Naval Artillery Detachment (Art. Det.): Marineartillerie-abteilung
Naval AA Regiment: Marineflakregiment
Naval AA Detachment (AA Det.): Marineflakabteilung
Naval Artillery Reserve: Marineersatzartillerie
Port Protection Flotilla: Hafenschutzflottille

TRAINING NEW RECRUITS

Before the end of the First World War, new recruits were trained by Naval Inspectorate (Marine Inspektion). These were allotted the suffixes 'I' for the Baltic and 'II' for the North Sea. Both Inspectorates were disbanded after the war and replaced by two new departments: Schiffsstammdivision der Ostsee and Nordsee. They, too, were later replaced by Schiffsstammregiment der Ostsee and Nordsee, each of which was sub-divided into Schiffsstammabteilung. In this book they have been translated as meaning 'Training Regiment' and 'Training Detachment'.

Training Regiments (Schiffsstammregiment)
The following list gives the Command (B = Baltic, N = North Sea) and main base for each regiment.
1. B; Stralsund. Disbanded, January 1944.
2. N; Wesermünde. Disbanded, November 1939.
3. B; Libau (Liepaja). Founded during January 1943 and moved to Epinal in April 1943.
4. N; Groningen. Moved to Steenwijk, October 1943.
5. B; Pillau. Only operational from January 1944 until February 1945.

1. Anyone finding these names difficult might like to know that there was a school called the Marinenachrichtenhelferinnenausbildungsabteilung.

German names are used in the singular throughout this section, even where they should be in the plural. As plurals are not simply formed by adding a 's' and as, usually, names on documents or on badges would have been in the singular, I hope this style will simplify matters for non-German readers.

Training new recruits was one of the major objectives of the two Naval Commands. Every man, no matter what line he wished to pursue, went through a land-based induction course. Some German officers have told us in their memoirs that this was hard and somewhat humiliating. Many people have stated that the initial training was of great value and some even admitted that it helped save their life during the war. The majority of men started their initial training with either the North Sea or Baltic Naval Commands. Officers had their own induction centre on the Island of Rügen. This shows the officer training centre with recruits before they were allowed to wear naval uniforms. Such courses also served as a selection net and a number of youngsters were usually rejected because they could not cope with the high demands made on them. Some of the promising failures were told to join a sports club and make another application in a year's time; those deemed impossible were diverted into some other occupation.

6. N; Belfont. Only operational from December 1943 until September 1944.

Training Detachments (Schiffsstammabteilung)
The following list gives the Command (B = Baltic, N = North Sea) and main base for each.
1. B; Kiel. Renamed 1st Naval Reserve Detachment, January 1944 (see also 7th Detachment).
2. N; Wilhelmshaven. Moved to Norden in April 1941; renamed 8th Naval Reserve Detachment during January 1944.

3. B; Kiel. Moved to Eckernförde, then to Waren near Müritz; it was renamed 9th Naval Reserve Detachment.
4. N; Wilhelmshaven. Renamed 4th Naval Reserve Detachment during 1944.
5. B; Eckernförde. Moved to Libau and later to Epinal.
6. N; Wilhelmshaven. Moved to Gotenhafen; renamed 16th Training Detachment during January 1940. Moved to Steenwijk and Wazep in Holland during April 1941.
7. B; Stralsund. Renamed 1st Training Detachment during January 1944 and moved to Epinal. Later moved to Fort Schiesseck near Bitsch.
8. N; Leer. Renamed 28th Naval Reserve Detachment, October 1944.
9. B; Stralsund. Renamed 3rd NCO Training Detachment, January 1944.
10. N; Wesermünde. Renamed 4th NCO Training Detachment, January 1944.
11. B; Stralsund. Renamed 3rd Training Detachment, January 1944.
12. N; Brake. Later renamed 6th NCO Training Detachment.
13. B; Sassnitz. Moved to Libau, then to Pillau and later to Epinal. Handed over to the Army during September 1944.
14. N; Glückstadt. Moved to Breda in Holland, September 1940.
15. B; Beverloo. Moved from near Beverloo to Copenhagen during January 1944 and re-named 5th NCO Training Detachment.
16. N; Bergen-op-Zoom. Moved to Gotenhafen June 1940. It was originally known as 6th Training Detachment.
17. B; Memel. Moved 1944.

18. N; Buxtehude. Moved from Buxtehude near Hamburg to Husum, May 1943; went to Belfont in December of that year. The detachment was handed over to the Army in September 1944.
19. B; Near Diedenhofen. Founded in July 1942. Later moved to Beverloo and afterwards to Hansted in Denmark.
20. N; Near Arnhem. Founded during July 1941 in Norden; moved to near Arnhem shortly afterwards. Later, the Detachment was also at Harkamm.
21. B; Leba. Moved to Copenhagen in 1944.
22. N; Beverloo. Later moved to Almelo in Holland.
23. B; Deutsch Krone. Known as the 3rd Naval Artillery Reserve Detachment before January 1944.
24. N; Groningen. Known as the 6th Naval Artillery Reserve Detachment before September 1943.
25. B; Pillau. Known as the 5th Naval Artillery Reserve Detachment before January 1944.
26. N; Helchteren. Originally founded in Wazep.
27. B; Ollerup (Denmark). Known as the 7th Naval Artillery Reserve Detachment before January 1944.
28. N; Sennheim. Only operational from October 1943 until October 1944. It was a special training unit for non-German naval volunteers.
29. Not operational.
30. N; Wittmund.
31. B; Windau. Moved to Windau during August 1942. It was disbanded during December 1944.
32. N; Stralsund. Renamed 2nd Training Detachment during January 1944. This was probably disbanded, because it was re-founded as 22nd Naval Reserve Detachment during October 1944.

NCO TRAINING DETACHMENTS

These units were first called Marineunteroffizierabteilung, until January 1944 when they were then renamed Marinelehrabteilung. Both were concerned with the training of non-commissioned officers. There were two regiments: Number 1 was in Eckernförde under the Baltic Command, and Number 2 was in Wesermünde under the North Sea Command. These two regiments were divided into seven detachments; the following list gives the command of each unit (B = Baltic, N = North Sea) and its main base.
1. B; Kiel. Moved to Glücksburg,[1] January 1944.
2. N; Wesermünde. Moved to Glückstadt, September 1940.
3. B; Stralsund. Moved to Aarhus in Denmark, July 1944.

1. Glückburg, complete with castle, lies near Flensburg and Glückstadt, (Matjes Herring Capital) is on the Elbe to the east of Brunsbüttel.

4. N; Lehe near Wesermünde. Founded in January 1944.

5. B; Copenhagen. Earlier, it was also known as the 15th Training Detachment.

6. N; Varel. Founded in January 1944 by renaming the 12th Training Detachment. Disbanded in October 1944.

7. B; Lütjenholm. Moved to Hirtenstall, September 1944. Later the Detachment moved to Norddorf on the island of Amrum; some members moved to Büsum and Sülzenholm.

NAVAL RESERVE UNITS

Naval Reserve Regiments (Marineersatzregiment):

1. Baltic Command, with headquarters in Kiel. This regiment dealt with personnel for special missions.

2. North Sea Command, with headquarters in Wilhelmshaven. Founded during January 1944. The following detachments were operational: 2, 4, 6, 8, 10, 12, 28, 42.

3. Baltic Command, with headquarters in Neustrelitz. This regiment was for armament specialists and technical personnel.

4. North Sea Command, with headquarters in Cuxhaven.

Naval Reserve Detachments (Marineersatzabteilung):
The following list gives the command of each detachment (B = Baltic, N = North Sea) and its base.

1. B; Kiel, Founded in January 1944 by changing the name of the 1st Training Detachment.

2. N; Wilhelmshaven. Founded in September 1944.

3. B; Neustrelitz. Founded during September 1944, it later moved to Schlochau.

4. N; Wilhelmshaven. Founded in 1944 by changing the name of the 4th Training Detachment.

5. B; Westerland. On the island of Sylt. Founded in September 1943.

6. N; Hörnum. On the island of Sylt. Founded in January 1944.

7. B; Schwesing. Founded in January 1944.

8. N; Norden. Founded in January 1944 by changing the name of the 2nd Training Detachment.

9. B; Waren. Probably also at Müritz. Founded in January 1944 by changing the name of the 3rd Training Detachment.

10. N; Near Godenstedt. Founded in January 1944 by changing the name of 2nd Naval Artillery Reserve Detachment.

11. B; Deutsch-Eylau (Ilawa). Founded in January 1944 by changing the name of the 11th Naval Artillery Reserve Detachment.

12. N; Cuxhaven. Founded in January 1944 by changing the name of the 4th Naval Artillery Reserve Detachment.

13. B; Sassnitz. Founded in January 1944 by changing the name of Marinestammkompanie. Also had bases in Neustrelitz and Bornholm.

14. N; Wilhelmshaven.

15. B; Swinemünde. Founded in January 1944.

16. N; Only operational for one month during 1944.

17. B; Flatow (Zlotow). Operational for one year from January 1944.

18. N; Leer. Founded in October 1944 by changing the name of the 2nd NCO Training Detachment.

19. B; Neustrelitz. Founded in January 1944 by changing the name of Ausbildungsstammkompanie Neustrelitz (Training Company Neustrelitz).

20. Probably not operational.

21. B; Memel.

22. N; Wyk/Föhr. Founded in December 1944 by changing the name of the 32nd Training Detachment.

23. B; Pilsen (?). Founded in June 1944.

24. N; Probably not operational.

25. B; Neustrelitz. Founded in May 1944.

26. N; Probably not operational.

27. B; Esbjerg. Founded in March 1945.

28. N; Leer. Founded in October 1944 by changing the name of the 8th Training Detachment.

29. B; Not operational.

30. N; Not operational.

31. B; Kiel. Founded in September 1944.

32. N; Hamburg. Founded in September 1944.

33. B; Stettin. Only operational for one month during 1944.

34. N; Bremen. Founded in November 1944.

35. B; Gotenhafen (Gdynia). Operational between November 1944 and March 1945. The name was then changed to 37th Naval Reserve Detachment.

36. N; Bremen. Founded in September 1944.

37. B; Königsberg. Founded in August 1944; moved to several other locations later.

38, 39, 40, 41. Not operational.

42. N; (?). Founded in December 1944.

COASTAL DEFENCE, NAVAL COMMAND NORTH SEA

Two Fortress Commanders had been responsible for coastal defence of the North Sea coast before the war: the East Friesian Area had its headquarters in Wilhelmshaven and the North Friesian Area was in Cuxhaven. But when war broke out the term Fortress Commander (Festungskommandant) was replaced by Coastal Commander (Küstenbefehlshaber). The two areas continued to function separately until they were amalgamated in February 1941, and a new post of Coastal Commander German Bight (Küstenbefehlshaber Deutsche Bucht) was created. Headquarters of the amalgamated section remained in Wilhelmshaven for some time, but the offices were later moved to Cuxhaven. The office of Coastal Commander German Bight existed until September 1944, when there was a drastic reorganization of Germany's coastal defences,

The following is an outline of the main units directly controlled by the Coastal Commander between September 1939 and September 1944. This is followed by an outline of the reorganized administration.

Section Borkum Island:
Borkum is a small island of about thirteen and a half square miles at the mouth of the Ems.
Port Protection Flotilla.
Naval Art. Det. 116.
Naval AA Det. 216.

The navy manned mobile and permanent land-based artillery units equipped with a variety of guns. The majority were of standard issue but once the war started Germany improvised by also using weapons from obsolete warships. The crews were particularly trained to cope with moving targets, rather than bombarding a stationary position.

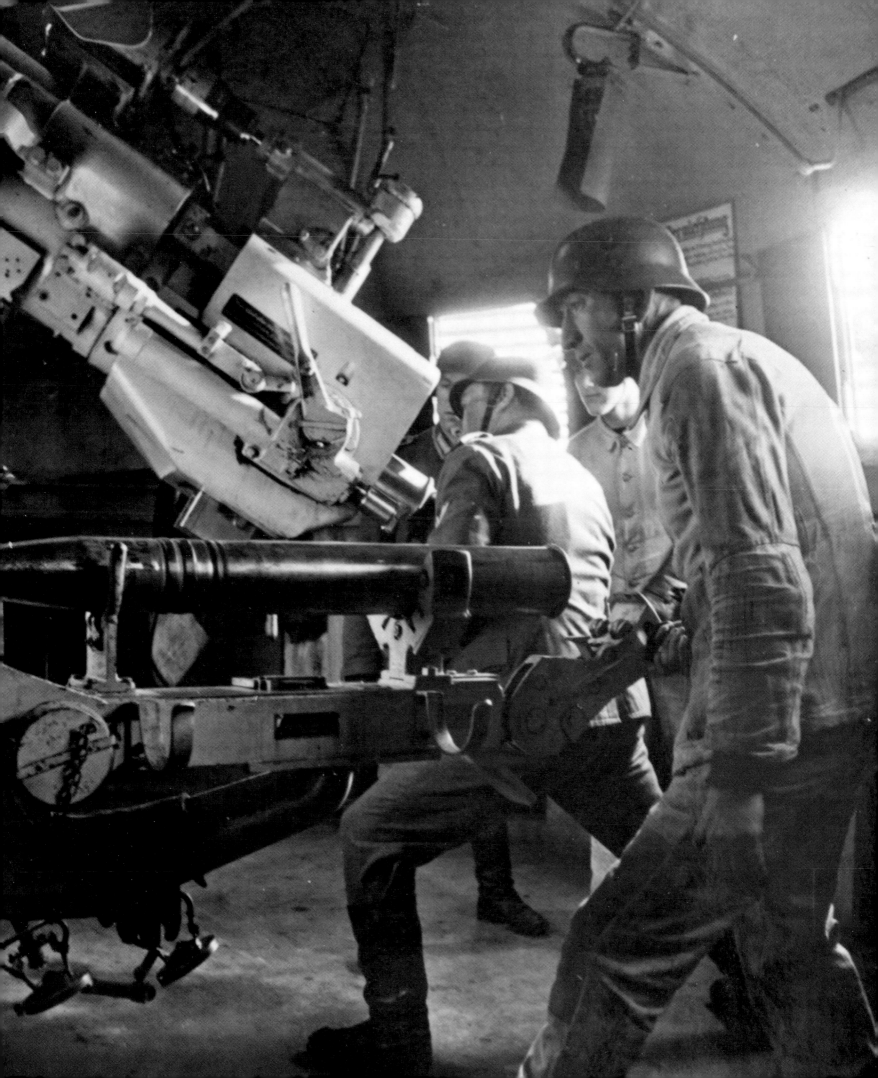

Although many men from land-based artillery units went through a period of training on ships and were allowed to wear naval uniforms, it was often more convenient and comfortable to be equipped with army-style clothing. This shows a youngster from a land-based anti-aircraft unit with a light 20mm anti-aircraft gun. The gun was balanced on its mount and could be fired in a similar fashion to a rifle and this made aiming easier than when having to wrestle with hand wheels to change the aim. However, it was not powerful enough to cope with new fast-flying and front-armoured aircraft.

Section Emden:
The five northerly Dutch provinces came under the jurisdiction of this section during May 1940.
6th Naval AA Regt. Founded in Emden during March 1942, the following detachments were operational:
Naval AA Det. 236; Emden.
Naval AA Det. 246; Harlingen.
Naval AA Det. 256; Delfzijl. (Founded, March 1942.)
Naval AA Det. 266; Westerhusen. (Founded, March 1942.)
Naval AA Det. 276; Kanalpolder. (Founded, December 1943.)
6th Naval Art. Res. Founded in Emden during August 1943. Also at Assen and Groningen. It was renamed 24th Naval Training Detachment during September 1943.
10th Naval Art. Res. Operational in Norden for a few weeks during January 1940.

8th Naval Motor Transport Det. Founded in Emden during March 1942.

Section Norderney:
Norderney is a small island, about eight and a half square miles, north of Emden.
Naval Art. Det. 126. Operational from October 1939 until July 1940.
Naval AA Det. 226. Operational from October 1939.

Section Wangerooge:
Wangerooge is an island of about five and three quarter square miles. This section also had small units on adjoining islands.
Naval Art. Det. 112. Operational from October 1939 until June 1940.
Naval Art. Det. 132. Naval AA Det. 232.
2nd Naval Training Det. for light AA guns.

Section Wilhelmshaven:
Port Protection Flotilla.
2nd Naval AA Regt. Wilhelmshaven. Renamed 2nd Naval AA Brigade (2. Marineflakbrigade) in May 1942. The following detachments were operational.
Naval AA Det. 212; Wilhelmshaven.
Naval AA Det. 222; Wilhelmshaven. Also the floating AA battery *Medusa*. (*Medusa* was an old pre-First World War cruiser.)
Naval AA Det. 232; Wilhelmshaven.
Naval AA Det. 252; Heidmühle.
Naval AA Det. 262; Wilhelmshaven.
Naval AA Det. 272; Tossens.
Naval AA Det. 282; Wilhelmshaven. Founded during the spring of 1940. The floating AA battery *Niobe* belonged to this detachment. (*Niobe* was a Royal Netherlands Navy cruiser.)
2nd Naval Art. Res.
2nd Naval Motor Transport Det.

Section Wesermünde (Bremerhaven):
Situated at the mouth of the River Weser. Wesermünde has been renamed Bremerhaven.
Naval AA Det. 244.
Naval AA Det. 264.

Section Heligoland:
Naval AA Det. 242.
Naval Art. Det. 122.

Section Cuxhaven:
Port Protection Flotilla.
Naval AA Det. 214.
Naval 4th Art. Res.

Section Brunsbüttel:
Brunsbüttel or Brunsbüttelkoog is a small town at the mouth of the River Elbe, where the Kiel Canal terminates. It is famous for the huge locks that control the canal's water level.
14th Naval AA Regt. The following detachments were operational.

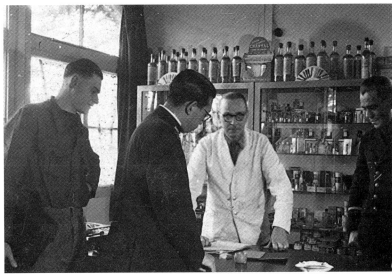

ABOVE: The quartermaster's store on land that issued ships with whatever they needed.

ABOVE: Although the navy provided many services, many men chose to visit a barber's shop in town, rather than having their hair cut on board. This shows one such barber who also provided a variety of luxury goods that could not be acquired aboard ships.

RIGHT: The German equivalent of the NAAFI stores where soldiers could buy all manner of goodies for private use.

BELOW: A radio room, probably at Stolpmünde on the Baltic coast. The large windows are of interest and indicate that this room is not inside a communications bunker, but located in an ordinary house.

Naval AA Det. 254; Sandhayn and later Friedrichshof.
Naval AA Det. 274; Brunsbüttel.
Naval AA Det. 294; Near Stade.
Naval AA Det. 224; Founded in Wilhelmsburg (Hamburg); moved to France during May 1943.

Section Sylt:
Sylt is an island in the North Sea near the Danish border. It is connected to the German mainland by the Hindenburg Dam which carries a railway line.
8th Naval AA Reg; Westerland. Disbanded during February 1942.
Naval AA Det. 204; Westerland. Moved to Esbjerg during April 1940.
Naval AA Det. 234; Westerland.
Naval AA Det. 264; Hörnum plus other locations. Disbanded during April 1943, after which the battery came under control of Naval AA Det. 234.
Naval Art. Det. 134; Vogelkoje and other locations.

Despite an impressive bunker building programme, the war was responsible for increasing the size of the workforce in the main ports beyond what could be accommodated in existing buildings and a number of obsolete passenger ships were brought in to provide living and office quarters. This shows the 16,732-ton Hapag liner *St. Louis* on the landing stage next to the Lützow Pier in Kiel while she served as headquarters for the 5th U-boat Flotilla. Although painted dark grey, such large ships were difficult to camouflage and were left to the mercy of the Allied air forces during air raids. There was a standing rule that all personnel had to seek shelter in air raid bunkers as soon as the sirens sounded. The U-boat on the right is a Type VIIC.

The 5th U-boat Flotilla's main entrance aboard the liner *St. Louis* in Kiel. This flotilla specialized in kitting out and provisioning U-boats going on their first war cruise.

ADMIRAL GERMAN BIGHT

There were drastic changes in coastal defence during September 1944. The Coastal Commander for the German Bight was renamed Commanding Admiral German Bight and the area was divided into three Sea Defence Regions, each subdivided as follows.

Sea Defence Region East Friesland:
    Headquarters at Tidefeld near Norden.
    Sections Borkum, Emden, Norderney, Wangerooge and Wilhelmshaven.

Sea Defence Region Elbe-Weser:
    Headquarters at Ottendorf, near Cuxhaven. Sections Cuxhaven, Brunsbüttel, Wesermünde and Heligoland.

Sea Defence Region North Friesland:
    Headquarters at Husum.
    Sections Friedrichstadt and Sylt.

Sea Defence Sections and their bases were as listed below.

Section Borkum:
    Port Protection Flotilla.
    Naval AA Det. 216.
    Naval Art. Det. 116.
    Naval Island Bttn. 350.

Section Emden:
    6th Naval AA Regt. with Naval AA Det. 236; Emden.
    Naval AA Det. 246; Harlingen.

Naval AA Det. 256; Delfzijl.
Naval AA Det. 266; Westerhusen.
Naval AA Det. 276; Kanalpolder.
Naval Art. Det. 126; Leer.
Naval Fortress Bttns: 363, 366, 367, 368.
Naval Island Bttn. 353. Founded in January 1945 on the island of Amrum and moved to Emden before the end of the war.

Section Norderney:
    Naval AA Det. 226.
    Naval Island Bttn. 355; Juist.

Section Wangerooge:
    Naval Art. Det. 631.
    Naval Island Bttn. Based on the islands of Wangerooge and Langeoog.
    (The Naval AA Training establishment in this section was disbanded during November 1944.)

Section Wilhelmshaven:
    Port Protection Flotilla.
    Naval AA Dets. 212, 222, 232, 272, 282; all based in the town.
    Naval AA Det. 252; Heidmühle.
    Three Naval Fortress Bttns.: 363, 364 and 365.

Section Cuxhaven:
    Port Protection Flotilla.
    Naval Art. Det. 114. Founded in September 1944.
    Naval AA Det. 214.
    Naval Fortress Bttns. 359 and 360.

Section Brunsbüttel
    14th Naval AA Regt. with
    Naval AA Det. 224; Wilhelmsburg.
    Naval AA Det. 254; Friedrichshof.
    Naval AA Det. 274; Zweidorf.
    Naval AA Det. 294; Near Stade.
    Naval Fortress Bttn. 358.

Section Wesermünde:
    Naval AA Det. 244.
    Naval AA Det. 264.
    Naval Fortress Bttn. 362; Nordenham.
    Naval Art. Det. 122 was also allocated, but probably not operational.

Section Heligoland:
    Naval AA Det. 242.
    Naval Art. Det. 122.
    Naval Island Bttn. 349 was also allocated, but probably not operational.

Section Friedrichstadt:
    Naval Art. Det. 124.
    Naval Fortress Bttn. 357; Tönning.

Section Sylt:
    Naval AA Det. 234; Westerland.
    Naval Art. Det. 134. Founded in September 1944.
    Naval Island Bttns. 351, 352 and 353.

COASTAL DEFENCE, NAVAL COMMAND BALTIC

The Baltic was divided into three autonomous defence zones: West Baltic, Pommern Coast and East Baltic. Each was headed by a Coastal Commander who was responsible for the following forces.
Coastal Commander West Baltic:
This post was later called Commander of Sea Defences for Schleswig-Holstein and Mecklenburg.
    Naval Art. Det. 121; Laboe. Operational from August 1939 until April 1940.
    1st Naval AA Regt. (Renamed 1st Naval AA Brigade during May 1942.)

The following detachments were operational:
    Naval AA Det. 211; Eckernförde.

GERMAN NAVAL BASES IN THE NETHERLANDS AND THE BALTIC

□ Port protection flotilla, Port commander
    and Naval fitting out base
▲ Port protection flotilla and Port commander
⊕ Port commander for the most part of the war
⊖ Port commander for only a short period of the war

Naval AA Det. 221; Kiel later also at Dehnhöft.
Naval AA Det. 231; Kiel. Moved to Brest.
Naval AA Det. 241; Kiel.
Naval AA Det. 243; Rendsburg. Disbanded early on in the war and later refounded.
Naval AA Det. 251; Kiel.
Naval AA Det. 261; Kiel.
Naval AA Det. 271; Kiel.
Naval AA Det. 281. Founded in March 1942.
1st Naval Motor Transport Det.
5th Naval Motor Transport Det. Founded during the summer of 1942. There were also several other major naval units in Kiel.

Coastal Commander Pommern:
The following units were based at Swinemünde unless otherwise stated.
3rd Naval AA Regt with:
Naval AA Det. 233.
Naval AA Det. 711.
Naval AA Det. 713.
(The last two were founded shortly before the end of the war.)
Light Naval Art. Det. 536; Wolin. Founded during March 1945.
Light Naval Art. Det. 537. Founded during January 1945.
Naval Art. Det. 123.

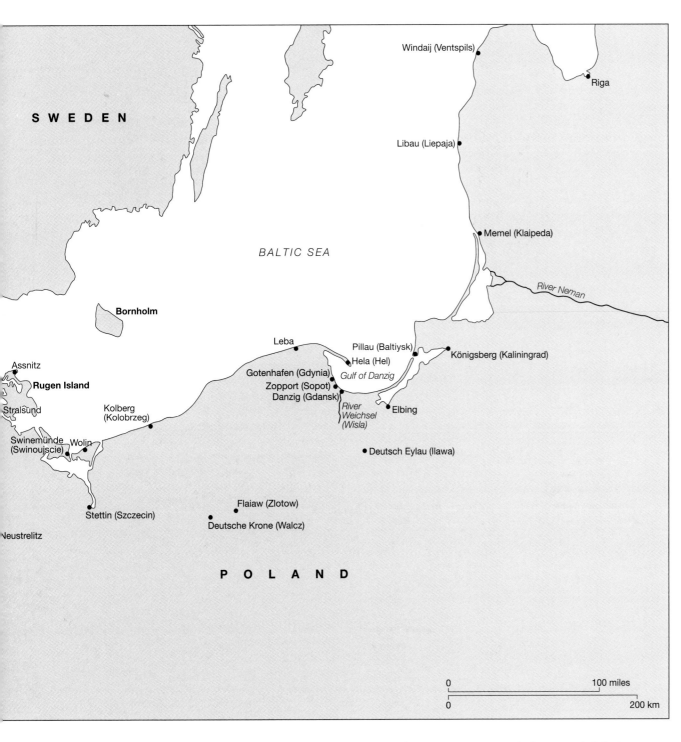

Windaij (Ventspils)

Riga

SWEDEN

Libau (Liepaja)

BALTIC SEA

Memel (Klaipeda)

River Neman

Bornholm

Leba

Pillau (Baltiysk)
Königsberg (Kaliningrad)

Assnitz

Hela (Hel)

Rugen Island

Gotenhafen (Gdynia)
Gulf of Danzig

Zopport (Sopot)
Danzig (Gdansk)

Stralsund

Kolberg
(Kolobrzeg)

River
Weichsel
(Wisla)

Elbing

Swinemünde
(Swinoujscie)   Wolin

Deutsch Eylau (Ilawa)

Flaiaw (Zlotow)

Neustrelitz

Stettin (Szczecin)

Deutsche Krone (Walcz)

P O L A N D

0   100 miles

0   200 km

3rd Naval Art. Res. Det.
3rd Naval Motor Transport Detachment.
There were also several other naval units based in
Swinemünde.

Coastal Commander East Baltic:
Section Gotenhafen:
  9th Naval AA Regt. (Founded during September 1942)
  with
  Naval AA Det. 219; Gotenhafen. Founded during
  February 1940.
  Naval AA Det. 229; Gotenhafen and also at Danzig
  (Gdansk). Later renamed Naval AA Det. 814 and
  moved to Denmark.

Naval AA Det. 259; Gotenhafen. Founded during
December 1942.
Naval AA Det. 818; Hela. Moved to Lorient (France)
during 1943.
Naval Art. Det. 119; Hela. Founded during February
1940.
Naval Art. Det. 629; Gotenhafen. Founded during
January 1944.
11th Naval Art. Res. Det.; Deutsch-Eylau. Founded
during August 1942, it was renamed Naval Art. Det. II
during April 1944.

Section Pillau:
> Naval AA Det. 215. Operational from September 1939 until January 1940. Refounded during February 1941.
> Naval AA Det. 225. Operational from September 1939 until January 1940. Refounded during June 1941, it was later disbanded, then refounded during August 1944.
> Naval Art. Det. 115. Operational from the start of the war until January 1940. Refounded during May 1940; it was renamed Naval Art. Det. 5 during September 1942.
> Naval Art. Det. 535. Founded during July 1944.

Section Memel:
> Naval AA Det. 217. Operational from September 1939 until October 1939. Refounded during March 1941 and then disbanded. It was refounded again in Zevern near Bremen, from where the Detachment moved to Memel.
> Naval Art. Det. 117. Renamed 7th Naval Art. Res. Det. and moved to Libau.

The following posts were created towards the end of the war:

Sea Defence Zone Estland:
> Naval AA Dets. 239 and 711.
> Naval Art. Dets. 530 and 532.

Sea Defence Zone Baltic Islands:
> Naval AA Det. 239.
> Naval Art. Dets. 531 and 532.

Sea Defence Zone Lettland:
> 10th Naval Art. Regt. with Art. Dets. 530, 532 and 534.
> Naval AA Div. 712.
> 9th Naval Motor Transport Det.; based mainly in Libau.

Sea Defence Zone East Prussia:
> Naval Art. Det. 533.
> Naval AA Dets. 215 and 225; all based at Pillau.

Sea Defence Zone West Prussia:
> Naval Art. Det. 629.
> 9th Naval AA Regt. with Naval AA Dets. 219, 249, 259 and 818. These were mainly based at Gotenhafen.

Sea Defence Zone Memel:
> Naval AA Dets. 217 and 218.

The type of pass needed to gain access to restricted areas. People passing in and out on a regular basis usually had their own private pass while occasional visitors and men from passing ships were issued with a pass each time they passed through the gate. This one was issued to Funkgefreiter Dorgögen in Constanta (Black Sea). For security reasons, field post numbers were used instead of the name of units. M31691, with M referring to Marine, was the staff of the 30th U-boat Flotilla. At the top it states that this pass must be placed inside the pay book, which also served as an identity card. If the pass was lost then it had to be reported right away to the soldier's own unit as well as to the Naval Coordination Officer. Lower down, below the name, it confirms that such a pass only worked in conjunction with a pay book, an identity card from a German Military Headquarters or a German passport.

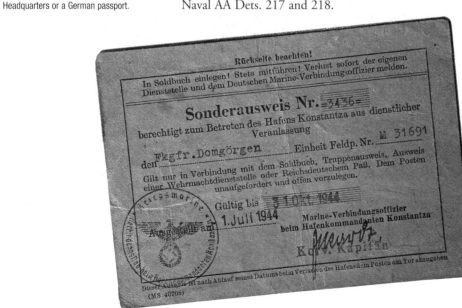

NAVAL COMMAND POSTS OUTSIDE GERMANY

DENMARK
Naval Anti-Aircraft Detachments (Marineflakabteilung): The following list gives the location and command section of each detachment.
204. Esbjerg (South Jutland). Moved from Sylt in April 1940.
716. Frederikshavn (North Jutland). Founded in November 1944.
717. Arhus (South Jutland). Founded in October 1944.
814. Hansted (North Jutland). Moved from Gotenhafen, as Detachment 229.

Naval Artillery Detachments (Marineartillerieabteilung): The following list gives the location and command section of each detachment.
118. Hansted (North Jutland). Founded in 1941.
508. Copenhagen (South Jutland). Founded during April 1940 as Artillery Detachment Seeland and renamed in July 1940.
509. Frederikshavn and Lökken (North Jutland). Founded in May 1940 by renaming Detachment 309.
518. Fanö (South Jutland). Founded in September 1944.
522. Copenhagen (Danish Islands). Founded in October 1944.
523. Grena (South Jutland). Founded in October 1944.
524. Arhus (South Jutland). Founded in January 1945 when Detachment 523 was split.
525. Fünen (Danish islands). Founded in January 1945.
814. Hansted (North Jutland). Moved from Gotenhafen, as Detachment 229.

Naval Artillery Arsenals:
> Copenhagen: Established during June 1940.
> Thisted: Established during September 1941.

NORWAY
Naval Artillery Detachments (Marineartillerieabteilung): The following list gives the location of each detachment.
501. Horten. Founded in March 1940.
502. Kristiansand Süd.
503. Near Stavanger. Founded in April 1940.
504. Near Horten. Founded in Bergen, April 1940.
505. Molde. Founded in June 1940.
506. Trondheim. Founded in May 1940.
507. Husöen. Founded in August 1940.
510. Bodo. Founded in August 1940.
511. Harstad. Founded in Narvik, July 1940.
512. Tromso. Operational for one year from October 1940.
513. Vardö. Founded in September 1940.
514. Lofoten. Founded in Narvik, March 1942.
516. Lodingen.

Naval AA Detachments (Marineflakabteilung): The following list gives the location of each detachment:
701. Trondheim. Founded in June 1941.
702. Trondheim. Founded in June 1940.
706. Narvik. Founded in June 1941.
709. Harstad. Founded in November 1941.
710. Narvik. Founded in Gotenhafen during October

WARTIME ORGANIZATION OF THE KRIEGSMARINE IN DENMARK

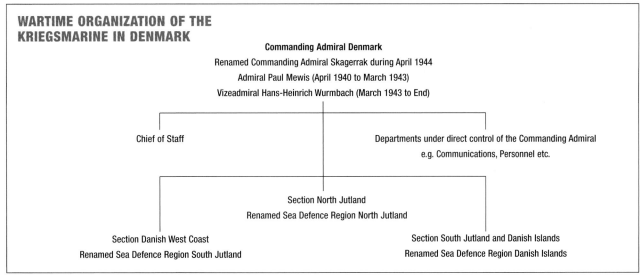

Commanding Admiral Denmark
Renamed Commanding Admiral Skagerrak during April 1944
Admiral Paul Mewis (April 1940 to March 1943)
Vizeadmiral Hans-Heinrich Wurmbach (March 1943 to End)

Chief of Staff

Departments under direct control of the Commanding Admiral
e.g. Communications, Personnel etc.

Section North Jutland
Renamed Sea Defence Region North Jutland

Section Danish West Coast
Renamed Sea Defence Region South Jutland

Section South Jutland and Danish Islands
Renamed Sea Defence Region Danish Islands

WARTIME ORGANIZATION OF THE KRIEGSMARINE IN NORWAY

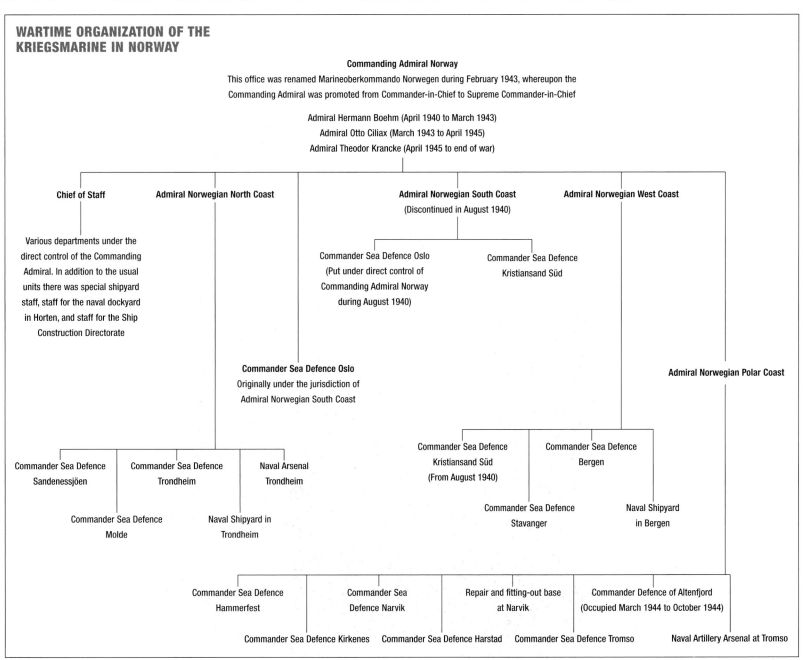

Commanding Admiral Norway
This office was renamed Marineoberkommando Norwegen during February 1943, whereupon the
Commanding Admiral was promoted from Commander-in-Chief to Supreme Commander-in-Chief

Admiral Hermann Boehm (April 1940 to March 1943)
Admiral Otto Ciliax (March 1943 to April 1945)
Admiral Theodor Krancke (April 1945 to end of war)

Chief of Staff

Admiral Norwegian North Coast

Admiral Norwegian South Coast
(Discontinued in August 1940)

Admiral Norwegian West Coast

Various departments under the
direct control of the Commanding
Admiral. In addition to the usual
units there was special shipyard
staff, staff for the naval dockyard
in Horten, and staff for the Ship
Construction Directorate

Commander Sea Defence Oslo
(Put under direct control of
Commanding Admiral Norway
during August 1940)

Commander Sea Defence
Kristiansand Süd

Commander Sea Defence Oslo
Originally under the jurisdiction of
Admiral Norwegian South Coast

Admiral Norwegian Polar Coast

Commander Sea Defence
Sandenessjöen

Commander Sea Defence
Trondheim

Naval Arsenal
Trondheim

Commander Sea Defence
Molde

Naval Shipyard in
Trondheim

Commander Sea Defence
Kristiansand Süd
(From August 1940)

Commander Sea Defence
Bergen

Commander Sea Defence
Stavanger

Naval Shipyard
in Bergen

Commander Sea Defence
Hammerfest

Commander Sea
Defence Narvik

Repair and fitting-out base
at Narvik

Commander Defence of Altenfjord
(Occupied March 1944 to October 1944)

Commander Sea Defence Kirkenes

Commander Sea Defence Harstad

Commander Sea Defence Tromso

Naval Artillery Arsenal at Tromso

GERMAN NAVAL BASES IN NORWAY

△ Main base with variety of services
□ Northern ports with Port protection flotilla
        Port commander
        Fitting-out base
        Landing flotilla
▲ Ports with Port protection flotilla
        Port commander
⊕ Ports with Port commander

NORTH SEA

N

Honningsväg
Hammerfest
Vardo
Kirkenes
Alta
Pechenga (Petsamo)
Tromso
Harstad
Lödingen
Narvik
Bodö
Sandnessjöen
Mosjöen
Brönnöysund
Rorwig
SWEDEN
FINLAND
Kristiansund
Trondheim
Molde
Alesund
Andalsnes
Malöy
Flora
Askvoll
Bergen
Leirvik
Haugesund
Kopervik
Stavanger
Oslo
Horten
Fredrikstad
Brevik
Larvik
Egersund
Arendal
Farsund
Kristiansand

NORWAY

0   100 miles
0   200 km

1941, the detachment moved to Narvik in January 1942 and later, in April 1943, to Altenfjord. The anti-aircraft cruiser *Nymphe* was operated by this unit. (She was the ex-Norwegian ship *Tordenskjold*, launched in 1897.)

714. Kristiansand Süd. Founded in November 1944.

715. Trondheim. Founded in February 1945.

801. Bergen. Founded in June 1940 as Detachment 301, it was renamed during the same month.

802. Bergen. Founded in June 1940, this unit amalgamated with Detachment 801 during January 1944.

822. Bergen. Founded in November 1944.

NETHERLANDS

Naval Artillery Detachments (Marineartillerieabteilung):
The following list gives the location of each detachment:

201. Den Helder and, later, Wijk aan Zee.

202. Vlissingen (Flushing) and, later, Domburg.

203. Ijmuiden.

204. Ostende.

205. Hook of Holland.

206. Blankenberge.

607. Den Helder.

Naval AA Detachments (Marineflakabteilung):
The following list gives the location of each detachment:

246. Harlingen.

German troops disembarking at Bergen on 9 April 1940. They had encountered only limited Norwegian resistance from coastal artillery on their passage in and by the 10 April the Bergen peninsula was in German hands. Bergen became the main breaking-out port for German ships before the fall of France; later in the war it was the last German naval base outside Germany. (Geirr H Haarr)

WARTIME ORGANISATION OF THE KRIEGSMARINE IN THE NETHERLANDS

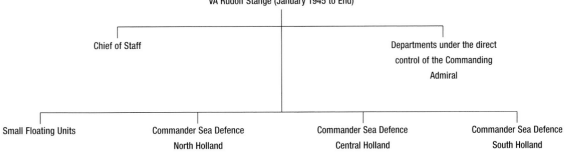

Naval Commander Netherlands / Belgium

This post was first known as Küstenbefehlshaber Südwest (Coastal Commander South-West) and Marineküstenbefehlshaber Südwest (Naval Coastal Commander South-West). Later it was renamed Commanding Admiral Netherlands.

VA Lothar von Arnauld de la Perière (May 1940 to June 1940)
KA Helmuth Kienast (June 1940 to June 1942)
KA Kurt Caesar Hoffmann (July 1942 to March 1943)
VA Gustav Kleikamp (March 1943 to December 1944)
VA Rudolf Stange (January 1945 to End)

Chief of Staff

Departments under the direct control of the Commanding Admiral

Small Floating Units

Commander Sea Defence
North Holland

Commander Sea Defence
Central Holland

Commander Sea Defence
South Holland

703. Vlissingen (Flushing).
808. Den Helder.
810. Vlissingen (Flushing).
813. Hook of Holland.
816. Ijmuiden.

Small Floating Units

Small flotillas in Holland came under the command of the Flag Officer for Motor-Boat Divisions (Führer der Motorbootverbände, or F.d.Mot.), whose office was founded during January 1941 and disbanded again in March 1945. The Flag Officer's headquarters were first in Den Haag and later in Dordrecht.

The following flotillas were operational:
Port Protection Flotilla North Holland. Founded, June 1941. At first based in Ijmuiden, the flotilla moved to Den Helder.
Port Protection Flotilla South Holland. Founded during

Generally, the German Navy was generous when providing port facilities for seagoing units, especially if they were small boats with poor accommodation. This shows a U-boat home near Lorient.

Lager Lemp in France. The Navy hardly ever named anything after a living person, so this complex was probably christened after May 1941 when Kptlt. Fritz-Julius Lemp lost his life when *U110* was boarded by the Royal Navy shortly before sinking. British aircraft became a far greater threat to this camp than local French Resistance and steps had to be taken to hide the main features, such as the conspicuous lake. It was later covered with massive tarpaulins.

June 1940 as Port Protection Flotilla Holland. It was later renamed. Main bases were at Vlissingen and the Hook of Holland.
River Clearing Flotilla. Founded during December 1940. The boats were passed on to the Rhine Flotilla when this command was disbanded in March 1945.
Rhine Flotilla. Founded in January 1940.
Danube Flotilla. Moved to Holland during January 1941 and returned to the Danube during April of that year.
Maas Flotilla. Founded during April 1941. When the unit was finally disbanded its boats were passed on to the Rhine Flotilla.
Waal Ferry Flotilla. Founded in autumn 1944, it was mainly used as an army support unit.
Boom Defence Flotilla North Sea Holland. (Netzsperrflottille). Main headquarters probably in Utrecht.

FRANCE

The German naval network in France was vast and its organization somewhat complicated. Details can be found in Volume II of Die deutsche Kriegsmarine, 1939-1945, by W. Lohmann and H. H. Hildebrand.

Naval Artillery Detachments (Marineartillerieabteilung): The following list gives the location of each detachment:
204. Ostende.
240. Wimeraux.
242. (?).
244. Calais.
260. Cherbourg.
262. Brest.
264. Lorient.
266. Le Havre.
280. Lorient and St. Nazaire.
282. Vendée.
284. Rouen.

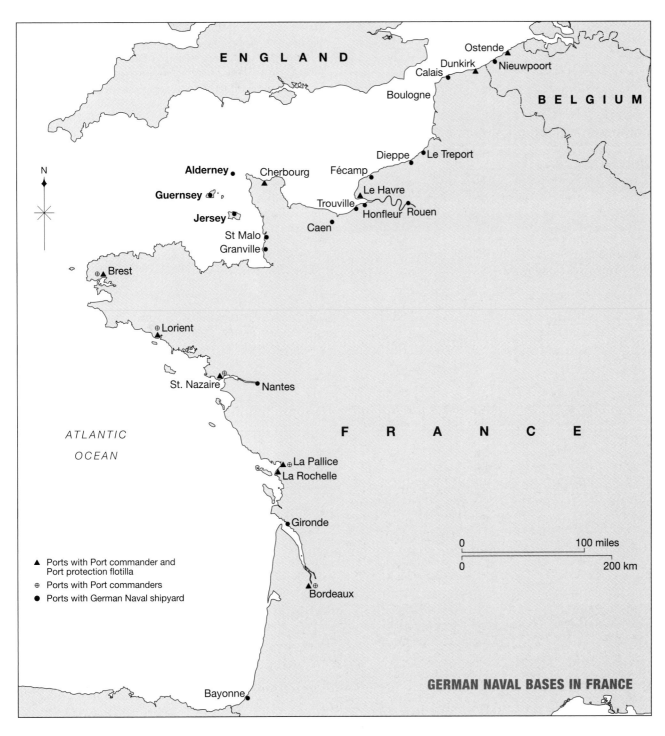

N

ENGLAND

Ostende
Dunkirk
Calais
Nieuwpoort
Boulogne

BELGIUM

Dieppe · Le Treport
Alderney
Cherbourg
Fécamp
Guernsey
Le Havre
Trouville
Honfleur Rouen
Jersey
St Malo
Caen
Granville
Brest

Lorient

St. Nazaire
Nantes

ATLANTIC

OCEAN

FRANCE

La Pallice
La Rochelle

Gironde

100 miles

0   200 km

▲ Ports with Port commander and
    Port protection flotilla
⊕ Ports with Port commanders
● Ports with German Naval shipyard

Bordeaux

GERMAN NAVAL BASES IN FRANCE

Bayonne

286. Bayonne.
610. Sète.
611. Marseilles.
612. Toulon.
618. Gironde.
682. Toulon.
683. (?).
684. Noirmoutier.
685. (?).
686. (?).
687. Ile d'Oléron.
688. Probably Toulon.
819. Toulon.

Naval AA Detachments (Marineflakabteilung):
703. St. Nazaire.
704. Lorient.
705. St. Nazaire.
803. Brest.
804. Brest.
805. Brest.
806. Lorient.
807. Lorient.
809. Nantes.
817. Lorient.
818. Lorient.
819. St. Nazaire.
820. St. Nazaire.

S-boats were used in every theatre of the war, even as far afield as the eastern Mediterranean and Black Sea.

MEDITERRANEAN AND BLACK SEA BASES

Although there were numerous German operational naval units in the Mediterranean and in the Black Sea, the majority belonged to Security Divisions rather than front line attack units. Much of their time was devoted to supporting merchant shipping which was carrying supplies for the army. Since U-boats were the only German units capable of passing though the Strait of Gibraltar, all other ships in the Mediterranean were either acquired from Italy, captured or were small enough to be carried overland. Both the Black Sea and the Mediterranean had their own German Naval Commanders who enjoyed more autonomy than their northern counterparts.

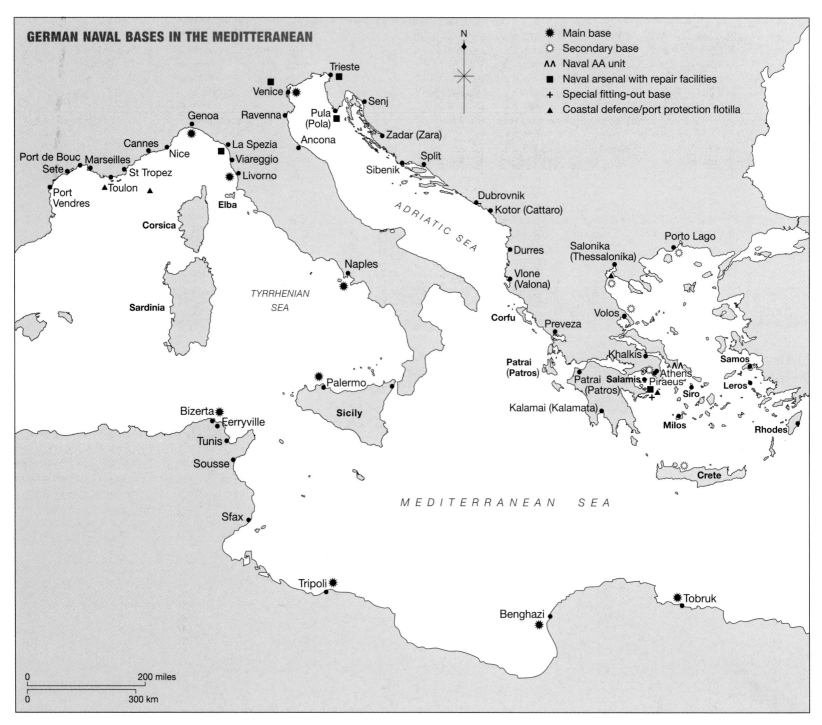

GERMAN NAVAL BASES IN THE MEDITTERANEAN

N

* Main base
☼ Secondary base
ʌʌ Naval AA unit
■ Naval arsenal with repair facilities
+ Special fitting-out base
▲ Coastal defence/port protection flotilla

Trieste
Venice
Ravenna
Genoa
Cannes
Nice
La Spezia
Viareggio
Port de Bouc
Marseilles
Sete
St Tropez
Livorno
Port Vendres
▲ Toulon ▲
Elba
Corsica
Pula (Pola)
Ancona
Zadar (Zara)
Split
Sibenik
Senj
ADRIATIC SEA
Dubrovnik
Kotor (Cattaro)
Durres
Salonika (Thessalonika)
Porto Lago
Sardinia
TYRRHENIAN SEA
Naples
Vlone (Valona)
Corfu
Preveza
Volos
Patrai (Patros)
Khalkis
Samos
Palermo
Patrai (Patros)
Salamis
Athens
Piraeus
Leros
Bizerta
Ferryville
Sicily
Kalamai (Kalamata)
Siro
Tunis
Milos
Rhodes
Sousse
Sfax
MEDITERRANEAN SEA
Crete
Tripoli
Tobruk
Benghazi

0   200 miles
0   300 km

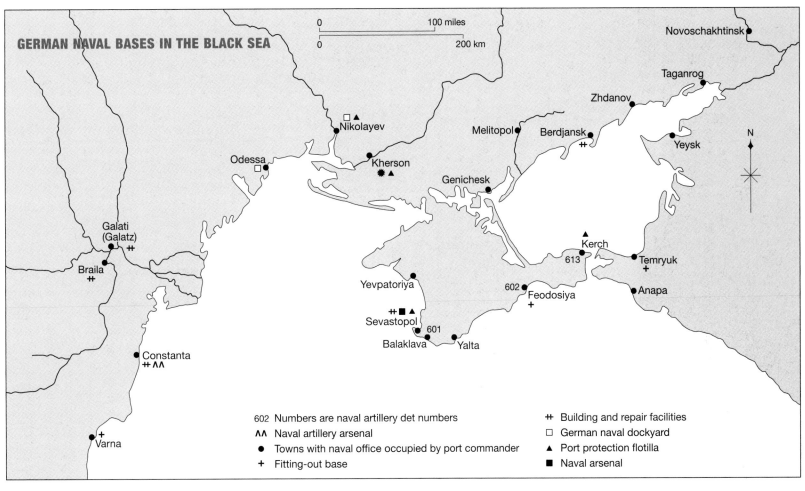

GERMAN NAVAL BASES IN THE BLACK SEA

0 ____ 100 miles
0 ____ 200 km

Novoschakhtinsk

Taganrog

Zhdanov

Nikolayev

Melitopol Berdjansk

Yeysk

Odessa

Kherson

Genichesk

Galati (Galatz)

Braila

Kerch

613

Temryuk

Yevpatoriya

602 Feodosiya

Anapa

Sevastopol

601

Balaklava Yalta

Constanta

Varna

602   Numbers are naval artillery det numbers

∧∧   Naval artillery arsenal

●   Towns with naval office occupied by port commander

+   Fitting-out base

+⊦   Building and repair facilities

□   German naval dockyard

▲   Port protection flotilla

■   Naval arsenal

U18 on the left, and another Type IIB on the right, in the German Naval Base at Constanta on the Black Sea coast during the summer of 1943. The stern of a boat just visible on the left is one of the small motor minesweepers which were needed to ensure that the harbour entrances were free from obstructions. The 1st Motor Torpedo Boat Flotilla was also stationed in the same port and there were several submarine chaser flotillas as well as escort groups and landing flotillas. Submarines and torpedo boats in the Black Sea were carried overland in sections from the river Elbe to the Danube and then rebuilt. Support of army activities was one of major naval functions in the Black Sea theatre.

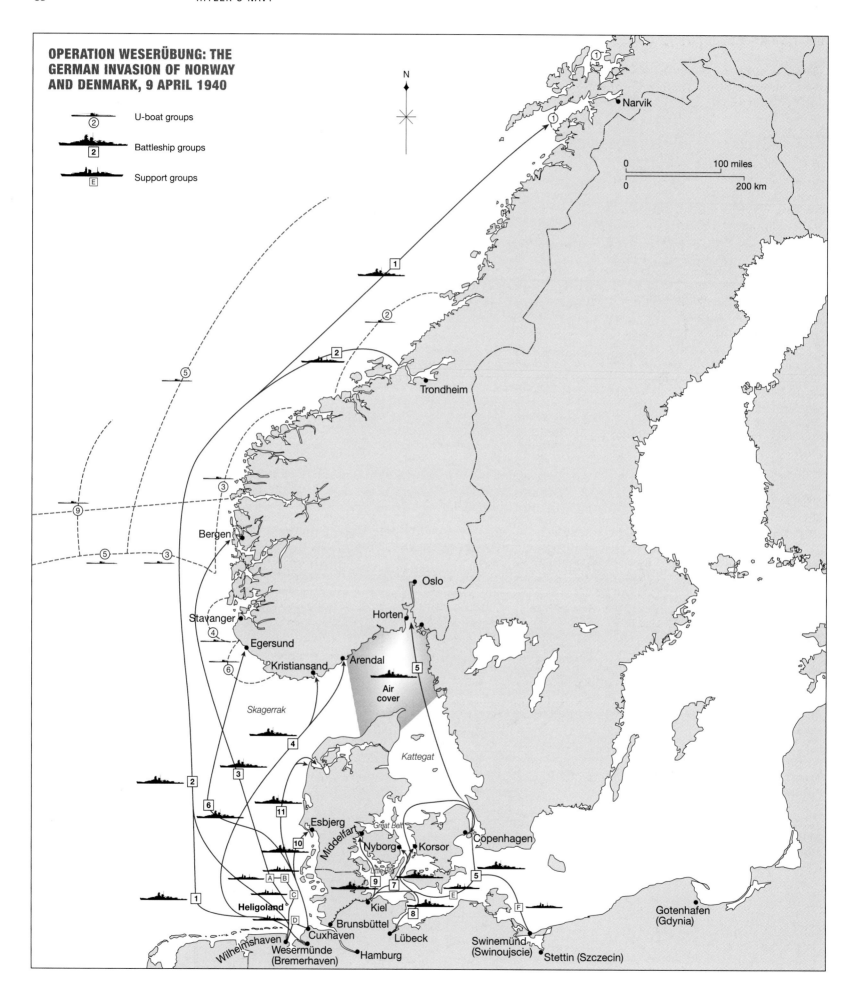

OPERATION WESERÜBUNG: THE GERMAN INVASION OF NORWAY AND DENMARK, 9 APRIL 1940

U-boat groups

Battleship groups

Support groups

N

Narvik

0   100 miles
0   200 km

1

2

2

Trondheim

5

3

9

Bergen

5   3

Oslo

Horten

Stavanger

4

Egersund

6

Kristiansand   Arendal

5

Air cover

Skagerrak

Kattegat

4

2

3

6

11

Esbjerg   Middelfart   *Great Belt*   Copenhagen

10   Nyborg   Korsor

A   B   9   7   E

C   Kiel

D

Heligoland   8   Lübeck

Wilhelmshaven

Wesermünde (Bremerhaven)   Hamburg

Cuxhaven   Brunsbüttel

Swinemünde (Swinoujscie)

Stettin (Szczecin)

Gotenhafen (Gdynia)

1

OPERATIONS WESERÜBUNG AND SEELÖWE

These two naval assault operations, both to be executed in 1940, involved massive organization and were to be the only major naval invasions planned by the Kriegsmarine during the war. Operation Weserübung, the invasion of Denmark and Norway, took place in April 1940 and was, ostensibly, a pre-emptive strike to prevent a Franco-British occupation of those countries. Surprise and speed were considered to be essential and, in addition, though it was predominantly a naval campaign, it was the first-ever successful combined operation in which the army, air force and navy operated together despite intense rivalries.

Operation Seelöwe, or Sea Lion to use the English term, was originally planned as a huge amphibious invasion, extending along the English Channel from Dorset to Kent, and the first studies for such an action were made by Raeder towards the end of 1939. In September 1940, it was postponed by Hitler indefinitely. The Kriegsmarine had lost a sizeable portion of its large surface units during the Norwegian campaign as well as a large number of destroyers. Attention was turned towards the Atlantic and the U-boat offensive. Debate continues as to whether Seelöwe could have succeeded and, indeed, whether Hitler seriously intended the invasion ever to go ahead.

OPERATION WESERÜBUNG: THE GERMAN INVASION OF NORWAY AND DENMARK, 9 APRIL 1940

Group 1 KS und Kommodore Friedrich Bonte
Z2 KK Max-Eckart Wolff
Z9 FK Gottfried Pönitz
Z11 KK Kurt Rechel
Z12 KK Karl Smidt
Z13 KK Alfred Schulze-Hinrichs
Z17 KK Erich Holtorf
Z18 KK Herbert Friedrichs
Z19 KK Friedrich Kothe
Z21 KK Hans Erdmenger (Group Commander's flagship)
Z22 KK Friedrich Böhme
Group 1 loaded Army troops in Wesermünde (Bremerhaven) and then sailed to the Schillig Roads, off Wilhelmshaven, to join Group 2 and its escorts.

Group 2 KS Hellmuth Heye
Admiral Hipper KS Hellmuth Heye
Z5 KK Hans Zimmer
Z6 KK Gerhardt Böhmig
Z8 KK Georg Langheld
Z16 KK Alfred Schemmel
Group 2 left Cuxhaven and sailed to the Schillig Roads to join Group 1 and its escorts.

Escorts for Group 1 and 2
Gneisenau KS Herald Netzbandt
Scharnhorst KS Kurt Caesar Hoffmann

Group 3 KA Hubert Schmundt
A: 1st Motor Torpedo Boat Flotilla KL Heinz Birnbacher
S19, S21, S22, S23, S24.
B: Karl Peters (tender) KL Otto Hinzke
Wolf (torpedo boat) OL Broder Peters
Leopard (torpedo boat) KL Hans Trummer
C: Königsberg (cruiser) KS Heinrich Rufus
Köln (cruiser) KS Ernst Kratzenberg
Bremse (artillery training ship) FK Jak Förschner

Group 4 Kpt.z.S. Friedrich Rieve
A: Karlsruhe (cruiser) KS Friedrich Rieve
Seeadler (torpedo boat) KL Franz Kohlauf
Luchs (torpedo boat). KL Karl Kassbaum
2nd Motor Torpedo Boat Flotilla KK Rudolf Petersen
S7, S8, S17, S30, S31, S32, S33.
Tsingtau (tender) KS Karl Klinger
B: Greif (torpedo boat) KL Wilhelm Freiherr von Lyncker

Group 5 Konteradm. Oskar Kummetz
KS August Thiele (after sinking of cruiser Blücher)
E: Lützow (heavy cruiser) KS August Thiele
F: Blücher (heavy cruiser) KS Heinrich Woldag
Emden (light cruiser) KS Werner Lange
Möwe (torpedo boat) KL Helmut Neuss
Kondor (torpedo boat) KL Hans Wilcke

Albatros (torpedo boat) KL Siegfried Strelow
1st Motor Minesweeper Flotilla KL Gustav Forstmann
R17, R18, R19, R20, R21, R22, R23, R24.

Group 6 KK Kurt Thoma
M2, M9, M13.

Group 7 KS Gustav Kleikamp
Schleswig-Holstein (old battleship) KS Gustav Kleikamp

Group 8 KK Wilhelm Schroeder
Hansestadt Danzig (minelayer) KK Wilhelm Schroeder
Stettin (icebreaker)

Group 9 KS Helmuth Leissner
Otto Braun (ex-M129)
Arkona (ex-M116) (experimental craft)
M757
V102
V103
R6
R7
UJ 107
Monsun and Passat (naval tugs)
Rugard (freighter) (Group Commander's flagship)

Group 10 KS und Kommodore Friedrich Ruge
2nd Motor Minesweeper Flotilla KK Gerhard von Kamptz
R25, R26, R27, R28, R29, R30, R31, R32.
Königin Luise (ex-F6)
M4, M20, M84, M102, M1201, M1202, M1203, M1204, M1205, M1206, M1207, M1208.

Group 11 KS Walter Berger
M89, M110, M111, M134, M136, M61.
R33, R34, R35, R36, R37, R38, R39, R40.
Von der Groeben (depot ship)
Mines laid during the night of 8/9 April by the following minelayers:
Roland KK Karl Kutzleben
Königen Luise KL Kurt Foerster
Cobra KK Karl Brill
Preussen KK Karl Freiherr von Recke
M6, M10, M11, M12.

U-boat Group 1
U25 KK Victor Schütze
U46 KL Herbert Sohler
U51 KL Dietrich Knorr
U64 KL Wilhelm Schulz
U65 KL Hans-Gerrit von Stockhausen

U-boat Group 2
U30 KL Fritz-Julius Lemp
U34 KL Wilhelm Rollmann

U-boat Group 3
U9 OL Wolfgang Lüth
U14 OL Herbert Wohlfahrt
U56 OL Otto Harms
U60 KL Peter Schewe
U62 OL Hans Michalowski

U-boat Group 4
U1 KL Jürgen Deecke
U4 OL Hans-Peter Hinsch

U-boat Group 5
U37 KK Werner Hartmann
U38 KL Heinrich Liebe
U47 KL Gunther Prien
U48 KL Herbert Schultze
U49 KL Curt von Gossler
U50 KL Max Bauer
U52 KL Otto Salmann
U21 KL Wolf Stiebler Ran aground on 27.3.40 and interned In Kristiansand Süd.

U-boat Group 6
U13 OL Max Schulte
U57 KL Claus Korth
U58 KL Herbert Kuppisch
U59 KL Harald Jürst

U-boat Group 8
U2 KL Helmuth Rosenbaum
U3 KL Gerd Schreiber
U5 KL Wilhelm Lehmann-Willenbrock
U6 OL Adalbert Schnee

U-boat Group 9
U7 OL Günther Reeder
U10 OL Joachim Preuss
U19 KL Joachim Schepke

Not attached to a group
U17 KL Udo Behrens
U23 KL Heinz Beduhn
U24 OL Udo Heilmann
U61 OL Jürgen Oesten

U-boat Transporters
U26 KK Heinz Scheringer (?)
U29 KL Otto Schuhart
U32 OL Hans Jenisch
U43 KL Wilhelm Ambrosius
U101 KL Fritz Frauenheim
UA KL Hans Cohausz

Support and Transport Ships to Narvik area (T = Tanker; F = Freighter)
F Alster
F Bärenfels
F Ravenfels
T Kattegat
T Jan Wellem

Support and Transport Ships to Trondheim area
F Levante
F Main
T Moonsund
F Sao Paolo

Support and Transport Ships to Bergen area
T Belt
F Curityba
F Marie Leonhardt
F Rio de Janeiro

Support and Transport Ships to Stavanger-Egersund area
T Dollart
F Mendoza
F Roda
F Tijuca
F Tübingen

Support and Transport Ships to Kristiansand–Arendal area
F August Leonhardt
F Kreta
F Westsee
F Wiegand

Support and Transport Ships to Oslo area
T Euroland
T Senator
F Antares
F Espana
F Friedenau
F Hamm
F Hanau
F Ionia
F Itauri
F Kellerwald
F Muansa
F Neidenfels
F Rosario
F Scharhörn
F Tucuman
F Wandsbek
F Wolfram

Karlsruhe played a significant part in the invasion of Norway, carrying troops and, together with the torpedo boats *Seeadler*, *Greif* and *Luchs*, forcing her way into Kristiansand in the early hours of 9 April. She was lost later in the day after being attacked by the British submarine *Truant*. Here she is shown in South American waters with virtually everything under wraps. Much of the deck was covered, not so much to protect it from the elements but to give the impression that there was highly secret modern gear underneath.

OPERATION SEELÖWE

Post-war research has revealed that the majority of barges were obsolete river craft and would never have crossed the open sea, except under the calmest of conditions; nor did the German Navy have any landing craft at this period of time.

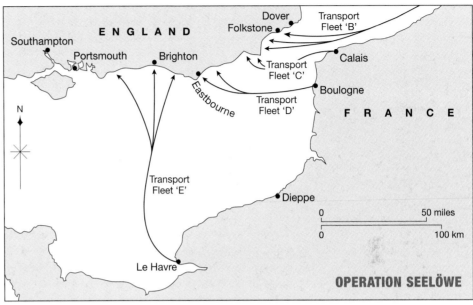

OPERATION SEELÖWE

LEFT The light cruiser *Königsberg* carried troops from Wilhelmshaven to Bergen – part of the plan was to use fast naval vessels rather than merchant ships for troop carrying in order to maximise surprise – but was attacked on 10 April by British Blackburn Skuas, launched from RNAS Haston in the Orkney Islands. They scored direct hits and *Königsberg* capsized and sank in Bergen, alongside the mole. She was later raised and used as a pier for U-boats.

Transport Fleet B
Commander: VA Hermann von Fischel
Departure base: Dunkirk
  3rd Minesweeper Flotilla
  11th Motor Minesweeper Flotilla
  3rd Coastal Defence Flotilla
  75 river barges
Departure base: Ostende
  3rd Minesweeper Flotilla
  2nd Coastal Defence Flotilla
  25 barges
Departure base: Ostende
  16th Minesweeper Flotilla
  8 steamers
  15 barges
  15 motor boats
Departure base: Rotterdam
  4th Minesweeper Flotilla
  50 steamers
  100 barges

Transport Fleet C
Commander KS Gustav Kleikamp
Departure base: Calais
  1st Minesweeper Flotilla
  32nd Minesweeper Flotilla
  4th Motor Minesweeper Flotilla
  7th Coastal Defence Flotilla
  100 barges
Departure base: Antwerp
  15th Minesweeper Flotilla
  50–60 steamers
  Approximately 100 barges
  14 motor boats

Transport Fleet D
Commander: KS Werner Lindenau
Departure base: Boulogne
  2nd Minesweeper Flotilla
  18th Minesweeper Flotilla
  2nd Motor Minesweeper Flotilla
  15th, 16th and 18th Coastal Defence
  Flotillas
  160 barges, to be towed four abreast

Transport Fleet E
Commander: KS Ernst Scheurlen
Convoy 4 Commander: KS Ulrich Brocksien
Departure base: Le Havre
  12th Minesweeper Flotilla
  25 steamers
  50 barges
  25 tugs

Convoy 5
Commander: KS Ulrich Brocksien
Departure base: Le Havre
  14th Minesweeper Flotilla
  25 steamers
  50 barges

Additional Forces
1st Motor Minesweeper Flotilla
4th, 13th and 20th Coastal Defence
Flotillas
200 motor boats
100 auxiliary sailing

THE ORGANIZATION OF THE GERMAN FLEET

THE HIGH SEAS FLEET (FLOTTENSTREITKRÄFTE)

THE FLEET COMMAND

The Fleet Commanders were as follows.

Adm. Hermann Boehm: Nov. 1938 to Oct 1939.

Adm. Wilhelm Marschall: Oct. 1939 to July 1940.

Adm. Günther Lütjens: July 1940 to May 1941; Lütjens and his entire staff went down with battleship *Bismarck* on 27 May 1941.

Genadm. Otto Schniewind: June 1941 to July 1944.

Vizeadm. Wilhelm Meendsen-Bohlken: July 1944 to end of war.

The office of 'Chief of the High Seas Fleet' was discontinued shortly after the First World War, and the few remaining ships were placed under the control of naval commanders within the Baltic and North Sea Naval Stations. A Supreme Commander-in-Chief of Seagoing Forces (Oberbefehlshaber der Seestreitkäfte) was appointed during 1923. Two years later, this rather long-winded title was condensed to Flottenchef (Fleet Commander).

Gneisenau was succeeded as flagship by *Bismarck* until her sinking, when it was planned to use her sister-ship *Tirpitz*. However, although she did fly the Fleet Commander's flag for a brief period, it was not long before a combination of circumstances made it impracticable. Her replacement was the tender *Hela*, which was used in this capacity for most of the remaining war years.

Before the Second World War, battleships and heavy cruisers came under the direct control of the Supreme Naval Command until summer 1939, when the Naval Group Commands were given operational control. At this time, light cruisers were commanded by the Commander-in-Chief Reconnaissance Forces (Befehlshaber der Aufklärungsstreitkräfte, or B.d.A.), who was also respon-

FLEET DIVISIONS

1. Flottenstreitkräfte	The High Seas Fleet
Schlachtschiffe und Kreuzer	Battleships and cruisers
Zerstörer	Destroyers
Torpedoboote	Torpedo-boats
Schnellboote (S-Boote)	Motor torpedo-boats (MTBs, E-boats)
Hilfskreuzer	Auxiliary cruisers
Flottentrosschiffe	Fleet supply ships
Schulschiffe	Fleet training ships

2. Sicherungsstreitkräfte	Security Forces
Flottillen:	Flotillas:
Minensuchboote	Minesweepers
Räumboote	Motor minesweepers
Sperrbrecher	Auxiliary minesweepers
Vorpostenboote	Patrol boats, coastal defence boats
Sicherungsboote	Picket boats, coastal defence boats
Unterseebootsjäger	Submarine hunters
Geleitboote	Escorts
Hafenschutzboote	Port protection boats
Küstenschutzboote	Coastal defence boats

3. Unterseeboote (Uboote)	U-boats[1]/Submarines

1. In the English language, the word 'U-boat' is used specifically when referring to a German submarine, whereas in German it embraces all submarines, whatever their country of origin. Originally spelt either 'U-Boot' or 'U-boot', the recognized German spelling is now 'Uboot'.

sible for destroyers, torpedo-boats and minesweepers. But this arrangement only lasted until the autumn of 1939, when further changes were implemented. The post of Commander-in-Chief Cruisers (Befehlshaber der Kreuzer, or B.d.K.) was created, and all cruisers were placed under his command. Disbanded again during October 1941, the position was renamed Admiral Northern Seas (Admiral Nordmeer). Destroyers and minesweepers were also given their own commands.

The position of Commander-in-Chief Battleships (Befehlshaber der Schlachtschiffe, or B.d.S.) was not created until June 1941, after the sinking of *Bismarck*, and the first to hold this office was Vizeadmiral Otto Ciliax. Later, during May 1942, he was made Commander-in-Chief Naval Forces in Norway, and his old job was taken over by Vizeadmiral Oskar Kummetz, who was given the new title Commander-in-Chief Cruisers (Befehlshaber der Kreuzer, or B.d.K.). The designation was later changed again by replacing the word 'Kreuzer' with 'Kampfgruppe' (Task Force), but the initials 'B.d.K.' remained the same. (This Command was also known as 1st Task Force and North Norway Naval Squadron.) Kummetz was absent for some periods, at which times Erich Bey held command. In February 1944, both men were replaced by Kpt.z.S. Rolf Johannesson, and Konteradmiral Rudolf Peters was commander of the Task Force from June 1944 until the post was disbanded in October 1944.

Operational Dates for Major German Warships

Name	Built	Commissioned	End of operational life
Battleships			
Bismarck	Hamburg	24 August 1940	27 May 1941
Gneisenau	Kiel	21 May 1938	26 February 1942
Scharnhorst	Wilhelmshaven	7 January 1939	26 February 1943
Tirpitz	Wilhelmshaven	25 February 1941	12 November 1944
Pocket Battleships			
Deutschland	Kiel	1 April 1933	4 May 1945
Admiral Graf Spee	Wilhelmshaven	6 January 1936	17 December 1939
Admiral Scheer	Wilhelmshaven	12 November 1936	10 April 1945
Heavy cruisers:			
Admiral Hipper	Hamburg	29 April 1939	3 May 1945
Prinz Eugen	Kiel	1 August 1940	Summer 1946
Blücher	Kiel	20 September 1939	9 April 1940
Light Cruisers			
Emden	Wilhelmshaven	15 October 1925	26 April 1945
Karlsruhe	Kiel	6 November 1929	9 April 1940
Köln	Wilhelmshaven	15 January 1930	31 March 1945
Königsberg	Wilhelmshaven	17 April 1929	10 April 1940
Leipzig	Wilhelmshaven	8 October 1931	16 December 1946
Nürnberg	Kiel	2 November 1935	6 January 1946[1]
Training ships (Old Battleships)			
Schlesien	Danzig	5 May 1908	4 May 1945
Schleswig-Holstein	Kiel	6 July 1908	20 December 1944
Warships not commissioned in the Kriegsmarine			
Graf Zeppelin	aircraft carrier		
Lützow	heavy cruiser sold to Russia		
Seydlitz	heavy cruiser; see page 26		

1. Renamed *Admiral Makarov* and commissioned in the Russian Navy

Destroyers

The post of Führer der Zerstörer or F.d.Z. (Flag Officer/ Commander for Destroyers) was held by the following officers.
Kommodore Friedrich Bonte: Nov. 1939 to April 1940.
Kpt.z.S. Alfred Schemmel: April 1940 to May 1940.
Konteradm. Erich Bey: May 1940 to Dec. 1943.
Kpt.z.S. Max-Eckart Wolff: Dec. 1943 to Feb.1944.
Vizeadm. Leo Kreisch: Feb. 1944 to End.

Before the war, destroyers came under the jurisdiction of the Flag Officer for Torpedo-Boats, whose immediate superior was Commander-in-Chief Reconnaissance Forces. By September 1939, there were some twenty separate and completely autonomous destroyer groups. However, this state of affairs did not last long, for in November 1939 there was a drastic reorganisation. Destroyers were formed into flotillas of six boats and given their own Flag Officer, who was responsible to the Fleet Commander. Many destroyers did not operate under his direct command because they were partly at the disposal of various task force commanders. There were major changes in the destroyer arm after the heavy losses incurred in the Norwegian Campaign of April 1940 (for details, see overleaf).

The bows of battleship *Gneisenau* with her main 11in (280mm) guns clearly visible. She was succeeded by *Bismarck* until her sinking in 1941.

Z25 at speed. Z25 was part of the 8th Destroyer Flotilla, sometimes referred to as the 'Narvik' flotilla.

Some destroyers were better known by an official traditional name, instead of their number. These names and their corresponding numbers are shown below.

Destroyers were also allocated a tactical number, which was painted on the side of the hull before the war and removed again by 9 November 1939. There appears to be no logic or reasonable sequence in this system, but it can be most useful when identifying destroyers in old photographs. Therefore the tactical numbers have been added in brackets after the Z number.

Z1	(–)	*Leberecht Maass.*
Z2	(13)	*Georg Thiele.*
Z3	(12)	*Max Schultz.*
Z4	(11)	*Richard Beitzen.*
Z5	(21)	*Paul Jacobi.*
Z6	(22)	*Theodor Riedel.*
Z7	(23)	*Hermann Schoemann.*
Z8	(63, 61)	*Bruno Heinemann.*
Z9	(61, 62, 63)	*Wolfgang Zenker.*
Z10	(62, 81)	*Hans Lody.*
Z11	(81, 62)	*Bernd von Arnim.*
Z12	(82)	*Erich Giese.*
Z13	(61, 83)	*Erich Koellner.*
Z14	(32, 33)	*Friedrich Ihn.*
Z15	(31, 32)	*Erich Steinbrinck.*
Z16	(33, 31)	*Friedrich Eckoldt.*
Z17	(51)	*Diether von Roeder*
Z18	(53)	*Hans Lüdemann.*
Z19	(52)	*Herman Künne.*
Z20	(42)	*Karl Galster.*
Z21	(43)	*Wilhelm Heidkamp.*
Z22	(41)	*Anton Schmitt.*

DESTROYER FLOTILLAS

1st Destroyer Flotilla:
Founded during the autumn of 1938 with the amalgamation of the 1st and 3rd Destroyer Divisions, this unit was disbanded in April 1940. The remaining boats were passed on to the 5th Flotilla.
Commanders: KS Wilhelm Meisel (Oct. 1938 to Oct. 1939); FK Fritz Berger (Oct. 1939 to end).
Ships: *Z2, Z3, Z4, Z14, Z15, Z16.*

2nd Destroyer Flotilla:
Founded during the autumn of 1938 when the 2nd Destroyer Division was renamed, the unit was disbanded in May 1940. The remaining ships went to the 6th Flotilla.
Commanders: KS Friedrich Bonte (Oct. 1938 to Oct. 1939); KK Rudolf von Pufendorf (Oct. 1939 to end).
Ships: *Z1, Z5, Z6, Z7, Z8.*

3rd Destroyer Flotilla:
This unit was founded in December 1939 by renaming the 5th Destroyer Division. It was disbanded four months later. The only remaining destroyer (*Z20*) was passed on to the 6th Flotilla.
Commander: FK Hans-Joachim Gadow (Dec. 1939 to end).
Ships: *Z17, Z18, Z19, Z20, Z22.*

4th Destroyer Flotilla:
The unit was founded during April 1939 by amalgamating the 6th and 8th Destroyer Divisions. It was disbanded again in April 1940, and its only remaining destroyer (*Z10*) was passed on to the 6th Flotilla. The 4th was reformed in October 1942.
Commanders: FK Erich Bey[1] (until April 1940); KK Georg Langheld (Oct. 1942 to April 1943); KS Rolf Johannesson (April 1943 to Dec. 1944); KS Hubert Freiherr von Wangenheim (Dec. 1944 to end of war).
Ships: (until 1940) *Z9, Z10, Z11, Z12, Z13;*
(after 1942) *Z31, Z32, Z33, Z34, Z37, Z38, Z39.*

5th Destroyer Flotilla:
This unit was founded during May 1940 with boats from the 1st Flotilla.
Commanders: FK Alfred Schemmel (May 1940 to Aug. 1940); KS Fritz Berger (Aug. 1940 to July 1942); KS Alfred Schemmel (July 1942 to Dec. 1942); KS Max-Eckart Wolff (Feb. 1943 to Feb. 1944); KS T. Freiherr von Mauchenheim genannt[1] Bechtolsheim (Feb.44 to April 44); KS Georg Langheld (April 1944 to end of war).
Ships: *Z4, Z14, Z15, Z16, ZH1*

6th Destroyer Flotilla:
The unit was founded during May 1940 with destroyers from the 2nd, 3rd and 4th Flotillas.
Commanders: KS Erich Bey[1] (May 1940 to Nov. 1940); KS Alfred Schulze (Nov. 1940 to April 1943); KS Friedrich Kothe (April 1943 to Dec. 1944); KS Heinz Peters (Jan. 1944(?) to end of war).
Ships: *Z5, Z6, Z7, Z8, Z10, Z20, Z35, Z36, Z43.*

1. Erich Bey was also Flag Officer for Destroyers at the same time.

2. Translates as 'known as'.

7th Destroyer Flotilla:
Probably not operational.

8th Destroyer Flotilla:
Also known as Flotilla Narvik, the unit was founded during December 1940. It was disbanded during August 1944, and refounded in November 1944.
Commanders: KS Gottfried Pönitz (Dec. 1940 to March 1943); KS Hans Erdmenger (March 1943 to Dec. 1943); FK Georg Langheld (Jan. 1944 to April 1944); KS T. Freiherr von Mauchenheim genannt[2] Bechtolsheim (April 44 to June 44); FK Georg Ritter und edler Herr von Berger (June 1944 to Aug. 1944); KS Heinrich Gerlach (Nov. 1944 to end of war).
Ships: *Z23, Z24, Z25, Z26, Z27, Z28, Z29, Z30.*

TORPEDO-BOATS

In German parlance, a torpedo-boat is a ship resembling a small destroyer, but the main armament of which is torpedoes. (The very small, fast, motor torpedo-boats, called Schnellboote, are dealt with in the next section.)

Until the autumn of 1939, when an administrative change altered things, the Flag Officer for Torpedo-boats had

The bows of *Z37* around the time of the commissioning ceremony. Before the war it was general practice for ships to go on trials with building yard staff plus key naval personnel. Commissioning then took take place afterwards, when the ship was accepted by the Navy. During the war, time-pressure and the lack of staff made it necessary for ships to be commissioned before trials.

also been responsible for destroyers and motor torpedo-boats. When the office was finally disbanded in April 1942, the remaining torpedo-boats were placed under the control of the Flag Officer for Destroyers. At the same time, a new post of Flag Officer for Motor Torpedo-Boats (Führer der Schnellboote, or F.d.S.) was created. However, the Flag Officer for Torpedo-Boats was only partly responsible for their operational control, because – as with destroyers – many boats were at the disposal of various task force commanders.

The post of Führer der Torpedoboote, or F.d.T. (Flag Officer for Torpedo-Boats) was held by the following officers.
Konteradm. Günther Lütjens: Oct. 1937 to Oct. 1939.
Kpt.z.S. Friedrich Bonte: Oct. 1939 to Nov. 1939.
Kpt.z.S. Hans Bütow: Nov. 1939 to April 1942.

Torpedo-Boat Flotillas
1st Torpedo-Boat Flotilla:
Operational from October 1939 until August 1941.
T1, T2, T3, T4, T9, T10.

2nd Torpedo-Boat Flotilla:
Founded October 1939.
T5, T6, T7, T8, T11, T12.

From August 1941 also: *T2, T3, T4, T9, T10.*
T1 joined the flotilla during late 1942.

3rd Torpedo-Boat Flotilla:
Founded in April 1941.
T13, T14, T15, T16, T17, T18, T19, T20, T21.

4th Torpedo-Boat Flotilla:
Operational from February 1943 until April 1944.
T22, T24, T25, T26, T27.
T28 and *T29* were later transferred from the 6th Flotilla.
T24 and *T25* joined the 5th Flotilla during April 1944.

5th Torpedo-Boat Flotilla:
T22, T23, T24, T25, T26, T28, T29, T34, T35, Albatros, Falke, Greif, Iltis, Jaguar, Kondor, Seeadler, Tiger.

6th Torpedo-Boat Flotilla:
Disbanded in February 1941.
Iltis, Jaguar, Leopard, Luchs, Seeadler, Wolf.
Refounded during November 1943 and operational until August 1944.
T28, T29, T30, T31, T32, T33.

Luchs, one of the Beast of Prey class torpedo-boats. The loop sticking up above the bridge is the rotating aerial of a radio direction finder.

7th Torpedo-Boat Flotilla:
   Operational from June 1940 until December 1940.
   Leopard, Löwe, Panther, Tiger.

8th Torpedo-Boat Flotilla:
   Not operational.

9th Torpedo-Boat Flotilla:
   Operational from September 1943 until October 1944.
   TA14,[1] *TA15, TA16, TA17, TA18, TA19.*
   Refounded during February 1945.
   TA14, TA41, TA42, TA43, TA44, TA45.

10th Torpedo-Boat Flotilla:
   Founded during January 1944.
   TA23, TA24, TA27, TA28, TA29, TA30, TA31, TA32, TA33.

Motor Torpedo-Boats (Schnellboote – E-Boats)

The post of Flag Officer for MTBs (Führer der Schnellboote or F.d.S.) was created during April 1942, when the office of Flag Officer for Torpedo-Boats was discontinued. The new position was held by Kpt.z.S. und Kommodore Rudolf Petersen throughout the remaining war years.

The 1st MTB Division was founded in July 1943 to operate in the Mediterranean with 3rd, 7th, 21st, 22nd and 24th flotillas. Motor torpedo-boats in other areas were not formed into divisions and they operated as autonomous flotillas.

The following flotillas were operational:
   1st, 2nd, 3rd, 4th, 5th, 6th, 7th, 8th, 9th, 10th, 11th, 21st, 22nd, 24th.

MTB Escort Ships:
   Adolf Lüderitz (June 1940 to end).
   Buea (May 1944 to end).
   Carl Peters (Jan. 1940 to end).
   Gustav Nachtigal (May and June 1944).
   Hermann von Wissmann (Dec. 1943 to end).
   Romania (March 1942 to Oct. 1943).
   Tanga (Jan. 1939 to end).
   Tsingtau (Sept. 1934 to end).

AUXILIARY CRUISERS

Auxiliary cruisers were originally known as Handels-schutzkreuzer or HSK (Trade Protection Cruisers). Later, they were called Hilfskreuzer or HK (Auxiliary Cruiser). During the war the initials HSK were also taken to mean Handelsstörkreuzer (Cruiser for Harassing Merchant Ships). These ships were first identified by using numbers from 1 to 8, prefixed by the letters HSK. Later, they were given a two-digit administration number, which was prefixed by the word 'Schiff' (ship). They were also given a traditional name, usually by their first commanders: HSK2, Schiff 16, for example, was also known as *Atlantis*. The British Admiralty chose to identify the German auxiliary cruisers by allotting a letter to each and these follow the sequence in which they were discovered. The following list gives the names and commanders of each ship, plus its name before conversion to auxiliary

cruiser and its name after its career as such.
Atlantis (HSK 2, Schiff 16, Raider C): KS Bernhard Rogge (Dec. 1939 to Nov. 1941). Before the war it was the merchant ship *Goldenfels.*
Coronel (HSK-, Schiff 14, Raider K): FK Rudolf Betzendahl (to April 1942); KS Ernst Thienemann (April 1942 to Feb. 1943); KK Rudolf Lück (Sept. 1943 to end). Ex-*Togo;* later became merchant ship *Svalbard.*
Hansa (HSK-, Schiff 5, Raider –): KS Hans Henigst (April 1943 to Aug. 1943); KS Fritz Schwoerer (Feb. 1944 to end). Ex-*Meersburg,* ex-*Glengarry;* later became merchant ship *Empire Humber,* then *Glengarry* again.
Komet (HSK 7, Schiff 45, Raider B): KA Robert Eyssen (Dec. 1939 to Feb. 1942); KS Ulrich Brocksien (Feb. 1942 to Oct. 1942). Ex-*Ems.*
Kormoran (HSK 8, Schiff 41, Raider G): FK Theodor Detmers (June 1940 to Nov. 1941). Ex-*Steiermark.*

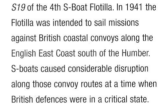

S19 of the 4th S-Boat Flotilla. In 1941 the Flotilla was intended to sail missions against British coastal convoys along the English East Coast south of the Humber. S-boats caused considerable disruption along those convoy routes at a time when British defences were in a critical state.

As far as possible, the main artillery of old 150mm guns was concealed behind shutters, as can be seen here. This photograph of *Atlantis* under Kpt.z.S. Bernhard Rogge was probably taken by his adjutant Oblt.z.S. Ulrich Mohr. Sailing around the cruiser for the purpose of taking photographs was an important test every time the disguise was changed. The shutters hiding the large guns were counterbalanced to lift up.

ABOVE Of all the German supply ships, *Altmark* ranks as the most famous. She was attacked in Jøssingfjord, then in neutral Norway, in February 1940 by ships of the Royal Navy in order to rescue prisoners of war who had been captured from ships sunk by the pocket battleship *Admiral Graf Spee*.

LEFT *Altmark* on the high seas. She was one of the few purpose-built vessels, especially designed for speed, to keep up with fast-moving warships. The tankers and supply ships taken over during the war from the merchant navy were designed more with economy in mind.

Michel (HSK 9, Schiff 28, Raider H): KS Hellmuth von Ruckteschell (Sept. 1941 to March 1943); KS Günther Gumprich (May 1943 to Oct. 1943). Ex-*Bielsko*.

Orion (HSK 1, Schiff 36, Raider A): FK Kurt Weyher (Dec. 1939 to Sept. 1941); KK Gerhard Meyer (Oct. 1942 to Oct. 1944); KK Wilhelm Kiesewetter (to Dec. 1944); KS Joachim Asmus (Dec. 1944 to May 1945). Ex-*Kurmark*; became artillery training ship *Hektor* in January 1944.

Pinguin (HSK 5, Schiff 33, Raider F): KS Ernst-Felix Krüder (Sept. 1939 to May 1941). Ex-*Kandelfels*.

Stier (HSK 6, Schiff 23, Raider J): KS Horst Gerlach (April 1940 to Sept. 1942). Ex-*Cairo*.

Thor (HSK 4, Schiff 10, Raider E): KS Otto Kähler (March 1940 to July 1941); KS Günther Gumprich (to Nov. 1942). Ex-*Santa Cruz*.

Widder (HSK 3, Schiff 21, Raider D): KK Hellmuth von Ruckteschell (May 1940 to Nov. 1940). Ex-*Neumark*; later became merchant ship *Ulysses*, then *Fechenheim*.

Naval Supply Ships

The ships listed below were built as naval supply ships, and they were used for that purpose between the dates indicated. During the war, more than a hundred other ships were also employed as supply vessels.

Dithmarschen (July 1938 to end of war). Used after the war under the names *Southmark* (GB) and *Conecuh* (USA).

Ermland (Aug. 1940 to Aug. 1944).

Nordmark (Dec. 1938 to end of war). Earlier known as *Westerwald*; after the war became HMS *Bulawayo*.

Uckermark (Nov. 1938 to Nov. 1942). Earlier known as *Altmark*.

Franken (March 1943 to April 1945).

SECURITY FORCES (SICHERUNGSSTREITKRÄFTE)

After the First World War, all security duties at sea came under the control of the Flag Officer for Minesweepers. During the 1930s, there was a tendency to divide these activities into two groups which resulted in the overall administration being taken over by the 2nd Admirals of the Baltic and North Sea Naval Stations. But, at the start of the Second World War, the Flag Officer for Minesweepers, Kpt.z.S. Friedrich Ruge, was back holding the reins again. At that time, only a war against Poland was envisaged, so Ruge moved into the Baltic with his flagship (*T196*). A similar post – filled by Konteradmiral Hans Stobwasser – was then created in the North Sea region.

During the war, coasts under German control were put under the jurisdiction of eleven Security Divisions (Sicherungsdivision), with the exception of Norway, which had a security force called Küstensicherungsverband (Coastal Security Unit).

Minesweeper Flotillas (Minensuchflottillen)

The numbers of the boats were prefixed by the letter 'M' meaning Minensuchboot (Minesweeper). Flotilla numbers 33, 35, 37, 39, 41, 43, 45, 47-51, 53, 55 and 57–69 were never operational.

1st Minesweeper Flotilla:
Operational from 1924 until the summer of 1946. *M1, M3, M4, M5, M7, M8, M14, M15, M17, M18, M20, M36, M37, M132, M155, M203, M204. M255, M256.*

2nd Minesweeper Flotilla:
Operational from 1936 until the summer of 1944. *M2, M6, M9, M10, M11, M12, M13, M21, M25, M38, M152, M153, M156.*
The flotilla was refounded during February 1945, and was kept operational until November 1947: *M606, M607, M608, M611, M805, M806.*

3rd Minesweeper Flotilla:
Operational from April 1940 until summer 1945. *M15, M16, M17, M18, M19, M22, M29, M30, M151* and Flakjäger *25* and *26*.

4th Minesweeper Flotilla:
Operational from the start of the war until spring 1945. *M61, M89, M136, M510, M511, M534, M582, M584.* Later also: *M1, M2, M36, M81, M101, M132, M151, M203, M204, M255.*

5th Minesweeper Flotilla:
Operational from late 1940 until October 1947. *M4, M23, M31, M35, M81, M154, M201, M202, M205, M251, M252, M253.*

6th Minesweeper Flotilla:
Operational from the start of the war until January 1942. *M4, M23, M31, M35, M81, M154, M201, M202, M205, M251, M252, M253.*
Refounded during May 1942, and kept operational until August 1944: *M38, M39, M82, M83, M102, M135, M155, M156, M206, M256, M265, M267.*

Cuxhaven on the estuary of the river Elbe was one of the main minesweeper bases and a minesweeper memorial still stands there, near the 'Alte Liebe' (Old Love) Pier. It lies on the seaward side of the dyke and the land around it is prone to flooding. This photo was taken before the Second World War.

7th Minesweeper Flotilla:
Operational from the start of the war until March 1940.
M75, M84, M102, M122, M126 and *Oxhöft* and
Westerplatte.
The 7th Flotilla was refounded in September 1942, and
kept operational until November 1947: *M23, M32,
M33, M82, M102, M103, M104, M201, F4, F5, F7.*

8th Minesweeper Flotilla:
Operational from early 1941 until 1945.
*M24, M26, M27, M28, M32, M34, M152, M254,
M256, M265, M277, M292, M329, M370.*

9th Minesweeper Flotilla:
Operational between March 1943 and summer 1947.
*M272, M273, M274, M276, M306, M326, M346,
M348, M364, M365.*

10th Minesweeper Flotilla:
Operational from April 1943 until September 1944.
*M263, M264, M275, M307, M347, M366, M367,
M385, M408, M428, M438.*

11th Minesweeper Flotilla:
Operational with twelve large fishing boats from the
start of the war until August 1942. The flotilla was
refounded during August 1943, and remained
operational until February 1945 with: *M264, M291,
M307, M327, M329, M347, M348, M368, M386.*

12th Minesweeper Flotilla:
Operational with about eight fishing boats from the
start of the war until late 1942. The flotilla was later
refounded, and remained operational until November
1947 with: *M601, M602, M603, M604, M605, M612,
M801, M803, M804.*

13th Minesweeper Flotilla:
Operational with about eight fishing boats from the
start of the war until December 1942.

14th Minesweeper Flotilla:
Operational from the start of the war until August 1941.
The flotilla was composed of converted drifters.

15th Minesweeper Flotilla:
Operational with about eight fishing boats from the
start of the war until early 1943.

16th Minesweeper Flotilla:
Operational with several fishing boats from October
1939 until January 1943.

17th Minesweeper Flotilla:
Operational with several fishing boats from September
1939 until November 1942.

18th Minesweeper Flotilla:
Operational with several fishing boats from September
1939 until November 1942.

19th Minesweeper Flotilla:
Operational with several fishing boats from September
1939 until October 1943.

20th Minesweeper Flotilla:
Founded during May 1945 to clear mines from the
Baltic. It was not operational during the war.

21st Minesweeper Flotilla:
Operational from January 1942 until shortly before the
end of the war.
*M261, M305, M323, M324, M327, M341, M342,
M343, M362, M383, M526, M545.*

22nd Minesweeper Flotilla:
Operational from September 1941 until early 1948.
*M301, M302, M303, M321, M322, M361, M368,
M381, M382, M436.*

23rd Minesweeper Flotilla:
Operational from August 1942 until 1947.
*M324, M401, M411, M421, M423, M441, M443,
M467, M468.*

24th Minesweeper Flotilla:
Operational from November 1942 until the end of the
war.
*M343, M402, M412, M422, M432, M442, M452;
M475; M483*

25th Minesweeper Flotilla:
Operational from December 1942 until the end of
1947.
*M278, M294, M295, M328, M330, M341, M342,
M403, M413, M423, M433, M443, M451, M453,
M459, M460.*

26th Minesweeper Flotilla:
Operational from January 1943 until August 1944.
*M404, M424, M434, M444, M454, M476, M486,
M495.*

27th Minesweeper Flotilla:
Operational from January 1943 until 1946.
*M261, M323, M327, M329, M369, M405, M414,
M425, M434, M455, M461, M469, M484.*

28th Minesweeper Flotilla:
Operational from December 1942 until August 1944.
*M262, M271, M304, M325, M344, M345, M363,
M384, M463.*

29th Minesweeper Flotilla:
Operational from October 1943 until June 1945.
*M265, M267, M293, M301, M386, M403, M406,
M415, M426, M436, M445, M455, M462, M470.*

30th Minesweeper Flotilla:
Operational until shortly after the end of the war.
*M266, M291, M348, M407, M416, M427, M437,
M446, M456, M489, M496.*

31st Minesweeper Flotilla:
Operational with several Dutch fishing boats and some German R-boats from September 1940 until the end of 1947.

32nd Minesweeper Flotilla:
Operational from June 1940 until shortly after the end of the war. This flotilla was equipped with Dutch fishing boats and a few German R-boats.

34th Minesweeper Flotilla:
Founded during the summer of 1940; the flotilla comprised several Dutch fishing boats.

36th Minesweeper Flotilla:
Operational from July 1940 until after the end of the war. It mainly comprised captured fishing boats.

38th Minesweeper Flotilla:
Operational from summer 1940 until after the end of the war. This flotilla mainly comprised of captured fishing boats.

40th Minesweeper Flotilla:
Operational from June 1940 until the autumn of 1944. It was made up mainly of French fishing boats. Possibly re-founded during 1945.

42nd Minesweeper Flotilla:
Operational from July 1940 until autumn of 1944. It mainly comprised French fishing boats.

44th Minesweeper Flotilla:
Operational with several French fishing boats from November 1940 until autumn 1944.

46th Minesweeper Flotilla:
Operational with a variety of fishing vessels from December 1941 until after the end of the war.

52nd Minesweeper Flotilla:
Operational in Norwegian waters from early 1941 until October 1944.
M1, M2, M534 and several Norwegian vessels.

54th Minesweeper Flotilla:
Probably first operational in early 1941 until about 1944. It was composed of Norwegian vessels.

56th Minesweeper Flotilla:
Operational with several Norwegian fishing boats from June 1940 until the end of the war.

70th Minesweeper Flotilla:
Operational in the Mediterranean from summer 1943. The name was changed to 13th Sicherungsflottille in October 1944.

One of the old minesweepers from the First World War.

First World War Minesweepers

Some of the First World War minesweepers were given a traditional name and most were renumbered.

Original number		New number
M28	Pelikan	M528
M50	Brommy	M550
M60	Hecht	M560
M61		–
M66	Störtebeker	M566
M72		M572
M75		M575
M81	Nautilus	M581
M82	Jagd	M581
M84		M584
M85		–
M89		M589
M98		M598
M102		M502
M104		M504
M107	von der Groben	M507
M108	Delphin	M508
M109	Sundewall	M509
M110		M510
M111		M511
M113	Acheron	M513
M115	Arkonda	M515
M117		M517
M122		M522
M126	Alders	M526
M129	Otto Braun	M529
M130	Fuchs	M530
M132		–
M133	Wacht	M533
M134	Frauenlob	M534
M135	Gazelle	M535
M136	Havel	–
M138	Nettelbeck	M538
M145		M545
M146	von der Lippe	M546
M157		M557

Motor Minesweepers (Räumboote)

Flotilla numbers 18–20, 22–24 and 26–29 were never operational.

1st Flotilla: Operational in the Baltic and North Sea until early 1948.

2nd Flotilla: This flotilla operated mainly in the North Sea until August 1944 when it was disbanded. Operational again during early 1945.

3rd Flotilla: Operational first in the eastern Baltic and later in Holland. From there the flotilla moved to France. Eventually the boats were taken overland to the Black Sea, where they operated until the summer of 1944.

4th Flotilla: Operational in the North Sea at the start of the war. Some boats went as far as Holland and Belgium. In 1944 they were taken to Norway, where they continued to work until the summer of 1945.

5th Flotilla: Operational in the Baltic and Norwegian waters from August 1939 until the end of 1945.

6th Flotilla: Operational for a few months of 1941 in the Mediterranean area. Refounded during the summer of that year, from when it probably remained in commission until the spring of 1945.

7th Flotilla: Operational from October 1940 until November 1946. Based at first in Holland and later in

Norway. It may also have served in Denmark.

8th Flotilla: Based in the North Sea from early 1942 it then moved westwards to France and, towards the end of the war, to Denmark. Disbanded in late 1947.

9th Flotilla: Operated mainly from Rotterdam in Dutch waters. Probably founded in 1942 and disbanded in 1947.

10th Flotilla: Operational from March 1942 until August 1944 in the North Sea region and in French waters.

11th Flotilla: Operational in the Baltic and probably Danish waters from before the war until October 1940.

12th Flotilla: Founded in Brugge (Belgium) during May 1942 and operational until early 1945. Based at first in the English Channel area and later in the Mediterranean.

13th Flotilla: Founded towards the end of 1943, its purpose was to clear mines from the German Bight. The flotilla continued to work in the North Sea and in the Baltic after the war. It was amalgamated into the Federal Armed Forces in 1957.

14th Flotilla: Operational from late 1943 until the summer of 1946, first in the German Bight and later in the Baltic. The flotilla worked in Danish waters and was eventually handed over to the Royal Danish Navy.

15th Flotilla: This flotilla operated in the Baltic and some

A flotilla of small minesweepers or 'Räumboote' in Norwegian waters.

of the boats went into Norwegian waters. Probably disbanded during the summer of 1945.

16th Flotilla: Based in Norway and later in Holland from October 1944 until the end of 1947.

17th Flotilla: Operational from July 1944 until the end of 1947 in the Baltic and later in Dutch waters.

21st Flotilla: Operational from the summer of 1943 until the end of 1945 in Norway and later in Russia.

25th Flotilla: Not operational during the war. The flotilla was founded during the summer of 1945 and operated until the end of that year in Danish waters.

30th Flotilla: Operational in the Black Sea for one year from summer 1943, probably with small Dutch boats.

Auxiliary Minesweepers (Sperrbrecher)

Flotilla number 7 was never operational.

1st Flotilla: Operational in the Baltic and North Sea from the start of the war until the summer of 1946.

2nd Flotilla: Founded towards the end of 1939 by amalgamating several auxiliary minesweeper groups. It was disbanded again during the summer of 1944. The flotilla operated in French waters and in the Baltic.

3rd Flotilla: Founded during late 1940 by amalgamating several groups. It then operated in the Baltic until 1946.

Coastal Defence Boats

Patrol Boats (Vorpostenboote)

The following flotillas were operational during the periods indicated; numbers 5, 21–50, 52, 54, 56, 58, 60 and 62 were never operational.

1st Flotilla: Oct. 1939 to Oct. 1940.

2nd Flotilla: Sept. 1939 to Dec. 1944.

3rd Flotilla: Probably operational for most of the war.

4th Flotilla: Sept. 1939 to Sept. 1944.

6th Flotilla: From early 1944 until about the end of the war.

7th Flotilla: From about the start of the war until Sept. 1944.

8th Flotilla: Operational for most of the war.

9th Flotilla: Operational for most of the war.

10th Flotilla: Operational from the start of the war until October 1943 when it was renamed 10. Sicherungsflottille (10th Security Flotilla).

11th Flotilla: Operational for most of the war.

12th Flotilla: Operational until the end of 1947.

13th Flotilla: Operational for most of the war.

14th Flotilla: Founded during Feb. 1943.

15th Flotilla: Operational for most of the war.

Sperrbrecher (barrier breakers) sailed ahead of other ships through minefields and detonated mines thereby creating a safe passage. They were filled with a variety of flotation aids and the crew was provided with cushioned quarters so that they would not be hurt by exploding mines. Many of these ships also carried an impressive array of anti-aircraft guns.

Patrol boats were (and still are) often confused with motor torpedo-boats but they had neither the torpedo tubes and seldom the three huge fuel-guzzling engines. These craft were found in many ports from the north of Norway to the coast of Africa.

4th Flotilla: Operational in the English Channel from summer 1940 until summer 1943.

5th Flotilla: Founded during the autumn of 1941, it was renamed 8th Flotilla before the end of the year.

6th Flotilla: Founded during July 1941 by splitting the 2nd Auxiliary Minesweeper Flotilla. It was then operational in France until September 1941.

8th Flotilla: Founded towards the end of 1941 to operate in Dutch waters and in the North Sea.

16th Flotilla: Founded in summer 1940.

17th Flotilla: Founded in summer 1940.

18th Flotilla: Operational from autumn 1940.

19th Flotilla: Operational from summer 1940 until autumn 1943.

20th Flotilla: Operational from July 1940.

51st Flotilla: Operational from early 1941.

53rd Flotilla: Operational from early 1941.

55th Flotilla: Operational from early 1941.

57th Flotilla: Operational from summer 1943.

59th Flotilla: Founded in 1940, but it may not have started operations until the following year.

61st Flotilla: Operational from November 1940.

63rd Flotilla: Operational from summer 1944.

64th Flotilla: Operational from summer 1944.

65th Flotilla: Operational from May 1944.

66th Flotilla: Operational from May 1944.

67th Flotilla: Operational from July 1944.

68th Flotilla: Operational from May 1944.

Picket Boats (Sicherungsboote)

The following flotillas were operational during the periods indicated.

1st Flotilla: Founded in the Baltic during October by renaming the 'Coastal Protection Flotilla: Western Baltic'.

2nd Flotilla: Operational in the central Baltic region towards the end of the war.

3rd Flotilla: Operational in the Danzig (Gdansk) area towards the end of the war.

4th Flotilla: Operational in southern Danish waters of the Baltic towards the end of the war.

5th Flotilla: Operational in the Great Belt towards the end of the war.

6th Flotilla: Operational in French Mediterranean waters during the middle war years. Either the boats were moved to the Baltic in 1945 or the flotilla was refounded there with new boats.

7th Flotilla: Probably not operational.

8th Flotilla: Founded during October 1943 and operational in the waters around Copenhagen.

9th Flotilla: Founded during October 1943 and operational in the Kattegat.

10th Flotilla: This flotilla was originally called 10th Patrol Boat Flotilla. It was renamed during October 1943 and operated in the Kattegat.

11th Flotilla: Operational in the Adriatic from the end of 1943 until early 1944.

12th Flotilla: Operational in the Great Belt from early 1944 until the end of the war.

13th Flotilla: Founded in the Mediterranean during early 1944.

14th Flotilla: Founded in the eastern Baltic during the summer of 1944.

15th Flotilla: Founded during the summer of 1944 and operated in the waters around Esbjerg.

16th Flotilla: Also founded during the summer of 1944 and also operated in the waters around Esbjerg.

Submarine-Hunters (Unterseebootsjäger)

Submarine-hunters had the numbers of their boats prefixed by the letters 'UJ'. Many other boats, especially minesweepers, were also engaged in hunting submarines. The following flotillas were operational; numbers 4–10, 13 and 18–20 were never operational; numbers 15 and 16 probably not operational.

1st Flotilla: Operational in the Black Sea from the summer of 1943 for one year. The flotilla was later refounded in the Baltic.

2nd Flotilla: Operational in the Adriatic Sea for the last nine months of 1944.

3rd Flotilla: Founded in the Black Sea region during the summer of 1944, but only operational for a few months. Later, the flotilla was refounded in the Baltic and remained operational until the end of the war.

11th Flotilla: Operational for most of the war, at first in the Baltic and later in Norwegian waters. Some boats went far north and worked along the northern coast of Norway.

12th Flotilla: Operational for most of the war. This was either a large flotilla with boats operating in different areas or the group moved around. Boats from this flotilla worked in the North Sea, in the approaches to the Baltic, along the French Atlantic coast, in the English Channel and along the northern coast of Norway.

14th Flotilla: This flotilla was originally founded as the 13th U-boat Hunting Group, and was renamed during 1940. It was operational in France and Norway.

17th Flotilla: Operational in the Baltic and in Norwegian waters for most of the years of the war.

21st Flotilla: Operational in the Mediterranean from early 1942 until early 1944.

22nd Flotilla: Operational in the Mediterranean from the end of 1942 until shortly before the end of the war.

23rd Flotilla: Operational in the Black Sea for a few months during the summer of 1944.

Escorts (Geleitboote)

Numbers 6–29 were never operational.

1st Flotilla: Also known as the 9th Torpedo-Boat Flotilla. Operational in the Adriatic towards the end of the war.

2nd Flotilla: Founded during March 1944. It was operational in the Adriatic Sea.

3rd Flotilla: Operational in the Mediterranean during the middle war years.

Patrol boats, minesweepers, escort boats and a variety of other small craft were modified to carry depth charges, seen here along the side under the torpedo grab. This crane was used for the recovery of training torpedoes. In addition to having a red and white striped head, training torpedoes were designed to float, rather than sink, at the end of their run.

Escort boat number 2, showing that they looked similar to torpedo-boats, but without the heavier armament on the deck.

4th Flotilla: Operational in the Mediterranean for a few months in 1943.

5th Flotilla: Operational in the Baltic during the last months of the war.

30th Flotilla: Operational in the Black Sea towards the end of 1943 and early 1944.

31st Flotilla: Operational in the Black Sea for part of the war.

THE U-BOAT ARM (UNTERSEEBOOTE)

The U-boat arm evolved from one small operational flotilla in 1935 to what has been described as the fourth branch of the armed forces (i.e., Navy, Army, Air Force and U-boats); as a result, its administration became very intricate. The following outline concentrates on the aspects that relate directly to a study of the war in the Atlantic.

HEADQUARTERS STAFF BEFORE THE WAR

Since many of the men mentioned in this section are more famous as U-boat commanders than as staff officers, the boats they commanded have been indicated after their names. The dates show when they were appointed.

Führer der Unterseeboote or F.d.U. (Flag Officer for Submarines): Kpt.z.S. und Kommodore Karl Dönitz,[1] Staff Officer for U-boats: Kpt.z.S. Hans-Georg von Friedeburg (July 1939).

Naval Staff Officers:

   1st Officer: KK Eberhard Godt (*U25*) Jan. 1938.

   2nd Officer: KL Hans Gerrit von Stockhausen (*U13* and *U65*) Oct. 1938.

   3rd Officer: KL Hans Cohausz (*U30* and *UA*) Jan. 1936.

   Chief Engineer: FK Otto Thedsen (Served during First World War) Jan. 1936.

   Medical Officer: Dr Gerold Lübben, Oct. 1938.

The pre-war administration pattern was changed on 18 August 1939, when the Supreme Naval Command ordered the immediate implementation of the 'Three Front War Programme' (details of which can be found on page 68).

Dönitz was chosen for the post of Flag Officer for Submarines with the Naval War Staff, and was made responsible for both the war in the Atlantic and any other area where U-boats played a major role. His first step was to move his headquarters to Swinemünde, for at that stage only war against Poland was on the cards. Western waters were con-

1. Dönitz held the office of Flotilla Commander until January 1936, when his post was upgraded to Flag Officer.

trolled by U-boat Flag Officer West from his headquarters at Wilhelmshaven. This position was held by Korvkpt. Hans Ibbeken (*U27* and *U178*).

Even before the war had begun, It was clear that no great submarine battles would be fought in the Baltic. So, on 1 September he moved his headquarters to Wilhelmshaven, where he held the position of Flag Officer U-Boats for all three theatres of war. At the same time the new post of Flag Officer East was created to help complete mopping-up operations in the Baltic. Fregkpt. Oskar Schomburg held this office until 19 September 1939, when operations in the Baltic came to a standstill and all resources were poured into the West.

Before the war, Dönitz had aimed to build a powerful and flexible submarine arm. In order to do this, he concentrated on putting flotillas in as many key positions as possible, rather than attempting to construct any system of effective fighting groups (which would have meant a few, large flotillas). Usually, he had training boats and fighting units in the same areas, and while at sea they were often controlled through the same channels. But when war broke out this entire concept was radically altered: training boats were removed from the enemy's reach, and the cumbersome flotilla structure was streamlined. The reorganization machinery ground into action in September 1939, and in the following month a temporary plan was introduced. Changes continued until Christmas, after which the established plan remained in effect until the end of the war. There were several alterations and expansions, but on the whole the administration pattern remained the same.

The U-boat arm was split into two main departments: Operations and Organization. (At that time, Dönitz was not responsible for U-boat construction, which was organized by a department under the Supreme Naval Command, called the U-bootsamt.)

The Operations Department, later called U-Boat Command (U-bootsführung) was responsible for virtually all operational boats. Its commander was Eberhard Godt, who later held the title of Commander-in-Chief U-Boats (Operations) (B.d.U.–Ops). Other aspects, such as training, weapons, supplies and personnel, were dealt with by the Organization Department headed by Hans-Georg von Friedeburg. No sooner had the war begun than he was despatched into the Baltic with Dönitz's flagship, *Erwin Wassner*, to find suitably safe venues for setting up shop.

Dönitz, with the title of Flag Officer U-boats, was promoted to the rank of Rear Admiral in October 1939, a few weeks before the famous raid by *U47* (Günther Prien) on Scapa Flow, where the battleship *Royal Oak* was sunk. At the same time, he was given the new title 'Commander-in-Chief U-boats'. Also appointed were three Flag Officers to be responsible for the important operation areas of West (for the Atlantic), Norway and Arctic. A fourth, Central, was added later. None of these Flag Officers had operational control of U-boats – only, occasionally, those that were in their immediate coastal waters – but were responsible for their organization. While at sea, the U-boats were usually controlled directly by the Operations Department; but, once they entered coastal waters, they came under the jurisdiction of the flotilla commander, who was responsible for 'domestic' details like replenishment, repairs and looking after the crews.

OPERATIONS DEPARTMENT LATER CALLED U-BOAT COMMAND (U-BOOTSFÜHRUNG)

Commander-in-Chief Operations: KA Eberbard Godt, Oct. 1939 to end of war.

1st Staff Officers:
> KL Victor Oehrn (*U14* and *U37*) Oct. 1939 to May 1940.
> KK Werner Hartmann(*U26, U37* and *U198*) May 1940 to Nov.1940.
> KK Victor Oehrn Nov. 1940 to Nov. 1941.
> FK Günther Hessler (*U107*) Nov. 1941 to end.
> KL Adalbert Schnee (*U6, U60, U201, U2511*) Nov. 1942 to July 1944.
> KL Heinrich Schroeteler (*U667, U1023*) July 1944 to Dec.1944.
> KK Ernst Hechler (*U870*) April 1944 to end of war.

2nd Staff Officers:
> KK Hans-Günther Looff (*U9, U122*) Oct. 1939 to April 1940.
> KL Karl Daublebsky von Eichein (*U9*) April 1940 to Feb.1943.
> KL Peter Cremer (*U152, (U333, U2519*) Feb. 1943 to April 1943.
> KK Alfred Hoschatt (*U378*) April 1943 to end of war.

3rd Staff Officers:
> KL Herbert Kuppisch (*U58, U94, U516, U849*) Sept. 1941 to June 1942.
> KL Johann Mohr (*U124*) June 1942 to end of war.

4th Staff Officers:
> KL Hans-Gerrit von Stockhausen (*U13, U65*) Oct. 1939 to Nov. 1939.
> KK Hans Meckel (*U13, U19*) Nov. 1939 to June 1944.
> KL Hermann Rasch (*U106*) June 1944 to Oct. 1944.
> KK Waldemar Mehl (*U62, U172, U371*) Oct. 1944 to end of war.

5th Staff Officer:
> KL Werner Winter (*U22, U103*) until June 1941.

6th Staff Officers:
> KL Herbert Kuppisch (*U58, U94, U516, U849*) June 1942 to Dec. 1942.
> KL Herbert Schultze (*U2, U48*) Dec. 1942 to March 1944.
> KK Hans Witt (*U161, U129, U3524*) March 1944 to Sept. 1944.
> KL Kurt Neide (*U415*) Sept. 1944 to end of war.

Engineer Officers:
> KL (Ing.) Hans Looschen.
> KK (Ing.) Karl Scheel.
> KL (Ing.) Gerd Suhren.
> KL (Ing.) Karl-Heinz Wiebe.

There were also several other posts, such as legal advisers and medical officers.

ORGANIZATION DEPARTMENT

Commander-in-Chief Organization: Hans-Georg von Friedeburg.

Chiefs of Staff:
> FK Heinz Beucke (*U173*) to May 1943.
> KA Ernst Kratzenberg June 1943 to just before end of war.
> KS Kurt Dobratz (*U1232*) During last few months of war.

Weapons Unit:
Torpedoes[1]:
    KK Klaus Ewerth (*U1, U35, U36, U26, U850*).
    FK Heinrich Schuch (*U37, U38, U105, U154*).
Artillery and Navigation:
    KK Hans Pauckstadt (*U193*).
    KK Claus Korth (*U57, U93*).
    KK Wilhelm Zahn (*U56, U69*).
    KL Helmut Möhlmann (*U143, U571*).
    KL Siegfried Lüdden (*U188*).
    Communications Unit:
    KL Kurt Grundke.
    KL Wilhelm Grundmann.
Technical Division:
    KA (Ing.) Otto Thedsen.
Personnel Department:
    KK Harald Jeppener-Haltenhoff (*U17, U24*).
    KK Wilhelm Müller-Arnecke (*U19*).
    KL Wilhelm Franken (*U565*).
Administration Office:
    FK Dr Walter Bucholz.
    FK Carl Wuttke.
    KK Heinz Mursch.

LOCATIONS OF HEADQUARTERS OF SUPREME COMMANDER-IN-CHIEF U-BOATS

Before the war: Mainly in Kiel.
August 1939, for a short period: Swinemünde.
1 Sept. 1939 to Nov. 1939: Wilhelmshaven Naval Radio Station in Toten Weg.
Nov. 1939 to Sept. 1940: Sengwarden near Wilhelmshaven at what is now called the Armin Zimmermann Kaserne. (The facilities there were still under construction when the war started and could not be occupied until later in the year.)
Sept. 1940 to Nov. 1940: Boulevard Suchet in Paris.
Nov. 1940 to March 1942: Kernevel near Lorient.
March 1942 to March 1943: Avenue Marechal in Paris.
March 1943 to Dec. 1943: Steinplatz in Berlin Charlottenburg.
Dec. 1943 to early 1945: Staff quarters at Bernau near Berlin (code-name 'Koralle'). The Naval Command Staff was split in February 1945. Part of the staff was moved to Sengwarden near Wilhelmshaven while the other half remained at 'Koralle'. Eventually, the staff met again at Plön and from there moved to Flensburg-Mürwik, where they were accommodated in Sport Complex of the Naval Officers' School.

U-BOAT FLOTILLAS

Flotilla numbers 15, 16, 17 and 28 were never operational.
1st Flotilla (Flotilla Weddigen): Kiel, later Brest.
2nd Flotilla (Flotilla Saltzwedel): Wilhelmshaven, later Lorient.
3rd Flotilla (Flotilla Lohs): Kiel, later La Pallice and La Rochelle.
4th Flotilla (Training): Stettin (Baltic).
5th Flotilla (Flotilla Emsmann): Kiel.

6th Flotilla (Flotilla Hundius): Wilhelmshaven, then Danzig and later St Nazaire.
7th Flotilla (Flotilla Wegener): Kiel, then St Nazaire and later Norway.
8th Flotilla (Training): Königsberg and later Danzig.
9th Flotilla: Brest.
10th Flotilla: Lorient.
11th Flotilla: Bergen.
12th Flotilla: Bordeaux.
13th Flotilla: Trondheim.
14th Flotilla: Narvik.
18th Flotilla: Only operational for the first three months of 1945.
19th Flotilla (Training): Pillau and Kiel.
20th Flotilla (Training): Probably Pillau.
21st Flotilla (Training): Pillau.
22nd Flotilla (Training): Gotenhafen.
23rd Flotilla (Training): Danzig.
24th Flotilla (Training): Danzig, Memel, Trondheim and back to Memel. Later also at Gotenhafen and Eckernförde.
25th Flotilla (Training): Danzig, Trondheim, Memel, Libau, Gotenhafen and Travemünde.
26th Flotilla (Training): Pillau and later Warnemünde.
27th Flotilla (Training): Probably never operational. There was only one boat attached to this flotilla.
29th Flotilla: La Spezia, Toulon, Pola (Pula), Marseilles and Salamis.
30th Flotilla: Constanta (Black Sea).
31st Flotilla (Training): Hamburg, Wilhelmshaven and Wesermünde (renamed Bremerhaven).
32nd Flotilla (Training): Königsberg and, towards the end of the war, Hamburg.
33rd Flotilla: Flensburg, with some boats in the Far East (Japan).

This building was used by the U-boat Command as their second headquarters of the war and now forms part of the Armin Zimmermann Barracks in Sengwarden, near Wilhelmshaven. Karl Dönitz occupied the two rooms by the side of the door. They were built to resemble north German farms in the hope of misleading enemy observers. The quarters were not ready at the beginning of the war and even when the U-boat Command moved in during November 1939 there was still much work to be finished off.

---

1. This unit was responsible for the submarines' torpedoes and had no connection with the department of the Supreme Command, which was partly responsible for the torpedo crisis mentioned on page 31.

SHIPS OF THE GERMAN FLEET

BATTLESHIPS

BISMARCK

Bismarck, the Fleet Commander's flagship, left Gotenhafen in East Prussia early in May 1941. Her commander, Kpt.z.S. Ernst Lindemann, had orders to break out into the Atlantic with the heavy cruiser *Prinz Eugen*. Both ships were to remain together until they had passed through the Denmark Strait – the waters between Iceland and Greenland – after which they would be free to go their separate ways. However, they were spotted by British forces and the subsequent action against HMS *Hood* and HMS *Prince of Wales* reached its height when shells from *Bismarck* pierced *Hood*'s magazine, causing her to blow up and sink instantly.

The next two days saw the now famous events that led to the sinking of the *Bismarck*. Although she managed to escape from the guns of the Royal Navy, her crew thought they were still being pursued and so they radioed a report to Germany.

This was her undoing, because the report was picked up by the British Navy, who then continued the hunt in earnest. *Bismarck* was located again by light aircraft from the carriers *Victorious* and *Ark Royal*. An aerial torpedo first damaged *Bismarck*'s steering gear and propeller shafts, and then she came under fire from the British battleships *King George V* and *Rodney*. Damage was too severe for *Bismarck* to continue and, after expending all her ammunition, she was eventually scuttled. Sinking was accelerated by a torpedo from the cruiser HMS *Dorsetshire*.

Latest research indicates that *Bismarck* was detected in Norwegian waters by the code breakers at Bletchley Park, and Michael Suckling flew out to make it appear that the detection had been due to a visual sighting.

TIRPITZ

This famous battleship's most valuable contribution to the war effort was her mere existence. Although she was only used for minor tasks and never took part in any real action, her potential posed such a threat that Britain injected terrific resources into effecting her destruction. In fact, the daring attacks on *Tirpitz* are far more interesting than her few aggressive sorties. *Tirpitz* was not fitted out for action until October 1941, and she underwent trials until the end of that year. Eventually, on 16 January 1942, she left Wilhelmshaven for Norwegian waters as flagship to Vizeadmiral Otto Ciliax (Commander-in-Chief Battleships). *Tirpitz* called at Trondheim in Norway and then went north to attack merchant shipping, but she returned two months later without having achieved anything noteworthy. Afterwards, she went on a short training cruise, and the following winter returned to dock for repairs. In January 1943, *Tirpitz* returned to an earlier anchorage near Narvik and from there moved to Kaafjord, an inlet of the famous Altenfjord. She sailed to Spitzbergen, flying the flag of the Commander-in-Chief of the North Norway Naval Squadron (Admiral Oskar Kummetz) and, on 6 September 1943, took part in the bombardment of shore installations with *Scharnhorst* and ten destroyers, which landed Army forces.

Tirpitz then returned to Altenfjord and was attacked by the famous British X-craft. This was, in fact, the second attack on *Tirpitz* by small submarines, for in October 1942 a pair of Royal Navy two-man human torpedoes ('Chariots') had been brought within striking distance, only to break away from their tow and sink. The X-craft attack on 22

Bismarck from *Prinz Eugen*, showing the massive beam of the class. It seems likely that this picture was taken close to port because the wings of the captain's bridge were usually dismantled once the ship was at sea. The Baltic camouflage is visible on the waterline just aft of the stem.

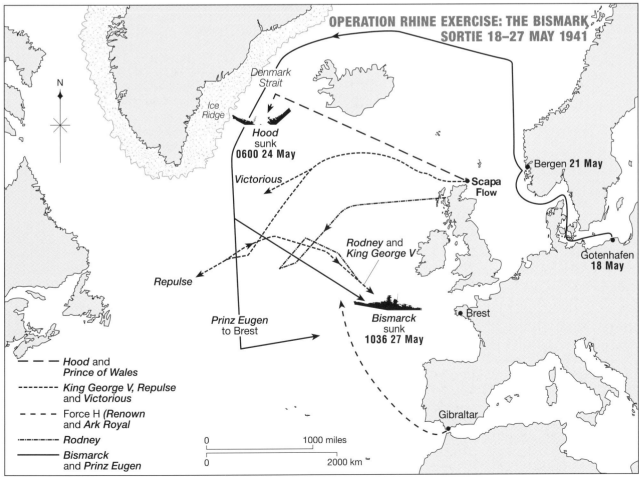

OPERATION RHINE EXERCISE: THE BISMARK SORTIE 18–27 MAY 1941

N

Denmark Strait

Ice Ridge

Hood sunk **0600 24 May**

Victorious

Bergen **21 May**

Scapa Flow

Rodney and King George V

Repulse

Prinz Eugen to Brest

Bismarck sunk **1036 27 May**

Brest

Gotenhafen **18 May**

Gibraltar

— · — · — *Hood* and *Prince of Wales*

– – – – *King George V, Repulse* and *Victorious*

— — — Force H (*Renown* and *Ark Royal*

— ·· — ·· — *Rodney*

——— *Bismarck* and *Prinz Eugen*

0   1000 miles
0   2000 km ≈

Bismarck in calm Norwegian waters before setting out for her one and only war cruise. This photograph was taken from her consort, the heavy cruiser *Prinz Eugen*. She originally had a straight stem, similar to *Scharnhorst* and *Gniesenau,* but was subsequently fitted with an 'Atlantic' bow, without which she would have been a very wet ship. She and her sister were the heaviest and probably the most capable European battleships ever built and the name *Bismarck* has a public recognition enjoyed by few other warships.

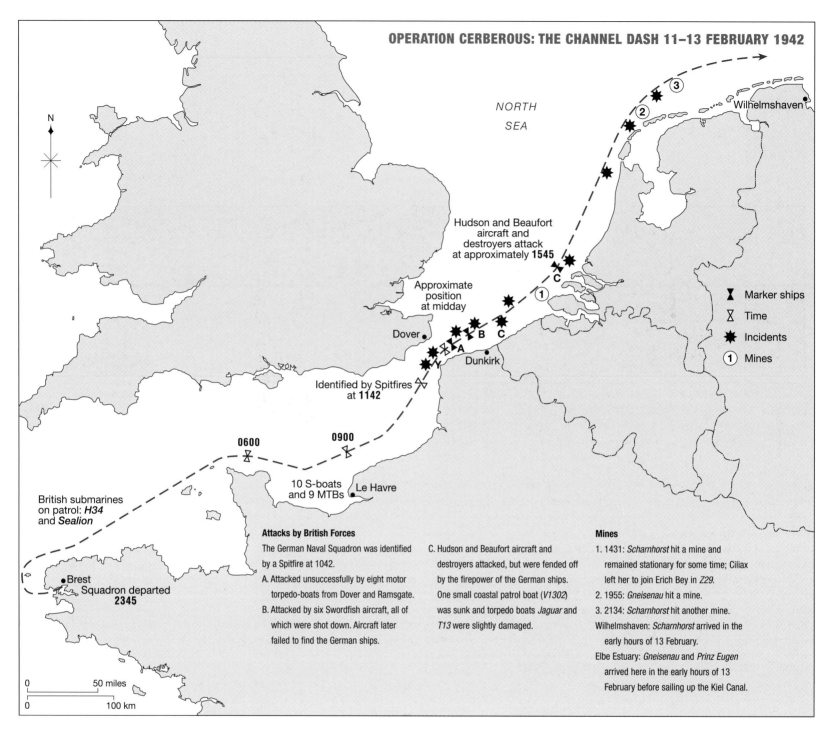

OPERATION CERBEROUS: THE CHANNEL DASH 11–13 FEBRUARY 1942

NORTH
SEA

Wilhelmshaven

Hudson and Beaufort
aircraft and
destroyers attack
at approximately **1545**

C

Approximate
position
at midday

B   C

Dover

A

Dunkirk

Identified by Spitfires
at **1142**

0600   0900

10 S-boats
and 9 MTBs   Le Havre

British submarines
on patrol: *H34*
and *Sealion*

Brest
Squadron departed
2345

N

Marker ships

Time

Incidents

(1) Mines

0   50 miles

0   100 km

Attacks by British Forces

The German Naval Squadron was identified
by a Spitfire at 1042.

A. Attacked unsuccessfully by eight motor
torpedo-boats from Dover and Ramsgate.

B. Attacked by six Swordfish aircraft, all of
which were shot down. Aircraft later
failed to find the German ships.

C. Hudson and Beaufort aircraft and
destroyers attacked, but were fended off
by the firepower of the German ships.
One small coastal patrol boat (*V1302*)
was sunk and torpedo boats *Jaguar* and
T13 were slightly damaged.

Mines

1. 1431: *Scharnhorst* hit a mine and
remained stationary for some time; Ciliax
left her to join Erich Bey in *Z29*.

2. 1955: *Gneisenau* hit a mine.

3. 2134: *Scharnhorst* hit another mine.

Wilhelmshaven: *Scharnhorst* arrived in the
early hours of 13 February.

Elbe Estuary: *Gneisenau* and *Prinz Eugen*
arrived here in the early hours of 13
February before sailing up the Kiel Canal.

Five minesweeper flotillas and three
motor minesweeper flotillas cleared
mines in critical areas of the English
Channel during the week preceding the
operation. The German Naval Squadron
(under the command of Admiral Otto
Ciliax) left Brest during the night of
11/12 February 1942, and consisted of
the following ships:

Scharnhorst KS Kurt Hoffmann

Gneisenau KS Otto Fein

Prinz Eugen KS Helmuth Brinkmann

Z4 (*Richard Beitzen*) KL Karl Kassbaum
(with KS Fritz Berger, Commander of
5th Destroyer Flotilla, on board)

Z6 (*Paul Jacobi*) KL Günther Bachmann

Z7 (*Hermann Schoemann*) KL Konrad
Loerke

Z14 (*Friedrich Ihn*) KL Theodor von Mutius

Z25 KK Kurt Haun

Z29 KL Wirich von Gartzen (with Erich
Bey, Officer Commanding Destroyers,
on board)

The German Naval Squadron was joined
by the following forces for part of the
operation:

X. From Le Havre

2nd Torpedo-Boat Flotilla (FK Heinrich
Erdmann)

T2 (KL Heinrich Gödecke)

T4 (KL Axel Bieling)

T5 (KL Rudolf Koppenhagen)

T11 (KL Georg Grund)

T12 (KL Thilo von Trotha)

Y. From Dunkirk

3rd Torpedo-Boat Flotilla (FK Hans Wilcke)

T13 (KL Werner Gotzmann)

T15 (KL Joachim Quedenfeldt)

T16 (KL Helmuth Düvelius)

T17 (KL Hans Blöse)

Falke (KL Heinrich Hoffmann)

Iltis (KL Walter Jacobsen)

Jaguar (KL Karl Paul)

Kondor (KL Franz Burkart)

(The named ships were torpedo-boats
that joined the German Naval Squadron in
the narrowest part of the English
Channel, off Cape Griz Nez.)

Z. After Cape Griz Nez

2nd Motor Torpedo-Boat Flotilla (KK Klaus
Feldt)

4th Motor Torpedo-Boat Flotilla (KK Niels
Bätge)

6th Motor Torpedo-Boat Flotilla
(KK Albrecht Obermaier)

Luftflotte 3 made more than 150 aircraft
available to escort the Naval Squadron. Of
these, there were usually at least 15
accompanying the ships while they
passed through the critical parts of the
English Channel.

September 1943 proved successful and caused considerable havoc: the rudder was damaged, all three propeller shafts were bent and some turbines were unseated from their mountings; cracks in the bottom caused flooding and even the rear 38cm gun turret was dislodged from its foundation. Repairs took five months, after which more trials were necessary. *Tirpitz* was just about ready for action when, on 5 April 1944, she came under attack from aircraft from the carriers *Victorious, Furious, Emperor, Searcher, Fencer* and *Pursuer*. More than a dozen bombs found their target, killing over 100 of the crew and wounding a further 316. Again, the ship was put out of action for several months.

The lonely queen of the north was the target of two more air strikes in August 1944. *Tirpitz* was then given a respite until mid-September, when she was attacked by RAF Lancasters. These aircraft carried special 12,000lb armour piercing bombs – designed by Barnes Wallis, inventor of the bouncing bomb used by the 'Dambusters' – which put *Tirpitz* completely out of action. However, her crew went to considerable lengths to disguise the fact that she was not seaworthy, and routine carried on as before. Unable to move under her own steam, *Tirpitz* was towed out of Kaafjord by warships instead of tugs, to give the impression she was setting out with escorts. The deception paid off, but on 12 November the RAF launched another attack and she finally capsized at her anchorage off Haakoy Island, near Tromsö. Only about fifty of her crew were saved.

Tirpitz had been commissioned on 25 February 1941 by Kpt.z.S. Karl Topp, who left her during February 1943 to become a departmental head at the Supreme Naval Command. He was replaced as commander by Kpt.z.S. Hans Meyer who remained in office until May 1944, when he became Chief of the Operations Department at the Supreme Naval Command. Wolf Junge took his place until November 1944, when he was made Admiralty Staff Officer, and the ship's First Officer, Robert Weber, was given command.

BATTLECRUISERS

GNEISENAU

In Britain, *Gneisenau* and *Scharnhorst* tend to be classified as battlecruisers, but in Germany they were referred to as battleships. *Gneisenau* was originally the flagship for the Fleet Commander, Vizeadmiral Wilhelm Marschall. During October 1939, she operated against shipping running between Britain and Scandinavia, but without any noteworthy success. Still under the command of Kpt.z.S. Erich Förste, her second cruise – in November 1939 – took her into the Atlantic, south of Iceland. Her main objective was to draw Allied forces away from the pocket battleship *Admiral Graf Spee*, which was operating farther south in Atlantic waters. On 23 November *Gneisenau* attacked and sank the British auxiliary cruiser *Rawalpindi*. Afterwards, she ran into bad weather, and serious storm damage forced her to return to Kiel for repairs.

Erich Förste was promoted to Chief of Staff at the Naval Construction Yard in Wilhelmshaven, and he was replaced as *Gneisenau*'s commander by Kpt.z.S. Harald Netzbandt who took her back into the North Atlantic – again as flagship to the Fleet Commander. This time, *Gneisenau* was accompanied by *Scharnhorst* and the heavy cruiser *Admiral Hipper*. During the Norwegian Campaign she served west of the Lofoten Islands as flagship to Vizeadmiral Günther Lütjens, Commander-in-Chief Reconnaissance Forces. There, she scored two hits on HMS *Renown*, and received light damage in return.

Her next cruise, during early June 1940, took her from Wilhelmshaven into the Arctic seas off Norway, where *Gneisenau, Scharnhorst, Admiral Hipper* and several destroyers searched for an Allied convoy. Although failing to find the convoy, they did manage to sink several ships, including the aircraft carrier HMS *Glorious*.

Gneisenau returned to Trondheim, where she remained until 20 June 1940. She did not go to sea during this brief

Tirpitz, the Lonely Queen of the North, showing off the full might of her artillery. Though the war was spent hiding in a Norwegian fjord, her latent threat made a significant contribution to the German war effort.

spell in port, except possibly for trials, but when she did put out, with *Admiral Hipper*, *Gneisenau* was hit by at least one torpedo from the British submarine *Clyde* and was forced to return to Trondheim for emergency repairs. Five days later she and the cruiser *Nürnberg* left for Kiel, to complete repairs in the naval dockyard. *Gneisenau* was out of action until 28 December 1940, when, under the command of Kpt.z.S. Otto Fein, she tried to break out into the Atlantic. (Her previous commander, Harald Netzbandt had been made Chief of Staff for the Fleet Command.) But, again, luck was not on *Gneisenau*'s side: heavy weather forced her to return for minor repairs. Eventually, at the end of January 1941, she managed to get out into the Atlantic to operate in the waters off Iceland. From there she went to Brest, arriving on 22 March. While in port she was damaged by aerial torpedoes, thus forcing her to stay put.

Gneisenau took part in the famous 'Channel Dash', ending up in Kiel, where, on 26–27 February 1942, she was

further damaged by the RAF. In April 1942, she was moved to Gotenhafen and withdrawn from active service for a large-scale refit. This idea was scrapped a year later and, at the end of the war, she was scuttled to block the harbour approaches. Her hulk was scrapped by the Russians between 1947 and 1951.

SCHARNHORST

Scharnhorst was commanded by Kpt.z.S. Otto Ciliax until October 1939, when the Navy's reorganization programme promoted him to Chief of Staff at Naval Group Command West. Kpt.z.S. Kurt Caesar Hoffmann replaced him as commander. During that first winter, *Scharnhorst* joined *Gneisenau* and *Admiral Hipper* for several combined operations. In June 1940 she and *Gneisenau* went into action against merchant shipping. On the 8th, *Scharnhorst* received a torpedo-hit from the destroyer HMS *Acasta* and, in addition to damaged gun turrets, both the central and starboard

Gneisenau, seen here, and her sister *Scharnhorst*, had four triple turrets with 11in (280mm) barrels, while *Bismarck* and *Tirpitz* were fitted with four double turrets, each containing 15in (380mm) guns.

engines were put out of action. Her commander had no alternative but to limp back to port. *Scharnhorst* tried to get back into the Atlantic with *Gneisenau* on 28 December 1940, but when *Gneisenau* was damaged by heavy seas, *Scharnhorst* accompanied her back to port. Their next attempt to break out into the Atlantic was successful and, on 8 February 1941, both ships passed through the Denmark Strait. After this cruise they both went to Brest, arriving there on 22 March. Once in port the ships were attacked by aircraft, and *Scharnhorst* was extensively damaged by several bombs.

During the famous 'Channel Dash' of 11–13 February 1942, *Scharnhorst* was flagship to Commander-in-Chief Reconnaissance Forces (Vizeadmiral Otto Ciliax). However, her old commander was out of luck, the ship ran onto two mines and remained stationary in the Channel for about thirty minutes, until her engineers managed to re-start the engines and she reached Germany under her own steam.

Scharnhorst's commander, Kurt Caesar Hoffmann, was

Scharnhorst, looking aft at the command tower. Note that the wings of the Captain's bridge have been dismantled. The general set up of these solid-looking command towers varied from ship to ship, but usually consisted of the following:

- The armour deck below the battery deck, seen here stretching away from the camera.
- Above that was the upper deck and then the superstructure deck. These two were often amalgamated into one aboard smaller ships.
- Next was the lower bridge deck or captain's bridge. The portholes of this are just visible above the turret.
- Above that was the admiral's bridge with chart room and meteorology office. Another huge rangefinder of the central fire control system was usually fitted inside stabilizing gimbals at the top.

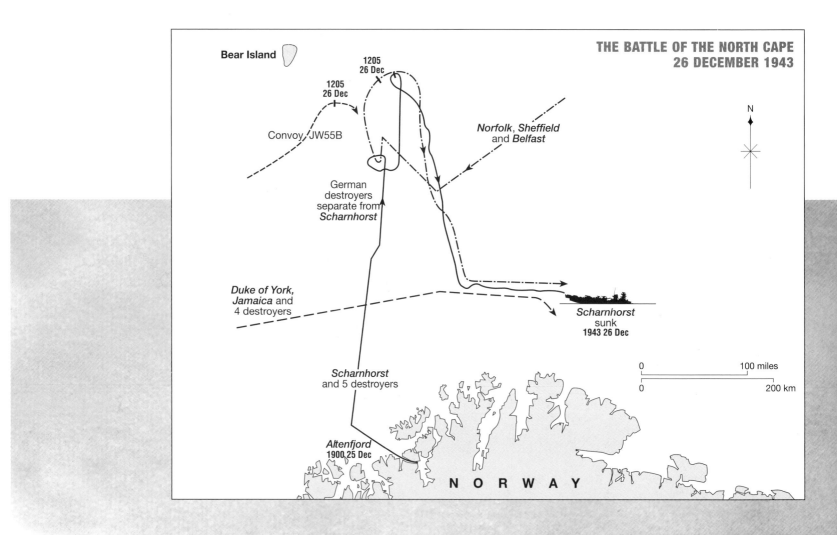

**THE BATTLE OF THE NORTH CAPE
26 DECEMBER 1943**

Bear Island

1205
26 Dec

1205
26 Dec

Convoy JW55B

Norfolk, Sheffield
and *Belfast*

N

German
destroyers
separate from
Scharnhorst

*Duke of York,
Jamaica* and
4 destroyers

Scharnhorst
sunk
1943 26 Dec

0   100 miles

0   200 km

Scharnhorst
and 5 destroyers

Altenfjord
1900 25 Dec

N O R W A Y

then put at the disposal of the Naval Station Baltic and later he was made Commanding Admiral in Holland. Meanwhile, *Scharnhorst* had been partly repaired and moved to Gotenhafen, where she was safe from RAF bombs. She then spent some time as a training ship under the command of Friedrich Hüffmeier. Later, during March 1943, he took her to Altenfjord in northern Norway to join *Tirpitz* and other warships for the Spitzbergen raid. *Scharnhorst* saw no further action for the rest of 1943. Hüffmeier was made a departmental head at the Supreme Naval Command and was

replaced by Kpt.z.S. Fritz Intze, who took the ship on an operation into the Arctic seas at the end of 1943. After attempting to intercept convoy JW55B, *Scharnhorst* was engaged by several British cruisers. She managed to break away, only to run into a group of four destroyers, one battle-ship and one cruiser.

Finally, at 1945 hours on 26 December 1943 *Scharnhorst* went down. Many of her crew were lost in the icy cold waters of the North Atlantic, and fewer than forty survivors were picked up.

Scharnhorst after completion, but before the impressive 'clipper' or 'Atlantic' bow was added. The wings of the captain's bridge are in position.

The pocket battleship *Deutschland* was later reclassed as a heavy cruiser and renamed *Lützow*. Like several other German capital ships, *Deutschland* was launched with a straight stem and had the 'Atlantic' bows added at a later date. Pocket battleships were the only class with a long deck sweeping back as an uncluttered line until it dropped down to the easily spotted lower part at the stern. This lower section contained two sets of torpedo tubes, each holding up to four torpedoes. The black, white and red stripes over the forward turret were an identification mark used during the Spanish Civil War.

Deutschland in port for repairs having been hit by a torpedo. This shows the stern of the ship well down in the water while the quadruple torpedo tubes have been removed from their circular mounts.

POCKET BATTLESHIPS[1]

DEUTSCHLAND (LATER RENAMED LÜTZOW)

The name of the world's first pocket battleship was changed from *Deutschland* to *Lützow* in February 1940. Another cruiser, named *Lützow*, had been built for the German Navy, but this vessel was sold to Russia and never served with the Kriegsmarine. The change of name was first suggested by Grand Admiral Erich Raeder shortly after the outbreak of the war, possibly to confuse Allied naval intelligence.

Deutschland left Germany for the North Atlantic before the start of the war, and did not return to Wilhelmshaven, with serious engine trouble, until late in 1939. From there she sailed up the Kiel Canal into the Baltic. *Lützow* (as she was now renamed) took part in the invasion of Norway and, on 9 April 1940, she sailed through the Great Belt with the heavy cruiser *Blücher*. Both ships came under heavy fire from Norwegian forces in Oslo Fjord, where *Lützow* was seriously damaged and *Blücher* sank. The pocket battleship managed to crawl on to her destination, Oslo, and shortly afterwards headed towards Horten, where better repair facilities were anticipated. Her commander was ordered to take the ship to Kiel. A day later, on 10 April, the unescorted *Lützow* was attacked by HM Submarine *Spearfish*, whose torpedoes put paid to both propellers. She had to be towed back to Germany, where she remained for over a year undergoing repairs. It was June 1941 before she put to sea again – but not for long. Trials in Trondheim Fjord were interrupted by a single British aeroplane, which fooled the escorts into thinking it was German and then scored a good torpedo hit. *Lützow* went back to port for further repairs and it was another year before she saw action again. But once again she was out of luck: *Lützow* ran aground, water seeped into some of her compartments, and she returned to dock for still more repairs. December 1942 found her back in Norway, first mooring in a fjord near Narvik and later taking up anchorage in Altenfjord. Later, she put out from there and saw action off Bear Island in the Battle of the Barents Sea. There was no noteworthy action after this and, eventually, in September 1943, she returned to Germany.

She sailed to Gotenhafen in October and from there on to Libau, where she underwent a complete refit. *Lützow* was then used as a training ship and did not see active operational service until the end of 1944, when she participated in the German evacuation of the eastern provinces – the largest operation of its kind in history, After arriving at Swinemünde from Hela, on 16 April 1945, *Lützow* was hit by several bombs, and she sank on an even keel in shallow water. Most of her guns remained above the water, and some of them were used until a serious fire on 4 May 1945 put everything out of action and she was blown up by German forces. After the war, the wreck was raised by the Russians.

Deutschland/Lützow had various commanders, all of whom held the rank of 'Kapitän zur See' (Captain) – with the exception of the First Officers who temporarily commanded her, holding the rank of 'Fregattenkapitän' (Captain, junior grade). Her first wartime commander was Paul Wenneker, who left in November 1939 to spend the remaining war years as the German Naval Attaché in Japan. His successor, August

Thiele, was originally meant to take command of an auxiliary raider, but these plans were scrapped and he ended up commanding *Lützow* for five months. Leo Kreisch moved command from the light cruiser *Nürnberg* to *Lützow* in March 1941, but he was absent for the last five months of that year, and the First Officer, Fregattenkapitän Bodo Knoke, took over from him. Kreisch returned during December 1941, but the following month he was made head of a training establishment in Romania. He was succeeded by Rudolf Stange, formerly a section leader with the Supreme Naval Command. After serving on *Lützow*, Stange went back there as Chief of Staff for Naval Group Command South. Another First Officer, Horst Biesterfeld, took command from November 1943 until January 1944. He then became an admiralty staff officer, and Bodo Knoke, promoted to Kapitän zur See, returned as commander, Knoke stayed until the end, but he was absent for a short period during November 1944, when Kpt.z.S. Gerhardt Böhmig held command.

ADMIRAL SCHEER

This pocket battleship first saw action in the Second World War when she shot down a British aeroplane while lying in the Schillig Roads off Wilhelmshaven. Her commander at the time was Kpt.z.S. Hans-Heinrich Wurmbach. In 1940 she was withdrawn from active service for a general refit: the solid, rather typical pocket battleship control tower and bridge were replaced by a lighter type of mast, and she was also given a clipper bow.

After trials, she eventually broke out into the Atlantic – during October 1940 – under command of Theodor Krancke and went into action against convoy HX84. During this engagement she sank the British auxiliary cruiser HMS *Jervis Bay*. Afterwards, *Admiral Scheer* refuelled from the supply ship *Nordmark*, and headed south, crossing the equator on 16 December 1940. She captured the refrigerated freighter *Duquesa*, which replenished the food stores of *Admiral Scheer*

The port side of pocket battleship *Admiral Scheer* with the unoccupied aircraft catapult visible on the extreme right. The two diagonal beams are cranes that were normally stowed along the side of the deck. Perhaps they are waiting to lift the aircraft back onto the catapult.

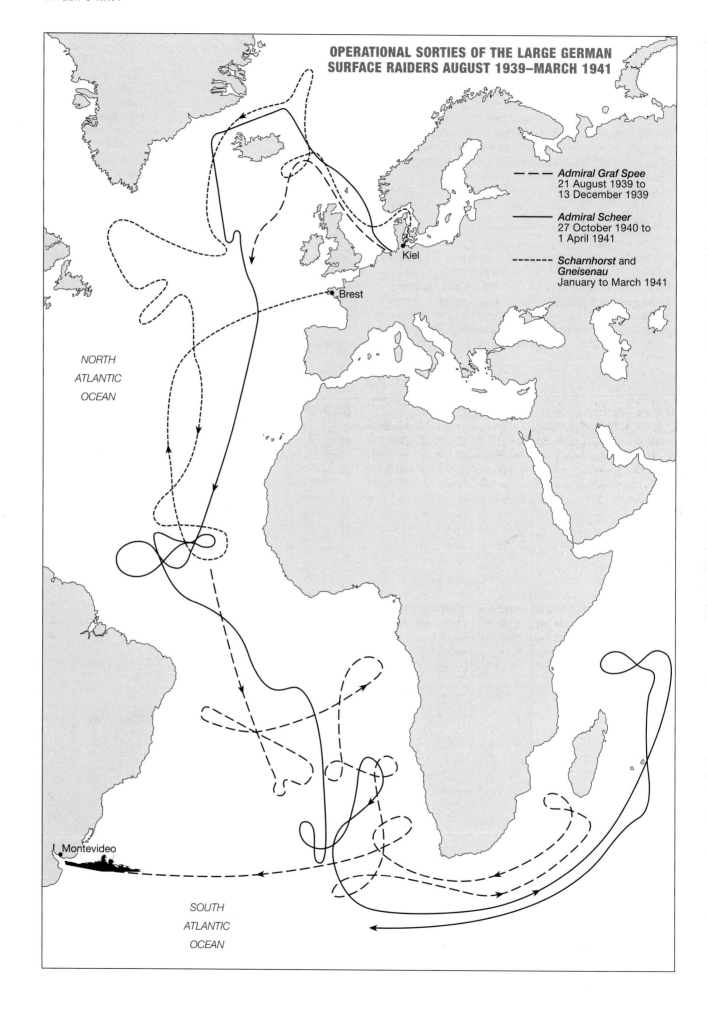

OPERATIONAL SORTIES OF THE LARGE GERMAN
SURFACE RAIDERS AUGUST 1939–MARCH 1941

– – –   *Admiral Graf Spee*
21 August 1939 to
13 December 1939

———   *Admiral Scheer*
27 October 1940 to
1 April 1941

- - - - -   *Scharnhorst* and
Gneisenau
January to March 1941

Kiel

Brest

NORTH

ATLANTIC

OCEAN

Montevideo

SOUTH

ATLANTIC

OCEAN

Pocket battleship *Admiral Graf Spee* exhibiting her stern anchor and emblem. The quadruple torpedo tubes can be made out below the row of standing men and the rangefinder is clearly visible.

Admiral Graf Spee seen from near the port bow with the main, triple 11in (280mm) gun turret swung sideways. The lower rectangular windows in the main control tower indicate the position of the captain's bridge. The four windows of the admiral's bridge are a feature of Spee – Scheer had only three. The rectangular shield with the name 'Coronel' is also a useful identification aid. This was where Admiral Maximilian Reichsgraf von Spee achieved victory before being killed at the Battle of the Falkland Islands in December 1914.

a reconnaissance aircraft from the British cruiser *Glasgow*, and a massive search operation was launched to engage the German pocket battleship. *Admiral Scheer* managed to dodge through the net of six cruisers and the aircraft carrier *Hermes* and, early in March 1941, she met up with the auxiliary cruisers *Kormoran* and *Pinguin*. She also rendezvoused with *U124*, under the command of Kptlt. Wilhelm Schulz, which had brought some vital spare parts for *Scheer's* radio. She then headed north, crossing the equator on 15 March 1941 and arriving in Bergen fifteen days later. During this successful cruise, she had sunk fourteen ships and one British auxiliary cruiser, and had captured two other ships.

After a complete overhaul, *Admiral Scheer* operated in the Baltic under the command of Kpt.z.S. Wilhelm Meendsen-Bohlken, who, towards the end of the war, was made Fleet Commander. There was no noteworthy action, and eventually the ship sailed to Trondheim, from where she continued up the coast to Narvik and joined a task force in search of convoy PQ17. She remained in the Arctic, near Bear Island, and after very little action she returned to Wilhelmshaven, passing through the Kiel Canal in November 1942.

After a refit, the ship came under the command of Fregkpt. Ernst Gruber, who had been the Communications Officer on the ill-fated *Blücher*. In February 1943, he was succeeded by Kpt.z.S. Richard Rothe-Roth, under whom *Admiral Scheer* served as a training ship in the eastern Baltic. From October 1944, when under the command of Kpt.z.S. Ernst Thienemann, she helped the Special Combat Units 'Rogge' and 'Thiele'. (These two units were created very hurriedly to help fight Russian forces in the East; they were named after their commanders, Bernhard Rogge of the legendary *Atlantis*, and August Thiele, who commanded the pocket battleship *Deutschland*, later renamed *Lützow*, shortly after the start of the war.) Towards the end of the war, *Admiral Scheer* headed west from Pillau, laden with a thousand refugees and wounded, bound for Kiel. There she was bombed and capsized on 9/10 April 1945.

ADMIRAL GRAF SPEE

This famous pocket battleship left Wilhelmshaven in August 1939, shortly before the outbreak of war. She remained in an isolated part of the South Atlantic until the end of September, when her commander, Kpt.z.S. Hans Langsdorff, was given orders to attack merchant shipping. This resulted in a relatively successful campaign, during which she sank nine merchant ships amounting to over 50,000 GRT.

The Battle of the River Plate began on 13 December, when *Graf Spee* came into contact with British cruisers. After a brief engagement, she put into the neutral South American port of Montevideo, where it was hoped some of the damage could be repaired. However, the Germans thought the town to be blockaded by superior British forces and, at 1815 on 17 December 1939, *Graf Spee* left Montevideo to be scuttled an hour later in the shallow waters of La Plata estuary. Langsdorff committed suicide and some of his crew remained in South America; only a few managed to escape back to Germany. Today, the wreck of *Admiral Graf Spee* can still be seen above the waterline, and one of her anchors lies in the town, forming a memorial to the Battle of the River Plate.

plus those of the raiders *Thor* and *Pinguin* and the supply ship *Nordmark*. All these ships met up on Boxing Day 1940 to exchange Christmas greetings.

Admiral Scheer continued on her own and managed to capture another ship – this time the Norwegian tanker *Sandefjord* which was taken to France by a prize crew. There was another meeting with *Nordmark* and, later, with the auxiliary cruiser *Atlantis*, commanded by Bernhard Rogge. Two other captured ships, *Speybank* and *Ketty Brovig*, were also present at this gathering on the high seas, plus the blockade-breaker *Tannenfels*.

Admiral Scheer then moved off on her own to operate in the Indian Ocean, off Mozambique, where she received orders to return home. On her way back, she was sighted by

HEAVY CRUISERS

ADMIRAL HIPPER

Admiral Hipper was undergoing a refit when war broke out. Trials lasted until the latter half of January 1940, and she was not ready for action until the end of that month.

In February 1940, *Hipper* sailed – under the command of Kpt.z.S. Hellmuth Heye – into the North Sea to operate with the battleships *Gneisenau* and *Scharnhorst*. Two months later she took part in the invasion of Norway, carrying mountain troops from Cuxhaven to Trondheim. During this voyage, *Hipper* was attacked by the destroyer HMS *Glowworm*. Both ships collided, causing *Hipper* to take on water and *Glowworm* to sink. The troops were then unloaded and the ship returned to Wilhelmshaven for repairs, after which *Admiral Hipper* operated in Norwegian, Arctic and Icelandic waters, only returning to Wilhelmshaven in autumn 1940. Heye was replaced as commander by Wilhelm Meisel, who tried to take the heavy cruiser to France via Norway and the Denmark Strait, but engine failure forced their return, and it was December before Meisel finally managed to get *Hipper* through the narrow gap between Iceland and Greenland. They finally arrived in Brest towards the end of January 1941. By the end of April, *Hipper* was back in Germany, where she remained in dock for the rest of the year.

During mid-March 1942, the ship moved to Trondheim, where she anchored next to the battleship *Tirpitz*. She remained in northern waters and, at the end of 1942, took part in the action against convoy JW51B. (It was the outcome of this operation that prompted Hitler's threat to 'throw the surface fleet into the dustbin'.) Kpt.z.S. Hans Hartmann replaced Meisel as commander of *Hipper* in February 1942. Hipper returned to Germany, accompanied by the light cruiser *Köln*, at the end of March 1943. She was decommis-

Admiral Hipper's impressive bows and her 8in (203mm) main armament. There was an option of having an open bridge around an armoured forward control centre with large optical range finder.

Heavy cruiser *Admiral Hipper* in her dark grey wartime colour. Although pocket battleships were later reclassed as heavy cruisers, there was a stark difference in the performance of these two classes, especially in the distance they could cover. Germany never managed to get the high-pressure steam turbines in cruisers to work efficiently, which inevitably influenced operations at sea. Note that both of the domes visible by the bridge and the rear mast appear to have a solid top and are situated on a solid-looking tube to indicate that they contain anti-aircraft rangefinders.

Prinz Eugen passing close to the torpedo boat *T21*. In the foreground is a nest for a 37mm semi-automatic anti-aircraft gun. Some shells for this gun can be made out lying in clips of four on top of the white box. One of the turrets has been elevated and shows the high angle at which it could still be fired.

and sank shortly before 0730 on the morning of 9 April. On this ill-fated operation, *Blücher* had been carrying Hermann Boehm, the Commanding Admiral for Norway designate, and the commander of her task force, Konteradmiral Oskar Kummetz, who had to move over to the heavy cruiser *Lützow* (ex-*Deutschland*). *Blücher*'s commander, Kpt.z.S. Heinrich Woldag, only outlived his ship by a few days, for on 17 April he was killed in an air crash.

PRINZ EUGEN

In many ways *Prinz Eugen* was an unlucky ship. First, she was damaged by bombs in Kiel before being commissioned and then, during her shakedown cruise, she ran onto a mine. After repairs, she left Gotenhafen on 18 May 1941, calling at Bergen before successfully breaking out into the Atlantic with the battleship *Bismarck*. *Prinz Eugen* took part in the action against the British battleships *Hood* and *Prince of Wales* and the cruisers *Norfolk* and *Suffolk*. Although *Bismarck* is credited with sinking *Hood*, German eye-witness accounts suggest that *Prinz Eugen* landed the first shells.

After this action, *Prinz Eugen* was dismissed by the Fleet Commander aboard *Bismarck*, and she sailed towards the South Atlantic to operate on her own. She appeared to have started her first lucky spell but, after refuelling from a supply ship, she developed engine trouble and had to return to port. *Prinz Eugen* arrived in Brest on 1 June 1941, only to suffer the torment suffered by all the German surface fleet stationed in France – being bombed by the RAF.

Six months later, *Prinz Eugen* took part in the 'Channel Dash', ending up at Trondheim, where she was torpedoed by HM Submarine *Trident*, causing considerable damage to the stern. Emergency repairs kept her afloat, and the heavy cruiser managed to limp back to Kiel under her own steam. She was in dock until October 1942, and thenceforward remained in German waters until the end of the war. *Prinz Eugen* was used as a training ship and, later, as an experimental vessel for testing new apparatus and weapons. She next saw action in June 1944, providing support for the Army against the Russians. On 15 October 1944, while travelling at twenty knots, she accidentally rammed the light cruiser *Leipzig*, a well documented event, for there was ample time to take photographs during the fourteen hours that the two ships remained locked together.

With repairs completed, *Prinz Eugen* left Swinemünde during April 1945 and made for Copenhagen, where she remained until after the cease-fire, when she was moved to Wesermünde. *Prinz Eugen* left Europe for Boston (USA) on 13 January 1946, arriving there on 22 January. She was damaged during the atom bomb tests at Bikini Atoll but, unlike some other warships; she remained afloat, and was anchored at Kwajalein Atoll until November 1947 when she was scrapped.

Prinz Eugen had four different commanders. Kpt.z.S. Helmuth Brinkmann commissioned her on 1 August 1940 and remained in charge for two years. He then became Chief of Staff at the Naval Group Command South, and was replaced by Kpt.z.S. Hans-Erich Voss, who remained in office until February 1943, when he was made Permanent Naval Representative at Hitler's headquarters. Werner Eckhardt took command from March 1943 until January 1944, when he was succeeded by Hans-Jürgen Reinicke.

sioned on 1 April 1943. At that time she was temporarily under the command of her First Officer, Kpt.z.S. Krauss. A year later she was recommissioned by Kpt.z.S. Hans Hengist, who had previously commanded the light cruiser *Emden*. However, *Hipper* was not fully operational and was only used for training purposes. At the end of the war, Hengist took his ship to Gotenhafen in the eastern Baltic, where he picked up one and a half thousand refugees and took them to Kiel. There, *Hipper* was immobilized by bombs and, on 3 May 1945, she was scuttled.

BLÜCHER

Blücher's first war operation was also her last. She left Swinemünde in April 1940 to take part in Operation Weserübung (the invasion of Norway and Denmark), and arrived off the coast of Norway without any noteworthy incidents. However, while trying to reach the Norwegian capital, she was seriously damaged by shore batteries in Oslo Fjord

LIGHT CRUISERS

EMDEN

Named after the famous First World War cruiser, *Emden* was the first large ship to be built for the Reichsmarine, with a design based on that of a promising cruiser from the Imperial Navy. Her armament came well within the limits of the Versailles Treaty, thus making it inadequate for modern warfare; but, although it had been designed with a view to increasing her firepower later, such a refit was never carried out and, as a result, *Emden* did not see much action during the war.

She was originally commissioned on 15 October 1925. Later, she was completely withdrawn from service for a lengthy overhaul until September 1934, when Karl Dönitz recommissioned her with a completely new crew. *Emden* then went on a long ambassadorial tour to the Far East. Although used as a training ship for most of her remaining life she did see a few brief periods of operational service including participation in the Norwegian Campaign of spring 1940, and her meagre armament was used to bombard shore batteries during the invasion of Russia in 1941. However her apparently uninteresting war service came to a dramatic climax during the winter of 1944/45 while she was undergoing a refit in Königsberg. After a great deal of her machinery, including parts of her engines, had been dismantled and taken ashore, thus leaving the ship partly immobilized, her commander (Kpt.z.S. Wolfgang Kähler) received orders to put to sea at once, to avoid being overrun by the advancing Russians. After instructing his men to gather as many replacement parts as possible Kähler managed to get the ship underway. *Emden* slowly crawled out to sea, laden with about a thousand refugees, including the stone coffin of Field Marshal Paul von Hindenburg, accompanied by his widow. The old ship made her way west at a painfully slow speed, but she reached Kiel where she was beached. *Emden* was eventually blown up by German forces shortly before British troops arrived. (Wolfgang Kähler, *Emden*'s commander, should not be confused with Otto Kähler, who commanded the auxiliary cruiser *Thor*.)

Emden held several records, besides that of being the first large warship of the Hitler era. First, members of her crew

Emden is seen here with the Iron Cross of the First World War, as well as the Emden coat of arms by the anchor.

were the first casualties of the German Navy to be sustained aboard ship in the Second World War. During an air attack while the ship was lying at anchor in the estuary of the River Jade, one of the aircraft was shot down and crashed onto *Emden*'s deck killing several men. Secondly, she must be the only German ship to have had one of her crew eaten by a lion! At least, one man disappeared while on the Far East tour, and a rather satisfied lion was the only plausible explanation. Thirdly, *Emden* was the last warship upon which Grand Admiral Raeder set foot as Supreme Commander-in-Chief of the Navy.

KARLSRUHE

Karlsruhe was undergoing a refit when the war began, and was not recommissioned until November 1939. She then underwent several trials before taking part in the invasion of Norway. On 9 April 1940, the British submarine *Truant* torpedoed her, putting paid to both engines and rudder, as well

The light cruiser *Karlsruhe*. A significant feature of these light cruisers was the 'well' in the deck by the foremost funnel to accommodate a set of torpedo tubes. The supporting offices were fitted behind or below the bridge, rather than inside a dominant control tower as found on larger ships.

Light cruiser *Köln* rolling at sea. The class suffered from stability problems that kept them confined to home waters, while the high percentage of welded joints – intended to keep down the weight – led to stress damage at sea, further reducing their cruising grounds. The inscription on the photograph of the hapless seasick sailor reads, 'This happens as well.'

This view of the *Köln* from astern clearly shows how the rear turrets of these cruisers were pushed as far to the sides as possible in order to give them the maximum angle for forward fire. The off-centre arrangement also helped with the engine-room layout. *Köln* is rolling badly in what appears to be a moderate sea.

until returning to the Baltic in the spring of 1943. Then she was decommissioned before being towed to Königsberg for a refit. In October/November 1944 she returned to operate in the waters around Denmark and Norway, as flagship for the Flag Officer for Destroyers. On the last day of 1944, *Köln* was put out of action by bombs; emergency repairs were carried out in Oslo, before she returned to Wilhelmshaven. Once there, she was subjected to further air attacks, which rendered her completely unseaworthy. However, some of her guns remained above the water and were used to bombard enemy troops after she was finally decommissioned on 5 April 1945.

KÖNIGSBERG

While being used by the Artillery Inspectorate before the war, Königsberg had a revolutionary new radio rangefinder (i.e., a radar set) installed on her forward gun turret. This efficient device differed slightly from British radar inasmuch that it was designed for use as an artillery rangefinder after the target had been sighted. *Königsberg*, under command of Kpt.z.S. Kurt Caesar Hoffmann, was operating off the Polish coast at the end of August 1939. On the day before the outbreak of war, she encountered two Polish destroyers: nerves on both sides must have been rather tense as the destroyers trained their torpedo tubes on *Königsberg*, which had her guns aimed at the destroyers. However, nothing developed from this 'sabre rattling', and the three ships parted company peacefully.

On 10 April 1940, whilst taking part in the Norwegian Campaign, *Königsberg* was sunk by three dive-bombers. Her wreck remained off Bergen until 1943, when it was raised and scrapped. Her commander, Kpt.z.S. Heinrich Rufus (who had relieved Hoffmann of command in September 1939) was understandably distressed at her loss, because she had been the second ship to sink under him, although on neither occasion had he been at fault: before the war, Rufus commanded the sail training ship *Niobe* until she capsized in a strong squall off the Island of Fehmarn.

LEIPZIG

Leipzig was torpedoed by HM Submarine *Salmon* in mid-December 1939, while laying mines off Newcastle. Heinz Nordmann, her commander managed to take her back across the North Sea, but she was attacked by another submarine, HMS *Ursula*, en route. The lookouts aboard *Leipzig* spotted the submarine and fired a salvo of torpedoes towards her, but these missed and the submarine went on to sink a German escort. *Leipzig* was repaired and, at the same time converted to a training ship. Some of her damaged boilers were removed to provide extra space for accommodation.

Shortly after leaving Gotenhafen on 15 October 1944, *Leipzig* was involved in a dramatic collision with the heavy cruiser *Prinz Eugen*. This happened some distance out, after she had stopped to change from diesel propulsion on the middle shaft to turbines on the two outer propeller shafts. This was quite a complicated procedure, usually taking at least twenty minutes; in the process, *Leipzig* drifted into bad weather and also into the wrong shipping lane – right in the path of *Prinz Eugen*. The resulting collision tore a deep hole in *Leipzig*, effectively putting her out of action for the rest of the war. However, her guns remained in use, and were used against the Russian Army. After the war, she was moved to

as most of her electrical equipment. Torpedo-boats then took off her crew and, at 2250 hours, *Karlsruhe* was sunk off Kristiansand by two torpedoes from the torpedo-boat *Greif*. *Karlsruhe*'s commander was Kpt.z.S. Friedrich Rieve.

KÖLN

At the start of the war, *Köln* served in the Baltic off Norway. She became the flagship to Commander-in-Chief Reconnaissance Forces, seeing service in the North Sea. Later, in spring 1940, she took part in the Norwegian Campaign and the invasion of Russia. She sailed to Narvik via Oslo during August 1942, and remained in these northern waters

LEFT The man is sitting on the port capstan, used for weighing anchor, the chain of which can be seen running towards the camera. In this case it is easy to identify the ship because the name (*Leipzig*) is engraved on the placards above the bridge windows. The one left (starboard side) also has the date 8.12.1914 and the name 'Falkland' – when the First World War ship with this name was sunk with a loss of 315 lives. The right hand placard refers to the battle at Coronel on 1.11.1914, where the German Naval Squadron, under Admiral Maximilian Reichsgraf von Spee, had one of its major victories.

ABOVE *Königsberg* was used for artillery training before the war and, at that time, had one of the first working radar sets fitted on top of the forward turret. It functioned well until the violent vibrations from the first salvo damaged the delicate glass valves and put the device out of action. It was also useful as a navigation aid, allowing the ship in and out of Wilhelmshaven during the thickest of fogs, when other ships could not move through the narrow channel. Karl Dönitz, the U-boat chief, was on board in 1938 but showed no interest in this invention and apparently did not even take up an offer to see it in action.

BELOW The guns of the light cruiser *Leipzig* with two torpedo boats following. The two triple turrets are the main armament, of 150mm, while the other gun is the multi-purpose, double-barrelled 88mm gun, although only one barrel is visible.

Nürnberg showing the typical light cruiser silhouette with the 'well' for torpedo tubes just forward of the funnel.

Wilhelmshaven, where the Allies filled her with outdated gas ammunition and, on 16 December 1946, scuttled her in the North Sea. She now presents a major ecological hazard.

NÜRNBERG

At the start of the war, *Nürnberg* served as flagship to the Commander-in-Chief Reconnaissance Forces. She was hit by a torpedo from the British submarine *Salmon* at about the same time that this submarine scored a hit on *Leipzig* (mid-December 1939). She was out of action undergoing repair until the summer of 1940, when she went north to serve in the Arctic seas. In August 1940, *Nürnberg* returned to Germany. She remained in home waters until November 1942, when she returned to Norway. *Nürnberg* was in

Wilhelmshaven at the end of the war, under the command of Kpt.z.S. Helmuth Giessler; after the cessation of hostilities, she was handed over to the Russian Navy, who then commissioned her under the name of *Admiral Makarov*.

OLD BATTLESHIPS

SCHLESWIG-HOLSTEIN AND SCHLESIEN

These veteran pre-dreadnoughts saw action at the Battle of Jutland in the First World War, and they both saw action during the Second World War. *Schleswig-Holstein* fired the first shots of the war at sea when she opened the bombardment of the Polish-held Westerplatte (a narrow spit of land between

Schleswig-Holstein, one of the old battleships left over from the First World War. The ship was launched in 1906 and took part in the Battle of Jutland. It served the German Navy faithfully until the end of March 1945 when it was destroyed by bombs. The long name was a bit of a mouthful and the ship was usually referred to as 'Sophie X' after its call sign of 'SX'.

the mainland and the open Baltic) near Danzig. The reason for the bombardment was to destroy fortifications erected with French support. Although both ships were used during the invasion of Norway and Denmark, for most of the war they served as training or accommodation ships and, occasionally, as icebreakers.

Schlesien saw active service again during the Battle of Gotenhafen in March/April 1945, when she ferried numerous refugees as far as Swinemünde; there she was scuttled on 4 May 1945.

Schleswig-Holstein was sunk by bombs on 19 December 1944. She went down on an even keel in shallow water in Gotenhafen. Her guns remained in use for some time, but a serious fire finally put her out of action completely. Her flags were lowered for the last time on 25 January 1945.

DESTROYERS

The German Navy used the term 'Zerstörer' (destroyer) somewhat differently from their British counterparts: German torpedo-boats of the First World War were large enough to act as destroyers and the first destroyers built after that war were very much larger than their British equivalents.

Destroyers were used during the Polish Campaign to line mine barrages near the German coast and later for mining British sea lanes. These mining operations were certainly the most important carried out by German destroyers during the first winter of war. Great care was taken to give the impression that the mines were the result of U-boat activities to prevent the Royal Navy from searching for surface ships close to her shores.

Two German destroyers were indirectly sunk by the German Luftwaffe during the first winter of war. This happened on 22 February 1940 when Kpt.z.S. und Kommodore Friedrich Bonte sailed to the Dogger Bank area with the 1st Destroyer Flotilla. Somehow aircrews were not informed and the flotilla was attacked. *Leberecht Maass*, commanded by Korvkpt. Fritz Bassenge, received a direct hit, which exploded inside her small launch. This saved the rest of the ship, but shortly afterwards the destroyer ran onto a mine laid by a British submarine in a German mine-free area. *Max Schultz*, commanded by Korvkpt. Claus Trampedach, suffered a similar fate during the same attack. She too ran onto a mine while trying to avoid an onslaught from the German Luftwaffe. Both commanders and most of the crews were lost.

Almost all available destroyers, as well as other small craft, were used during the invasion of Norway and Denmark – so many in fact, that at one time there were hardly any ships left in German waters. The Norwegian fjords became a bloody battleground for destroyers; although it was a successful campaign overall, Germany lost many of her small fighting ships during the confused fighting. As a result the destroyer arm had to be drastically re-organised.

After the Norwegian Campaign, destroyers dealt with a variety of tasks over a wide operational area. After the Polish Campaign of 1939, there were virtually no destroyers in the Baltic until the end of 1944, when the 6th Flotilla was sent east for security and mining operations.

The main operation areas for destroyers were as follows:

+ Sunk in operation area
* Moved to another area, but sunk before the end of the war
• Sunk near Narvik during the invasion of Norway in April 1940

No symbol indicates that the boat survived the war

This photograph, taken in Norway, shows the effectiveness of camouflage schemes. The destroyer, moving at speed, was photographed from *Z24*.

The Polish Campaign, 1939
Z1*, Z8*, Z9*, Z11*, Z14, Z15, Z16*

Norwegian waters
Z2+•, Z6*, Z8*, Z9+•, Z10, Z11+•, Z12+•, Z13+•, Z15, Z16*, Z17+•, Z18+•, Z19+•, Z20*, Z21+•, Z22+•

Arctic/Northern Seas
Z4, Z6, Z7*, Z10, Z14, Z15, Z16+, Z20, Z23*, Z24*, Z25, Z26+, Z27*, Z28*, Z29, Z30, Z31, Z33, Z34, Z38

Skagerrak
Z4, Z6, Z14, Z20

North Sea
Z3+, Z4, Z6, Z8*, Z9*, Z10, Z11*, Z12*, Z13*, Z14, Z15, Z16*, Z17*, Z18*, Z19*, Z20, Z21*, Z22*, Z34+

Western France (English Channel and French Atlantic Coast)
Z4, Z5, Z6, Z7*, Z8+, Z10, Z14, Z15, Z16*, Z20, Z23+, Z24+, Z27+, Z32+, Z37+, ZH1+

The Baltic, late 1944
Z5, Z10, Z20, Z25, Z28, Z31, Z34+, Z35*, Z36+, Z39, Z43+

AUXILIARY CRUISERS

Auxiliary cruisers were sent to sea with the main aim of tying up enemy forces and diverting naval ships away from the main theatre of war.

ATLANTIS

In March 1940, *Atlantis*, the first auxiliary cruiser of the Second World War, left German waters disguised as a Russian freighter. Shortly before she was permitted to start aggressive action, on 29 April 1940, her appearance was changed to resemble that of a Japanese ship. Four days later, she bagged her first victim in the still bustling shipping lanes between Cape Town and Freetown. *Atlantis* kept to the shipping lanes and sailed south, eventually laying mines near Cape Agulhas, the most southerly point of Africa. After completing this operation, on 10 May, she changed her identity to that of a Dutch ship, and sailed into the Indian Ocean, which remained her hunting ground for the rest of the year. In December 1940, she met up with the auxiliary cruiser *Pinguin* and her prize, the tanker *Storstad*. *Atlantis* then sailed on to the Kerguelen Islands for a general overhaul of her machinery and to replenish her fresh water supplies.

At the end of January 1941, *Atlantis* encountered the pocket battleship *Admiral Scheer*, which passed within a few hundred yards of the raider, and in April she met the auxiliary cruiser *Kormoran*. Another, far more dramatic meeting took place in the South Atlantic in mid-May, when *Atlantis*

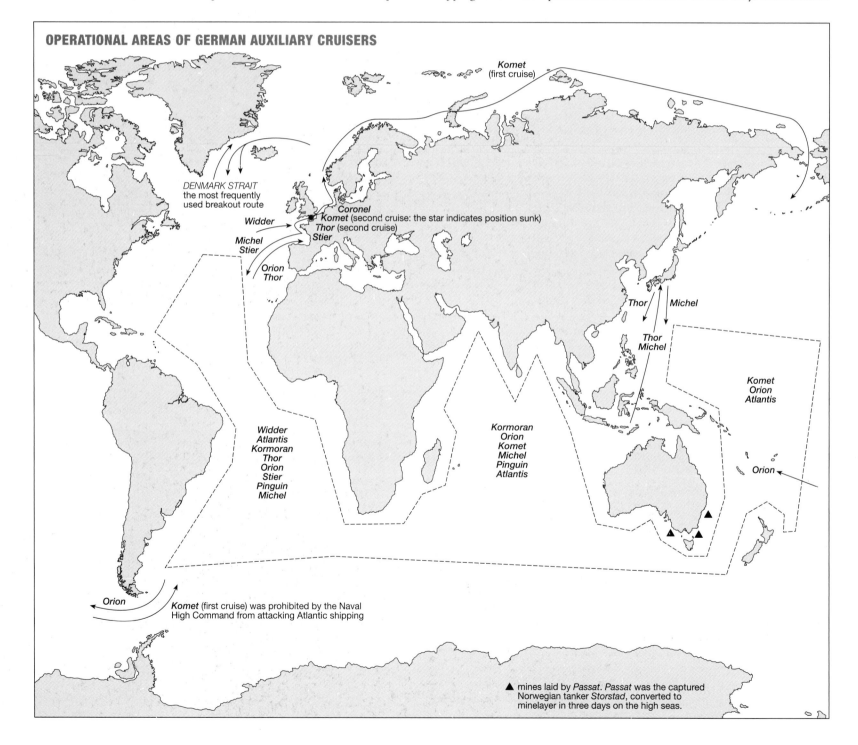

OPERATIONAL AREAS OF GERMAN AUXILIARY CRUISERS

Komet (first cruise)

DENMARK STRAIT the most frequently used breakout route

Widder

Michel Stier

Orion Thor

Coronel
Komet (second cruise: the star indicates position sunk)
Thor (second cruise)
Stier

Thor   *Michel*

Thor Michel

Komet Orion Atlantis

Widder Atlantis Kormoran Thor Orion Stier Pinguin Michel

Kormoran Orion Komet Michel Pinguin Atlantis

Orion

Orion

Komet (first cruise) was prohibited by the Naval High Command from attacking Atlantic shipping

▲ mines laid by *Passat*. *Passat* was the captured Norwegian tanker *Storstad*, converted to minelayer in three days on the high seas.

was suddenly surprised by the aircraft carrier HMS *Eagle* and the battleship HMS *Nelson*. Either the two warships did not spot *Atlantis* in the darkness or the four and a half miles between them was sufficient to deceive the Royal Navy, for she was not challenged. In such situations, the auxiliary cruiser had to rely completely on her disguise, because her armament was barely sufficient to take on even a small cruiser. Meanwhile, further problems were brewing on the high seas, because the supply ship *Babitonga* had been sunk by a British cruiser. As a result, the auxiliary cruiser *Orion* had almost run out of fuel, and Bernhard Rogge (commander of *Atlantis*) had no choice other than to hand over some of his 'liquid gold'. This meeting took place on 1 July, after which *Orion* headed for home and *Atlantis* continued hunting in southern waters. Another supply ship, *Münsterland*, reached *Atlantis* and the auxiliary cruiser *Komet* in mid-September 1941.

At about this time, *Atlantis* received orders to cease operating as an auxiliary cruiser and to concentrate on supplying U-boats, which were starting operations in the southern seas. By this time, however, it was possible for Royal Navy intelligence to understand a fair proportion of the Germans' secret radio code, and the heavy cruiser HMS *Devonshire* was dispatched to intercept a German refuelling rendezvous. *U68*, commanded by Korvkpt. Karl-Friedrich Merten, and *U126*, commanded by Kptlt. Ernst Bauer, had just been supplied some 470 miles north-west of Ascension Island when the cruiser appeared. *U68* saw the ensuing action, but was too far away to help, and *U126* dived very quickly. The commander of *U126* was aboard *Atlantis* when *Devonshire* appeared, and the boat dived without him. Once submerged with no commander (who was the only person in the submarine trained to carry out an attack) and untrimmed because of the newly loaded stores, *U126* was no threat to the British cruiser. *Atlantis* was scuttled and abandoned while under fire from *Devonshire*, but Rogge and a large proportion of the crew were picked up by the two U-boats. Later, these survivors were taken aboard the supply ship *Python*, but she was sunk and another rescue operation had to be mounted to bring the men back to France. When *Atlantis* was scuttled, she had been at sea for 622 days without putting into port and had covered some 112,500 miles.

The raider code was never broken by Bletchley Park in England, but Britain obtained the positions of raiders because they were transmitted to submarines using the U-boat code. It is often thought that *Atlantis* went down with guns ablaze, which is not the case. Bernhard Rogge knew retaliation was pointless and decided it would be better if the enemy thought they might have sunk an innocent merchant ship, rather than an armed cruiser.

On 11 November 1940 *Atlantis* had captured the 7528 GRT freighter *Automedon*, which was a significant event because highly secret and important British papers were taken from the ship that provided impetus for the Japanese attack on Pearl Harbor. This event is well covered in the book *Mrs Ferguson's Tea-Set* by Eiji Seki, but the significance of the action is still largely unknown. The master of the *Automedon* was given several boxes of confidential documents for locking in the ship's strong room and more material, so secret that it was sewn into lead-weighted bags. The instructions were to leave these in his desk on the bridge and to throw them over-

board if there was a danger of the enemy boarding the ship. When *Atlantis* put her first shot across the bows to stop the *Automedon*, the master ordered full speed ahead and immediately sent distress signals with his call sign GBZR. As a result the second salvo, aimed at the radio room, wiped out the entire bridge, instantly killing all the officers there. Consequently there was no one left who knew about the highly sensitive mail in the desk and it fell into German hands. It was then taken to the German Naval Attaché in Tokyo and provided the Japanese with information to formulate their attack on the United States.

CORONEL

Coronel was used as a minelayer before being converted to an auxiliary cruiser during the winter of 1941/42. She underwent trials and, during January 1943, tried to break out into the Atlantic. She sailed from the central Baltic around Denmark and stopped near the island of Sylt for four days, before heading south through the English Channel. But luck was not on her side: one of the escorts hit a mine and *Coronel* twice ran aground. This caused considerable delay, making it impossible for her to pass through the Strait of Dover under cover of darkness, so she remained in Dunkirk until the next night. *Coronel* left Dunkirk on the night of 8 February 1943, when she came under attack from British forces and was forced to go back to Dunkirk for repairs. *Coronel* was then ordered back to Germany, where she was refitted as an auxiliary minesweeper and served as such in the Baltic.

HANSA

In 1940 this ship was under construction for the Glen Line in Copenhagen when it was commandeered by the Germans. *Hansa* was first employed in the Baltic as a target ship for U-boat training and only later fitted out as an auxiliary cruiser. Most of this work was done in Rotterdam, with only the armament and the finer details being added in Hamburg. However, this was never completed because the ship was damaged during an air raid, and conversion plans were therefore scrapped. The ship was subsequently used for target practice and training in the Baltic.

KOMET

Komet, the smallest German auxiliary cruiser, was fitted with specially strengthened bows to negotiate polar pack ice, and undertook one of the most dramatic voyages of the Second World War. Leaving Gotenhafen, in the eastern Baltic, she called at Bergen in Norway on 9 July 1940, and then sailed around the North Cape to go through the Siberian sea passage into the Pacific Ocean. *Komet* crossed the Kara Sea with the help of two Russian icebreakers, *Stalin* and *Lenin*. A third icebreaker later took over, but proved too slow. Diplomatic relations were also rapidly deteriorating between Russia and Germany, so the auxiliary cruiser continued alone on the three and a half thousand mile voyage, arriving in the Bering Strait (between Russia and America) on 5 September 1940. A good quarter of this distance had been made more difficult by thick ice. Her Russian icebreaker escorts remained stuck in ice for several months until the thaw of the following spring.

Komet then sailed south into warmer waters to meet the supply ship *Kulmerland*, which had sailed from Japan. They were joined by the auxiliary cruiser *Orion* and also by another supply ship *Regensburg*. *Komet* and *Orion* then operated together for a short period.

Komet's first success against enemy shipping came on 25 November 1940, when she sank the New Zealand ship *Holmwood*. *Komet* then called at Nauru Island, north-east of Australia, during the last days of 1940, to set prisoners ashore. (Another part of the island group was later bombarded by *Orion*; the ships had parted company by this time and were operating separately.)

All German auxiliary cruisers, despite having a fairly free hand, were under the direct control of the Naval High Command, who instructed *Komet* to meet *Pinguin* and supply ships before heading south to look for whaling ships. *Komet* did not remain long in whaling waters before being instructed to head for home, with strict orders to avoid further conflict. She went to France, sailed up the English Channel and eventually arrived in Hamburg after 516 days at sea. All this time she had been under the command of Vizeadmiral Robert Eyssen. It would appear that Eyssen was the only auxiliary cruiser commander who volunteered for the job instead of having been selected for an especially difficult command by the Naval War Staff.

Komet did not manage to break out into the Atlantic for a second time. On 14 October 1942, she came under attack from the Royal Navy's *MTB236*, and was sunk near Cape de la Hague. Her last commander, Kpt.z.S. Ulrich Brocksien, went down with his ship.

KORMORAN

Kormoran left Gotenhafen on 3 December 1940 under the command of Fregkpt. Theodor Detmers and passed into the South Atlantic through the Denmark Strait. A meeting with *U124*, commanded by Kptlt. Wilhelm Schulz, took place during early March (when a considerable volume of cargo was passed from the U-boat to the cruiser). *Kormoran* had been experiencing problems with her radar, and this equipment was later dismantled and given to the heavy cruiser *Admiral Scheer* to take back. (These radar sets were not used for locating enemy ships, as in the Royal Navy, but more as artillery rangefinders after the target had been sighted. Radar impulses could be picked up by the target long before there was a response on the German radar screen, so that poorly equipped auxiliary cruisers could accidentally give their presence away to superior enemy forces.) *Kormoran* supplied *U105*, commanded by Kptlt. Georg Schewe, and *U106*, commanded by Kptlt. Jürgen Oesten, with fuel and provisions before meeting the auxiliary cruiser *Atlantis* and passing into the Indian Ocean. She was supplied by the *Kulmerland* shortly before encountering the Australian cruiser *Sydney*. *Kormoran* played her disguised role to the last, managed to fool her adversary, get within range and sink the cruiser after a short duel. HMAS *Sydney* also landed four hits on *Kormoran*, one of which exploded in the engine room, causing considerable damage. Over seventy of the crew were killed and the ship had to be scuttled, bringing her voyage of 350 days to an end. Most of the survivors managed to reach the Australian mainland.

MICHEL

This ship was originally commandeered by the Naval High Command with a view to fitting it out as a hospital ship, and only much later was it considered for conversion to auxiliary cruiser. *Michel* left Germany on 9 March 1942 and passed through the Strait of Dover during the night of 13/14 March. Then she sailed into the South Atlantic, where she had her first success on 19 April 1942, sinking the 7,000-ton motortanker *Patella*, which was loaded with oil. The raider carried a small motor torpedo-boat (*LS4*) – in addition to the usual antiquated armament – which was first used against the enemy on 22 April 1942, when the merchant ship *Connecticut* was stopped and sunk.

Michel met the auxiliary cruiser *Stier* on 29 July, and then operated alone until she was ordered home in January 1943. But the presence of several Allied ships near the French coast prompted the Naval High Command to reconsider their decision, and *Michel* was instructed to make for Japan. She called at Djakarta and Singapore before arriving at Kobe, where she was refitted from 2 March to 21 May 1943. On 4 June 1943, *Michel* set sail on her second cruise from Yokohama, by which time she was the only German auxiliary cruiser left on the high seas. But her days were numbered. On 17 October 1943, she was sunk by the United States submarine *Tarpon*.

Michel's first commander had been Kpt.z.S. Hellmuth von Ruckteschell. He was replaced by Kpt.z.S. Günther Gumprich, who commanded her from May 1943 until she was sunk.

ORION

Orion, the second auxiliary cruiser to leave Germany during the Second World War, sailed from Kiel on 30 March 1940. *Atlantis* was waiting for suitable conditions before breaking out into the South Atlantic via the Denmark Strait and, as the Naval High Command did not want to run the risk of two cruisers bumping into British forces at the same time, *Orion* was ordered to remain in coastal waters for another week, Eventually, on 6 April, she headed west disguised as the Dutch freighter *Beemsterdijk*.

Orion had not gone very far before the Naval High Command issued another revision of orders to her commander, Fregkpt. Kurt Weyher. Instead of heading straight for the Pacific, he was instructed to sink some merchant ships. The Germans hoped this would fool the Royal Navy into thinking that a pocket battleship was on the prowl, in which event they might draw some forces away from Norway, where Germany was anticipating a heavy sea battle during the invasion of that country. The auxiliary cruiser eventually passed Cape Horn on 27 May 1940, and she arrived off Auckland on 13 June to lay mines in the Hauraki Gulf. The most noteworthy victim of this enterprise was the freighter *Niagara*, which was carrying a vast hoard of gold ingots. Later, *Orion* arrived at Lamutrek Atoll to meet the supply ships *Kulmerland* and *Regensburg*, as well as the raider *Komet*. Afterwards, both auxiliary cruisers operated along the east coast of New Zealand. *Orion* eventually headed west, only to find herself in real difficulties; her designated supply ship had been sunk, she was low on fuel and her crew had not sighted a suitable ship – with fuel – to capture. In the end, *Atlantis* supplied sufficient 'liquid gold' to enable her to pass north through the Atlantic to France. She arrived there on 23 August 1941, having left Kiel some 511 days earlier. *Orion* went on to Germany, where she was converted to a

repair and workshop ship. In 1944, she was commissioned as the artillery training ship *Hektor*. Her end came on 4 May 1945, when she was bombed off Swinemünde by Allied aircraft.

PINGUIN

Pinguin – although not named until she was approaching the South Atlantic – left Gotenhafen on 15 June 1940, with some 350 mines below decks and a mining expert on the bridge. Kpt.z.S. Ernst-Felix Krüder, her commander, lived up to his reputation by capturing the Australian-bound Norwegian tanker *Storstad* and converting her into an auxiliary minelayer in three days. Renamed *Passat*, she was then taken along her planned route and was used to lay mines off Melbourne, Sydney and Adelaide. Afterwards, both ships met up again, with *Passat* acting as an additional set of eyes for *Pinguin*. Her name now changed back to *Storstad*, the tanker was sent back to Europe with a 'prize crew' and prisoners from *Pinguin* and *Atlantis*.

Pinguin sailed on into Antarctic waters and captured three whale factory ships plus their fleets of small hunters. She then headed north again into warmer waters, and met the heavy cruiser *Admiral Scheer*, which provided food, fuel and men to take the prize whaling ships back to Europe. Repairs to the engine room were carried out at the Kerguelen Islands in March 1941, during which time *Pinguin* was joined by *Komet*. Krüder then went on the prowl for another ship suitable for conversion to auxiliary minelayer, but his luck had run out. *Pinguin* crossed the bows of the heavy cruiser HMS *Cornwall* on 8 May 1941 – her 357th day at sea. One of

Cornwall's shells exploded among the remaining mines, detonating them and blowing *Pinguin* to smithereens.

STIER

Stier was taken over by the German Navy during November 1939 to be used as an icebreaker. The following summer, she was converted to a minelayer and employed as such in the Bay of Biscay until the latter half of 1941, when it was decided to refit her as an auxiliary cruiser. She eventually left Kiel early in May 1942 to pass through the Baltic-North Sea Canal and on to Rotterdam. At this stage, she was still known under her old identity of Sperrbrecher *171*. After arriving in the South Atlantic, *Stier* spent several weeks operating with the auxiliary cruiser *Michel*, and then headed south alone, reaching a point roughly half way between the Equator and the South Pole. The necessity to overhaul parts of her engines led *Stier* to explore the waters around Gough Island, but no suitable anchorage could be found and the repair attempt was abandoned. Instead, *Stier* took fuel from the supply ship *Charlotte Schliemann* and headed for Japan. On 27 September 1942 she engaged the US armed freighter *Stephen Hopkins* which, although eventually sunk, severely damaged *Stier*. So, after a total of 140 days at sea, she was abandoned and scuttled.

At the time *Stier* sank, *Michel* had been relatively close and had even picked up the ship's SOS; but her commander, not convinced by the signal and suspecting a trap, quickly sailed out of the area. Some of *Stier*'s crew were later picked up by the supply ship *Tannenfels*. (In order to understand the action taken by *Michel*'s commander, one should be aware of the

The *Santa Cruz* photographed before the war. This ship, belonging to the Oldenburg–Portugiesischen Dampfschiffahrts Reederei, was later converted into the raider *Thor*, which sailed on two highly successful voyages to far-off waters and tied up considerable Allied resources.

HMS *Carnarvon Castle* and, later, HMS *Voltaire*. *Thor* encountered the first of this trio, the 22,000-ton *Alcantara*, on 28 July 1940. In the ensuing skirmish, *Thor* was slightly damaged by two hits and broke off the action. She fared better against *Carnarvon Castle*: during this engagement, on 5 December 1940, *Thor* hit the British vessel many times and forced her to break off the action. *Thor* completed her 'round' of British auxiliary cruisers with a flourish when, on 4 April 1941, *Voltaire* sank under a barrage of artillery fire. *Thor* also met the heavy cruiser *Admiral Scheer* in the South Atlantic before returning to the Bay of Biscay during April 1941. The German raider reached Hamburg on 30 April 1941, ending a 329-day cruise, during which *Thor* had either sunk or captured 12 ships. She managed to break out into the South Atlantic from Kiel a second time on 30 November 1941 and sailed on to the Indian Ocean, eventually arriving in

Santa Cruz after conversion to auxiliary cruiser *Thor* with paint brushes hanging out to dry. Painting was one of the major occupations aboard raiders and even involved heeling the ship so that the waterline could be attended to.

extraordinary events that dictated it. Commanders of German auxiliary cruisers employed a great deal of cunning in catching their quarry, including sending false messages to Allied merchant ships persuading them to change course towards the predator. One such message had even been weighted and dropped onto a ship from a seaplane. The British ship's crew obeyed – not having noticed the swastika on the aeroplane! So, expecting to be treated in a like manner, raider commanders treated all signals with the utmost suspicion.)

THOR

Thor left Kiel early in June 1940 on what may well appear to have been a general inspection of British auxiliary cruisers, for she came into conflict with three of them: HMS *Alcantara*,

Yokohama on 9 October 1942. *Thor* was moored next to the supply ship *Uckermark* when an explosion and subsequent fire gutted both ships. *Thor*'s second voyage had lasted 321 days, during which time she had captured or sunk 10 ships.

WIDDER

Widder sailed from Cuxhaven on 5 May 1941 and, before breaking out into the central Atlantic, had a minor skirmish with HM Submarine *Clyde*. Engine trouble eventually forced her to make for France, where she arrived some 180 days after leaving Germany. But, despite the engine trouble, the voyage had not been a wasted one, for *Widder* had sunk 10 enemy ships. Afterwards, her commander, Kpt.z.S. Hellmuth von Ruckteschell, became commander of the auxiliary cruiser *Michel*.

SAIL TRAINING SHIPS

A tremendous shock wave echoed throughout Germany when the sail training ship *Niobe* sank off the Baltic island of Fehmarn on 26 July 1932, taking sixty-nine lives with her. Peacetime accidents of such magnitude were rare, and there had not been a similar disaster since 16 December 1900, when the training ship *Gneisenau* went down in a gale off Malaga for the loss of about a hundred lives. The loss of *Niobe* triggered off several reactions. The general public, in good Prussian tradition, needed a scapegoat, but the court martial found everybody, including the captain, completely innocent. *Niobe* was thought to have been uncapsizable, but nature had obviously been stronger than anticipated. In naval circles, there was a great debate about the future of sail training ships, which ended with the Navy determining to build better ships. As a result, a new design, *Gorch Fock*, was laid down at the Blohm & Voss shipyard in Hamburg. She was launched on 3 May 1933, and two similar vessels followed: *Horst Wessel* on 13 June 1936 and *Albert Leo Schlageter* on 30 October 1937. The quality of these ships can be assessed by the fact that they not only survived the war, but were still sailing the oceans long after the end of the war.

The sinking of *Niobe* had some far-reaching effects on naval history, for it deprived the German Navy of a whole year's intake of officer cadets, who were lost at a time when the Navy was starting to expand. Admiral Raeder, Supreme Commander-in-Chief of the Navy, wrote to Germany's civil shipping companies, requesting their best men to volunteer for the naval officer corps. It was by this route that many famous men joined the Navy, among them Günther Prien,

The sail training ship *Niobe*, seen here, began life as a Danish timber ship and was captured by a German submarine in 1916 and then purchased by the German Navy in 1922. She was converted from a four-masted schooner and served the Navy well as a training ships for cadets, until she foundered in a squall in the narrow Fehmarn Belt of the Baltic in 1932. Sixty-nine crew lost their lives. The U-boat commander Claus Korth (*U57* and *U93*) was one of the few to have survived the *Niobe* sinking. He happened to have been on deck when the ship capsized and was washed into the open sea.

Cadets doing knots and rope work on the *Horst Wessel*.

the hero of Scapa Flow, and 'Ajax' Bleichrodt, also one of the top U-boat commanders.

Horst Wessel went to the United States in May 1945 and, under the name of *Eagle*, continued sailing the major oceans. During the war, *Albert Leo Schlageter* ran onto a mine in the Baltic and had to be towed to Swinemünde; she was repaired after the war and went first to the United States, then to Brazil, and finally to Portugal. *Gorch Fock* was scuttled at Stralsund during May 1945; she was later salvaged by the Russians and renamed *Tovarisch*. The Federal German Navy's sail training ship *Gorch Fock*, which is similar to the original, was launched by Blohm & Voss at Hamburg in 1958. It has been stated that *Gorch Fock* was named after one of Hitler's early supporters, but, as the gentleman in question died long before the Nazi Party was founded, this is obviously untrue. In fact, Gorch Fock was a poet, whose real name was Johann Kienau. He went down with his ship, SMS *Wiesbaden*, on 31 May 1916 during the Battle of Jutland.

U-BOATS

In Germany, the different submarine classes were referred to as 'Types', which were identified by a number – usually written as a roman numeral. Numbers were designated to projects before they reached the drawing-board and, as many of the ideas were never considered for construction, some numbers did not appear. That is also the reason why boats were not launched in numerical order and why some numbers were missing. It is sometimes thought that the boats were numbered to confuse the Allies but the numbering simply reflected the project designations.

Each Type started as a basic design, and many of them were modified as time went on. Such modifications were distinguished by a letter after the number.

The most important of the German submarines was Type VIIC; more than 600 were commissioned, making it the largest class of submarine ever built. Throughout the war, they were used for a wide variety of duties, remaining in pro-

duction long after they became obsolete in 1943. Several of them were taken over by Allied navies after the war and used for active service until the end of the 1950s.

The other Type that played an important role in the Battle of the Atlantic was Type IX, which, although similar to Type VII, was considerably larger. These long-range vessels were also designed as 'flagships' for U-boat packs, the idea being that they would carry the task force commander, who would conduct the convoy battles at sea. The extra space enabled the boats to carry the additional staff and communications equipment necessary. However, such a system of command was hardly ever utilized, and most of the actions were led directly from U-boat headquarters on land, with the most senior U-boat commander usually taking command of the whole pack if and when conditions demanded it.

All existing operational U-boats became obsolete in 1942. They were to be replaced by electro-submarines, which were an interim measure until Walter's true submarines could be commissioned. There were two operational types: Type XXI,

An early Type VIIC boat. Construction of this type began in 1938 and the first boat was commissioned in 1940. Around 650 were built throughout the war. They were the workhorse of the North Atlantic and they continued to be built despite the development of more advanced submarines.

Loading a Type VIIC U-boat. The webbing over the top was a simple type of camouflage, Most of the crates would have been too large to fit through hatches and so emptied before being taken on board. Tins were often marked with numbers rather than words and had no paper labels which would have soon disintegrated in the wet conditions . The two gun platforms aft of the conning tower and a 37mm anti-aircraft gun indicate that this photo was taken during the latter part of the war.

Small, Type II coastal submarines moored at the Tirpitzquay of Kiel naval harbour on a rainy day. Mooring side by side like this was prohibited after the start of the war so as to avoid offering too large a target to enemy aircraft.

which was a large ocean-going boat to replace Type VII; and Type XXIII, which was a small coastal submarine to help fill the gap until bigger boats could be built.

U-BOAT TYPES IN COMMISSION DURING THE WAR

- Type IA: Ocean-going boats based on the design of the Turkish submarine *Gür*; only two boats, *U25* and *U26* were launched.
- Type II: Small coastal submarines based on the UBII Class of 1915, UF of 1918 and on the prototype *Vesikko*, which was built for Finland by the German Submarine Development Bureau; most of these were used for training during the war.
- Type VII: Ten experimental prototypes were launched between June and December 1936, based on the UBIII design of 1915/1916 and on the prototype *Vetehinen*, which had also been built for Finland before the Second World War.
- Type IX: Developed from the *U81* design of 1915, the first three versions (Types IXA, B and C) were

straightforward conventional submarines. Type IXD, however, was not planned as a fighting submarine, but rather as a long-distance cargo carrier, without torpedo tubes. Torpedo tubes were later added and another long-distance fighting version built as Type IXD2. These long-range boats could cover distances up to about 32,000 nautical miles and were used for voyages to the Far East. Once there, only the boats' defensive armament was retained and they took on cargo which was then ferried back to Europe.

- Type XB: Type XA, a design based on Type I, was not very successful and was never built, but the plans were modified to build a minelayer. These boats had a capacity of about 88 mines, but were often used as supply vessels for other fighting U-boats.
- Type XIV: These boats had no torpedo tubes, but were designed and built as supply submarines.
- Types XXI and XXIII: These were the electro-submarines, which only became operational shortly before the end of the war.

The minelayers of Type XB were the largest U-boats built in Germany during the Second World War and can be identified because they had a row of mineshafts along both sides of the pressure hull and another set in a raised section running through the bows. Most of these huge minelayers were used as supply submarines or for long-distance, cargo-carrying voyages to the Far East. For that reason they were fitted with pressure-resistant containers on top of the side mineshafts, as can be seen here. Mines could still drop out of the bottom, but the containers would need to be removed before the tubes could be loaded from the top. The cargo-carrying boats also had special containers fitted inside the mineshafts. The few special mining operations carried out by these boats have been poorly documented.

U-BOATS AT SEA

The U-boat campaign, particularly in the North Atlantic, was the Kriegsmarine's most potent threat to the Allies at sea, but it was carried out at a great cost to those who commanded and crewed the submarines. The hostility of the enemy was one threat but so too were the conditions at sea, and life onboard the small vessels was supremely testing; long-distance navigation, temperamental technology and Allied code-breaking also hindered the fighting ability of the U-boat crews.

Helmuth Köppe of *U613* using an extension pushed into the end of the speaking tube on the top of the conning-tower during manoeuvres in port. The speaking tube usually terminated under the top of the conning-tower wall and had a small lid to prevent too much water washing down it. If this did happen, there was a 'trap' to catch most of it to prevent it flying in the helmsman's face. Köppe's clean uniform suggests he is on his way out rather than coming back from a mission.

When the war started, many of the men in U-boats had been through a three-year induction. The officers had experienced life at sea on sail training ships and many had been on tours to far-off lands, flying the flag onboard cruisers before they joined the crew of a submarine. When the first wartime emergency intake of volunteers were sworn in, however, they found that the highly-regarded sail training ships were being moth-balled and that any sea-going experience was going to be limited to the Baltic. Many of the youngsters were in for a nasty shock when they faced the challenge of the North Atlantic, a wilder and far more hostile environment than they had been used to. This chapter describes what happened to those men at sea, and what their experience was of the most significant and drawn-out naval battle of the war, the U-boat war. (Continued on page 145)

Like many car engines of the period, those in U-boats were sometimes temperamental and considerable coaxing was required to make them burst into life. This seems to be one of those occasions when the mechanics used a little too much throttle and with the subsequent pall of smoke. The exhaust was close to the vents, so it was easy for smoke to blow between the pressure hull and the upper deck, making it look as if the whole boat is on fire.

Naval operations continued all the year round without regard to the weather, but the winter temperatures of the Baltic were often cold enough to freeze the salt water so solid that it even became difficult for huge ships and impossible for submarines. The camouflage on the ship in the background, probably a barrier breaker, suggests this picture was taken during the war years but the fact that U-boats are lying side by side suggests that they are out of reach of enemy aircraft. The submarine in the middle is a long-range variety of Type IXC and Atlantic boats of Type VIIC are moored on both sides of it.

INSIDE THE U-BOAT

RIGHT The rear torpedo tube with its surrounding machinery. The door, opening towards the left, is hardly visible because it is pointing directly at the camera.

1. A torpedo would have been pushed into the tube and the piston fitted in behind before closing the door. The tube would then be flooded and the outside doors opened; compressed air would be injected into the rear, hollow part of this piston to force it along the tube and eject the torpedo. The piston would stop at a lip on the far end of the tube to prevent air from escaping into the sea.
2. Trim tank
3. Compressed air cylinder
4. Diesel compressor
5. Electric motor for rudders. (The two rudders worked only in unison. The rudders, one on each side of the torpedo tube, were fitted so that the

heavy torpedo could be discharged along the central axis of the boat.)
6. Device for ejecting asdic 'foxers'.
7. Torpedo 'mixer' to adjust the torpedo settings inside the tube, while waiting to be fired. There were two sets of pointers; one showed the information sent from the fire control system inside or on top of the conning-tower. Making adjustments was a simple case of rotating a couple of wheels until the pointers from this box matched the other two.
8. Torpedo tank. There was another tank on the port side. The boat would become considerably lighter after a 1.5-ton torpedo had been discharged and these tanks were then filled with water to compensate for the difference. This prevented the boat from rising during submerged attacks and made a dive after a surface attack more efficient.

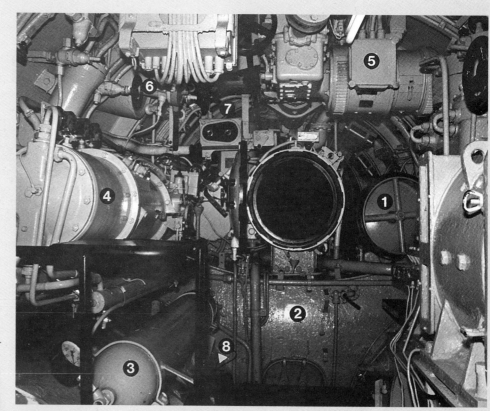

ABOVE A close-up of the torpedo adjuster, showing the two different pointers: one pointer radiating out from the centre and the other 'running' around the outside of the dial.

BELOW A close-up of the device for ejecting asdic 'foxers'. These consisted of a small tin, which produced a mass of bubbles once it came into contact with seawater. The device was called 'Bold' – short for Kobolt (elf or goblin). The dials, left bottom, are part of the diesel compressor.

LEFT Looking forwards from the rear torpedo tube towards the emergency steering wheel. This was hinged at the top and could be swung sideways, into the middle of the boat, when required. The indicator needle showing the position of the rudder on the shaft above the wheel is missing. To the left of the shaft is a repeater from the gyrocompass.

The interior photographs are of *U995*, which is now a technical museum near the naval memorial in Laboe (Kiel).

Looking forwards from the rear torpedo tube into the main electro-compartment. The emergency steering wheel can just be seen on the left. The controls for the electric motors are clearly visible on both sides of the central passageway and the tops of the motors can be seen at floor level. Between these, below the floor, is room for one spare torpedo. The wall with the rectangular doorway, at the far end, was there to cut off some of the noise from the diesel engines beyond it. The electric controls of later boats were inside insulated boxes and worked by a set of wheels, as can be seen here. Some earlier boats had a more open wiring system with levers instead of wheels.

ABOVE The speed indicator dial. Note that the instructions for forwards (right-hand side of the dial) and reverse are not identical. There were cases where officers used to giving the order 'Grosse Fahrt forwards' gave the order 'Grosse Fahrt backwards' during emergencies. This confused some inexperienced helmsmen long enough for them to hesitate and to make the recovery of a man overboard more difficult. The words on the dial translate as follows:

Äußerste Kraft – Not used in the British Navy. There the order would have been Full speed: emergency.

Große Fahrt – Full speed

Halbe Fahrt – Half speed

Langsame Fahrt – Slow speed

Kleine Fahrt – Dead slow

Laden – Charge (batteries)

Beide Maschinen 10 weniger – Both engines ten revolutions less

Voraus – Forwards

Zurück – Reverse

Bb – Backbord – Port

Sb – Steuerbord – Starboard

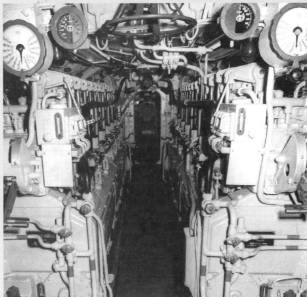

LEFT The diesel engine controls on the port side.

1. Starter handle and throttle.
2. Wheel for controlling the air flow to the engine.
3. Temperature gauges, one for each cylinder and one for the exhaust.
4. Telegraph from central control room.
5. Diesel engine.

ABOVE Looking backwards from the diesel engine controls.

RIGHT Petty officers' compartment, immediately forward of the galley. The circular doorway, leading to the central control room, is both water- and pressure-resisting. Most men slept in a 'hot bunking' system, meaning that a man coming off duty would occupy a bed vacated by someone going on duty. The ladder-like railings could be folded away and were usually only raised during bad weather to stop men falling out. Note that the lower sets also served as seats. It would have been difficult to get along this central passageway once the tables were folded out for meals.

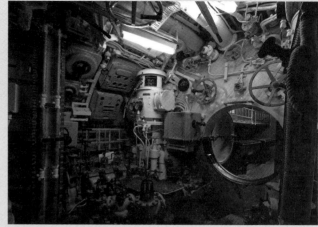

ABOVE Looking backwards from the stern of the central control room, with petty officer accommodation on the other side of the circular, pressure-resistant door. The main ballast pump occupies much of the corner. Below it are a number of pipes for controlling water in several areas and to clear the bilges. Each of these pipes had a cover so that they could be opened for cleaning or dealing with occasional blockages. One of these covers was removed to flood the boat shortly before *U505* was captured by the United States Navy. An astute American sailor, standing in several inches of water, searched for the missing cover, found it and had the sense to screw it back in position, to prevent the boat from sinking. The floor along this central part of the boat was almost halfway up the pressure hull. Below it was a series of tanks and the petty officer's room was above a massive space filled with batteries.

ABOVE Looking forwards into the central control room from the circular hatch by the petty officers' compartment. The dome-like object in front of the periscope and aerial well is the main gyrocompass. To the left is a large still for making distilled water and beyond it is the navigation area. The distilled water could be used for topping up batteries or, in an emergency, for drinking.

RIGHT AND BELOW The engineer officer's desk with the main trimming panel beyond. Engineer officers had to be able to work these taps in total darkness. Therefore each wheel was slightly different, with a different feel. These details are illustrated in the operating instructions carried by each boat, one page of which has been reproduced here.

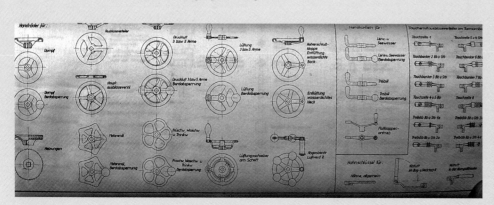

LEFT The helmsman's position, looking forwards from the middle of the central control room. On the left is the forward, pressure-resisting hatch with the commander's corner beyond it on the left and the radio room towards the right.

1. Wheels for operating the forward diving tanks.
2. Port and starboard engine telegraphs.
3. Speaking tube running up to the conning-tower.
4. Loudspeaker.
5. Magnetic compass. The compass was situated outside the boat, in a bulge by the base of the conning-tower and this picture of the dial was transmitted down through an illuminated periscope.
6. A 'slave' from the main gyrocompass.
7. An electrical box controlling the rudder. There were two handgrips and a button below each one: one for turning to the right and the other to the left.
8. At first U-boats were without any form of ventilation or air purification system, but from 1943 onwards some elementary carbon-dioxide removal tins were installed. Tins containing potash can be seen here.
9. Indicator showing the position of the rudder. (The two rudders could only be used in unison. The reason for having two was to be able to eject torpedoes along the central axis of the boat. The double rudders were not fitted to improve the turning circle.)

ABOVE This shot, taken during the summer of 2007, shows that thieves have been at work to remove some of the fittings in the central control room. The helmsman's position and the seats for the two hydroplane operators are clearly visible.

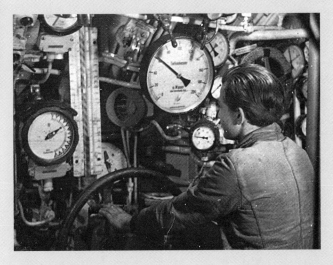

ABOVE The hydroplane controls with depth gauges. The operators sat at right angles to the helmsman (whose position is just visible towards the left) and faced 'outwards' towards the wall of the pressure hull.

1. Compressed air bottles.
2. Electric hydroplane controls (bows on the left and stern on the right)
3. Wheels for operating the hydroplanes manually if there was a serious electrical failure. There was another set of emergency hydroplane controls below the floor of the stern and bow compartments. Although these were not often used, men were always standing by during action and access had to be kept unobstructed. Each set of controls also had a depth gauge.
4. Shallow water depth gauge for up to 25 metres (approx 82 feet).
5. Indicators to show the positions of the hydroplanes.
6. Main depth gauge indicating 0–200 metres (656 feet).
7. Telegraph indicating engine revolutions (left black for forward and right red for reverse).
8. Waterproof fuse boxes with telephone-like locking lever.
9. A manometer. A liquid inside a glass tube would rise and fall to show the position of the water surface in relation to the boat. There was an extended periscope drawn along its side and this manometer was used when running at periscope depth.

ABOVE A wartime shot of the stern hydroplane operator in action with the large depth gauge indicating 45 metres.

LEFT Looking up from the central control room to the commander's control room inside the conning-tower. This would only have been used for submerged attacks, otherwise the commander would have been on top of the conning-tower supervising proceedings while the first watch officer shot torpedoes. U-boat commanders took an active part in attacks and did not work a torpedo calculator in the control room, as has been claimed. Each building yard produced a slightly different hatch locking mechanism. After the war, some lucky chap from the Royal Navy was given the fascinating task of blowing open all the various fittings to find out which was best.

ABOVE The sound detection room with some post-war equipment.

RIGHT The bow torpedo compartment.

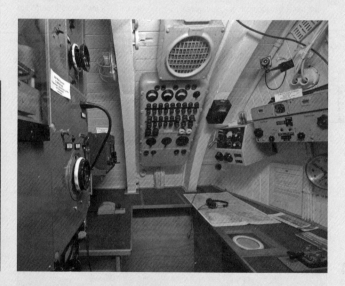

RIGHT The four bow torpedo tubes with many of the dials removed by thieves. The grey box towards the front, between the two upper tubes, was the original torpedo adjustment box. The one further back and lower down was a later addition to cope with looping anti-convoy torpedoes of Type FAT.

ABOVE The radio room. The black circular fittings on the board at the back were fuses. German fuses were fitted inside a small porcelain holder and when one 'blew' it was a simple case of inserting a new one with the right colour code for the correct current.

The first U-boats set sail towards the end of August 1939 to take up positions in deep water out in the ocean. The big incentive for leaving Germany before the outbreak of hostilities was to prevent ships being blockaded inside their own bases by superior surface forces. Departing Germany by sea was no easy matter and boats had to cope with either the Danish Belts or pass through the narrows and shallows of the German Bight. Whichever route they chose there was no room for deviation because they had to stay out of sight of land, and avoid potential observers, until there was sufficient water to dive safely.

Returning to port was often even more difficult because the old, well-used routes had been laced with mines by both sides and complicated detours became necessary. Despite some remarkable early successes, the majority of U-boats came home with a full, or nearly full, load of torpedoes. For many it was a monotonous life of rolling and pitching where only mechanical breakdowns added some deviation from the daily routine. For those who did see action, the encounter was usually short and sharp and only the few men on the top of the conning-tower would witness the events. The word 'routine' is important; the majority of men never saw the sky, the sun or the stars because they were incarcerated inside the steel confines of a narrow tube, where their life revolved around one monotonous procedure after another. In all navies it is important that crews carry out orders quickly, without questioning the reason for the action; in U-boats, this teamwork had to be even more engrained. Reactions had to be instant if the men were to survive the hostility of their surroundings and the attacks of the enemy.

At the start of the war there was still an abundance of cargo ships, many of them belonging to neutral countries, as well as fishing boats and aircraft making life uncomfortable for U-boats in home waters. The voyage from Germany, in the relative openness of the North Sea, to the Shetland Islands took about three days. From there, another two or three days were needed to get further west and south and into the shipping lanes of Britain's Western Approaches. This sea area could be very inhospitable and many U-boats found themselves driving hard against heavy seas, but making little progress over the ground. Kptlt. Kurt von Gossler, in *U49*, recorded the men's frustrations in the log, noting that the first four days had cost 16 per cent of their fuel and that they had not even reached the operations

A twenty-four-hour leave pass for the Gotenhafen dockyard in the far eastern Baltic near Danzig, now known as Gdynia. Such passes were an essential part of personal equipment during the training and build-up periods.

U128, looking towards Kiel with the city on the right and the dockyards with their hammerhead cranes on the left. The rusty drum by the small boat is the buoy of a deepwater, mid-stream mooring.

This is probably a Type IX with the 105mm quick-firing deck gun. The 88mm gun was used on the smaller craft.

RIGHT The first diving tests were carried out somewhere near the dockyard where the U-boat was built, usually in an out-of-the-way spot that had been dredged especially deep for the purpose. U-boats undergoing diving tests flew a red flag from the extended periscope as can be seen here. The ace of clubs symbol on the side of the conning-tower was one of many marks used to identify U-boats during their training days and was usually removed once they had been declared 'Frontreif' or ready for the front.

FAR RIGHT The stern of *U302* (a Type VIIC under Kptlt. Herbert Sickel) heading out for one of its early training voyages during the summer of 1942. Identification of the stern is by the two wires running down from the top of the gun platform; there was usually only one wire running down to the bows.

LEFT *U128*, under Korvkpt. Ulrich Heyse, shortly after commissioning, in the sheltered waters near Kiel. The characteristic tower of the Naval Memorial is visible in the far background on the right and there is open sea beyond the Friedrichsort lighthouse (towards the left). This indicates that the photograph was taken from somewhere close to the large locks of the Kiel Canal. The deck of this Type IXC is considerably wider than a Type VIIC. Also note the 37mm quick-firing gun aft of the conning-tower.

U128, ballasted bow up in order to gain access to damage on the bow. The stalk with the bulbous top in the foreground is the microphone (or hydrophone) end of an underwater sound detection system. In good conditions, this could detect ships below the horizon and still not visible to lookouts. The hydrophone only worked when submerged. The black and white badge painted on the front of the conning-tower, just below the jumping wire and above the spray deflector, shows the coat of arms of the City of Ulm, which had adopted the boat.

area. Much of a boat's valuable fuel was used on the passages to and from Germany to the operations area and back again. The number of days required for this journey was variable and depended on the opposition, the weather and other irritants, notably fishing boats. *U37*, under Korvkpt. Werner Hartmann, which was lying close to St Kilda at 0000 hours on 1 November 1939, found himself desperately short of fuel and had to return at the most economical speed, managing only 8 knots over the ground, to arrive in Wilhelmshaven at about 0900 hours on the 8th.

In 1940, after the fall of France, the U-boat Command was quick to establish bases along the Biscay coast. A train loaded with materials and men was ready to roll as soon as the High Command gave permission, and the first U-boat to be replenished there was *U30* under Kptlt. Fritz-Julius Lemp, who had sunk the first ship of the war, the liner *Athenia*. *U30* arrived in Lorient on 7 July and remained in port for four days before setting out again. Now, suddenly, Germany had bases on the doorstep of the Atlantic and there was no need for long and dangerous commuting. So far, the men had been used to being at sea for about thirty to thirty-five days for each trip. The availability of the French bases meant that long voyages now usually lasted about three weeks while many boats were back in much less than two. Furthermore, they were no longer returning with a load of unused torpedoes because they had had to abandon operations, having run short of fuel. Instead, it became a case of running out of torpedoes while there was still an abundance of fuel and targets. Those boats that did not meet opposition straight away made themselves more deadly by being able to remain longer in the shipping lanes and being able to hunt down ships further west. During the autumn of 1940, when U-boats attacked

RIGHT *U128* was commissioned in May 1941 at Flender Werft in the old Hansa town of Lübeck and this photograph was probably taken a few weeks later. It is unlikely that an inexperienced crew would have taken the boat into the more dangerous waters of the North Sea. The boat is using its own tanks, as well as the weight of the crew, to lift the bows clear of the water.

LEFT The damage revealed. The ship in the background is the 187 GRT freighter *Feistein*, which was launched way back in 1896 and originally belonged to a Norwegian shipping line in Stavanger until it was moved to Kiel.

on the surface at night, each boat was sinking on average almost six ships per month; and this was at a time when torpedo failures were still having a significant impact. The Prize Ordinance Regulations had been eased during October 1939, but not fully removed until August 1940, after which U-boats were free to sink any ship in the war zone around the British Isles.

Not all U-boats operated in the North Atlantic; some headed south to Spanish waters and some sailed even further to the warmer seas off Africa. The first U-boat operations there were unsuccessful and boats came home almost empty handed because of problems the U-boat Command had in locating shipping, but this was soon remedied. When the second and subsequent waves were sent they found ample targets in those far-off waters.

Britain was quick to react and this 'happy time' did not last long. It was all over in less than six months and the number of ships sunk per U-boat at sea dropped dramatically from its peak in October 1940. Escorts and aircraft drove the U-boats further away from the coasts into the open ocean where it was much more difficult to find targets. Earlier it had been a case of waiting in the funnel where shipping had

ABOVE The back or landward side of the U-boat bunker at La Pallice in France showing the corner that used to contain a massive power plant to keep the installation running.

BELOW The bows of *U128* with the head of the hydrophone on the right and the capstan on the left. The capstan could be operated mechanically from inside the boat, but in an emergency it could also be turned by manpower on the upper deck. In the foreground is the 105mm quick-firing deck gun.

U-boats were wet vessels. Lack of freeboard when surfaced, even in a moderate sea as depicted here, made them resemble a half-tide rock more than a ship. The conning-tower 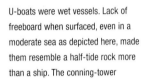 offered the crew something to hold on to and, during rough weather, they would be chained in position. Nonetheless, around 1,000 men were lost overboard during the war.

Lookout on the bridge of *U562*. The emblem of the two daggers has been attached to the partly extended attack periscope. This was the one with the small head lens. The rod on the right is the so-called commander's flagpole, flying a long narrow pennant. The men on the left are wearing special, navy issue sunglasses.

to squeeze through the North Channel to reach British ports. Now, with operations having moved further west, U-boats had to scour larger areas to find their quarry. This was the time when patrol lines or wolf packs were formed to intercept anticipated shipping movements.

Group attacks had already taken place during the 'happy time' but often there was so much shipping that there was no need to search for it; it was a case of one U-boat reporting a convoy and then all the U-boats in the area converging on it. An attack did not usually start until the majority were in place. Now it was harder to find ships in the vastness of the ocean. Then, when something was reported zealous escorts were ready to defend convoys and force U-boats beneath the surface. The tactic employed at this time was for U-boats to sail at a slow, economical speed towards the convoy dur-

ing daylight and then turn to sail in the same direction as the expected ships during the hours of darkness. This made it more difficult for shipping to slip past unseen. By the autumn of 1941, however, it was clear to the U-boat Command that convoys were making determined efforts to avoid patrol lines. Far too often a line was established right in front of a large convoy, but then the merchant ships just vanished, as if by magic. The only possible explanation for such drastic evasion was that they must have known about the U-boats ahead of them. A breach of the radio code was thought to be responsible, but the Naval High Command did not immediately recognize this and the fourth wheel for the Enigma machine was not introduced until February 1942. It was hard work for the crews, who were achieving less with each succeeding month. During 1941, the number of

ships sunk per U-boat at sea dropped dramatically to less than two.

The U-boat Command reacted by creating a different type of wolf pack. In September 1941 it was decided to create the so-called 'fast-moving wolf pack', in which all boats sailed at a fast, instead of a slow, cruising speed. Furthermore, there was no turning back when darkness came. The boats headed further and further west, sailing not only towards Canada but also into the most ferocious weather that the North Atlantic winter had to offer. The crews suffered rough, wet and cold, conditions but there was no noteworthy increase in the number of ships attacked.

The next major development came with America's entry into the war in December 1941. The U-boats had another heyday on the American East Coast. But there was a down-

On the surface, perpetual vigilance was an imperative. Lookouts scan the horizon.

LEFT AND RIGHT Those boats that crossed the Equator made a point of keeping up tradition by having a crossing of line ceremony where Triton and his court came on board to cleanse the dirty mortals from the north, before allowing them to proceed south. The treatment meted out could be harsh but the majority of sailors, in time-honoured tradition, took it all in good humour.

BELOW The bows of U128. Note the area of calm water on the starboard side, a result of the boat turning in a tight circle. This calming attribute was exploited by large warships in order to create a flat sea for their small aircraft to land on.

ABOVE These men are wearing U-boat overalls, the design of which was based on British battledress captured at the fall of France. The caps, called 'Schiffchen' (little ships), were favoured because they folded flat and thus did not occupy a great deal of locker space.

BELOW *U128* at sea. The only way onto the upper deck was from a ladder at the back of the conning-tower and struggling along this narrow, slippery deck required considerable agility, as can be seen here. The large 105mm gun was not used very often because then men also had to carry heavy shells along this precarious route. *U128* was an ocean-going boat of Type IXC with a comparatively wide upper deck. The majority of Atlantic boats were much narrower at this critical point. This photo shows why U-boats had railings along this part of the deck.

The collar braiding indicates that this is a 'Maat' or petty officer. In U-boats, men were usually allowed to smoke on top of the conning-tower or under the open hatch inside the commander's control room. Smoking was not allowed inside submarines because much of the crew quarters were on top of batteries, which gave off a mixture of hydrogen and oxygen which is highly flammable.

side as well. The men had to cross the whole stretch of the Atlantic to reach the new hunting grounds and, with the extra time at sea, there was only a slight increase in the sinking rate when calculated per U-boat. Each U-boat was sinking on average less than two ships per month, and this modest bonanza did not last for long before U-boats were driven away from the lucrative eastern seaboard and forced into the Air Gap of the mid-Atlantic or into the hot waters further south.

1942 saw the appearance of submarine supply boats and the launching of the first very long-range U-boats, which embarked upon voyages to Japanese-held territory in the Far East. The supply boats had a good year. Bletchley Park in England had been locked out of the radio code since the beginning of February, when the fourth wheel was introduced for the Enigma machine. This was not cracked until the end of the year, when one of these machines, together with its rotors and code books, was captured in the eastern Mediterranean from *U559* under Kptlt. Hans Heidtmann. Meanwhile, Britain had introduced a new and potent device which made it very difficult for U-boats to get within attack-

The man on the left is wearing his own, standard U-boat leathers while the one on the right is dressed in rubberized rain gear. This was issued to the boat and not to individual men, although key officers such as the commander and the three watch officers had their own set. Usually each boat carried only enough wet weather gear for two watches and the heavy garments had to be shared.

Welding gear was among the standard issue for the majority of boats. In the vastness of the oceans self sufficiency was critical.

Guns required constant maintenance. Each one had about eighty greasing points. Greasing them and keeping the gun in good order required considerable time and became more difficult as the war progressed and Allied aircraft made surfacing increasingly uncomfortable; much of this work had be carried out in total darkness.

The commander of *U177*, Kptlt. Robert Gysae, at the periscope. This was a very-long-range boat of Type IXD2, with similar fittings to the standard Type IXC. In both types the eye pieces for the periscopes were inside the conning-tower. On the smaller Type VII boats, only the attack periscope (seen here) with the single lens terminated inside the conning-tower. The larger navigation, or sky periscope, was viewed from the central control room, one deck further down.

The quarry. The sinking of the 7,176 GRT freighter *Alice F. Palmer* some twenty-six degrees south of the Equator on 11 July 1943, by *U177* under Kptlt. Robert Gysae.

U858, a Type IXC/40, under Kptlt. Thilo Bode, after she had surrendered to American forces at the end of the war. The sky, or navigation periscope, with the large head lens, has been partly extended to hold a navigation light as she sails through coastal waters.

ing range. It was a small box known as a High Frequency Direction Finder, or H/F D/F, which determined the direction from which even short radio signals were coming. Installed aboard escorts and some merchant ships, it informed the convoy exactly when the shadowing U-boat broke radio silence to start its attack and, most important of all, the direction from which the radio signal was emanating. This made it possible to place an escort with radar in the vulnerable area to force the boat under before locating it with asdic, the primary underwater detection device used by the Allies.

The short-range attack on the surface at night was no longer feasible. The majority of U-boats now simply failed to make contact with convoys. Those that did manage to find a quarry had to attack quickly, firing as many torpedoes as possible in the shortest possible time, before escaping the Allied depth charges. The slightest hesitation resulted in retaliation from fast and powerful escorts against which U-boats had no defence other than hiding in the depths.

Long-distance journeys to the Far East were not initially planned but the operations in waters off South Africa were made to help draw Allied warships away from the North Atlantic, and these voyages developed into longer tours into the Indian Ocean. One of the first boats to make for the Indian Ocean, *U178* under Kptlt. Wilhelm Dommes, had just about reached its limits, and was in the process of turning round to head back to France, when a radio signal asked whether it was possible to reach Penang. Despite the crew's reluctance they set off further east and Dommes reached Penang on 27 August 1943, having been at sea since 28 March, a full five months. He was lucky in one way. He remained in the Far East as German co-ordinator and Wilhelm Spahr (who started the war as Obersteuermann (Warrant Officer Navigator) of *U47* under Kptlt. Günther Prien, and

Men from *U302* on the upper deck.

was on board when HMS *Royal Oak* was sunk in Scapa Flow) brought the boat back home to Bordeaux. That journey extended from 27 November 1943 to 25 May 1944, a period of six months.

This very long-range boat of Type IXD2 was virtually identical to an ordinary Type IXC, except that the aft section was stretched to add another set of economical cruising engines and this weight was balanced in the bows with an additional compartment for the crew. Much of the machinery, including the periscopes, remained the same so that it was impossible to mount a submerged attack in winds of over force four without the bows and stern breaking through the surface of the water. Everything else was much slower, too, including diving. *U37*, mentioned earlier, was a Type IXA, which could vanish in about thirty seconds. A Type IXD2, on the other hand, could take as long as fifty to sixty seconds.

This may not sound critical, but *U37*'s baptism of fire came when an aircraft dropped out of clouds at a range of four kilometres to release a series of depth charges. Able to reach the U-boat in less than a minute there was no margin of error for the U-boat crew and had *U37* been a very-long-range type, it would most likely have been hit.

For these U-boat crews in their small craft, and for the Allied crews on the little escorts like the Flower class corvettes, it was the harsh conditions at sea that represented perhaps the greatest challenge. The conditions met with varied from the heat of the tropics to the extreme cold of the Arctic, with the storms of the North Atlantic in between. Of the 1,171 U-boats commissioned during the Second World War, only about 325 fired torpedoes; the other 850 or so never came close enough to even see the enemy in their sights, but the sea was with them all the time.

The Kriegsmarine's ensign flying atop the conning-tower.

These conning-towers show the early variation with only one platform containing a 20mm anti-aircraft gun. The lip at the top of the structure, the so-called wind deflector, was of a type installed some time after the beginning of the war. Note how the lip points down, rather than curving upwards as can be seen in other photos. The two boats at the front are Types IXC while the one behind appears to be a Type VIIA.

TECHNICAL DATA

BATTLESHIPS

Scharnhorst and *Gneisenau* were often classed as battlecruisers by foreign navies but the Germans referred to them as battleships.

	Scharnhorst, Gneisenau	Bismarck	Tirpitz
Displacement, standard	31,850 tons	41,700 tons	43,000 tons
Displacement, full load	38,900 tons	50,900 tons	52,600 tons
Waterline length (metres)	226 m	242 m	242 m
Overall length	235 m	251 m	251 m
Beam	30m	36 m	36 m
Draught	9.9 m	10.5 m	10.2 m
Machinery	12 boilers in 3 sets	12 boilers in 3 sets	12 boilers in 3 sets
Number of shafts	3	3	3
Maximum SHP	160,000 shp	138,000 shp	138,000 shp
Maximum speed	31.5 knots	31 knots	31 knots
Cruising speed	17 knots	19 knots	19 knots
Range (nautical miles)	10,000 nm	8,100 nm	9,000 nm
Crew	1,800 men	2,090 men	2,600 men
Deck armour	50–105 mm	50–120 mm	50–120 mm
Side armour	45–350 mm	up to 320 mm	up to 320 mm
Armament:			
20mm	10–38	12–52	12–52
37mm	16	16	16
88mm	0	0	0
105mm	14	16	16
150mm	12	12	12
203mm	0	0	0
280mm	9	0	0
380mm	0	8	8
Torpedo tubes	6	8	8
Aircraft catapults	2 later 1	1 double	1 double
Aircraft carried	4	6	6

Scharnhorst being launched at the naval dockyard in Wilhelmshaven on 3 October 1936, just one year after Hitler repudiated the Treaty of Versailles. An Atlantic bow, higher and drier, was added later.

POCKET BATTLESHIPS AND HEAVY CRUISERS

Heavy cruisers were: *Admiral Hipper, Blücher* and
Prinz Eugen

	Deutschland	*Admiral Scheer*	*Admiral Graf Spee*	Heavy Cruisers
Displacement, standard	11,700 tons	12,000 tons	12,000 tons	14,050 tons
Displacement, full load	16,000 tons	16,000 tons	16,000 tons	18,200 tons
Waterline length (metres)	182 m	182 m	182 m	195 m
Overall length	188 m	188 m	188 m	206 m
Beam	20.7 m	20.7 m	21.7 m	21.3 m
Draught	7 m	7 m	7 m	7.7 m
Machinery	8 x 9 cylinder diesel engines	8 x 9 cylinder diesel engines	8 x 9 cylinder diesel engines	12 boilers in 3 sets
Number of shafts	2	2	2	3
Maximum SHP	54,000 shp	54,000 shp	54,000 shp	132,000 shp
Maximum speed	28 knots	28 knots	28 knots	32 knots
Cruising speed	20 knots	20 knots	20 knots	20 knots
Range (nautical miles)	10,000 nm	9,000 nm	9,000 nm	6,800 nm
Crew	1,150 men	1,150 men	1,150 men	1,600 men
Deck armour (mm)	18–40 mm	18–45 mm	18–45 mm	30 mm
Side armour	up to 60 mm	up to 80 mm	up to 80 mm	80 mm
Armament:				
20mm	10–28	10–28	10–28	28
37mm	8	8	8	12
88mm	0	0	0	0
105mm	6	6	6	12
150mm	8	8	8	0
203mm	0	0	0	8
280mm	6	6	6	0
380mm	0	0	0	0
Torpedo tubes	8	8	8	12
Aircraft catapults	1	1	1	1
Aircraft carried	2	2	2	3

Heavy cruiser *Prinz Eugen*.

LIGHT CRUISERS

	Emden	*Karlsruhe*	*Königsberg*	*Köln*	*Leipzig*	*Nürnberg*
Displacement, standard	5,600 tons	6,650 tons	6,650 tons	6,650 tons	6,515 tons	6,520 tons
Displacement, full load	6,990 tons	8,350 tons	8,130 tons	8,130 tons	8,250 tons	8,380 tons
Waterline length (metres)	150 m	167 m	167 m	150 m	166 m	170 m
Overall length	155 m	174 m	174 m	155 m	177 m	181 m
Beam	14.3 m	16.6 m	15.3 m	14.3 m	16.2 m	16.4 m
Draught	5.9 m	6 m	6 m	5.9 m	5.7 m	5.7 m
Machinery	10 boilers	2 sets boilers 2 x 10 cyl diesel	2 sets boilers 2 x 10 cyl diesel	10 boilers	2 boilers	2 boilers
Number of shafts	2	2	2	2	3	3
Maximum SHP	46,500 shp	66,800 shp	66,800 shp	46,500 shp	60,000/12,400 shp	60,000/12,400 shp
Maximum speed (knots)	29 knots	30 knots	32 knots	29 knots	32 knots	32 knots
Cruising speed	18 knots	19 knots	19 knots	18 knots	19 knots	19 knots
Range (nautical miles)	5,300 nm	5,700 nm	5,700 nm	5,300 nm	5,700 nm	5,700 nm
Crew	636 men	850 men	850 men	636 men	850 men	896 men
Deck armour (mm)	20 mm	40 mm	40 mm	20 mm	20–25 mm	40 mm
Side armour	50 mm	50 mm	50 mm	50 mm	50 mm	50 mm
Armament:						
20mm	0	0?	0?	0	10	4
37mm	4	8 twins	8 twins	4	8	8
88mm	3	6 twins	6 twins	3	6	6
105mm	0	0	0	0	0	0
150mm	8	9	9	8	9	9
203mm	0	0	0	0	0	0
280mm	0	0	0	0	0	0
380mm	0	0	0	0	0	0
Torpedo tubes	4	12	12	4	12	12
Aircraft catapults	0	1[1]	1	0	1	1
Aircraft carried	0	1[1]	2	0	1	2

1. Removed in 1942

The light cruiser *Karlsruhe*.

DESTROYERS

Type: number	1934: *Z1* to *Z4*	1934: *Z5* to *Z8*	1934: *Z9* to *Z13*	1934: *Z14* to *Z16*	1936: *Z17* to *Z22*	1936A: *Z23, Z24*
Displacement, standard	2,232 tons	2,171 tons	2,270 tons	2,301 tons	2,411 tons	2,603 tons
Displacement, full load	3,156 tons	3,100 tons	3,190 tons	3,221 tons	3,415 tons	3,605 tons
Waterline length	114 m	116 m	116 m	116 m	120 m	122 m
Overall length	119 m	121 m	121 m	121 m	123/125 m	127 m
Beam	11.3 m	11.3 m	11.3 m	11.3 m	11.8 m	12 m
Draught	4.2 m	4.2 m	4.2 m	4.2 m	4.5 m	4.7 m
Maximum speed	38.2 knots	38.2 knots	38.2 knots	38.2 knots	36 knots	36 knots
Cruising speed	19 knots	19 knots	19 knots	19 knots	19 knots	19 knots
Range (nautical miles)	4,400 nm	4,400 nm	4,400 nm	4,400 nm	4,850 nm	5,000 nm
Crew	325 men	325 men	325 men	325 men	313 men	332 men
Armament:[1]						
20mm	8	8	8	8	7	14
37mm	4 to 14	4 to 14	4 to 14	4 to 14	4	4
127/128mm	5	5	5	5	5	0
150mm	0	0	0	0	0	5
Torpedo tubes	8	8	8	8	8	8
Mines carried	60	60	60	60	60	60

Type: number	1936A: *Z25* to *Z27*	1936A: *Z28*
Displacement, standard	2,543 tons	2,595 tons
Displacement, full load	3,545 tons	3,519 tons
Waterline length	122 m	122 m
Overall length	127 m	127 m
Beam	12 m	12 m
Draught	4.4 m	5 m
Maximum speed	36 knots	36 knots
Cruising speed	19 knots	19 knots
Range (nautical miles)	5,000 nm	5,900 nm
Crew	321 men	327 men
Armament:[1]		
20mm	14	14
37mm	4	?
127/128mm	0	0
150mm	5	5
Torpedo tubes	8	8
Mines carried	60	60

The commissioning of *Z33* at Deschimag AG Weser in Bremen on 6 February 1943. The caption on the back of the photo must be a mistake, or it was an exceptionally warm February day but there are no natural indications, such as trees, to show the time of year. No one seems to be wearing coats, not even the civilians on the upper part of the deck. A woman wearing what looks like a thin blouse can just be made out on the extreme left. Perhaps it depicts *Z37*, which was commissioned on 16 July 1942.

Type: number	1936B: *Z29* to *Z34*	1936B: *Z35, Z36*	1936A(Mob): *Z37* to *Z39*	1936A(Mob): *Z43* to *Z45*
Displacement, standard		2,527 tons	2,600 tons	2,527 tons
Displacement, full load	2,603 tons	3,507 tons	3,597 tons	3,507 tons
Waterline length	3,597 tons	108 m	108 m	122 m
Overall length	122 m	112 m	112 m	127 m
Beam	127 m	11.3 m	11.3 m	12 m
Draught	12 m	4.3 m	4 m	4 m
Maximum speed	4.6 m	36 knots	36 knots	36 knots
Cruising speed	36 knots	19 knots	19 knots	19 knots
Range (nautical miles)	19 knots	6,200 nm	5,900 nm	5,900 nm
Crew	5,900 nm	332 men	332 men	321 men
Armament:[1]	321 men			
20mm		16	up to 14	15
37mm	14	4	4	4
127/128mm	4	0	4	0
150mm	0	5	0	5
Torpedo tubes	0	8	8	8
Mines carried	8	76	60	76

1. The exact number of guns varied and there were especially drastic modifications during the war years.

AUXILIARY CRUISERS

Name	Atlantis	Coronel	Komet	Kormoran	Michel
Crew	350 men	350 men	270 men	400 men	400
Displacement	17,600 tons	12,700 tons	7,500 tons	19,900 tons	11,000 tons
Length	155 m	134 m	115 m	164 m	132 m
Beam	18.7 m	17.9 m	15.3 m	20.2 m	16.6 m
Draught	8.7 m	8 m	6.5 m	8.5 m	7.4 m
Max shp	7,600 shp	5,100 shp	3,900 shp	16,000 shp	6,650 shp
Max speed	16 knots	16 knots	14.5 knots	18 knots	16 knots
Armament:					
20mm	4	?	4	5	4
37mm	2	?	2	4	4
75mm	1	0	0	0	1
150mm	6	6	6	6	6
Torpedo tubes	4	4	6[1]	6	6[1]
Aircraft carried	2	2	2	2	2
Mines carried	92	0	30[2]	360	0[2]

Name	Orion	Pinguin	Stier	Thor	Widder
Crew	376 men	420 men	324 men	345 men	363 men
Displacement	15,700 tons	17,600 tons	11,000 tons	9,200 tons	16,800 tons
Length	148 m	155 m	133 m	122 m	152 m
Beam	18.6 m	18.7 m	17.3 m	16.7 m	18.2 m
Draught	8.2 m	8.7 m	7.2 m	7.1 m	8.3 m
Max SHP	6,200 shp	7,600 shp	3,750 shp	6,500 shp	6,200 shp
Max speed	14 knots	17 knots	14 knots	18 knots	14 knots
Armament:					
20mm	4	4	4	4	4
37mm	6	2	2	2	4
75mm	1	1	0	0	1
150mm	6	6	6	6	6
Torpedo tubes	4	4	2	4	4
Aircraft carried	1	2	2	1	2
Mines carried	228	380	?	?	?

1. Four tubes above the waterline and two below.

2. *Komet*, *Kormoran* and *Michel* also carried *MTB2* (LS2), *MTB3* (LS3) and *MTB4* (LS4). These were 11.5 ton, 45 knot boats with a range of 300 nautical miles at 30 knots. Each had two 45.7 mm torpedo tubes, 3–4 mines and a crew of six.

The supply ship-cum-blockade breaker *Tannenfels* photographed from one of the auxiliary cruisers during a rare meeting in southern waters.

TORPEDO BOATS

Type	1935	1937	Fleet Torpedo Boats, 1939	Fleet Torpedo Boats, 1941	Fleet Torpedo Boats, 1944
	T1 to *T8*[1]				
Number/name	*T9* to *T12*	*T13* to *T21*	*T22* to *T36*	*T37* to *T51*	*T52* to *T60*[3]
Displacement, standard	844 tons	853 tons	1,294 tons	1,493 tons	1,418 tons
Displacement, full load	1,088 tons	1,098 tons	1,754 tons	2,155 tons	1,794 tons
Waterline length	82 m	82 m	97 m	97 m	97 m
Overall length	84 m	85 m	102 m	102 m	102 m
Beam	8.6 m	8.9 m	10 m	10 m	10 m
Draught	2.9 m	3.1 m	3.2 m	3.2 m	3.2 m
Maximum speed	34.5 knots	34.5 knots	32.5 knots	34 knots	37.2 knots
Cruising speed	19 knots	19 knots	19 knots	19 knots	19 knots
Range (nautical miles)	2,400 nm	3,000 nm	2,100 nm	2,350 nm	4,500 nm
Crew	119 men	119 men	206 men	210 men	222 men
Torpedo tubes	6	6	6	6	6
Mines carried	30	30	50	?	50
Armament:					
20mm	8	7	7–12	9	0
37mm	0	1	4	4	10
105mm	1	1	4	4	4
127mm[2]	0	0	0	0	0

1. *T1–T8* were some 5-10 tons heavier than *T9–T12*.
2. Armament was modified during the war.
3. Not completed.

A torpedo-boat of the Beast of Prey class at sea.

Torpedo boats (continued)

Type Number/name	Fleet Torpedo Boats, 1940 *T61 to T64, T67 to T70*	1923 *Seeadler, Möwe*	1923 *Albatros, Falke, Greif, Kondor*	1924 *Wolf, Jaguar, Leopard. Luchs, Iltis, Tiger*
Displacement, standard	1,931 tons	924 tons	924 tons	933 tons
Displacement, full load	2,566 tons	1,290 tons	1,290 tons	1,320 tons
Waterline length	97 m	85 m	86 m	89 m
Overall length	102 m	87 m	88 m	93 m
Beam	10 m	8.4 m	8.4 m	8.7 m
Draught	3.2 m	3.7 m	3.7 m	3.5 m
Maximum speed	34.8 knots	32 knots	33 knots	34 knots
Cruising speed	19 knots	17 knots	17 knots	17 knots
Range (nautical miles)	6,000 nm	3,600 nm	3,600 nm	3,100 nm
Crew	231 men	122 men	122 men	129 men
Torpedo tubes	6	Variable	6	6
Mines carried	50		?	?
Armament:		Variable		
20mm	8		4	4
37mm	4		?	?
105mm	0		3	3
127mm	4		0	0

Type Number/name	Old Boats[1] *T107, T108, T110, T111*	Old Boats[1] *T151, T153, T155, T156, T157, T158*	Old Boat[1] *T185*	Old Boat[1] *T190*	Old Boat[1] *T196*
Displacement, standard	750 tons	650 tons	760 tons	750 tons	750 tons
Displacement, full load	875 tons	800 tons	860 tons	860 tons	875 tons
Waterline length	75 later 80 m	73 m	74 m	74 m	74 m
Overall length	–	–	–	–	–
Beam	7.5 m	7.5 m	8 m	8 m	8 m
Draught	3 m	3 m	3 m	3 m	3 m
Maximum speed	31 knots	30 knots	30 knots	30 knots	32 knots
Cruising speed	17 knots	17 knots	17 knots	17 knots	19 knots
Range (nautical miles)	2,000 nm	3,500 nm	1,400 nm	1,400 nm	1,850 nm
Crew	85 men	85 men	85 men	100 men	100 men
Torpedo tubes	–	–	–	–	–
Mines carried	–	–	–	–	–
Armament:					
20mm	2	1	0	2	2
37mm	0	0	0	0	0
105mm	1	1 x 88mm	0	1	2
127mm	0	0	0	0	0

1. The old torpedo boats were launched before the First World War and were not used as torpedo boats during the Second. Instead they served as tenders, training vessels and general workhorses for coastal protection activities. They were originally coal burning, but converted to oil after the First World War. A shortage of oil after 1939 meant they were then converted back to run on coal.

Torpedo boat *T58*. The flag of the Reichsmarine on the stern indicates that this photo was taken before the swastika was introduced in 1935.

MOTOR TORPEDO BOATS (SCHNELLBOOTE)

Almost all of these boats could cruise at a speed of only a few knots slower than their maximum. They were armed with two torpedo tubes, plus light anti-aircraft weapons; some had machine guns as well.

Number	S1	S2–S5	S6–S9	S10–S13	S14–S17	S18–S25	S26–S29	S30–S37, S54–S61
Crew	14 men	14 men	21 men	21 men	21 men	16 men	21 men	23 men
Launched	Pre-war	1937/38	1933/34	1934/35	1936/37	1938/39	1940	1940
Displacement	50 tons	50 tons	80 tons	78 tons	97 tons	85 tons	95 tons	82 tons
Length	28 m	32.5 m	35 m	35 m	35m	35 m	35 m	33 m
Beam	4.3 m	5 m	5 m	5 m	5 m	5 m	5 m	5 m
Draught	1.4 m	1.4 m	1.7 m	1.4 m	1,6 m	1.6 m	1.6 m	1.5 m
Maximum speed	33 knots	33 knots	36.5 knots	35 knots	38 knots	40 knots	39 knots	36 knots
Range	350 nm	350 nm	600 nm	600 nm	600 nm	700 nm	700 nm	800 nm

Number	S38–S53, S62–S99, S101–S135, S137	S100, S136, S138–S150, S159–S169, S171–S185, S187–S194	S151–S158	S170, S186, S195–S218	S219–S788
Crew	23 men	23 men	21 men	23 men	23 men
Launched	1942/43	1942/43	1941/42	1944	1944
Displacement	95 tons	95 tons	55 tons	95 tons	100 tons
Length	35 m	35 m	28 m	35 m	35 m
Beam	5 m	5 m	4.3 m	5 m	5 m
Draught	2 m	2 m	1.6 m	2 m	2 m
Maximum speed	39 knots	39 knots	32 knots	39 knots	39 knots
Range	700 nm	700 nm	350 nm	750 nm	750 nm

S11 was one of four S-boats delivered in 1936 which were fitted with the Daimler-Benz MB502 sixteen-cylinder four-stroke diesel engines which proved much more reliable than the older MAN diesels fitted in earlier vessels.

MINESWEEPERS

Not all of these boats were commissioned and *M613* to
M800 were never built.

Number	*M1* to *M260*	*M261* to *M500*	*M601* to *M612, M801* to *M806*
Crew	90–120 men	60–80 men	107 men
Displacement	682–875 tons	545–775 tons	580–820 tons
Length	67–68 m	58–62 m	63–68 m
Beam	8.3 m	8.5 m	9 m
Draught	2.6 m	2.8 m	2.7 m
Maximum speed	18.3 knots	16.8 knots	16.7 knots
Range	5,000 nm	4,000 nm	3,600 nm
Armament:			
20mm	6	7	8
37mm	2	1	2
105mm	2	–	2
Torpedo tubes	0	2	0
Mines carried	30	?	24

MOTOR MINESWEEPERS

Numbers *R291–R300* were not completed. Armament:
1–4 x 20mm AA guns, 3–6 x 37mm AA guns plus other
variations.

Number	*R1*	*R2–R7, R9–R16*	*R8*	*R17–R24*	*R41–R129*	*R130–R150*	*R151–R290*
Launched	1930	1932	1934	1934	1939	1943	1940
Crew	40 men	18 men	18 men	34 men	34 men	34 men	34?men
Displacement	45 tons	63 tons	63 tons	115 tons	125 tons	150 tons	110 tons
Length	42.5 m	24.5 m	26 m	27.8 m	34.5 m	37.8 m	35.4 m
Beam	5.2 m	4.4 m	4.5 m	4.5m	5.6 m	5.8 m	5.6 m
Draught	2.5 m	1 (?) m	1.1 m	1.3 m	1.4 m	1.4 m	1.4 m
Max. speed	17 knots	17 kts	?	21 kts	20 kts	19 kts	23 kts
Range	800 nm	800 nm	?	900 nm	900 nm	900 nm	1,100 nm

A minesweeper with paravane in the
foreground. The boats could also be used
as minelayers and many served in a
variety of other functions; they were the
general workhorses for the Navy.

The 37mm anti-aircraft gun aboard a
small minesweeper, or Räumboot, with a
sailor using a rangefinder on the left.

TRAINING SHIPS

Name	*Schlesien, Schleswig-Holstein*	*Albert Leo Schlageter*	*Gorch Fock*	*Horst Wessel*
Type	Battleship	Sailing ship	Sailing ship	Sailing ship
Launched	1906	1937	1933	1936
Crew	c. 800 men	298 men	265 men	298 men
Displacement	14,900 tons	1,634 tons	1,500 tons	1,634 tons
Length	126 m	89 m	74 m	89 m
Beam	22.2 m	12 m	12 m	12 m
Draught	7.7 m	5 m	4.8 m	4.8 m
Maximum speed	16 knots	10 knots[1]	8 knots[1]	8 knots[1]
Range	5,900 nm	3,500 nm[1]	3,500 nm[1]	3,500 nm[1]
Armament	4 x 280 mm	8 x 20 mm AA	8 x 20 mm AA	8 x 20 mm
	6 x 105 mm			
	10 x 40 mm AA			
	20 x 20mm AA or more			

1. Running on engines only.

PURPOSE BUILT ESCORTS (GELEITBOOTE)

Larger boats were projected but never built. The 'F' comes from the German Fangboot meaning 'catching boat'.

Number	*F1* to *F10*
Crew	120 men
Displacement	770–1,150 tons
Length	73–76 m
Beam	8.8 m
Draught	3.2 m
Max. speed	28 knots
Range	1,500 nm
Armament	2 x 105 mm
	4 x 37 mm
	8 x 20 mm

ABOVE The German Navy invested heavily in sail training ships and these played a central part during the pre-war Kiel Week, the annual sailing regatta held in June each year. Here is *Gorch Foch* with *Horst Wessel* behind.

RIGHT Deck work on the *Horst Wessel*. After the war she was taken as a war prize by the United States and was commissioned in 1946 into the United States Coast Guard as the USCGC *Eagle*. She is still in service today.

U-BOATS

V80 was an experimental boat with a Walter turbine. Type XXIII was a small coastal electro-submarine. Type XXI was an ocean-going electro-submarine.

Type	IIC Coastal boat[4]	VIIC Sea-going boat[5]	IXC Ocean-going boat[5]	V80[6]
Crew	25 men	44–56 men	c. 48 men	4 men
Displacement, surface	314 tons	770 tons	1,120 tons	71 tons
Displacement, dived	460 tons	1,070 tons	1,540 tons	80 tons
Length	44 m	67 m	76 m	22 m
Beam	5 m	6 m	7 m	2 m
Draught	4 m	5 m	5 m	3 m
Maximum speed, surface	13 knots	17 knots	18 knots	4 knots
Maximum speed, dived	7.5 knots	7.5 knots	7 knots	28 knots
Cruising speed, surface	8 knots	10 knots	10 knots	–
Cruising speed, dived	4 knots	4 knots	4 knots	–
Range, cruising surface[1]	5,650 nm	8,500 nm	13,450 nm	–
Range, cruising dived	56 nm	80 nm	63 nm	50 nm
Maximum diving depth	150 m	250 m	200 m	–
Torpedo tubes – bows	3	4	4	–
Torpedo tubes – stern	0	1	2	–
Torpedoes carried[2]	5	12[7]	22	–
Mines carried[2]	18	39	66	–
Guns:				
105mm[3]	0	0	1	–
88mm[3]	0	1	0	–
37mm	0	1	–	–
20mm	2–4	2 twins	–	–

1. Range could be increased by going onto diesel/electric drive. This meant charging batteries with one engine and using the other to move the boat.

2. The total number of torpedoes and mines could not be carried at the same time. Boats usually carried about half a dozen torpedoes and used the other space for storing mines.

3. The large deck guns of 88mm and 105mm could not be used against aircraft.

4. Type IIC was used mainly for training, but a few did see service as minelayers and as attack boats in the Western Approaches of Britain.

5. Type VIIC and IXC carried the main burden of the war in the Atlantic. Type VIIC was the largest submarine class ever built. Both Types VIIC and IXC were later modified and identified as VIIC/41, VIIC/42 and IXC/40.

6. Anti-aircraft armament varied. At first boats had only one 20mm AA gun, but later the common variations were 2 x 20mm twins and 1 x 20mm quadruple AA or 1 x 37mm AA gun. Other combinations appeared towards the end of the war, when an effective twin 37mm AA gun came into service.

7. Torpedoes in a Type VIIC were stored as follows:
   4: Bow tubes
   1: Stern tube
   4: Below floor in bow compartment
   2: Above floor in bow compartment
   1: Under the floor, between the two electric motors
   1: In external tube under the upper beck bows
   1: In external tube under upper deck stern.

Torpedoes could not be fired from the upper deck tubes and had to be man-handled into the interior before they could be used. This was a long and hard job, which could only be carried out during the first few years of the war.

The long sleek bows of a Type VIIC with jumping wire running from near the camera to the top of the conning-tower. This served as an aerial and was also intended to help the boat slide under anti-submarine netting, though few submarines during the Second World War encountered this. It could also be used for attaching personal safety harnesses.

XVIIA[6]	XXIII	XXI
12 men	14 men	57 men
240 tons	235 tons	1,620 tons
280 tons	275 tons	2,100 tons
34 m	35 m	77 m
3.5 m	3 m	8 m
4.5 m	4 m	6 m
9 knots	10 knots	15.5 knots
26 knots	12 knots	17 knots
–	6 knots	10 knots
–	4–10 knots	5–10 knots
–	4,450 nm	15,500 nm
80 nm	35 nm 10 kt	110 nm 10 kt
	200 nm 4 kt	365 nm 5 kt
–	150 m	Over 250 m
2	2	6
0	0	0
4	2	24
–	–	–
0	0	0
0	0	0
0	0	0
0	0	4

A Type VIIC inside locks, probably at La Pallice in France.

U14, a Type IIB, with the black, white and red neutrality markings painted onto the conning-tower during the Spanish Civil War, and the hats suggest that the boat has just come back from Spanish waters. Although the distances involved were quite a challenge for these small coastal submarines, they did have the advantage of being able to sail unhindered through the English Channel and to stop off at any port en route. The heavy weather the boats encountered off Spain provided excellent experience for later operations, when small Type IIC and IID boats were sent into the shipping lanes to the west of Britain.

RANK, UNIFORMS, AWARDS AND INSIGNIA

RANKS

The basic ranks in 1938 and their approximate British equivalents were as follows. (The German words were often written as one compound word, but they have been broken up here, to make reading easier.)

Seamen[1]

Matrose	Ordinary Seaman
Matrosen-Gefreiter	Able Seaman
Matrosen-Obergefreiter	Leading Seaman
Matrosen-Hauptgefreiter	Leading Seaman with 4½ years' service

Junior Non-Commissioned Officers without Swordknot (Unteroffiziere ohne Portepee)

– maat[2]	Petty Officer
Ober – maat[2]	Chief Petty Officer

Warrant Officers with Sword Knot (Unteroffiziere mit Portepee)

Bootsmann[3]	Boatswain
Oberbootsmann[3]	Chief Boatswain
Stabsoberbootsmann[3]	Senior Chief Boatswain

Trainee Officers

Fähnrich zur See	Midshipman/Cadet
Oberfähnrich zur See	Sub-Lieutenant

Commissioned Officers

Leutnant zur See	Lieutenant (Junior)
Oberleutnant zur See	Lieutenant (Senior)
Kapitänleutnant	Lieutenant-Commander
Korvettenkapitän	Commander
Fregattenkapitän	Captain (Junior)
Kapitän zur See	Captain
Konteradmiral	Rear Admiral
Vizeadmiral	Vice Admiral
Admiral	Admiral
Generaladmiral	No equivalent
Grossadmiral	Admiral of the Fleet

Kommodore (Commodore) – a Captain in a position usually held by an admiral but it was not a rank. The title would have been Kpt.z.S. und Kommodore.

Trade names used with Ranks

The name of a man's trade formed the main part of his rank and the following are the main trades, given for a Warrant Officer with Sword Knot (Portepee). All of these are the equivalent of Boatswain.

Bootsmann
Fernschreibmeister
Feuerwerker
Funkmeister
Maschinist
Mechaniker
Signalmeister
Steuermann
Feldwebel
Kraftfahrfeldwebel
Marineartilleriefeldwebel
Musikfeldwebel
Sanitätsfeldwebel
Schreiberfeldwebel
Verwaltungsfeldwebel
Zimmermeister

RANK INSIGNIA

The German Navy used a far wider range of rank insignia than any other branch of the armed forces. These fell into the four basic types mentioned above: Seamen, Petty and Chief Petty Officers, Warrant Officers with Swordknot (Portepee) and Commissioned Officers.

SEAMEN

Seamen wore their badges of rank as chevrons on the left sleeve. These chevrons were often combined with trade insignia as a one-piece badge. Seamen also wore plain cornflower blue collar patches on the pea jacket as a further indication of rank.

---

1. Ranks introduced later during the war included Matrosen-Stabsgefreiter and Matrosen-Stabsobergefreiter, which was a more senior position of Leading Seaman.
2. A man's trade prefixed the word, to give ranks such as Maschinenmaat, Signalmaat, Funkmaat or Obermaschinenmaat, Obersignalmaat, Oberfunkmaat.
3. The man's trade would have been used instead of Bootsmann, to give ranks such Maschinist, Steuermann, Funkmeister or Obermaschinist, Obersteuermann, Oberfunkmeister.

RIGHT The parade jacket is shown here to good effect, worn by Matrosengefreiter Bruno Vowe of the Reichsmarine's sail training ship *Niobe*. It is worn with the white sailor's shirt and the blue 'Nelson' collar with its three white edge stripes is worn outside of the jacket. Note also the black silk knot with crossed white tapes and the thin white diagonal line running from *his* top left hand corner to *his* bottom right hand corner of the scarf knot. This signified that the wearer belonged to the Baltic Naval Command. Men from the North Sea wore the diagonal line the other way around, from *their* top right to *their* bottom left.

Hans Schulze wearing a pea jacket with cornflower blue collar patches.

LEFT Two shoulder straps for warrant officers. The pips indicated the rank and the badge in the middle the man's trade.

The standard working gear for the German Navy when not engaged in dirty activities. These radio operators from the radio outpost at Stolpmünde are obviously on a railway station platform and the lightning flash of the man's trade can just be made out on the right. The man on the right is also displaying the National Sports' Badge.

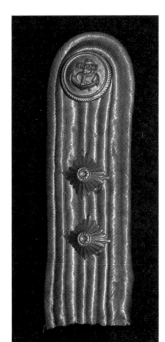

LEFT Two shoulder straps for commissioned officers. Deck officers tended to have plain straps while other trades had an additional emblem. In this case it is a cog wheel for an engineer officer.

RIGHT A Maat, or petty officer, showing the gold braiding along the edge of his collar and the gold strip over the cornflower blue lapel patches.

The two Maate (petty officers) shown here are both wearing the sailor's blue wool pea jacket. Note that in contrast to the parade jacket the blue collar is worn inside the jacket. On the sleeve is a high-quality gilt metal version of the rank insignia for a Maschinenmaat under which both are wearing the red embroidered specialist's badge for an electrical artificer.

RANK INSIGNIA

WORN ON THE PULLOVER, UNIFORM JACKET AND PEA JACKET

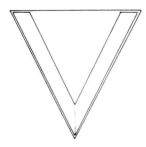

Matrosen-gefreiter.

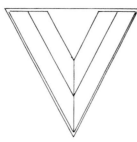

Matrosen-obergefreiter.

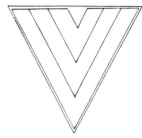

Matrosen-hauptgefreiter.

Collar patch for ranks from Matrose to Matrosen-stabsobergefreiter.

Matrosen-stabsgefreiter.

Matrosen-stabsgefreiter.

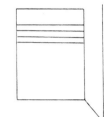

Collar patch for Maat.

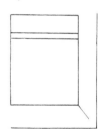

Collar patch for Obermaat.

SHOULDER STRAPS AND SLEEVE RINGS

Shoulder straps worn on the white summer jacket, white mess jacket, greatcoat and U-boat clothing; also unofficially, on the reefer jacket towards the end of the war. Sleeve rings worn on the reefer jacket, mess jacket and frock coat.

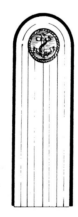
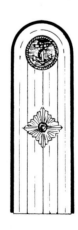

Shoulder strap and sleeve ring for Leutnant zur See.

Shoulder strap and sleeve rings for Oberleutnant zur See.

Shoulder strap and sleeve rings for Kapitänleutnant.

Shoulder strap and sleeve rings for Korvettenkapitän.

Shoulder strap and sleeve rings for Fregattenkapitän.

Worn on the reefer jacket, greatcoat, white summer jacket and on U-boat clothing

Field Grey Uniform collar patches

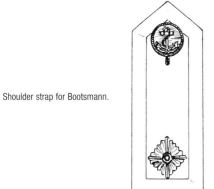

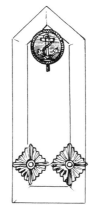

Shoulder strap for Bootsmann.

Shoulder strap for Stabsbootsmann.

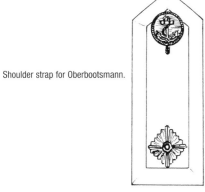

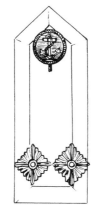

Shoulder strap for Oberbootsmann.

Shoulder strap for Stabsoberbootsmann.

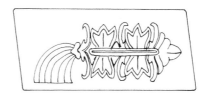

Field Grey Uniform: Collar patch for Admiral ranks.

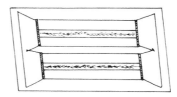

Field Grey Uniform: Collar patch for Officers.

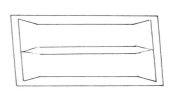

Field Grey Uniform: Collar patch for seamen, Petty Officers and Warrant Officers.

Shoulder strap and sleeve rings for Kapitän zur See.

Shoulder strap and sleeve ring for Kommodore.

Shoulder strap and sleeve rings for Konteradmiral.

Shoulder strap and sleeve rings for Vizeadmiral.

Shoulder strap and sleeve rings for Admiral.

Shoulder strap and sleeve rings for Generaladmiral.

Shoulder strap and sleeve rings for Grossadmiral.

LEFT Senior NCOs or warrant officers with Portepee (swordknot) wore reefer jackets cut in the same manner as officer jackets. Rank was shown by shoulder straps, as can be seen here: an Oberbootsmann displaying a single pip and gilt fouled anchor on his strap. The national emblem is an officer quality piece in hand embroidered gold wire.

ABOVE The man on the left is a warrant officer with Portepee, which can be seen by his elaborate shoulder strap. The anchor on the strap and the large lapels indicate that he is probably the Obersteuermann, or navigator, who also served as third watch officer. Engineer officers wore leather gear without lapels because the protection these offered on the bridge got in the way when working in confined spaces. Note that the man on the left is wearing a plain peaked cap and that the officer on the right has gold scalloped edging to his peak.

An officer's peaked cap showing the embroidery of scalloped edging for ranks from Oberleutnant zur See to Kapitänleutnant.

Korvettenkapitän Leo Wolfbauer of *U463* wearing the higher grade of officer shoulder straps and a row of oakleaves on the peak of his cap. *U463* was one of the large purpose-built supply boats, which required a mature commander with plenty of patience rather than aggressiveness.

ABOVE An interesting collection of uniforms with the U-boat commander, Hans-Peter Hinsch on the left. The artillery officer (note the badge above the sleeve rings) at the back is wearing a so-called 'Monkey's Swing' to indicate that he is an adjutant (or aide de camp) to a senior officer.

RIGHT Grand Admiral Dönitz with the double row of oakleaves for admirals on his cap. The badges on his left breast are (from top to bottom): The Second World War U-boat Badge, the eagle indicating he won the Iron Cross First Class during the First World War, the Iron Cross First Class of the Second World War and, at the bottom, the U-boat Badge from the First World War. Around his neck he is wearing a Knight's Cross with Oakleaves.

PETTY AND CHIEF PETTY OFFICERS

Petty Officer grades displayed their rank by means of an anchor on the left sleeve, upon which their trade badge was superimposed. Flat, woven, gold braid was worn on the collar of the pea jacket and on the cuffs of the uniform jacket. The collar patches on the pea jacket had a single bar of silver cord for Petty Officers and two bars for Chief Petty Officers. The silver colour was changed to gold on 1 December 1939. Petty Officers and Chief Petty Officers wore the same uniform as junior ranks, with sailor's cap.

WARRANT OFFICERS

Warrant Officers displayed their rank by means of shoulder straps. These were in dark blue cloth with flat gold braid edging and various combinations of aluminium pips to denote ranks. Warrant Officers wore collar and tie with a peaked cap, but without any gold embroidery on the peak.

COMMISSIONED OFFICERS

On the blue uniforms, rank groups were shown on the peaks of the caps, and specific ranks were indicated by rings on the jacket sleeves. On white summer uniforms and greatcoats (and also on the reefer jackets towards the end of the war), there were no sleeve rings; rank was shown by the peak of the cap and by shoulder straps.

Sleeve rings were made from flat, woven, gilt wire braid. The peaks of the caps were covered with dark blue cloth on which a pattern of scallops or oak leaves was embroidered in gilt wire.

Shoulder straps were based on the Army pattern, being made from matt silver braid on a dark blue cloth base. Admirals had a triple cord, the centre one in gilt and the outer cords in silver. Aluminium pips were used to denote specific ranks. Only the highest rank of Grand Admiral had crossed admiral's batons instead of pips.

THE FIELD GREY UNIFORM (FELDGRAUE BEKLEIDUNG)

Seamen wore chevrons on the left sleeve and field grey coloured shoulder straps, with their unit designation embroidered in yellow cotton thread.

Petty Officers and Warrant Officers wore shoulder straps similar to those worn by Warrant Officers on the blue uniform, but generally with slightly wider gilt braid, and on a field grey base.

Officer styles of shoulder straps followed those for the blue uniform, but the base colour was dark green. Officers from Leutnant to Kapitän zur See wore silver-wire-embroidered collar patches with two yellow stripes. Admirals wore collar tabs based on the design for Army generals, but the gold wire was based on blue instead of red.

No peak embroidery was worn on the cap for the field grey uniform and the peaks could be with or without leather binding to the edge.

THE STANDARD BEARER'S ARM SHIELD

This embroidered shield insignia was worn by Naval Standard Bearers on the upper left arm. It was produced as shown on a white backing for the summer uniform, and on a dark blue backing of a slightly differing shape (indicated on this illustration by a broken line) for wear on the winter uniform.

TRADE BADGES (LAUFBAHNABZEICHEN)

Trade badges or Laufbahnabzeichen for Seamen and Petty Officers were worn on the upper left arm; those for Warrant Officers on the shoulder strap; and those for Commissioned Officers on both arms. (There were only five trades for Commissioned Officers.)

Trade badges for Seamen consisted of a circular piece of navy blue badge cloth, approximately 6cm (2¼in) in diameter, with the appropriate insignia machine-embroidered in golden yellow cotton thread. For wearing during the summer months (April to September) or in tropical waters, the insignia was machine-embroidered in cornflower blue on a white linen disc, and the edges were bound to prevent them from fraying. Lower-deck ratings wore a specialist badge to denote their specific duty (e.g., specializing in anti-aircraft gunnery within the naval artillery branch) below the trade badge.

Trade badges for Petty Officers were identical to those for Seamen, but were superimposed on an anchor. The design was also machine-embroidered in golden yellow thread on blue badge cloth, forming an oval of about 9cm x 7cm

This Steuermannsmaat is wearing the Bordmütze, or Schiffchen, on his head, which folded flat and therefore used less space in his locker than the large cap with long trailing ribbon. This shot also shows the gold braid worn to the jacket collar by the ranks of Maat and Obermaat.

A Bootmannsmaat with special training in artillery using the portable rangefinder to assist small calibre anti-aircraft guns.

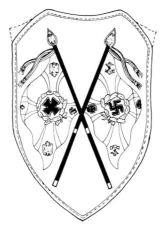

The Standard Bearer's Arm Shield.

(3½in x 2¼in). The summer version was of similar design, but embroidered in blue cotton on a white linen base. Insignia for Chief Petty Officers was the same, but with the addition of a single chevron below the anchor.

Petty Officers and Chief Petty Officers could, at their own expense, purchase fine quality versions of their trade insignia in gilt metal alloy. This was fixed to a badge-cloth base by four prongs, which fastened behind a metal backing plate. It was covered on the reverse side with black linen.

Warrant Officers wore their trade insignia in gilt metal alloy on their shoulder straps.

Commissioned Officers wore their trade insignia, hand-embroidered in gilt wire, on a small blue cloth patch immediately above their sleeve rings. Officers with a specialist trade, i.e. those other than line officers, also wore gilt metal trade insignia on the shoulder straps of appropriate uniforms.

CLOTHING

THE PULLOVER SHIRT (BLUSE)

This was the most commonly worn item of clothing in the German Navy. The blue, winter version was made in navy blue Melton cloth, with button fastening cuffs, and was worn with a cornflower blue collar, edged with three white bands

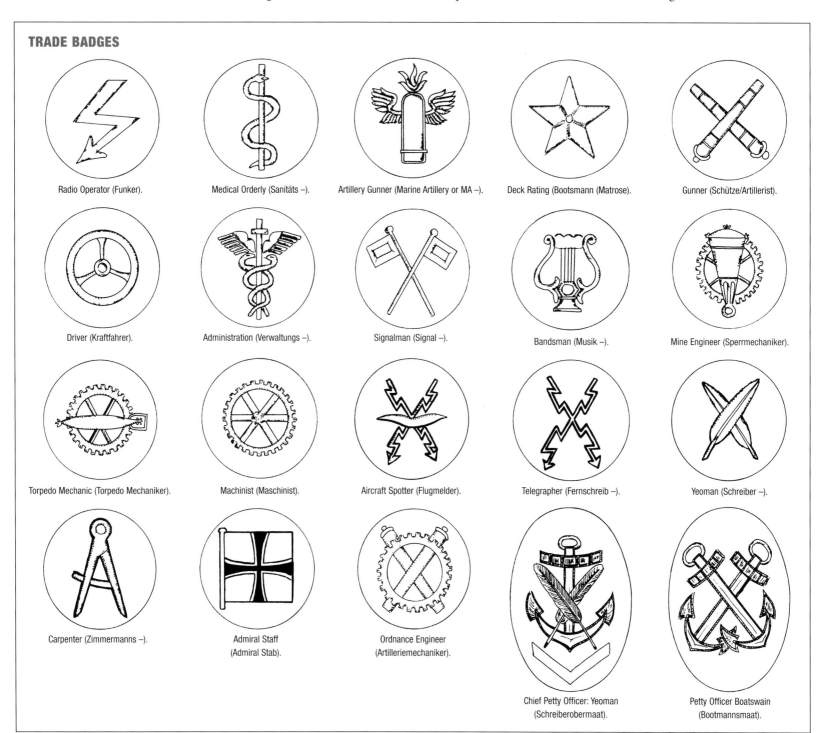

TRADE BADGES

Radio Operator (Funker).

Medical Orderly (Sanitäts –).

Artillery Gunner (Marine Artillery or MA –).

Deck Rating (Bootsmann (Matrose).

Gunner (Schütze/Artillerist).

Driver (Kraftfahrer).

Administration (Verwaltungs –).

Signalman (Signal –).

Bandsman (Musik –).

Mine Engineer (Sperrmechaniker).

Torpedo Mechanic (Torpedo Mechaniker).

Machinist (Maschinist).

Aircraft Spotter (Flugmelder).

Telegrapher (Fernschreib –).

Yeoman (Schreiber –).

Carpenter (Zimmermanns –).

Admiral Staff (Admiral Stab).

Ordnance Engineer (Artilleriemechaniker).

Chief Petty Officer: Yeoman (Schreiberobermaat).

Petty Officer Boatswain (Bootmannsmaat).

and a black silk. The national emblem, in yellow silk weave or in yellow cotton embroidery, was worn over the right breast, and rank/trade badges on the left sleeve. Navy blue trousers made from the same material were worn with this shirt. (The three white bands represented the same as in the British Royal Navy – the major injuries of Vice Admiral Horatio Nelson.)

A white version of the pullover was worn during the summer months (April to September) or in tropical waters. The appearance of this was slightly more elaborate, with cornflower blue cuffs, trimmed in white and fastened by gilt anchor buttons. The insignia for this version were in cornflower blue on white backing.

A further version of the pullover, in a very strong white woollen cloth, was used as working rig. Much simplified, this version had a plain collar and was of a closer fit than the normal pullover.

THE UNIFORM JACKET (DIENSTJACKE OR PARADEJACKE)

Worn as service dress, this elaborate jacket resembled the officers' mess jacket and was worn by Sailors and Petty Officers only. It was worn over the pullover, with the pullover's collar outside the jacket. The jacket was fastened by means of a small chain link.

The insignia on this jacket were worn in the normal man-

A naval bandsman with pea jacket and the Matrosenmütze. Note the sleeve insignia, in gilt metal, showing the Lyre superimposed on an anchor, the rank badge of a Musikmaat.

A petty officer with special training as carpenter or cabinet maker with the war badge for minesweepers in his left breast.

A petty officer with special training as artillery mechanic.

A petty officer with special training as mine mechanic.

A petty officer with special training as medical orderly.

A sailor wearing the trade badge of a torpedo mechanic. The pea jacket for junior ranks was worn without braid around the collar, and with plain cornflower blue collar patches. This Torpedomechaniker wears a torpedo over a cogwheel in place of the five-pointed star of the seaman's branch.

A sailor wearing a chevron to indicate that he is a Matrosengefreiter with driver as specialist trade.

This trade badge for an administration able seaman was worn by men holding a variety of different jobs, including cooks who were always high in demand. Note that this trade badge looks fairly similar to the Medical Trade Badge.

The greatcoat worn by naval land units was similar to those worn by the army, being made of field grey wool. This early example features a contrasting dark green collar whilst later examples had a plain field grey collar. Note the insignia on his dark green shoulder strap, a winged shell superimposed on an anchor.

CLOTHING

The Pullover Shirt.

The Uniform Jacket.

The Pea Jacket.

The Reefer Jacket.

The White Summer Jacket.

The Mess Jacket.

The Field Grey Tunic.

Naval Artillery Officers'
NCOs' Tunic

ner, with national emblem over the right breast and trade/rank badge on the sleeve. The cuffs for Petty and Chief Petty Officers were decorated with flat, woven, gilt wire braid. The metal version of the Petty Officer rank/trade badge was typically worn on this jacket.

The Pea Jacket (Überzieher)

Designed to be used over the service dress or over the pullover, this jacket was worn by all grades of seamen and petty officers in place of the greatcoat. A warm garment, it was made from thick, blue, Melton cloth, was double-breasted and fastened by five anchor buttons. The national emblem and rank/trade badges were worn in the usual manner, and collar patches were also worn (it being the only form of naval clothing, apart from the field grey naval artillery dress, to use collar patches). The pea jacket for Petty and Chief Petty Officers had flat, woven, gilt wire braid around the collar embroidered with gilt wire for Commissioned Officers.

The Reefer Jacket (Jackett)

This double-breasted garment was similar to the pea jacket in style but of much finer cloth, usually worsted, serge or even doeskin. It also had two rows of five gilt anchor buttons, but with the top button in each row being non-functional. The top two buttons were also normally set farther apart than the others.

Warrant Officers had shoulder straps with this jacket to indicate their rank, and Commissioned Officers also wore sleeve rings. It was not uncommon to find officers also wearing shoulder straps during the latter months of the war, but this was purely a fad and was against the written regulations. It was usual to wear a white shirt and black tie under this jacket.

The White Summer Jacket (Weisses Jackett)

This smart uniform jacket was worn by Commissioned and Warrant Officers during the summer months (April to September) and in tropical waters. It was single-breasted, fastened by four gilt anchor buttons, with an open collar and with four pleated patch pockets. Rank was indicated by shoulder straps, and the national emblem was made from gilt metal with a pin-back attachment. All insignia and the buttons could easily be removed for cleaning. Earlier versions of the jacket had a high collar and six button fasteners at the front. White trousers, white shirt and black tie were usually worn with this jacket. When this jacket was worn, the peaked cap would be worn with the white cover.

The Mess Jacket (Messejacke)

Two types of mess jackets were produced, but exclusively for officer ranks. The standard type was made from fine quality blue material, with four buttons at the front, and fastened with a small chain. Rank was indicated by sleeve rings. The jacket was usually worn with a matching waistcoat (often replaced by a white one for formal dress occasions), a stiff white shirt and a black bow tie.

A white version of this mess jacket was produced for wear in tropical waters and during the summer months. It was identical in design to the other garment, but rank was indicated by means of shoulder straps instead of the sleeve rings.

This shows the normal manner of wearing the naval dagger. It was suspended from black silk straps adorned by gilt lion's head buckles and hooks, and attached to a blue webbing belt worn under the jacket. The pommel (swordknot), or Portepee, was worn by commissioned officers and warrant officers with Portepee.

Korvkpt. Kümpel, commander of the sail training ship *Niobe* in 1931, wearing a frock coat and the old pattern of cap, with the Weimar Republic's eagle in the cockade. The U-boat Badge and the Wounded Badge can be seen below the Iron Cross of 1914. Just visible on the right breast is the Iron Half Moon, a star-shaped badge awarded by Turkey to men who served there during the First World War. Kümpel does not feature in the Second World War because he committed suicide shortly before it started.

Three officers displaying a variety of ways of wearing awards. The Oberleutnant zur See in the middle is wearing the Minesweeper Badge above the brocade belt, above that the U-boat Badge and then the Iron Cross First Class. The ribbon for the Iron Cross Second Class can be seen just below the pocket. The man on the right, who has not yet been awarded the Iron Cross First Class, is wearing the ribbon for the Iron Cross Second Class through the top buttonhole. This medal was usually worn only on the day of issue or during official occasions.

The traditional naval uniform had long trousers and lace-up shoes to accompany the officer's reefer jacket but matching dark blue breeches were also authorized for wear with jackboots, though this form of dress was not often used. This Korvettenkapitän is a veteran of the First World War with the Imperial Navy U-Boat badge worn just under his Iron Cross.

This interesting shot shows the white summer tunic worn by a Fähnrich zur See. All insignia and buttons for this jacket were designed to be easily removable to facilitate cleaning. Both warrant officers with Portepee and Fähnriche zur See had plain peaks without embroidery.

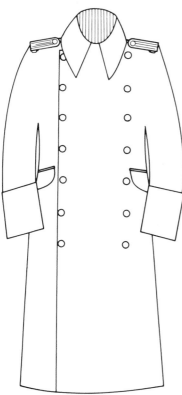

The regulation naval greatcoat worn by a Fähnrich zur See. The greatcoat was buttoned up to the neck by all ranks except admirals or men who were wearing a Knight's Cross.

and was usually buttoned up to the top unless left open to display a neck decoration (such as the Knight's Cross). The coat had cornflower blue lapels for Admirals, who never buttoned their coats right to the top; ranks were indicated on all coats by shoulder straps only, there being no sleeve rings.

Grand Admiral Karl Dönitz had the habit of wearing his coat open and he carried his gloves, instead of wearing them. One day, while sitting among a group of junior officers, he invited questions and was asked why he wore his coat and gloves against the written regulations. Looking the man straight in the eyes, Dönitz replied, 'I look like every other sailor, and somehow you have got to notice that I am in charge.' Dönitz also occasionally wore a non-regulation greatcoat with the collar and cornflower blue lapel panels covered in fur, which also lined the entire interior. This coat was exceedingly heavy, but useful when having to stand around waiting for boats to berth.

THE FIELD GREY TUNIC (FELDBLUSE)

A field grey tunic, with high collar and four patch pockets, was worn by naval artillery land units, by seamen undergoing initial training and by numerous sailors towards the end of the war, because crews from obsolete ships were drafted into land units. (This explains why there are so many photographs of what are obviously land uniforms showing naval badges.)

Various styles were available. From photographic evidence, it appears that officers often wore army-pattern tunics. Non-commissioned ranks wore a similar tunic, but of inferior quality, with a shorter skirt and a 'slash' rather than patch pockets. Both the collar and shoulder straps were edged with gilt braid, whereas lower ranks had none on either. The jacket for lower ranks had a plain collar and often a much shorter skirt.

Buttons were identical for all ranks. Normal anchor buttons and the national emblem were worn as mentioned before, but the buttons were painted field grey rather than being gilt, and the motif was hand embroidered on a dark blue-green backing for officers and machine woven or machine embroidered on dark green or field grey cloth for the lower ranks. Collar patches comprised army style 'Litzen' and had a yellow stripe down the centre of each bar. There were two types of collar patches: machine woven for lower ranks and NCOs and hand embroidered for commissioned officers up to the rank of Captain.

Collar patches for Admirals were embroidered in gilt wire on a blue backing, and were identical to those worn by Army Generals.

THE FROCK COAT ('GEHROCK', OR PLAIN 'ROCK')

This was a three-quarter length coat worn only by officers. It was slightly shorter than the greatcoat but considerably longer than any naval jacket. It also differed from the jacket and greatcoat in that both shoulder straps and sleeve rings were worn. An elegant silver brocade belt was usually worn on the outside of this garment.

Epaulettes could be attached to the shoulder scraps, but these were usually only worn by an Officer in foreign waters or at the officer's own wedding (for which there was also a special pair of trousers with a broad golden band along the outside seams of the legs).

THE GREATCOAT (MANTEL)

The greatcoat was worn by all ranks from Warrant Officer upwards. It was double-breasted with seven button fastenings, and there were a further seven buttons on the half belt and scalloped panels on the rear. It had deep turn-back cuffs

BELOW The leather coat as issued to deck personnel in U-boats, with shoulder straps to suggest this is the third watch officer holding the rank of Warrant Officer with Portepee. The majority of men had large lapels, as can be seen here, to help protect them from the weather. Men from the technical division were without lapels to prevent these getting in the way when working in confined spaces.

ABOVE A group of men during their initial training, wearing full field grey combat gear. Although most naval troops only wore field grey during basic training, there were also small numbers of land-based naval assault troops operational throughout the war with this type of gear.

During the later part of the war entire divisions of naval infantry were equipped with this clothing. The Navy did not have special head protection of its own and used the same standard M35 and M42 helmets as the other branches of the armed forces.

LEFT Gun drill with plenty of evidence that the white working rig often got pretty dirty.

ABOVE The two soldiers flanking their tall comrade are wearing field grey uniforms of the Naval Artillery. The principal differences between these uniforms and those of the Army are the lower pockets. Army tunics had external patch pockets similar to the breast pockets. The soldier in the centre is wearing the tough cotton drill work rig.

BELOW U-boat crews seldom all wore the same gear. The middle figure is the commander of *U431*, Dietrich Schöneboom, wearing the olive green work tunic. Crew member Walter Kimmelmann on the left wears the plaid shirt and the engineer officer, Leutnant zur See Brockerhoff, on the right, the naval tropical tan-coloured tunic.

LEFT These two sailors are wearing white working rig. This was similar to the normal white shirt but lacks the contrasting blue cuffs. It was made from thick cotton twill and was usually worn without the national emblem and without the blue 'Nelson' collar. Note also that the white work shirt featured a pocket on the right breast, which is missing from this working rig

ABOVE Officer cadets wearing the white sports uniform, with national eagle on the vest. The vest they wore under shirts was usually plain white, without an eagle.

ABOVE Naval personnel serving in the tropics normally wore a tan-coloured shirt and matching long baggy trousers or, as here, tan shorts. The matching tan version of the visor cap, shown here, was also produced for the tropics.

RIGHT A new set of German U-boat overalls. This design was based on the British army battledress.

The Dräger submarine escape apparatus in action. This could be used as closed-circuit breathing gear when the atmosphere became poisonous from smoke, or for escaping from submerged submarines. This photo looks as if it was taken inside an escape tank, of which there were several in Germany.

The frock coat was worn for official functions and for walking-out on Sundays by officers only. The early design of the coat was called 'Gehrock' (frock coat), but the style was changed later and it became known simply as 'Rock' (coat).

The Cloak ('Umhang', nickname 'Spanier')

This was rather like an elaborate opera cloak, it was secured with a small chain attached to two lion-head buttons, and the whole cloak was lined with silver-grey silk. Pre-war garments such as this received a new lease of life during the war when many were 'requisitioned' by the men's wives for making into dresses.

WAR BADGES

A vast range of war badges was created from 1939 until 1945. Many of them were designed by well-known artists, engravers and designers to reflect the branch of service to which the wearer belonged. All naval units were eligible for some type

Kptlt. Heinrich Schonder with men wearing inflated life jackets. Even many of the simple life saving aids were equipped with a gas bottle to fill the air bag quickly, but for most of the time men would have inflated it by blowing down the mouthpiece.

Men aboard a U-boat wearing standard rain gear consisting of a coat and sou'wester and heavy rough-weather gear on the left. In addition to this they are equipped with standard life jackets in case they are washed overboard. The circular dipole aerial of a radar detector can also be seen.

of award, although not every department was covered by an individual badge. Crews of supply ships, which supported raiders such as *Atlantis*, *Thor* and *Pinguin*, were eligible for the Auxiliary Cruiser Badge.

Method of wear

These war badges were produced in two basic forms: either as a badge to be worn on the breast or as a clasp (Spange) worn above the left breast pocket (or in that position, if there were no pockets). The only exceptions to this rule were the seven grades of awards for the Midget Weapons Unit (Kleinkampfverband), which was fixed to the sleeve. All these badges ranked lower than decorations; an Iron Cross, for example, was worn above the war badge.

Attachment

The majority of these badges were made of metal, although in some cases cloth variants could be purchased at the wearer's expense. The first mentioned were attached to the uniform by means of a hinged pin fitting, of which there were two common types: the early badges were mostly produced with a broad flat pin, which passed through thread loops sewn on the tunic; later examples had round pins and could be pushed through the material of the tunic. These pins ran either vertically or horizontally.

Materials

During the early stages of the war, these badges were generally made from a bronze alloy (called Tombakbronze) or brass, with a very high quality mercuric fire-gilded finish. Later, they were produced in fine-grain zinc and, towards the end of the war, in very poor quality pot metal known in Germany as war metal (Kriegsmetall). The gilt finish of these later types deteriorated remarkably quickly and it is not uncommon to find these badges today in mint condition, but with hardly any traces of their original gilt colouring. These late war badges used a cheap gold lacquer known as Brennlaq (Brennlack).

THE AWARDS

A certificate or some type of document usually accompanied the badge itself at the award ceremony. These pieces of paper ranged from fairly plain designs to most impressive and elaborate works of art. There was no real attempt to standardise the documents, as was the case with certificates for decorations, and it is quite possible that, towards the end of the war, no documents were awarded. However, such awards were recorded in the man's pay book.

The badges themselves were handed over in anything from a brown paper bag or small box to an elaborate velvet-lined case. In many cases, the badge was pinned directly onto the recipient's tunic, without any box or case being given with it.

Miniature stick pin versions of these badges exist, for wearing as lapel pins on civilian clothing.

Variant Awards

Naval war badges were also produced on a limited scale in occupied France. Several types are known, including the

EAGLE SYMBOLS TO BE
FOUND IN THE HERALDRY
OF THE GERMAN NAVY

The eagle of the Reichsmarine.

The political eagle of the NSDAP which was
often used by the Kriegsmarine.

The eagle of the Kriegsmarine.

E-boat, High Seas Fleet, U-boat, Destroyer and Coastal Artillery. These badges were considered controversial for some time but are now generally accepted to have been produced by a manufacturing concern in Paris during the period of the German occupation.

The detail on these badges differed greatly from their German counterparts, the most striking difference being their smaller size. It can be assumed from their relative scarcity that these badges were only produced on a small scale.

U-Boat Badge (Uboots-kriegsabzeichen)

This was the first war badge introduced during the Second World War. It was instituted on 13 October 1939 – the day that Günther Prien and *U47* started their famous attack on the battleship HMS *Royal Oak* in Scapa Flow. Paul Casberg designed the badge to follow the First World War pattern of a U-boat superimposed on an oval wreath of laurel; the only noteworthy change was the substitution of an eagle and swastika for the old imperial crown.

The basic requirement for the award of the badge was that the recipient had served on at least two operational cruises, although this could be waived for wounded men.

The badge itself measured 48mm x 40mm (about 2in x 1½in) and was worn on the left side of the tunic or shirt. It was usually made from gilt metal, but embroidered cloth versions can also be found.

A special gilded, solid silver version of this badge was produced by Schwerin of Berlin. It can be identified by the

U-Boat Badge.

nine small diamonds that were set into the swastika. Unfortunately, this form is very rare: only 29 were awarded to outstanding U-boat commanders. It appears that Schwerin also made the badge in solid gold with the swastika and laurel wreath encrusted with diamonds. Only one was made, which was awarded to Karl Dönitz.

The original version of the U-boat Badge was introduced on the orders of Grand Admiral Raeder, and the silver version was added later on by Grand Admiral Dönitz.

Destroyer Badge (Zerstörer-kriegsabzeichen)

The Destroyer Badge was instituted during June 1940 as an award for men engaged in the Battle of Narvik, during the Norwegian Campaign. In October of the same year, it was authorized for crews of other destroyers and for men serving in torpedo-boats who could fulfil one of the following conditions.

1. Participation in three engagements against the enemy.
2. Participation in twelve sorties without engaging the enemy.
3. Being wounded in action.
4. Service in a vessel that had been sunk by enemy action.
5. Especially meritorious service.

The designer, Paul Casberg, based the ship depicted upon the badge on the destroyer *Z21* (*Wilhelm Heidkamp*). The award was worn on the left side of the shirt or tunic and measured 54mm x 44mm (about 2in x 1¾in).

Badge for Minesweepers, Submarine-Hunters and other Security Forces

In Germany this is called the 'Kriegsabzeichen für Minensuch, Ubootsjagd und Sicherungsverbände'. It was instituted on 31 August 1940 for crews of minesweepers, submarine-chasers and escort vessels who could fulfil one of the following conditions.

1. Participation in three operational sorties.
2. Participation in one successful sortie.
3. Six months active service.

Destroyer Badge.

Badge for Minesweepers, Submarine-Hunters and other Security Forces.

4. Being wounded in action.
5. Service in a vessel sunk by enemy action.

The badge, in gilt and measuring 55mm x 44mm (about 2in x 1¾in) was designed by Otto Placzek and worn on the left side of the tunic or shirt.

MOTOR TORPEDO-BOAT BADGE (SCHNELLBOOTS-KRIEGSABZEICHEN)

This was instituted on 30 May 1941 for crews of torpedo and motor torpedo-boats to replace the Destroyer Badge for which they had been eligible.

There was a split in the organization, with torpedo-boats leaving Destroyer Command and forming their own arm. Conditions for its receipt remained similar.

The badge was originally designed by Wilhelm E. Peekhaus of Berlin to depict a silver-coloured, early type of motor torpedo-boat speeding through a gilt wreath. It was redesigned, with help from Kpt.z.S. Rudolf Petersen (Commander-in-Chief for Motor Torpedo-Boats) during January 1943 to show a more modern boat. The first design measured 45mm x 57mm (about 1¾in x 2¼in) and the later version 52mm x 60mm (about 2in x 2¼in).

A special badge, in gilted solid silver with nine diamonds on the swastika and depicting the later type of boat, was produced by Schwerin of Berlin, It was awarded eight times to outstanding motor torpedo-boat commanders, all of whom also held the Knight's Cross of the Iron Cross with Oakleaves.

Motor Torpedo-Boat Badge (early type).   Motor Torpedo-Boat Badge (later type).

AUXILIARY CRUISER BADGE (HILFSKREUZER-KRIEGSABZEICHEN)

This badge was instituted on 24 April 1941 for crews of auxiliary cruisers and also for the crews of their supply ships who had taken part in at least one long-distance cruise. It was designed by Wilhelm E. Peekhaus to show a gilt metal wreath with a silver-coloured globe. A number were also made in Yokahama (Japan) on behalf of the Germans, and awarded to crew members of vessels operating in far eastern waters.

A special edition of this badge was commissioned, with fifteen small diamonds and made from solid silver, but only one confirmed award is known, that being the one given to Kpt.z.S. Bernhard Rogge, commander of the legendary *Atlantis*.

U-BOAT CLASP (UBOOTS-FRONTSPANGE)

This clasp was introduced by Grand Admiral Dönitz in May 1944 to recognize further merit on the part of U-boat per-

Badge for Auxliary Cruisers.

sonnel who had already been awarded the U-boat Badge. No fixed criteria were laid down for this award, except that each application had to be approved personally by Dönitz.

The clasp was initially only made from bronze, but a silver grade was added during November 1944. They were designed and made by Schwerin of Berlin and measured 71mm x 24mm (about 2¾in x 1in). Whilst it seems that issue of the bronze version was initially controlled, it is said that a large number of the silver awards were given to U-boat men who simply happened to have been in port, during the last days of the war when supplies of the clasp had become surplus to requirements.

ABOVE U-Boat Clasp.   BELOW Naval War Clasp.

NAVAL WAR CLASP (MARINEFRONTSPANGE)

This clasp was introduced on 19 November 1944 for all crews other than U-boat personnel. Requirements were five times those needed for the appropriate war badge. The only original examples of this clasp extant are crude, and were probably made aboard ships.

BADGE FOR MIDGET WEAPONS UNIT (KAMPFABZEICHEN DER KLEINKAMPFMITTEL)

This badge was introduced during November 1944. There were seven grades:

1. A yellow embroidered swordfish within a rope circle on a blue cloth backing; awarded for participation in one action.
2. As above, but with the addition of a single sword, pointing forty-five degrees to the left; awarded for participation in two actions.

Badge for Midget Weapons Unit (lower grades)

LEFT Badge for Midget Weapons Unit (upper grades)

Motor Boat Rescue Badge (Air, Sea Rescue, controlled by the Luftwaffe). Probably not awarded; but photographs of the badges testify that at least some were manufactured.

RIGHT Naval Artillery Badge.

3. As above, but with two crossed swords; awarded for completing three actions.
4. As above, but with a third, vertical sword added; awarded for completing four actions.
5. A bronze metal clasp showing the swordfish superimposed on a knotted rope; awarded for participation in five actions.
6. As above, but made from a silver-coloured metal; awarded after completing seven missions.
7. As above, but in a gilt metal; awarded after completing at least ten missions.

The cloth awards were worn on the upper right sleeve and the metal clasps on the left breast.

FLEET WAR BADGE (FLOTTEN-KRIEGSABZEICHEN)

Introduced during April 1941 for crews of battleships and cruisers who could fulfil one of the following conditions:
1. Twelve weeks active service at sea.
2. Service in a ship lost at sea.
3. Being wounded in action.
4. Participation in one particularly successful cruise.

The badge, in gilt metal with the battleship in dark grey, was designed by the marine artist Adolf Bock. It measured 44mm x 57mm (about 1¾in x 2¼in).

LEFT Fleet War Badge.

BELOW Blockade-Breakers Badge.

BLOCKADE-BREAKERS BADGE (ABZEICHEN FÜR BLOCKADEBRECHER)

This was awarded to crews of merchant ships that were in foreign ports at the start of the war and managed to bring their vessels into a German-held port. Men serving in ships lost at sea by enemy action or men who prevented their ship from falling into enemy hands by scuttling were also eligible.

The badge was 51mm (2in) in diameter and was usually awarded together with a half-size miniature for wearing with

civilian clothing. It was dark grey in colour, with the eagle and swastika silvered.

NAVAL ARTILLERY BADGE (KRIEGSABZEICHEN FÜR MARINEARTILLERIE)

This badge was awarded to crews of naval artillery batteries engaged in either anti-aircraft or coastal defence duties. It first appeared during June 1941 and was awarded on a points basis, a total of eight being required for the badge. Two were given for shooting down an aeroplane unassisted, one point if helped by another gun, half a point for detecting enemy aircraft, and so forth. The badge, in gilt colour with a dark grey gun emplacement motif, was designed by Otto Placzek and measured 55mm x 42mm (about 2¼in x 1¾in).

THE NARVIK SHIELD (NARVIKSCHILD)

The Narvik Shield was designed by Professor Klein of Munich and was instituted during August 1940 for men involved in the Battle of Narvik between April and June of 1940. Two different versions were produced: a gilt metal badge for the Navy and a silver-coloured type for Army and Air Force.

Of a total of 8,577 distributed throughout the Navy, 2,670 went to destroyer personnel; 411 of these were posthumous awards.

The badge measured 92mm x 40mm (about 3½in x 2½in) and was fixed to a piece of navy blue backing cloth, which was sewn onto the upper left arm of the tunic.

THE LORIENT SHIELD (LORIENTSCHILD)

The idea to commemorate the stand of the Lorient garrison with a badge was only approved at local level and it probably never received official backing. Apparently, the shield was made from a variety of materials, and was somewhat crudely manufactured. There were four pairs of small holes around the edge for attaching to the sleeve. The author talked to at least half a dozen men who were in Lorient at the time, but none of them had heard of this award.

CLASP FOR THE ROLL OF HONOUR OF THE NAVY (EHRENTAFELSPANGE DER KRIEGSMARINE)

This clasp was intended to recognize those men whose names were recorded in the Ehrentafel der deutschen Kriegsmarine, a roll of honour recording heroic deeds by German seamen.

The clasp consisted of a gilt metal wreath of oak leaves with an anchor, upon which a swastika was superimposed. It was clipped to the ribbon of the Iron Cross Second Class and worn from the buttonhole. Very few were ever awarded.

The Narvik Shield.

Lorient Shield.

Clasp for the Roll of Honour of the Navy.

HEADGEAR

Headgear for the Kriegsmarine followed the traditional naval design, the principal innovation of the Third Reich period being the introduction of gilt wire embroidery on the peaks of officers' caps to indicate rank groupings.

The most frequently worn type of headgear among the lower ranks was the sailors' cap with tally ribbon. This consisted of a rigid band with a floppy, wide-brimmed top fitting over it. The colour was dark blue for winter, white for summer and for tropical waters. The hat band was fitted with a long ribbon, which had the name of the wearer's ship or shore establishment woven upon it in gold-coloured gothic letters. Insignia, in the form of a gilt eagle and swastika over the national cockade, was worn on the front of the brim.

All these ribbons with names should have been withdrawn during the war and replaced by one bearing the legend 'Kriegsmarine', but this did not occur until about November 1939. Named ribbons continued to be worn after this within barracks or for special occasions such as weddings or having portrait photographs taken.

The sailors' cap became less popular as the war progressed, and it was gradually replaced by the forage cap or Schiffchen

U-boat leathers for technical divisions were without large lapels as shown here. The men are also wearing the 'Bordmütze' forage caps also called 'Schiffchen' which was favoured because it folded flat.

ABOVE This photograph of Oberleutnant zur See Heinz Ehrich of *U334* typifies the appearance of a wartime submarine commander. He has added a pin-on metal breast eagle, plus his Iron Cross and U-Boat War Badge to his cotton twill U-boat blouse and sports a bow tie. The blouse was based on British battledress, captured after the fall of France and initially issued only to U-boat crews because they were unlikely to be accidentally shot as a result of being confused for the enemy. The white cap cover instantly identifies him as the boat's commander.

This sailor is wearing the standard sailors' cap or Matrosenmütze, which had a simple cap ribbon bearing the title 'Kriegsmarine' during the war years.

LEFT These men are wearing naval issue woollen bobble hats.

(meaning small ship, because of its shape). This was made from blue woollen cloth with a black lining, and it was worn by all ranks from Ordinary Seaman to Grand Admiral.

Lower ranks had the insignia woven in yellow silk on blue; officers had gilt wire instead of silk, and also had gilt piping around the flap.

A forage cap was produced in the same pattern for the naval field grey uniform. This had the insignia woven in yellow on green for lower ranks and in gilt wire for officers, who also had the gilt piping around the flap. Some examples of the field-grey forage cap have an inverted, lemon-coloured chevron over the cockade.

The peaked cap, called 'Schirmmütze', was similar in basic appearance for all ranks. It had a black, or cloth-covered peak, a woven mohair band and a wide-brimmed floppy top in blue cloth. The chin strap was made from leather and fastened by two small anchor buttons. The insignia consisted of an embroidered eagle and swastika, either in yellow cotton or gilt wire, on the front of the floppy top. A red/silver/black national cockade, surrounded by a wreath of oak leaves, was attached to the cap band, which was also embroidered in either yellow cotton or gilt wire.

The peak of the cap was in plain black (usually with leather edge binding) for non-commissioned officers and officer candidates. Those ranking from Leutnant zur See to Kapitänleutnant had a thin row of gilt wire scallops embroidered along the edge of the blue cloth of the peak; officers from Korvettenkapitän to Kapitän zur See had a row of oakleaves; and Admirals had two wide rows of oakleaves.

White covers, removable and fixed types, were worn on the peaked cap during summer months and also in tropical waters. Sometime after the start of the war, U-boat commanders wore a white cover to their caps. This started as fad and was not included in written regulations.

The peaked cap for wearing with the field grey uniform was similar in design to the normal blue cap. It had a plain black peak for all ranks, with the top in field grey and with dark green piping. The cap band was also dark green and normally had dark green piping only along the top edge. Silver cord chin straps were worn by officers and leather chin straps by NCOs. The insignia were similar to those on the blue cap, but were embroidered in gilt on green for officers, while NCOs had plain metal badges.

BELTS AND BUCKLES

The belt buckle for the lower ranks of the German Navy was identical in design to the buckle worn by the Army and was made from steel with a gold plate. An aluminium buckle with gilt wash (a thin anodised coating) was used for parades; the front of this was pebbled and there was often a separate centrepiece. Examples of this buckle with a dark blue painted finish also exist; these were used for front-line field service duty. All these buckles were usually worn with a brown leather belt.

There were several variations in the general appearance of the buckle. Officers normally wore a gilt finish, pebbled aluminium, double-clawed buckle; a circular buckle consisting of an oak leaf wreath surrounding an anchor, was worn for dress occasions, with a black and silver brocade belt. The

Belt Buckle for Lower Ranks.

Officers' Pattern Belt Buckle.

A close-up of the brocade belt buckle.

buckle was cast in aluminium and had a gilt finish. A similar buckle, only much smaller, was worn with the blue canvas dagger or sword belt inside the greatcoat or jacket, while the brocade belt was worn on the outside.

SMALL ARMS AND EDGED WEAPONS

There appears to have been no hard and fast rule about the issue of guns. They were often given to a ship or unit and distributed by the commander when required, and then collected again after use. Some men carried their own personal – but naval issue – pistols either for self defence or to ensure a quick death should they find themselves in an impossible situation faced with a slow and painful end.

PISTOLS
The hand-guns used by the Navy were standard pieces issued to other branches of the armed services. There were no special naval pattern guns, like the naval P08 of the Imperial Navy. However, the Mauser HSc automatic appears to have been very popular during the Third Reich period.

Although pistols were only rarely issued to naval personnel, officers on duty in port (both commissioned and non-commissioned) could usually be identified because they wore a belt with pistol or bayonet. Lower ranks on guard duty in port were more often given a rifle or some other large large-calibre hand weapon.

RIFLES AND OTHER SMALL ARMS
Standard issue infantry weapons, such as the Mauser Kar 98k, MP38/40, MG34/41, were issued to naval personnel when required. It appears that obsolete weapons, such as the Mauser Gewehr 98, were issued to naval units, so that front-

A few automatic weapons, such as this 9mm machine pistol, were issued to U-boats for use by guards when in port.

line Army units could be given preference for new weapons. Bayonets:

The standard Mauser 98 bayonet, with either wood or Bakelite grips and worn in a brown leather frog, was issued to naval personnel.

DAGGERS AND SWORDS

Two basic forms of naval daggers were produced, either with a beaten or an engraved scabbard. The dagger itself had a long double-edged blade, with two fullers, and was either plain or with a large variety of etch patterns of naval motifs. Blades were made in both plain and Damascus steel, although the latter were not usually issued by the Navy – they had to be purchased. The cross-piece, with anchor motif, was in gilt cast brass, as was the pommel, which was in the form of an eagle and swastika. The grip was in white celluloid with a gilt wire wrap over a wooden base. Special scabbard designs with ornate oak leaf designs were also produced.

The dagger was suspended from two black satin straps, which were fitted with gilt alloy, lion-head motif buckles. Administration officials had silver buckles.

Naval daggers, virtually indistinguishable from the original, are still being produced today to meet the demand from collectors, and a new version with the swastika replaced by an anchor is being made for the Federal Navy.

Unless on special operations, U-boats were usually issued with old rifles which were no longer needed by the army.

A German naval dagger with Portepee, or swordknot, correctly attached.

The Honour Dagger

This highly ornate version of the naval dagger was instituted by Grand Admiral Raeder, and it is known to have been awarded at least six times. It was manufactured by the firm of Carl Eikhorn in Solingen. The swastika on the pommel was encrusted with small diamonds and the ivory grip had an ornate oak leaf wrap. The blade was made from Damascus steel with a raised gilt dedication on the ricasso. The scabbard was also very ornate, with fine oak leaf decorations.

The Sword

The naval sword was traditional in appearance, with a gilt lion-head pommel, a white grip with gilt wire wrap and a fouled anchor on the folding shell guard. The scabbard was in black leather with gilt brass fittings. Swords could be carried by warrant officers with swordknot (Portepee) and by commissioned officers. The naval version can be identified because the lion's head on the handle had one red and one green eye.

MARKSMANSHIP AWARDS

Marksmanship was recognized by awarding a lanyard made from plaited blue cord, which was worn from the right shoulder. The type of weapon with which proficiency had been achieved was indicated by a miniature device hung from the end of the lanyard. An acorn indicated rifle and machine-gun marksmanship. Other symbols were as follows:
- Shell: Deck guns, anti-aircraft and coastal artillery.
- Shell with wings: Anti-aircraft machine-guns.
- Torpedo: Torpedo shooting.

These awards were of gun metal colour for the first award and silver and gold for the second and third awards. The lanyard itself also differed for each higher award:
- 1st Award: Plain blue lanyard with a black miniature.
- 2nd Award: Blue lanyard with a silver interwoven stripe and a silver miniature.
- 3rd Award: Blue lanyard with a silver interwoven stripe and a gilt miniature.
- 4th Award: Blue lanyard with a silver interwoven stripe and a gilt metal miniature.

NAVAL OFFICIALS (MARINEBEAMTEN)

Marinebeamten were officials who carried out administrative duties, and were given status equivalent to the appropriate naval rank. Their uniforms were in the same style as those of regular officers, but the insignia were in silver rather than gold colour. Their trade speciality was indicated by a small embroidered badge on each sleeve, worn just above the sleeve rings: this insignia consisted of an eagle and swastika over the appropriate trade badge.

The peaked cap for officials was similar to the standard naval cap, but it also had the silver insignia. The peak was plain leather with wire chin cords, rather than plain leather ones, and admirals had gilt wire chin cords.

Naval officials were further distinguished by the use of coloured piping on uniforms where epaulettes were worn: black for technical personnel, carmine red for legal officials,

NAVAL CHAPLAIN'S INSIGNIA

Collar Patch for Marinedekan (Naval Dean) 1942-45.

Collar Patch for Marinepfarrer (Minister) Oberpfarrer and Dekan pre-1942 pattern.

Cap band emblem for naval chaplains.

and cornflower blue for administrative officials, pharmacists and all other non-technical personnel.

Naval chaplains were also classed as officials and wore the uniform of the Marinebeamten with a few minor changes. There was, for example, a silver wire, embroidered cross above the national cockade on the peaked cap. Collar patches, showing a cross surrounded by oak leaves in wire embroidered on purple velvet, were also worn on the reefer jacket.

The silver rather than traditional gold naval insignia worn by these non-seagoing personnel often led to them being somewhat scathingly referred to by sailors as 'Silberlings'.

COASTAL POLICE (MARINE-KÜSTENPOLIZEI)

This was a coastal security unit performing similar duties to the United States Coastguards. The men wore standard naval uniforms with special police insignia in gilt colour. A gorget, bearing the luminous inscription 'Marineküstenpolizei', was worn when on duty, as was a cuff title with the same inscription. After 1943, the police pattern insignia was replaced by standard naval rank insignia.

AWARDS AND INSIGNIA FOR INDIVIDUAL UNITS

Some units created their own unofficial awards and badges, usually incorporating their own insignia in the design. There were two main types: lapel badges, worn in a similar manner to Air Force insignia; and non-portable badges in the form of shields, plaques or paintings on sides of ships. One example of lapel insignia was created by Korvkpt. Hans Bartels, commander of minesweeper *M1*. When he became Chief of Naval Defence Units in part of Norway, he instituted his own Pin of Honour, a small pin that was presented with an elaborate award document in colour.

The 3rd Motor Torpedo-Boat Flotilla was one of the units that produced its own shield, which was finely cast in aluminium and hand-painted. The insignias or emblems painted directly on to the sides of the ships were either done by hand or, if the insignia were elaborate, the boat carried a sheet metal stencil. Officially, the Naval Command did not object to such insignias; they specified that they should be removed before the boat went to sea, but many boats disregarded the directive and proudly carried their badges into battle. Even so, the emblems had to be repainted frequently and, as a result, the exact details of the design tended to differ.

NAVAL HITLER YOUTH (MARINE-HITLERJUGEND)

The Naval Hitler Youth played an important part in the training of future recruits for both the Kriegsmarine and the merchant navy. They wore the standard naval rating's uniform with the following insignia:

1. An enamelled red, silver and black diamond-shaped Hitler Youth badge in place of the national insignia on the rating's cap.
2. A tally ribbon, in pale blue, with block or gothic letters woven to show the district.
3. A Hitler Youth armband on the left arm.
4. Also on the left arm, above the armband, a woven triangular badge with the district designation.

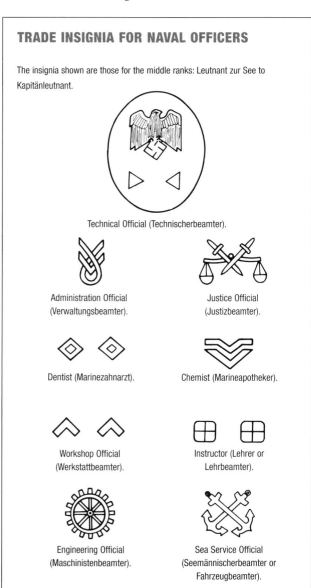

TRADE INSIGNIA FOR NAVAL OFFICERS

The insignia shown are those for the middle ranks: Leutnant zur See to Kapitänleutnant.

Technical Official (Technischerbeamter).

Administration Official (Verwaltungsbeamter).

Justice Official (Justizbeamter).

Dentist (Marinezahnarzt).

Chemist (Marineapotheker).

Workshop Official (Werkstattbeamter).

Instructor (Lehrer or Lehrbeamter).

Engineering Official (Maschinistenbeamter).

Sea Service Official (Seemännischerbeamter or Fahrzeugbeamter).

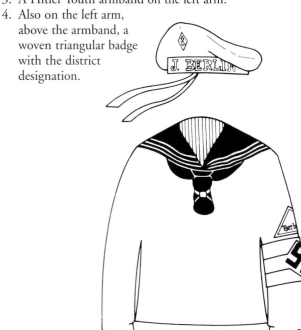

Uniform for Naval Hitler Youth.

Achievement Badge for Shipyard
Workers.

ACHIEVEMENT BADGE FOR SHIPYARD WORKERS (WERFTLEISTUNGSABZEICHEN)

This was introduced during 1944 to recognize appreciation of the work done by those involved in the U-boat construction and repair programme. It was a semi-official award and was accompanied by a formal award document. Original examples of the badge are relatively scarce.

NON-NAVAL AWARDS

THE IRON CROSS

This old Prussian award was originally instituted in 1813 and was re-introduced later by Kaiser Wilhelm I for the war against France in 1870. It reappeared in 1914, and next emerged in 1939. On the latter occasion it appeared in four grades.

1. Iron Cross (2nd Class) – abbreviated EK2 in Germany from Eisernes Kreuz.
2. Iron Cross (1st Class) – abbreviated EK1 in Germany.
3. The Knight's Cross of the Iron Cross.
4. The Grand Cross of the Iron Cross.

The Iron Cross (2nd Class)

The Iron Cross (2nd Class) was awarded with a red, white and black ribbon, and usually presented in a small blue or cream-coloured envelope inscribed 'Eisernes Kreuz 2. Klasse 1939'. The cross measured 44mm (1¾in) and consisted of a blackened centre, with the date '1813' on the otherwise blank

A Knight's Cross of the Iron Cross with Oakleaves.

reverse. The front had a swastika in the centre and the date '1939' on the lower leg of the cross. The rim was made from a separate piece of silver-coloured metal, which could have been anything from real silver to nickel silver or plated brass.

The cross was normally only worn immediately after the award had been made. Thereafter, only the ribbon was worn through the buttonhole of the tunic. If the wearer had only the one medal, the cross would be worn on a ribbon bar or on its own for dress occasions.

There were several people who won EK2 in both the First and Second World War. In that case, they wore the black and white ribbon of the 1914 Cross in the buttonhole and attached to it a small eagle and swastika with a bar bearing the date '1939'. This was attached to the ribbon by four prongs and usually measured 30mm x 30mm (about 1⅛in x 1⅛in).

Approximately 2,300,000 Second Class Crosses and Clasps were awarded during the years 1939 to 1945.

The Iron Cross (1st Class)

The Iron Cross (1st Class) was issued in a small black case lined with white flock or velvet and with a silver 'iron cross' printed on the lid. The front was identical to that of the 2nd Class version, but the reverse side was plain silver-coloured, with a hinged pin fitting to attach it to the tunic. Variations exist with a screw back fitting, and some crosses also had brass centres (which were popular with naval personnel because they did not rust as quickly). Some of these brass-centre crosses were also convex in shape, which was popular during the First World War, but fairly rare during the Second.

One major and extremely rare variation was the Japanese-produced type. Obermaat Conrad Metzner and some twenty-five other men, from the auxiliary cruiser *Michel*, were awarded the EK1 by Admiral Paul Wenneker, (the Naval Attaché in Tokyo). These were made from pure Japanese silver with a copper centre.

Men who had won the EK1 in 1914 and were awarded it again during the Second World War wore the 1914 version on the left breast of the tunic and above this a clasp similar to that for the EK2, but this one had a hinged pin fitting and it was slightly larger, 45mm x 31mm (1¾in x 1¼in). The clasp was presented in a small black case lined with black velvet, and there was a silver clasp embossed on the lid.

Approximately 300,000 EK1s and Clasps were awarded during the Second World War.

The Knight's Cross

The Knight's Cross of the Iron Cross was a new award introduced to bridge the previously enormous gap between the EK1 and the Grand Cross. It was almost identical to the EK2. The Knight's Cross was slightly larger, at 48mm (nearly 2in), and the rim was made from genuine 800 fine silver. The medal was worn from a red, white and black neck ribbon.

The Cross was awarded with a black oblong fitted case lined with black velvet, and was, in the early stages of the war at least, accompanied by a most elaborate hand-finished citation. The wording was on vellum and presented inside a large red and brown leather folder with a gilt metal eagle and swastika on the front. The original notification of the award was usually accompanied by a preliminary certificate.

It should be noted that some Knight's Cross holders purchased duplicates, or they even wore a EK2 at the neck, for

KNIGHT'S CROSS AWARDS TO THE GERMAN NAVY

	Knight's Cross	Higher grades
OKM (Supreme Naval Command) and Staff Officers	18	3 Oakleaves
Battleships and cruisers	44	5 Oakleaves
Destroyers and torpedo-boats	44	9 Oakleaves
Minesweepers	37	4 Oakleaves
Coastal Security Craft	9	1 Oakleaves
Small battle groups	6	–
Coastal artillery and Anti-aircraft gunners	14	3 Oakleaves
Merchant navy	1	–
U-boats	145	28 Oakleaves, Swords and Diamonds

fear of losing their real medal in action. Ships' crews, especially submarines, often made their own Knight's Crosses for their officers, which could be worn until the proper presentation. Many men wore this home-made version in preference to the correct naval issue one.

318 Knight's Crosses were awarded to Kriegsmarine personnel and the majority of these went to U-boat men.

Contrary to popular belief, the Knight's Cross was not liberally awarded; the higher grades of the Knight's Cross were certainly just as rare as the higher Allied awards. Only two Knight's Crosses with Oakleaves, Swords and Diamonds were awarded to the Navy during the entire war.

Oakleaves to the Knight's Cross

The Oakleaves were instituted on 3 June 1940, and consisted of a small pure silver cluster of three oakleaves, mounted on a replacement ribbon loop, which was clipped on to the Knight's Cross. The Leaves were awarded in a small black case lined in black velvet, and accompanied by an elaborate certificate and a white leather folder, similar to the one presented with the Knight's Cross. Fifty-three such awards were made to the Kriegsmarine during the war.

Swords and Oakleaves to the Knight's Cross

The Swords were instituted on 2I June 1941, and consisted of two small pure silver swords, 24mm (approx. 1in) long, crossed at an angle of forty degrees. They were soldered to the bottom of a replacement set of oakleaves, and presented in a black case similar to the others. The certificate was a little more elaborate. All five Swords awarded to the German Navy went to U-boat commanders:

- Fregkpt. Otto Kretschmer (26 December 1941). This was the 5th set of Swords awarded to German Armed Forces.
- Fregkpt. Erich Topp (17 August 1942), the 17th set of Swords awarded to the German Armed Forces.
- Fregkpt. Reinhard Suhren (1 September 1942), the 18th set of Swords awarded to the German Armed Forces.
- Kpt.z.S. Wolfgang Lüth (15 April 1943), the 29th set of Swords awarded to the German Armed Forces.
- Fregkpt. Albrecht Brandi (9 May 1944), the 66th set of Swords awarded to the German Armed Forces.

Diamonds to the Knight's Cross

This rare and beautiful hand-made version of the Swords and Oakleaves was studded with real diamonds on the front. Only two men in the Kriegsmarine were awarded them: Albrecht Brandi and Wolfgang Lüth.

THE WAR MERIT CROSS (KRIEGSVERDIENSTKREUZ OR KVK)

This was awarded for meritorious service contributing to the war effort. It could be won 'with Swords' for military service that did not involve actual combat with the enemy (for which the Iron Cross would be appropriate) or without Swords for non-military actions. The awards without Swords were often bestowed upon civilians, but could occasionally be given to military personnel serving on the home front. The War Merit Cross was also awarded in two classes (like the Iron Cross), and there was a Knight's Cross with or without Swords. These medals were worn in a similar manner to the corresponding Iron Crosses.

The War Merit Cross is relatively uncommon in the Navy when compared with the other branches of the military. The first Knight's Cross was awarded, with swords, to Generaladmiral Carl Witzel on 5 October 1942, and the next one, to Oberfunkmeister Klaus Hoelck, was not authorized until 21 February 1944. Another fifteen or so were awarded in 1944, and only about eleven in 1945.

In photographs, especially poor-quality prints, it could be possible to mistake the Knight's Cross of the Kriegsverdienstkreuz for the Pour le Mérite of the First World War. The Knight's Cross of the Distinguished Service Cross had a distinct disc bearing a swastika in the centre, and there was no such disc on the Pour Ie Mérite. There were about sixteen men serving during the Second World War who also held this famous First World War medal.

THE GERMAN CROSS (DEUTSCHES KREUZ)

This large dominant medal was introduced in 1941 to acknowledge effort above the degree normally recognized by the Iron Cross (1st Class), but not sufficient to merit a Knight's Cross. The German Cross was large, 63mm (2½in) in diameter, a heavy and most impressive pin-backed medal, which was worn on the right breast of the tunic.

It consisted of a central silver-coloured disc with a black swastika in enamel, surrounded by a wreath of oakleaves, bearing the date '1941'. Radiating out from this was a sunburst star. The Cross was also manufactured in cloth, with a metal central core surrounded by embroidery.

The oakleaves surrounding the central swastika were in silver if the award was for non-combat related service (in which case the recipient must have already earned the War Merit Cross First Class), or gold where the award was for combat-related actions (where the recipient must already have earned the Iron Cross First Class).

THE SPANISH CROSS (SPANIENKREUZ)

This award appears occasionally in wartime photographs. It was presented as a result of some noteworthy participation in the Spanish Civil War during 1937. The Cross consisted of a Maltese cross with central swastika, and between the four arms there were small Luftwaffe-type flying eagles.

THE IRON HALF MOON (EISERNER HALBMOND)

Commonly referred to by the Germans as the Iron Crescent or even as the Gallipoli Star, the correct name for this award is the Turkish War Medal. It was bestowed upon many German personnel serving in the Dardanelles, by Germany's Turkish allies during the First World War.

The award consisted of a red five-pointed star with a crescent moon in the centre, above which was portrayed the 'Tughra' or seal of the Ottoman emperor Mehmed V and the date 1333 (1915 in the Ottoman calendar), this being the date of institution of the award.

The original Turkish awards were of very poor-quality metal with a crude painted finish and it was not long before firms in Germany were manufacturing high-quality versions in silver plate or even real silver with high-quality enamelled centres.

Those naval personnel who earned this award in the First World War continued to wear it on the right breast of their naval uniform in the Second World War.

The War Merit Cross.

The Iron Half Moon.

BIOGRAPHICAL NOTES

The people in this section have been selected because their names appear fairly frequently in post-war literature, but little tends to be known about their careers. This is not, therefore, intended as a roll-call of the most famous men. (Certain outstanding people have been omitted because they held a few easily distinguishable offices and it is not too difficult to trace their careers from books listed in the Bibliography.)

The rank shown at the head of each entry was the last position held by that individual in the Kriegsmarine.

When the first edition of this book was written, historians were allowed access to personal military records, but this is now longer possible due to the European Data Protection Act, which seems to have imposed tighter restrictions than the official censor. Therefore, it has not been possible to verify or add dates.

BACKENKÖHLER, OTTO, ADMIRAL
1892–1967. Chief of Staff of the Baltic Naval Station and later of the Fleet Command. He later held several posts connected with weapons and armament.

BARTELS, HANS, KORVKPT
Joined the Navy in 1931 and commanded *M1* at the beginning of the war. Was awarded the Knight's Cross of the Iron Cross in May 1940 and later became the First Officer aboard a destroyer because, as Grand Admiral Raeder said, he needed to relearn naval discipline. Towards the end of the war he worked with the midget weapons unit and designed the one-man submarine of Type Biber. He had a British mother and is said to have died in a car accident shortly after the war, but his friends think that he committed suicide. A colourful character whose application to join the U-boat arm was turned down more than once. He was responsible for building a flotilla of small minesweepers in Norway and created the 'Tiger of the Fjords' award. See also 'Early Wartime Surface Vessels' on page 30.

BASTIAN, MAX, ADMIRAL
1883–1958. President of the National War Court until November 1944.

BEHNCKE, PAUL, ADMIRAL
13.8.1866–4.1.1937. Born near Lübeck, he joined the Imperial Navy at Easter 1883. At the start of the First World War, he occupied several influential positions,

Admiral Paul Behncke, who joined the Navy in 1883 and was awarded the Pour le Mérite during the First World War, became the Navy's Supreme Commander-in-Chief for four years from 1920 until 1924.

and became commander of the Third Battle Squadron of the High Seas Fleet, with which he saw action at the Battle of Jutland. He was awarded the Pour le Mérite (Blue Max) in 1917. Although Behncke held several important posts at the end of the First World War, today he is probably best remembered as the first Commander-in-Chief of Germany's post-First-World War Navy, a position he held from 1920 until his retirement in September 1924.

BERGER, FRITZ, KPT.Z.S.
Joined the Navy in 1917 and was awarded the Knight's Cross as Commander of the 1st Destroyer Flotilla. Later with the 5th Destroyer Flotilla and Sea Commander for parts of Norway.

BEY, ERICH, KONTERADMIRAL
23.3.1898–26.12.1943. Born in Hamburg, he joined the Navy after the start of the First World War. At the outbreak of the Second one, Bey was Flag Officer for Destroyers and Commander of the 6th Destroyer Flotilla. Later, while still holding these posts, he also commanded the North Norway Naval Squadron. Bey was killed on 26 December 1943, when *Scharnhorst* went down during the Battle of the North Cape. He was one of the most famous destroyer leaders.

BOEHM, HERMANN, GENERALADMIRAL
18.1.1884–11.4.1972. Boehm joined the Imperial Navy in 1903. He was Fleet Commander until October 1939, when he worked in the Supreme Naval Command, and was later made Commanding Admiral for Norway.

BONTE, FRIEDRICH, KPT.Z.S. UND KOMMODORE
1896–10.4.1940. Bonte commanded the 2nd Destroyer Flotilla and was later made Flag Officer for Torpedo-Boats, a title he held briefly until the reorganization of October 1939 changed it to Flag Officer for Destroyers. He was killed off Narvik while taking part in the Norwegian Campaign.

BRANDI, ALBRECHT, FREGKPT.
20.6.1914–6.1.1966. Born in Dortmund, Brandi served under Hans Bartels, as First Officer of the minesweeper *M1* at the start of the war. Afterwards he went to submarine school, and commanded: *U617*, *U380* and *U967*. Brandi had the distinction of being only the second naval man to receive the Knight's Cross of the Iron Cross with Oakleaves, Swords and Diamonds, a feat he achieved with *U967*. (The other award went to Wolfgang Lüth.) Brandi then served as Admiralty Staff Officer, before being made commander of the Midget Weapons Unit in Holland.

BRINKMANN, HELMUTH, VIZEADMIRAL
12.4.1895–?. Born in Lübeck, Brinkmann was Chief of the Naval Defence Department at the Supreme Naval Command until July 1940, when he joined the heavy cruiser *Prinz Eugen* as her first commander.

After this, he was Chief of Staff for Naval Group Command South. In November 1943 he was made Commanding Admiral for the Black Sea, and he returned to Germany towards the end of the war to take up the post of Commanding Admiral for the Baltic and North Sea. Brinkmann was discharged from the Navy towards the end of November 1947.

BURCHARDI, THEODOR, ADMIRAL
1892–?. Burchardi was commander of the cruiser *Köln*, and went on to become Chief of Staff at the Naval Construction Yard in Kiel. Subsequently, he held several posts connected with coastal defence.

CANARIS, WILHELM, ADMIRAL
1.1.1887–9.4.1945. Born in Dortmund, Canaris was appointed Chief of the Abwehr in January 1935. He held this position until July 1944, when he was appointed Chief of the Special Staff for War Economy and War Economic Measures. On 23 July, Canaris was arrested for complicity in the Bomb Plot and sent to Flossenburg concentration camp, where he was executed shortly before the end of the war.

CARLS, ROLF, GENERALADMIRAL
18.5.1885–15.4.1945. Born in Rostock, Carls joined the Imperial Navy in 1903. At the start of the First World War, he was aboard the cruiser *Breslau*. Subsequently, he served on the battleship *König*, commanded *U9* and, later, *U124*. After the war he was made Chief of the Training Division at the Supreme Naval Command and was then given command of the old battleship *Hessen*. From 1933 until his appointment in the following year to the posts of Commander-in-Chief Battleships (Linienschiffe) and C-in-C of German Naval Forces in Spanish waters, Carls was Chief of Staff of the Fleet Command. He was Fleet Commander from 1937 until 1938, when he became Commanding Admiral for the Baltic; at the same time he held the post of Commander-in-Chief of the Naval Group Command East. Afterwards, he became Chief of the larger Naval Group Command North, which he commanded until 1943. Both Rolf Carls and Karl Dönitz were nominated to succeed Grand Admiral Raeder. Hitler chose Dönitz and Carls later resigned, possibly to prevent friction among the naval leadership. He was killed by enemy action on 15 April 1945, less than three weeks before the end of the war.

CILIAX, OTTO, ADMIRAL
30.10.1891–12.12.1964. Ciliax commanded the battlecruiser *Scharnhorst* until October 1939, when he became Chief of Staff at Naval Group Command West. This was followed by a spell as Commander-in-Chief Battleships. He then worked with the Torpedo Inspectorate. Ciliax was promoted to Admiral on 1 February 1943 and, in the following month, was made Supreme Commander-in-Chief of the Supreme Naval Command for Norway. He was discharged in February 1946.

CREMER, PETER-ERICH, KORVKPT.
Commander of *U333* and *U2519*; collided with three Allied ships during separate actions and headed Dönitz's bodyguard at the end of the war and shortly afterwards.

DENSCH, HERMANN, ADMIRAL
1887–24.8.1963. Born in Königsberg, Densch held the post of Commander-in-Chief Reconnaissance Forces until October 1939, when he was made Commanding Admiral for the North Sea Naval Station, later known as Supreme Naval Command North Sea. After that he worked in Berlin as a Naval Commissioner.

DÖNITZ, KARL, GROSSADMIRAL AND HEAD OF STATE
16.9.1891–24.12.1980. Born at Grünau, which was then a small village south-east of Berlin and is now part of the city, Dönitz joined the Navy as an officer cadet on 1 April 1910 at Kiel-Wik. After his initial training, he spent a year aboard the training ship SMS *Hertha*, and was later posted to the cruiser *Breslau*, then the fastest and most modern cruiser in the Imperial Navy. *Breslau* operated in the Mediterranean with the battlecruiser SMS *Goeben*, as the core of the German Mediterranean Naval Squadron, commanded by the famous Admiral Wilhelm Souchon. However, the squadron was never fully developed and, at the outbreak of the First World War, *Goeben* and *Breslau* were the only two German ships in this theatre. They managed to evade the numerically superior forces hunting them and made their way to neutral Turkey, where the ships were eventually handed over to the Turkish Navy, an action that helped bring Turkey into the war on Germany's side.

Dönitz married lngeborg Weber, daughter of General Weber, in May 1916. In October of that year, the newly-weds returned to Germany and took up residence in Kiel. Dönitz was made First Officer of *U39*, commanded by the ace submariner Walter Forstmann, and a year later was given command of *UC25*. Later, he was transferred to the larger and faster *UC68*, which was depth-charged and sunk by HMS *Snapdragon*. Dönitz and some of his crew managed to evade a watery grave to be taken prisoners. Dönitz was first held in a prison camp on Malta and later at Redmires, near Sheffield, England. He eventually returned to Germany in July 1919 in a poor state of health.

Dönitz remained in the Navy, and was given an administrative position in the Personnel Department. In March 1920, he took command of the old torpedo-boat *T157*. In 1921, the Dönitz family, now with the addition of a daughter, Ursula (born 1917), and son, Klaus (born 1920), moved to Swinemünde – one of the major torpedo-boat bases. Two years later, they moved back to Kiel when Dönitz was appointed adviser at the Torpedo, Mine and Artillery Inspectorate. The family moved again in 1923 – by which time another son, Peter, had arrived (born 1922) – this time to Berlin, where Dönitz was adviser at the Naval Office. In 1927, on Dönitz's appointment the post of Navigation Officer of the cruiser *Nymphe* – flagship for the Commander-in-Chief Seaforces Baltic – the family returned to Kiel. The position of C-in-C Seaforces Baltic was held by

Karl Dönitz, the U-boat chief, after he had been promoted to Supreme Commander-in-Chief of the Navy. The admiral's baton, which he is holding, was taken from his baggage after the war and is now on display in Shrewsbury Castle (England).

Admiral Wilfried von Loewenfeld, whom Dönitz had known since he joined the training ship SMS *Hertha*.

In 1928, Dönitz became Chief of the 4 Torpedo-Boat Half Flotilla, which consisted of four brand new boats: *Albatros, Kondor, Möwe* and *Greif*. This gave Dönitz a golden opportunity to show what he could do, since the crews were also new and Dönitz was free to train them as he wished.

During 1930, Korvkpt. Karl Dönitz was appointed to the post of First Admiralty Staff Officer at the Naval Station in Wilhelmshaven. There, he won a naval scholarship to visit any country of his choice and, as a result, went to Ceylon and several other countries in the Far East. This was an interesting experience, especially as it came just before the National Socialists' rise to power. He revisited the region in 1934 as captain of the light cruiser *Emden*, the first large ship built after the First World War, and noticed a considerable improvement in the attitudes towards Germans. *Emden* had, by this time, been commissioned a second time after a long refit with a new crew.

A year later, he held the rank of Fregattenkapitän and returned to Germany with *Emden* hoping to take the ship on another cruise to the Far East. Instead, however, he was ordered to take command of the U-boat flotilla in Kiel. He expanded this initially small group of half a dozen coastal submarines to become what has been described as the fourth branch of the armed forces: Army, Air Force, Navy and U-boat arm.

Dönitz succeeded Grand Admiral Erich Raeder as Supreme Commander-in-Chief of the Navy in January 1943. On 30 April 1945 at 1935 hours, Dönitz received a radio signal from Berlin, telling him that Hitler had appointed him second Führer of the Third

Reich. Dönitz did not want to accept this office, and he carefully considered the alternative – including suicide – but in the end be concluded that it was his duty to accept the office of Head of State. Dönitz and his entire staff were arrested by British forces on 23 May 1945, when the German government was dissolved and the armed forces disbanded. Dönitz stood trial at Nuremberg where he was found to be not-guilty of the charges against him. But a new law, that of training men for a war of aggression was introduced, for which he was found guilty and sentenced to ten years imprisonment. No other military or political leader has ever had to face this charge. Several German writers have described how Dönitz whipped his men into action, at a time when everybody should have known that it was pointless to go on. Yet, the people making this claim do not seem to know that he instigated a secret ballot among U-boat crews, asking them to vote in complete anonymity whether they wanted to continue. Furthermore, any officer agreeing to the Allied terms of unconditional surrender would have been labelled as a traitor.

EYSSEN, ROBERT, KONTERADMIRAL
2.4.1892–31.3.1960. Eyssen was Chief of the Military Department at the Supreme Naval Command Defence (OKM Wehr) and later commanded the auxiliary cruiser *Komet*. Interestingly enough, this post had not been foreseen by the Naval Command. It was his own idea to negotiate the Siberian Seaway and he was one of the few men to approach his bosses to carry out a seemingly impossible task. Afterwards, he worked as liaison officer, followed by a spell as Chief of the German Naval Office in Oslo, and then went to the Regional Defence Office in Vienna.

FISCHEL, HERMANN VON, ADMIRAL
1.1887–1950. Born in Kiel, von Fischel was Chief |of the General Naval Office. Later, he became head of the Command that tested new warships (Erprobungskommando für Kriegsschiffneubauten). This was followed by a period as Commanding Officer for Sea Defences at Ostende. Afterwards, von Fischel held several posts connected with coastal defence. He commanded pocket battleship *Deutschland* before the war and at the same time, during the Spanish Civil War, served as Commander-in-Chief of the German Forces in those waters. Von Fischel died a miserable death, together with tens of thousands of others, a prisoner-of-war in Russia in 1950.

FREIWALD, KURT, KAPITÄN ZUR SEE
29.10.1906–?. Born in Berlin, Freiwald was one of the Third Reich's early U-boat commanders. In 1935 he

Kapitän zur See Kurt Freiwald was Adjutant to both Grand Admirals. He commanded *U7* and *U21* early in his career. Towards the end of the war, he took on *U181* to make a voyage to the Far East, where a senior officer was required to negotiate with the Japanese authorities.

commanded their first operational boat, *U7*. He was made adjutant to Generaladmiral Raeder in October 1938 and later became adjutant to Karl Dönitz – the other Supreme Commander-in-Chief of the Navy. Freiwald returned to the submarine school during the summer of 1943, and afterwards took command of the long-distance boat, *U181*, in which he sailed to Japanese-held bases in the Far East. The reason for this appointment was that high ranking officers were required to negotiate with the Japanese.

FRIEDEBURG, HANS-GEORG VON, GENERALADMIRAL

15.5.1895–23.5.1945. Von Friedeburg joined the staff of the Flag Officer for U-boats in 1937. It was intended that he should take over the U-boat arm, thus releasing Dönitz for a post with cruisers, but the war started before such plans could be implemented and, instead, von Friedeburg became Chief of the U-boat arm's large Organization Department. Von Friedeburg held the title of Commanding Admiral for U-boats from February 1943 until April 1945, when he was made Supreme Commander-in-Chief of the Navy. It was von Friedeburg who negotiated surrender with the Allies and, with others, signed the official surrender document. Von Friedeburg, who was described by his colleagues as 'the perfect gentleman – correct to the last degree', committed suicide in May 1945 after mistreatment by the British who had arrested him.

Admiral Hans-Georg von Friedeburg, head of the U-boat arm's large and most complex Organization Department. At the end of the war he headed the delegation which that signed the Instrument of Surrender at Field Marshal Montgomery's headquarters in the Lüneburg Heath. He killed himself shortly after the war to avoid ill treatment from British forces.

FUCHS, WERNER, ADMIRAL

1891–?. Admiral Fuchs was Chief of the Fleet Department at the Supreme Naval Command (Flottenabteilung), and especially dealt with new construction problems. He was made Chief of the

Office for Warship Construction shortly before the start of the war. Fuchs worked in ship construction for most of the war until 1944, when he held the post of Flag Officer for Reserves. (He was moved because, during 1943, ship construction was placed under the control of the Ministry of Armament.)

GODT, EBERHARD, KONTERADMIRAL

5.8.1900–?. This man – almost unknown throughout the war and after – was the driving force behind the all-important Operations Department of the U-boat arm. Born in Lübeck, he joined the Navy at the end of the First World War and, after commanding a U-boat during the 1930s, became a staff officer. Later, he was made head of the Operations Department, at that time still a small, relatively unimportant post. But, as the war progressed, both the department and Godt's responsibility grew. The post was later re-designated 2nd Chief of Naval War Staff, although most men referred to the department as 'U-boat Command' (Ubootsführung). Eberhard Godt was the driving force behind nearly all the convoy battles, directing the U-boat commanders from the U-boat arm's nerve centre – the Operations Room. He was made Konteradmiral on 1 March 1943, when his office was renamed Commander-in-Chief for Submarines (Operations) – Befehlshaber der Unterseeboote (Operationen) or B.d.U. (Ops). He told the author that he had never considered himself as having been a driving force and always looked upon Dönitz as being the key person, but he did agree that he formulated many of the orders for boats at sea.

HESSLER, GÜNTER, KORVKPT.

A successful U-boat commander (*U107*) and Knight of the Iron Cross who married Ingeborg Dönitz to become the U-boats chief's son-in-law. After the war he collaborated with the Royal Navy to write a three-volume work about the war at sea, which has since been published and is one of the outstanding books about the U-boat war.

HEYE, HELLMUTH, VIZEADMIRAL

1895–1970. At the outbreak of the Second World War, this colourful character was commander of the heavy cruiser *Hipper*. He then held several administrative posts, and in 1944 he was made Admiral for the Midget Weapons Unit.

KRANCKE, THEODOR, ADMIRAL

30.3.1893–18.6.1973. Krancke was born in Magdeburg and was Chief of the Naval Academy (Naval Officers' School – Mürwik) shortly before the start of the Second World War, and was later made Chief of Staff for the Commander-in-Chief Security Forces of the North Sea. Afterwards, he took command of the pocket battleship *Admiral Scheer* and, simultaneously, held the post of Chief of Staff for the Commanding Admiral in Norway. From January 1942 until March 1943, Krancke was the Permanent Representative of the Supreme Commander-in-Chief of the Navy at Hitler's headquarters. He then moved on to become Supreme Commander-in-Chief of the Naval Group Command West. Shortly before the war ended he held the post of Supreme Commander-in-Chief of Naval Command Norway.

KRANZBÜHLER, OTTO, A RANK IN THE NAVAL LEGAL SERVICE EQUIVALENT TO KPT.Z.S.

8.7.1907–?. Born in Berlin, Kranzbühler's main claim to fame was in being Dönitz's defence counsel at Nuremberg. Dönitz was given a list of German lawyers willing to act for him at the Trials, but he rejected all of them because of their inexperience regarding maritime law. Dönitz had retained the memory of Kranzbühler's adept handling of a pre-war collision case, and the Grand Admiral decided he was the one person capable of defending him. Not surprisingly, Kranzbühler was difficult to find, and he had to be virtually dug out of the ruins of the Third Reich. Although Dönitz was convicted, after the trial he reaffirmed his belief that he could not have hoped for a better lawyer.

KRETSCHMER, OTTO, FREGKPT.

1.5.1912–20.8.1998. Otto Kretschmer, the 'Tonnage King', was the most successful U-boat commander of the Second World War. He sailed on sixteen operational war cruises and sank 238,000 GRT, which included one destroyer and at least 41 merchant ships. (An earlier figure puts the number of ships sunk at 44, and the gross registered tonnage at 266,629.) Kretschmer was born near Liegnitz (now called Legnica), lying west of Wroclaw (Breslau), and joined the Navy in 1930. At the start of the war, Kretschmer commanded the small boat *U23* and later took over *U99*. Both *U99* and *U100* (Kptlt. Joachim Schepke) were sunk simultaneously on 17 March 1941: *U100* was located on the surface by Type 286 radar fitted in HMS *Vanoc*; and *U99*'s lookouts failed to spot HMS *Walker* until the U-boat had run across the destroyer's bows. Kretschmer was not on the bridge at the time, and the duty officer gave the order to dive, after which *U99* was saturated with depth charges and only just managed to re-surface. Fortunately, quite a number of her crew got out before she sank – including Otto Kretschmer who spent the remaining war years in a prison camp and was not released until the end of 1947. He was awarded the Knight's Cross with Oakleaves and Swords. (A detailed account of Kretschmer's career has been drawn by Terence Robertson in *The Golden Horseshoe*.) He served as Flotillenadmiral in the Federal German Navy and died on 20 August 1998 as a result of falling down the steps of a pleasure cruiser. Kretschmer could, and often did, talk as much as anyone else. His nickname of 'Silent Otto' came about because he was one of the early U-boat commanders who did not make a great deal of use of his radio.

KUMMETZ, OSKAR, GENERALADMIRAL

21.7.1891–?. Oskar Kummetz was born in East Prussia and was Chief of Staff of the Fleet Command until October 1939, when he joined the Torpedo Inspectorate. During the invasion of Norway, he held the position of Commander of Task Force Oslo and, after this, held the office of Commander-in-Chief Cruisers and Commander-in-Chief North Norway Naval Squadron. Shortly before the end of the war, he was Supreme Commander-in-Chief of the Supreme Naval Command Baltic.

LÜDDE-NEURATH, WALTER, KORVKPT.

15.5.1914–?. Although Walter Lüdde-Neurath had a

most distinguished naval career, his name did not become famous until the end of the war, when he was the last adjutant to Grand Admiral Dönitz. After the war, he recorded a valuable set of records, outlining the events leading to the end of the Third Reich (see Bibliography).

Born in Huningen, just north of Basel, he joined the Navy in 1933. His wartime duties included the posts of Watch Officer and Torpedo Officer aboard the destroyer *Karl Galster*. He then became First Officer of *Z30*, and went on to command torpedo-boats *Greif, Möwe* and the destroyer *Richard Beitzen*. Lüdde-Neurath next held the post of First Admiralty Staff Officer with the Flag Officer for Destroyers, shortly after which he became Dönitz's adjutant.

Lüth, Wolfgang, Kpt.z.S.

15.10.1913–14.5.1945. Wolfgang Lüth was one of two men in the German Navy to be awarded the Knight's Cross of the Iron Cross with Oakleaves, Swords and Diamonds. (The other medal was awarded to Albrecht Brandi.) This famous U-boat commander was born in Riga, and died after being accidentally shot by one of his own guards. He failed to reply to the guard's challenge – and paid the penalty. Lüth commanded *U9, U138, U43* and *U181*. He was also Chief of the 22nd U-boat Flotilla and, towards the end of the war, was head of the naval school in Mürwik. His official quarters there have now been turned into a magnificent naval museum.

Lütjens, Günther, Admiral

25.5.1889–27.5.1941. Lütjens was born in Wiesbaden, and held the post of Flag Officer for Torpedo-Boats from October 1937 until October 1939, after which he was made Commander-in-Chief Reconnaissance Forces. He was Fleet Commander from the spring of 1940 until he went down with the battleship *Bismarck* in May 1941.

Admiral Günther Lütjens, the Fleet Commander who went down with battleship *Bismarck*.

Marschall, Wilhelm, Generaladmiral

30.9.1886–20.3.1976. Born in Augsburg, Marschall joined the Navy in 1906. He was Commander-in-Chief Pocket Battleships at the start of the war, and Fleet Commander from October 1939 until June 1940. At the same time, he was Commander-in-Chief Naval Forces West (Seebefehlshaber West). After this he became an inspector with Education Units and, from August 1942 until a year later, when the post was renamed Commander-in-Chief Naval Group Command West, he held the office of Commanding Admiral France. Wilhelm Marschall was made the Führer's Special Naval Delegate for the Danube after

his spell of duty in France, returning to the Supreme Naval Command shortly before the end of the war. He was discharged from the Navy in June 1947.

Meckel, Hans, Fregkpt.

15.2.1910–?. Meckel was a U-boat commander at the submarine arm's re-founding in 1935, after which he held the post of Admiralty Staff Officer for the Flag Officer for U-boats. In 1944, he became Chief of the Radar Division. After the war, he contributed considerably to the understanding of radar and radio related subjects.

Puttkammer, Karl-Jesko von, Konteradmiral

24.3.1900–?. Von Puttkammer was 39 years old when he moved from the destroyer *Hans Lody* to Berlin, just before the start of the war, to become a liaison officer at Hitler's headquarters. He was Hitler's Naval Adjutant from October 1939 until the end in April 1945.

Raeder, Dr. h.c. Erich Grossadmiral/Admiral Inspekteur

24.4.1876–1960. Erich Raeder was born in Hamburg-Wandsbek, the eldest son of a language teacher, who was also the headmaster of a grammar school. He joined the Navy as an officer cadet in 1894 and, after three and a half years training, 'passed out' as best student of his year. Raeder first served in the Far East aboard the battleship *Deutschland*, the flagship of Prince Heinrich of Prussia (Commander-in-Chief of the 2nd Cruiser Division). Later, Raeder was made Wachoffizier (Watch-Keeping Officer) of the battleship *Kaiser Wilhelm der Grosse*. Afterwards he went to the Naval Academy, from where he travelled to Russia in order to improve his Russian. (He also spoke fluent English and French.) Raeder held several interesting land-based positions before being made Navigation Officer of the armoured cruiser *Yorck*. Then, also in the capacity of Navigation Officer, he was transferred to the Kaiser's yacht *Hohenzollern* (a post he disliked, because the ship spent most of its time lying at anchor).

In 1912, Raeder was appointed to the post of First Admiralty Staff Officer to the Commander-in-Chief Reconnaissance Forces (a position first held by Admiral Hans Bachmann, who was replaced by the famous cruiser pundit, Admiral Franz Ritter von Hipper). Raeder saw several important actions from the command bridge of the battlecruiser SMS *Seydlitz*, including the Battle of Jutland. He was given command of *Köln* shortly before the end of the war, but did not spend much time aboard the small cruiser because of his appointment as Naval Representative to the Armistice Commission.

Grand Admiral Dr. h.c. Erich Raeder, Supreme Commander-in-Chief of the Navy 1928–1943.

After the war, he was transferred to 'Archives', because of his suspected involvement in the Kapp Putsch while he was Chief of Staff to Admiral von Throtha. However, it was not long before his innocence was established and he returned to normal duties, initially as Commander-in-Chief of Sea Forces North Sea and later as Commanding Admiral in Kiel. He then succeeded Admiral Hans Zenker as Chief of the German Navy, a position he held until his resignation in January 1943. This position was known by a variety of names which could lead to some confusion. He still held the honorary rank of Admiral Inspekteur der Kriegsmarine after his resignation, but this did not involve any command duties. Raeder received a ten year sentence at the Nuremberg Trials.

Rogge, Bernhard, Vizeadmiral

1899–?. Rogge was born in northern Germany, and was commander of the sail training ship *Albert Leo Schlageter*, and of the auxiliary cruiser *Atlantis* – with which he remained at sea for an incredible 622 days without putting into a port. Rogge held administrative posts after the sinking of *Atlantis* and, towards the end of the war, founded and commanded the Special Task Force 'Rogge', which operated in the eastern Baltic.

Rösing, Rudolf, Kpt.z.S.

28.9.1905–?. Rösing's name crops up in various places, and at times it is difficult to keep track of his career. Born in Wilhelmshaven, be joined the Navy in 1924, making his way to the U-boat arm before its re-founding in 1935, and becoming one of its early commanders. At the start of the war, Rösing commanded U-Flotilla 'Emsmann', which was renamed 7th U-Flotilla during the reorganization of October 1939. He then had another spell as a U-boat commander – a step that many people have interpreted as demotion. 'Vaddi' (Herbert) Schultze, the commander of *U48*, was taken ill and Dönitz quickly needed a tough replacement to control the U-boat's crew: *U48* had been in the thickest action since the start, and her men had earned the reputation of being 'an uncontrollable wild bunch, who did not take kindly to inexperienced newcomers'. Obviously, Dönitz thought Rösing the man for the job. After his spell of duty in *U48*, Rösing became Liaison Officer with the Flag Officer for U-boats in Bordeaux. In 1941, he took control of the 3rd Flotilla and later was made Commander of the Central Department (Zentral Abteilung). From July 1942 until the end of the war, he was Flag Officer for U-boats West (F.d.U. West), which had its headquarters first in France, then Norway and finally Germany. One U-boat commander has written a book in which Rösing was accused of having issued a suicide order, but this is not true. The *suggestion* of attempting a suicide raid was made by a U-boat commander but it had never been an order.

Ruckteschell, Hellmuth von, Kpt.z.S.

23.5.1890–1948. Born in Hamburg, Ruckteschell was commander of the auxiliary cruisers *Widder* and, later, *Michel*. He handed over command of *Michel* to Günther Gumprich in May 1943, and then worked with the German Naval Attaché in Japan. Before serving in auxiliary cruisers he had commanded the minelayer *Cobra*. After the war he was convicted as a war criminal because it was claimed that he attacked too aggressively, but such a rule was never applied to those Allied commanders who destroyed much more than von Ruckteschell.

RUGE, FRIEDRICH, VIZEADMIRAL
25.12.1894–?. Ruge was born in Leipzig, and his varied career spanned the following positions: Flag Officer for Minesweepers, Chief of Staff for the Naval Group Command in Italy, Admiral with Army Group B and, towards the end of the war, Chief of the Armaments Office at the Supreme Naval Command. Ruge was made Commander-in-Chief of the Federal German Navy. After the war he became a professor and prominent historian.

SCHNIEWIND, OTTO, GENERALADMIRAL
12.12.1887–26.3.1964. Born in the Saar Region, Schniewind joined the Navy in 1907. At the outbreak of the Second World War, he was both Chief of Staff to the Chief of Naval War Staff (SKL) and Chief of

Admiral Otto Schniewind, Chief of Staff and Fleet Commander (left) and KptLt. Herbert Sohler, Commander of the 7th U-boat Flotilla in St Nazaire from September 1940 until February 1942 (right).

the Naval Command Office (Marinekommandoamt). He was made Fleet Commander after the sinking of the battleship *Bismarck* and, at the same time, held the office of Commander-in-Chief of Naval Group Command North. Schniewind briefly occupied several other posts before the end of the war, when he was arrested by the Allied Powers, tried for war crimes and found to be not guilty.

STOBWASSER, HANS, VIZEADMIRAL
1884–30.5.1967. He was Flag Officer for Minesweepers and later Commander-in-Chief for the Security of the Baltic.

THEDSEN, OTTO, KONTERADMIRAL (ING)
1886–11.2.1949. Born in Hamburg, Thedsen became Flotilla Engineer with the U-boat arm in 1935, and was later Chief of the Technical Division of the U-boat arm.

THIELE, AUGUST, VIZEADMIRAL
28.8.1893–?. Thiele was commander of the heavy cruiser *Lützow* (ex-*Deutschland*) and, later, held the position of Sea Commander at Trondheim. Afterwards,

he was made Admiral of the Norwegian North Coast. He was also Chief of Staff to the Fleet Command. Thiele founded and commanded the Special Task Force 'Thiele', a raiding force that operated in the eastern Baltic towards the end of the war.

TOPP, ERICH, FREGKPT.
2.7.1914–2005. Born in Hannover, Topp served as a U-boat commander, leaving the Navy in August 1945, having reached the rank of Fregattenkapitan. His commands included *U57*, *U552* and *U2513*. He was also Chief of the 27th U-Flotilla. Topp held the Knight's Cross of the Iron Cross with Oakleaves and Swords. He was the first U-boat commander to put the idea of the short range attack on the surface into practice, when he sank three ships on 23 August 1940 after having fired all three torpedoes from his three bow tubes in less than five minutes.

TOPP, KARL, VIZEADMIRAL
29.8.1895–1981. At the start of the war Topp worked at the Supreme Naval Command and, between February 1941 and February 1943, he commanded the battleship *Tirpitz*. The most important office he held after relinquishing command of *Tirpitz* was Chairman of the Shipbuilding Commission at Dr. Speer's Armaments Ministry.

TOPP, RUDOLF, FREGKPT.
1896–unknown. A Rhinelander, Topp began the Second World War at the Naval School in Wilhelmshaven, but later held several other posts, including command of a battalion of naval marksmen. He was discharged in 1945.

VOSS, HANS-ERICH, VIZEADMIRAL
1897–1973. Born near Stettin, Voss commanded the heavy cruiser *Prinz Eugen*, after which he became Permanent Naval Representative at the Führer's headquarters – a position he held until the end of the war. He was then sent to a Russian prison camp for nine years, from which he was not released until the end of 1954.

WAGNER, GERHARD, KONTERADMIRAL
1898–?. At the start of the war, Wagner held the post of Group Commander with the Supreme Naval Command. He became Head of the Operations Department of the Supreme Naval Command in June 1941, and later worked as Admiral with the Supreme Commander-in-Chief for a short time before becoming Permanent Representative to the Head of State. He was a member of the delegation that signed the surrender document at Lüneburg Heath in 1945. After the war he helped with research at the United States Naval Historical Branch and, among other things, edited the German edition of the 'Fuehrer Conferences'.

WARZECHA, WALTER, GENERALADMIRAL
1891–30.8.1956. Warzecha was Chief of the General Naval Office at the Supreme Naval Command and later Chief of the Naval Defence Department. He replaced Hans-Georg von Friedeburg as Supreme Commander-in-Chief of the Navy after von Friedeburg's suicide on 23 May 1945.

WENNEKER, PAUL, ADMIRAL
27.11.1890 – 17.10.1979. Wenneker was commander of the pocket battleship *Deutschland* until November 1939, when he became German Naval Attaché to Japan. He held this post from March 1940 until the end of the war.

WEYHER, KURT, KONTERADMIRAL
30.8.1901–?. Weyher was nicknamed 'The Singing Captain' by his cadets when he was commander of the sail training ship *Gorch Fock*. Afterwards, he commanded the auxiliary cruiser *Orion*. He then became First Admiralty Staff Officer with the Staff of the Commanding Admiral Aegean Region, after which he held a similar position with Naval Group Command South. He was moved to the Black Sea at the start of 1944 as Chief of the Security Forces. At the same time he was Chief of the German Naval Command at Constanta. He also served in Crete before returning to Germany to become Naval Commander of the East Friesian Region. He annoyed British naval officers after the war by playing German tunes on a saw with a violin bow. He was also an accomplished artist, having produced a number of fascinating paintings showing his activities with auxiliary cruisers.

WITZEL, CARL, GENERALADMIRAL
1884–31.5.1976. Witzel was Chief of the Main Weapons Department with the Supreme Naval Command for most of the war.

WURMBACH, HANS-HEINRICH, ADMIRAL
12.5.1891–?. Wurmbach was commander of the pocket battleship *Admiral Scheer*. He also held the positions of Commander of the Naval Station for the Baltic at Kiel and Chief of Staff to Naval Group Command East. After that he was first Commanding Admiral for the Black Sea and later Commanding Admiral for Denmark – a post that was renamed Commanding Admiral Skagerrak.

ZENKER, HANS, ADMIRAL
1870–1932. Zenker joined the Imperial Navy in 1889, commanding the small cruisers *Lübeck* and *Köln* before the First World War, when he also gained experience as departmental head in the Admiralty. During the war, he commanded the battlecruiser *von der Tann* and also held several other important posts. In 1920, he became Commander of the North Sea Naval Station and, in 1924, succeeded Paul Behncke as Commander-in-Chief of the Navy, a position that be held until Raeder was appointed in September 1928. Zenker retired in September 1928, and died in 1932, just five months before Hitler came to power. (His son, Karl Adolf, was the first Commander-in-Chief of the Federal German Navy.)

Admiral Hans Zenker, the Supreme Commander-in-Chief of the Navy from 1924 until 1928. He joined the navy Navy in 1889 and took part in the Battle of Jutland.

CHRONOLOGY

1918
11 Nov: the official end of the First World War.

1919
28 June: Treaty of Versailles was signed.

1920
10 Jan: Treaty of Versailles came into effect. The more moderate Germans called it the 'Dictate of Versailles' and the majority referred to it as the 'Betrayal of Versailles'.

1921
1 Jan: Foundation of the new German Navy, called Reichsmarine. (There had been great turmoil after the end of the First World War, with suggestions to scrap the Navy completely and to put the few ships under command of the Army. Naval forces had been known as the 'Provisional Navy' (Vorläufige Reichsmarine) from 11 August 1919 until the end of 1920.)
11 April: Reichsmarine Ensign was hoisted for the first time.
29 May: Salzburg (Austria) voted in an unofficial referendum to become part of the German state, but the Allies opposed the move. The vote in favour of joining Germany gained a majority of over 95 per cent. Other Austrian regions held similar votes and the results were all similar, with the majority wanting to join Germany as one nation.
13 Dec: Washington Treaty was signed.
31 Dec: Kaiser's Flag was officially hauled down for the last time. It reappeared in later years and was also flown during Hitler's time.

1925
7 Jan: Light cruiser *Emden* was launched in Wilhelmshaven. She was the first large warship built in Germany after the First World War.

1926
1 Oct: The first post-First World War torpedo-boat, *Möwe*, was commissioned.

1928
1 Oct: Erich Raeder was promoted to Commander-in-Chief of the Navy.

1929
17 April: Light cruiser *Königsberg* was commissioned.
22 July: The new passenger ship *Bremen* gained the Blue Riband for the fastest crossing of the Atlantic.
6 Nov: Light cruiser *Karlsruhe* was commissioned.

1930
15 Jan: Light cruiser *Köln* was commissioned.
6 March: Grand Admiral Alfred von Tirpitz died.

1931
19 May: Pocket battleship *Deutschland* was launched.
8 Oct: Light cruiser *Leipzig* was commissioned.

1933
Early in year: German Naval Attachés were appointed to London, Washington and Paris.
30 Jan: Adolf Hitler was appointed as Chancellor.
14 March: President of Germany, Paul von Hindenburg, ordered a slight change in the Naval Ensign; the removal of the small canton in the upper left-hand corner.
1 April: Pocket battleships *Deutschland* was commissioned and *Admiral Scheer* was launched.
14 Oct: Germany resigned from the League of Nations and German delegates walked out of a disarmament conference.
12 Nov: There was a national referendum in Germany to determine whether it was right for the country to have left the League of Nations; 95 per cent voted in favour of remaining out of the League.
23 Nov: Motor torpedo-boat *S6* was commissioned, the first post-First World War MTB to see service in the Second World War.

1934
3 June: Pocket battleship *Admiral Graf Spee* was launched.
2 Aug: The German President, Paul von Hindenburg, died and Hitler became leader or Führer. There followed a referendum in Germany asking whether one person should hold both offices of President and Chancellor; almost 90 per cent of the voters agreed.
12 Nov: Pocket battleship *Admiral Scheer* was commissioned.

1935
16 March: Hitler repudiated the Treaty of Versailles; National Conscription was re-introduced.
21 May: German Navy was renamed Kriegsmarine.
18 June: Anglo-German Naval Treaty was signed.
29 June: First of the new submarines, *U1*, was commissioned.
18 Aug: *Leberecht Maass, Z1*, the first post-war destroyer, launched.
27 Sept: 1st U-boat Flotilla (Flotilla 'Weddigen') commissioned by Fregkpt. Karl Dönitz (who had previously been commander of the light cruiser *Emden*).
2 Nov: Light cruiser *Nürnberg* commissioned.
9 Nov: New Ensign, with swastika, was hoisted for the first time.

1936
6 Jan: Pocket battleship *Admiral Graf Spee* was commissioned.
30 May: The naval memorial at Laboe, near Kiel, was officially opened. (The initial idea for a memorial was conceived by Obermaat – Petty Officer (Imperial Navy) Wilhelm Lammertz, and

the money was raised by members of the Marine Kameradschaft (Naval Comradeship Association) – quite an impressive feat when one considers that those were the years of deep depression.)
3 Oct: Battlecruiser *Scharnhorst* was launched.
6 Nov: Germany joined the London Submarine Protocol (Prize Ordinance).[1]
22 Nov: *U18* sank after a collision with the tender *T156*. This was the first U-boat to sink after the end of the First World War.
8 Dec: Battlecruiser *Gneisenau* was launched.

1937
14 Jan: Destroyer *Z1 (Leberecht Maass)* was commissioned.
6 Feb: Heavy cruiser *Admiral Hipper* was launched.
8 June: Heavy cruiser *Blücher* was launched.

1938
4 Feb: Hitler appointed himself Supreme Commander-in-Chief of the armed forces, and soldiers took a new oath, swearing obedience to him.
13 March: The Austrian Anschluss; Austria became part of the Greater German Empire.
21 May: Battlecruiser *Gneisenau* was commissioned.
22 Aug: Heavy cruiser *Prinz Eugen* was launched.
Sept: The 'Z' Plan was formulated.
1 Sept: *M1* was commissioned, the first new minesweeper since the First World War.
29 Sept: The famous meeting in Munich, after which Neville Chamberlain returned to England waving a piece of paper and expressing confidence in 'peace in our time'. The reason for this meeting was that many public services in Czechoslovakia had either collapsed or never been developed and it was agreed that Germany should be allowed to continue looking after the well-being of her nationals who had been forced to abandon their German nationality at the end of the First World War.
Dec: Britain agreed to Germany increasing her submarine force.

1939
27 Jan: Hitler gave the 'Z' Plan highest priority.
14 Feb: Battleship *Bismarck* was launched.
1 April: Battleship *Tirpitz* was launched.
1 April: Erich Raeder was promoted from Generaladmiral to Grand Admiral, a rank unused since the First World War.
27 April: Hitler repudiated the Anglo-German Naval Treaty.

1. This international treaty was originally signed by the major naval powers in 1930 and sought to impose rules on submarine warfare. Surprise submerged attacks on merchant vessels were prohibited; instead, the submarine had to surface, stop the ship and inspect its papers. The vessel could only be sunk if its cargo came under a specified list of contraband and the safety of the crew could be ensured. As lifeboats were not considered suitable accommodation on the high seas, therefore the ship's crew was supposed to have been taken aboard the submarine.

29 April: *Admiral Hipper* was commissioned.

18 Aug: German Naval High Command ordered 14 submarines leave Germany and sail to their war stations in the North Atlantic.

21 Aug: Pocket battleship *Admiral Graf Spee* left Wilhelmshaven.

24 Aug: Two more U-boats departed to their war stations; pocket battleship *Deutschland* (later renamed *Lützow*) left Wilhelmshaven.

25 Aug: Warning telegrams of a possible war were sent to German merchant ships not in German ports.

27 Aug: German merchant ships were instructed to get home to Germany in four days or to run into the nearest neutral port.

Aug–Sept: Germany agreed to take part in several peace initiatives and considerable diplomatic activities continued behind the scenes, but these were rejected by the Allies and the details have hardly been published.

1 Sept: 0445, start of the German attack on Poland.

3 Sept: Britain and France declared war on Germany. German ships started laying mines in the North Sea, concentrating on the defence of the German Bight. Such mining operations continued throughout the year, and became one of the Navy's most important contributions to the war during its first winter; the merchant ship *Hannah Böge* was attacked by HMS *Somali*, to become the first ship of the war to be captured.

4 Sept: The first bombing raid of the war took place: the RAF attacked Wilhelmshaven and Cuxhaven.

7 Sept: Operational submarines were withdrawn from the Baltic.

16 Sept: *U31*, commanded by Kptlt. Hans Habekost, was the first U-boat to attack a convoy.

17 Sept: British aircraft carrier HMS *Courageous* was sunk by *U29* (Kptlt. Otto Schuhart).

20 Sept: Heavy cruiser *Blücher* was commissioned.

25 Sept: Royal Navy started to lay mines in the English Channel (An international sea passage) to block the route for all shipping. (These operations continued until the end of the year.)

26 Sept: Two heavy German ships (pocket battleships *Admiral Graf Spee* and *Deutschland*) at sea since before the start of the war were given permission to start offensive action. This had been withheld because peace negotiations were still underway, but Britain and France refused to take part.

4 Oct: The war against Allied merchant shipping intensified by the German Naval Command lifting various restrictions on the types of vessels that could be attacked.

13 Oct: U-boat War Badge was instituted by Grand Admiral Raeder; *U47*, commanded by Günther Prien, penetrated the defences of Scapa Flow during the night of 13th/14th and sank the battleship HMS *Royal Oak*.

29 Oct: German Naval High Command gave permission for passenger ships to be attacked by U-boats if they were sailing with a convoy.

Oct: U-boats started to lay magnetic mines in British shipping lanes.

20 Nov: First mines were dropped in British coastal waters by German aircraft.

23 Nov: A German magnetic mine, dropped in shallow waters off Shoeburyness in Essex, was

defused by Lieutenant-Commander Ouvery; auxiliary cruiser HMS *Rawalpindi* was sunk by battlecruiser *Scharnhorst*.

13/14 Dec: British submarine *Salmon* scored torpedo hits on cruisers *Leipzig* and *Nürnberg*.

15 Dec: The damaged *Leipzig* was torpedoed again by HM Submarine *Ursula*.

13 Dec–17 Dec: Battle of the River Plate and scuttling of pocket battleship *Admiral Graf Spee*.

20 Dec: The German passenger liner *Columbus* was trailed by an American cruiser that broadcast its position so that the Royal Navy destroyer *Hyperion* could attack. The master of *Columbus* set his ship on fire rather than hand it over to the Allies.

1940

22/23 Feb: Destroyers *Leberecht Maass* and *Max Schultz* (commanded by Korvkpt. Fritz Bassenge and Korvkpt. Claus Trampedach), ran onto mines laid by a British submarine, while they were trying to avoid attack from German aircraft.

31 March–1 April: Auxiliary cruiser *Atlantis* (commanded by Bernhard Rogge) left German coastal waters, the first auxiliary cruiser to do so.

3 April: Transports left German ports for the invasion of Denmark and Norway.

6 April: *Orion*, under command of Kpt.z.S. Kurt Weyher, became the second auxiliary cruiser to leave Germany.

7 April: German warships left German bases for the invasion of Norway and Denmark.

8 April: British destroyer HMS *Glowworm* was sunk by *Admiral Hipper*.

9 April: Heavy cruiser *Blücher* was sunk in Oslo Fjord.

10 April: Light cruisers *Karlsruhe* and *Königsberg* were sunk in Norwegian waters.

11 April: First Battle of Narvik (Norway).

13 April: Second Battle of Narvik.

14 April: *U49* (commanded by Kptlt. Johann Egbert von Gossler) was sunk by HMS *Brazen* and HMS *Fearless*; secret documents, probably connected with the 'Enigma' ciphering machine, floated to the surface and were captured.

10 May: German forces invaded Holland, Belgium and France.

15 May: Dutch forces capitulated.

24 May: Allied Supreme Command decided to evacuate Norway.

27 May: German auxiliary cruiser *Orion* passed Cape Horn on her outward voyage.

4 June: Destroyer Badge was instituted.

5 June: Dunkirk evacuation completed.

8 June: British aircraft carrier *Glorious* was sunk by *Scharnhorst* and *Gneisenau*.

10 June: Evacuation of British forces from Norway completed; Italy declared war on Britain and France.

17 June: First U-boats arrived in France, to use the French Atlantic ports for refuelling.

22 June: Franco-German armistice concluded at Compiegne; auxiliary cruiser *Pinguin* passed through the Denmark Strait on her outward voyage.

25 June: Ceasefire in France came into effect at 0135 hours.

27 June: Britain announced a blockade of the Continent and stopped food imports to countries occupied by German forces. As a result many civilians in neutral countries had to live on starvation diets.

3 July: Auxiliary cruiser *Komet* left Gotenhafen in the Baltic for the Pacific Ocean. The ship, under the command of Konteradmiral Robert Eyssen, sailed around the North Cape of Norway and headed east via the Siberian Sea passage. This was the first non-Russian ship to complete the hazardous voyage against the flow of ice.

1 Aug: Heavy cruiser *Prinz Eugen* was commissioned.

17 Aug: Germany announced a total blockade of the United Kingdom, and an area in which all ships were to be sunk without warning.

19 Aug: The Narvik Shield award was instituted.

20 Aug: German High Command planned to capture Gibraltar (Operation Felix).

24 Aug: Battleship *Bismarck* commissioned.

27 Aug: Plan to mount an initially large-scale invasion of Great Britain was abandoned in favour of landings on a small front from Eastbourne to Folkestone.

30 Aug: Invasion of Great Britain postponed.

31 Aug: War Badge for Minesweepers, Submarine-Hunters and Security Forces was instituted.

18 Sept: The 11,081-ton British steamer *City of Benares* was attacked at one minute past midnight by *U48* under Kptlt. Heinrich Bleichrodt.

9 Oct: Start of one of the most important and critical convoy battles – 21 ships were sunk from convoy SC7 and another 12 from convoy HX79, making this also one of the most successful 'wolf pack' attacks.

23 Oct: Pocket battleship *Admiral Scheer* left Gotenhafen for the Atlantic under command of Kpt.z.S. Theodor Krancke.

31 Oct: Auxiliary cruiser *Widder* arrived in Brest after a cruise in American waters.

18/19 Nov: First U-boat was located by radar fitted in a Sunderland aircraft (but not sunk).

30 Nov: Auxiliary cruiser *Komet* returned to Hamburg after 516 days at sea.

3 Dec: Auxiliary cruiser *Kormoran* left Gotenhafen.

1941

4 Feb: Forty Fw 200 Condor long-range bombers came under the direct control of the U-boat arm. They were used for reconnaissance purposes.

25 Feb: Battleship *Tirpitz* was commissioned.

3 March: British forces captured an 'Enigma' cipher machine from V-boat *Krebs*.

17 March: HMS *Vanoc* located *U100* on the surface with radar. This was the first success with Type 286 radar and led to the sinking of *U100* (Joachim Schepke) and *U99* (Otto Kretschmer).

1 April: War Badge for Blockade-Breakers was instituted.

23 April: Auxiliary cruiser *Thor* (commanded by Kpt.z.S. Otto Kähler) arrived in the Bay of Biscay after a successful cruise in the South Atlantic.

24 April: Auxiliary Cruiser Badge instituted.

30 April: Fleet War Badge instituted; auxiliary cruiser *Thor* arrived in Hamburg from France after 329 days at sea.

7 May: German floating weather station *München* was sunk by a British cruiser force; men from the destroyer HMS *Somali* managed to get aboard before she went down, and captured valuable radio equipment, including a naval cipher machine of the 'Enigma'-type plus various important documents.

8 May: Auxiliary cruiser *Pinguin* was sunk.

10 May: *U110* (Fritz-Julius Lemp) was captured by British forces; valuable secret material fell into British hands, including a working model of the secret cipher machine set up with the code of the day.

18 May: *Prinz Eugen* and *Bismarck* left Gotenhafen for *Bismarck*'s first and only war cruise.

24 May: The old British battlecruiser *Hood* was sunk by *Bismarck*. Some eye witnesses say that *Prinz Eugen* landed the first hits.

27 May: 1035, *Bismarck* went down, with the Fleet Commander and the entire Fleet Command on board.

30 May: Motor Torpedo-Boat Badge instituted.

4 June: German tanker *Gedania* was abandoned and scuttled when the British auxiliary cruiser *Marsdale* appeared. Royal Navy personnel managed to get on board before the tanker sank, and captured secret material relating to the secret cipher machine.

15 June: German supply ship *Lothringen* was captured by the British cruiser *Dunedin*; once again, secret documents fell into British bands. (By this time, Britain had captured vital documents and machinery for understanding large proportions of the German secret code.)

20 June: An incident occurred between USS *Texas* and *U203* (Rolf Mützelburg); as a result, Dönitz forbade German submarines to attack American warships, even if they appeared inside the blockade area around the British Isles.

22 June: *U48*, the most successful U-boat of the war, returned to port from her last operational war cruise. She was subsequently used for training. (It has been stated that *U99* was the most successful U-boat of the war, but this is not correct: her commander, the famous Otto Kretschmer, was the most successful commander, but he commanded two boats (*U23* and *U99*) and *U48* was responsible for sinking more tonnage than either of these two.)

24 June: Naval Artillery War Badge instituted.

June: During this month, U-boat Command began to suspect that some Allied convoys were being deliberately routed around the German 'wolf packs'.

June: The following supply ships, sent out to support the *Bismarck* and U-boat operations were sunk during this month as a direct result of Britain being able to read the German radio code: *Alstertor, Babitonga, Belchen, Egerland, Esso Hamburg, Friedrich Breme, Gedania, Gonzenheim, Lothringen* and *Spichern*.

End of June: German floating weather station *Launenburg* was sunk in the North Atlantic; men from the British destroyer *Tartar* managed to get on board before she went down, and captured yet more secret documents.

5 July: U-boats started to operate in the Arctic seas.

July: The first sea trials with the High Frequency Direction Finder (H/F D/F) were carried out by British forces.

23 Aug: Auxiliary cruiser *Orion* returned to France after a voyage lasting 511 days.

28 Aug: *U570* was captured by British forces. (She later became HMS *Graph*.)

Sept: U-boats experienced noteworthy difficulties in finding and attacking enemy convoys.

Oct: H/F D/F sets (High Frequency Direction Finders) were installed by the Allies in fairly large numbers.

14 Nov: British aircraft carrier *Ark Royal* was sunk by *U81* (Kptlt. Friedrich Guggenberger).

15 Nov: *U459*, the first purpose-built supply submarine, commissioned by Korvkpt. Georg von Wilamowitz-Möllendorf, who had seen service during the First World War.

22 Nov: Auxiliary cruiser *Atlantis* was sunk by HMS *Devonshire* after a voyage lasting 622 days.

29 Nov: Auxiliary cruiser *Kormoran* was sunk by HMAS *Sydney* after 350 days at sea. The *Sydney* went down as well without a single survivor.

6 Dec: A Japanese submarine was sunk in the approaches of Pearl Harbor.

7 Dec: Pearl Harbor was attacked by Japanese forces and part of the United States Pacific Fleet destroyed.

11 Dec: Germany and Italy declared war on the United States.

Dec: A dramatic and very significant convoy battle took place in the Atlantic; Swordfish aircraft from the British escort carrier *Audacity* succeeded in keeping U-boats away from convoy HX76. *U751* (Korvkpt. Gerhard Bigalk) managed to sink *Audacity* after a ferocious battle, but not before Dönitz recorded in his war diary: 'The risk of being sunk is greater than the possible success. The presence of aircraft make wolf pack tactics impossible.' U-boat High Command issued standing directives to U-boat commanders telling them to make the location and destruction of aircraft carriers their prime objective; previously, the main aim of U-boats encountering convoys had been to shadow the enemy while calling in other boats.

1942

1 Feb: The U-boat arm introduced a new four-wheel Enigma coding machine. Consequently British cryptanalysts were locked out of the German radio code until the end of the year, after one of these machines was captured on 30 October from *U559* (Kptlt. Hans Heidtmann) by men from HMS *Petard*.

11 Feb: Start of the 'Channel Dash'; German warships (*Gneisenau, Scharnhorst* and *Prinz Eugen* with heavy escorts) sailed through the English Channel from Brest (France) to Germany and Norway.

26/27 Feb: Battlecruiser *Gneisenau* was put out of action by bombs and remained in Kiel until 4 April, when she was moved to Gotenhafen.

13/14 March: German auxiliary cruiser *Michel* passed through the Strait of Dover on the outward voyage of her first operational cruise.

20 April: Motor torpedo-boats were given their own autonomous command under Kpt.z.S. und Kommodore Rudolf Petersen. (Previously, they had been under the jurisdiction of the Flag Officer for Destroyers.)

12 May: *Stier* leaves Kiel on her first war cruise as an auxiliary cruiser.

June: The British secret Anti-Submarine Report (issued to officers hunting U-boats) stated: 'The conning tower opened and about ten men appeared with their hands raised in surrender. As they made no attempt to man the gun, the aircraft did not feel justified in opening fire on them, though the proper course would have been to have machine gunned the men on the conning tower and any others who might have come up after this had been done.'

1 July: Battlecruiser *Gneisenau* decommissioned.

11 Aug: British aircraft carrier *Eagle* sunk by *U73* (Kptlt. Helmuth Rosenbaum).

12 Sept: Liner *Laconia* torpedoed and sunk by *U156* (Korvkpt. Werner Hartenstein).

27 Sept: Auxiliary cruiser *Stier* was scuttled after damage caused by action with American freighter *Stephen Hopkins*.

28 Sept: Naval High Command, including leader of the U-boat arm, met Hitler in Berlin to discuss new trends in the Battle of the Atlantic and the deterioration of the U-boat impact on convoys.

8 Oct: Auxiliary cruiser *Komet* left Hamburg for her second war cruise, under command of Kpt.z.S. Ulrich Brocksien.

9 Oct: Auxiliary cruiser *Thor* arrived at Yokohama at the end of her second cruise.

14 Oct: Auxiliary cruiser *Komet* was torpedoed by a British MTB while on way out for her second voyage.

30 Oct: *U559* under Kptlt. Heinz Heidtmann was sunk in the eastern Mediterranean by British destroyers. Men from HMS *Petard* managed to get on board and captured the four four-wheel Enigma code writer, together with code books on how to adjust its settings. This made it possible for Bletchley Park to get back into reading the U-boats' secret radio code.

19 Nov: The Russians launched their attack on German forces at Stalingrad; this battle became one of the great turning points of the Second World War.

31 Dec: A battle off the North Cape of Norway; Hitler threatened to 'throw the surface fleet into the dustbin' as a result of the failure of the German North Norway Naval Squadron to drive home its attack on convoy JW51B.

1943

30 Jan: Grand Admiral Erich Raeder resigned as Supreme Commander-in-Chief of the Navy and was succeeded by Karl Dönitz.

2 Feb: The Battle of Stalingrad ended in a shattering defeat for the Germans.

12 Feb: 'Rotterdam Radar', from a crashed British aeroplane near Rotterdam in Holland, fell into German hands.

2 March: German auxiliary cruiser *Michel* arrived at Kobe in Japan to end her first war cruise.

16 March: The start of the largest convoy battle of war, with U-boats attacking convoys HX229 and SC122.

23 March–8 April: Battle for convoy HX231, the first time since the fighting began that a convoy managed to cross the Atlantic and beat off almost all attacking U-boats, despite the 'air gap' still being 450 miles wide.

May: U-boat losses rose dramatically, and Grand Admiral Dönitz withdrew U-boats from the troubled waters and instigated a secret vote for the men to vote whether they wished to continue or not.

21 May: German auxiliary cruiser *Michel* left Yokohama in Japan, after fitting out.

31 May: U-boat construction was handed over to Dr Speer's Department of Military Armament.

4 June: The last German auxiliary cruiser still operational, *Michel*, left Yokohama for her second war cruise, under command of Kpt.z.S. Günther Gumprich.

20 Sept: *U338* (Kptlt. Manfred Kinzel) was sunk by aircraft which had dropped an acoustic torpedo, making this probably the first U-boat to have been sunk with such a weapon.

22 Sept: British midget submarines (X-craft) launched a successful attack on the battleship *Tirpitz* in Altenfjord.

17 Oct: *Michel*, the last German auxiliary cruiser on the high seas, was sunk by the American submarine *Tarpon*.

26 Dec: *Scharnhorst* was sunk in the Battle of North Cape.

1944

5 April: The British mounted a large-scale air attack on the battleship *Tirpitz*, moored in Kaafjord.

13 May: Clasp for the Roll of Honour of the German Navy was instituted.

15 May: U-boat Clasp instituted.

May: Schnorkels, fitted to U-boats, came into widespread use.

20 May: The Dragoner U-boat Group was at sea as the first Wolf Pack where every boat was equipped with a schnorkel.

6 June: D-Day – The Allied landings in Normandy.

11 June: Last remaining supply U-boat, *U490*, was sunk.

12 June: First electro-boat was commissioned – *U2321*, of Type XXIII, a small coastal submarine carrying only two torpedoes.

27 June: First large electro-submarine was commissioned – *U2501*, of Type XXI.

July: 'Versuchskommando 456' (Experimental Command 456) founded under Admiral Helmuth Heye to experiment with all types of midget craft.

15 Aug: *Tirpitz* was again bombed in Kaafjord.

15 Oct: *Tirpitz* left Kaafjord for Haakoy Island, near Tromsö.

12 Nov: *Tirpitz* sank at her anchorage, off Haakoy Island.

13 Nov: War Badge for Midget Weapons was instituted in seven grades.

19 Nov: Naval War Clasp (Marine Front Spange) was instituted.

24 Dec: Eight hundred American soldiers lost their lives when the British troopship *Leopoldville* was torpedoed by *U486* (Oblt.z.S. Gerhard Meyer). It would seem that many of the men could have been saved, had the authorities reacted more promptly.

1945

Evacuation of Germans from the eastern provinces proceeded throughout early 1945 and continued until the end of the war.

30 Jan: The German evacuee ship *Wilhelm Gustloff* was sunk, with what originally was thought to have been a loss of just over five thousand lives. Recent research has shown that there were probably about twice this number on board.

30 April: Hitler committed suicide. Grand Admiral Dönitz became Head of State.

30 April: The first large electro-boat of Type XXI (*U2511* under command of Adalbert Schnee) left port for its first operational war cruise.

4 May: German delegation signed the surrender document at 1830 in Field Marshal Montgomery's headquarters on Lüneburg Heath to the south of Hamburg.

23 May: The German Government, under Grand Admiral Karl Dönitz, was arrested at its headquarters in the sport hall of the Naval Officers' School in Mürwik near Flensburg.

1 Aug: German Minesweeping Administration founded.

APPENDICES

'Enigma' (Schlüsselmaschine 'M')

Germany's armed forces used a machine known as 'Enigma' to encode most of their day-to-day secret communications. 'Enigma' was such a complex piece of apparatus that it was thought the codes could not be broken. Yet the Polish Secret Service knew about 'Enigma' some ten years before the start of the war, and their knowledge was passed on to Britain shortly before the Germans entered Warsaw. British cryptologists, working in conjunction with mathematicians and scientists, continued the work started by the Poles. They reconstructed an 'Enigma' machine and, by mid-1941, were able to break the majority of German secret codes. Initially, they were able to decode German signals for up to two to three days a week, but the decodings became more frequent as time passed. Consequently, the British High Command knew almost every move the Germans were about to make. Obviously, it did not tell them everything, but it did give them a pretty good idea of German positions, and what they were doing. The information must have given them the locations of many secret meeting places in isolated parts of the Atlantic and enabled British forces to surprise and then destroy German ships while they were refuelling and taking on fresh provisions. So, deciphering 'Enigma' played an important role in the war.

Schlüsselmaschine 'M' (Cypher Machine 'M'), used only by the German Navy, worked on the same principle as the 'Enigma' machine used by the Army and Air Force. It was usually housed in a small portable box, about the size of an office typewriter. It had a typewriter keyboard, above which was a set of small windows, each one with a letter of the alphabet printed on it. If one of the keys were pressed, this would light up the relevant letter of the alphabet. Above the windows were three (later four) wheels rotating inside the box, with their outside edges just visible through the holes in the cover. These wheels rotated in the same way as a typewriter roller and could be set manually in any position; a set of serrations protruded above the surface of the box for this purpose. Each wheel had fifty-two electrical contacts: twenty-six on one side wired up to another twenty-six on the other side. The wiring pattern differed on each wheel. When a key was depressed, an electrical contact would be made to any one of the first wheel's twenty-six terminals and the electric current would flow through the wiring of all three wheels, pass through a system of complicated loops at the end and return through the wheels to light up a bulb in one of the windows above the keyboard. Meanwhile, one of the wheels would rotate by one position, so that when the same key was depressed a second time, the electric current would follow a slightly different circuit and light up a different letter of the alphabet.

To make matters more complicated, there was a plug board at the front that had to be wired up correctly with the 'code of the day' before the set

A three- and a four-wheel naval Enigma machine of the types used for coding all manner of radio messages. These examples are on display at the Aeronauticum Museum in Nordholz near Cuxhaven, Germany. The one on the right is the same machine as the one used in the film *Das Boot*.

The early (three-wheel) Enigma machine used throughout the German Navy.

could be used. From 1 February 1942, the Navy had a choice of four wheels from a total of eight. These could be shuffled around to fit any position, and the starting position of each wheel was pre-set by hand according to that day's code. It was, therefore, almost impossible to break the code manually. Even with a captured machine, it would have been necessary to know the plug board settings at the front, which wheels to insert, the order of these wheels and their starting positions. In addition to this, the ring with letters that identified each contact could be rotated by hand to start at any one of the twenty-six positions. A modern computer could crack a complicated problem like this, but such advanced electronics were not available in 1939 – although Britain did construct the first modern computer to help break the code.

The details of how this was done are dealt with in two books included in the Bibliography: one by Patrick Beesly and the other by F. W. Winterbotham.

ABOVE The coding wheels of the Enigma machine were detachable and towards the end of the war operators had to choose four from a set of eight. The wheel without finger grips (on the left) is the 'reflector' which did not rotate.

BELOW One of the rotating wheels from an Enigma machine with flat terminals and the letter strip visible. There was a tiny, spring-loaded plug on the other side of each terminal to make good contact with the next wheel. The Navy usually identified the starting position of each wheel by a ring of letters, while other branches of the armed services used numbers. This ring of letters could be rotated to start at any one of the twenty-six contacts.

Jürgen Rohwer also gives a valuable insight into radio telegraphy and the workings of Schlüsselmaschine 'M' and how German models were captured in his book *The Critical Convoy Battles of 1943*. Numerous other publications have appeared since the above was written for the first edition of this book.

Historians have given the cracking of the German Radio Code almost God-like characteristics and many have forgotten that the secret Submarine Tracking Room at The Admiralty in London (led by Commander Rodger Winn) was fed with information from a number of other important channels. At sea, the combination of High Frequency Direction Finders, radar and asdic probably contributed more to the U-boats' destruction than the breaking of the radio code.

FLAGS

The Grand Admiral's Flag
The flag for the Grand Admiral was introduced in 1939, at the same time that the rank was reintroduced into the German Navy. (Previously, the Supreme Commander-in-Chief of the Navy had held the rank of Generaladmiral.) The Flag consisted of a white square with a large black iron cross, edged in white. Behind the iron cross were two admiral batons crossed, and a gold eagle with swastika was superimposed on the cross.

Flag for Commander-in-Chief of the Navy
This flag was introduced in 1935 to be flown from vessels, shore establishments, and vehicles in which the Commander-in-Chief was travelling. It consisted of a white square with a large black iron cross, edged in white and superimposed upon two golden-yellow coloured crossed swords.

Command Flags
Command flags were flown from the flagships of various admirals to indicate their presence on board – they were also flown at shore bases and from the wing of the admiral's car. This flag was in a miniature form on vehicles and it was either flown from a small staff on the wing or was painted directly on to the wing itself. These vehicle flags were about 30cm (12 in) square. The flag featured a black disc in the upper and lower staff-side hand corners for Konteradmiral; only one disc for a Vizeadmiral; a full admiral had a cross without any discs; and a Generaladmiral had a pair of crossed swords in the lower staff-side corner.

Flags for Naval Land Units
The first flag awarded to a naval land unit was presented during September 1936. Similar Army flags utilized a variety of different colours and patterns for various units, but the Navy only produced one pattern. This was a blue square with a white central disc carrying a black swastika. The disc was edged in gold-wire embroidered oakleaves. Gold-edged white 'wedges' ran from the centre to each corner, and there were black and silver iron crosses in the top right and bottom left hand corners. The opposing corners showed gold, fouled anchors. The reverse of the flag was similar, but with a black

and silver iron cross in the centre and a gold eagle in place of the iron cross.

Pennants
Whereas the command flags, mentioned before, were flown from, or painted onto, the right hand wings of vehicles, other officer ranks flew a blue triangular pennant. These blue pennants were edged in gold, and had the national emblem, also in gold, in the centre. Admirals flew a similar pennant, but theirs had more elaborate edging in gold wire and there was a woven swastika design.

GERMAN NAVAL CHARTS
Standard German naval charts were based on a system of artificial squares covering the earth's surface. The actual size of each square on the ground differed slightly because the maps were drawn to Mercator's projection: the same area of ground was represented by squares that gradually decreased as they neared the equator. Furthermore, some areas were a little irregular to enable the pattern to be used more conveniently.

Each large square, of about 900km (486 nautical miles) each side, was identified by two letters: 'EG', 'EH', 'EQ', 'ER' and so on. These letters followed a consecutive sequence over the earth's surface. The square was then subdivided into 9 further squares –

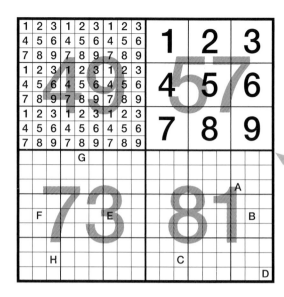

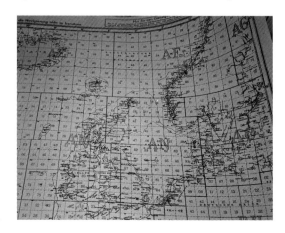

German Navy chart.

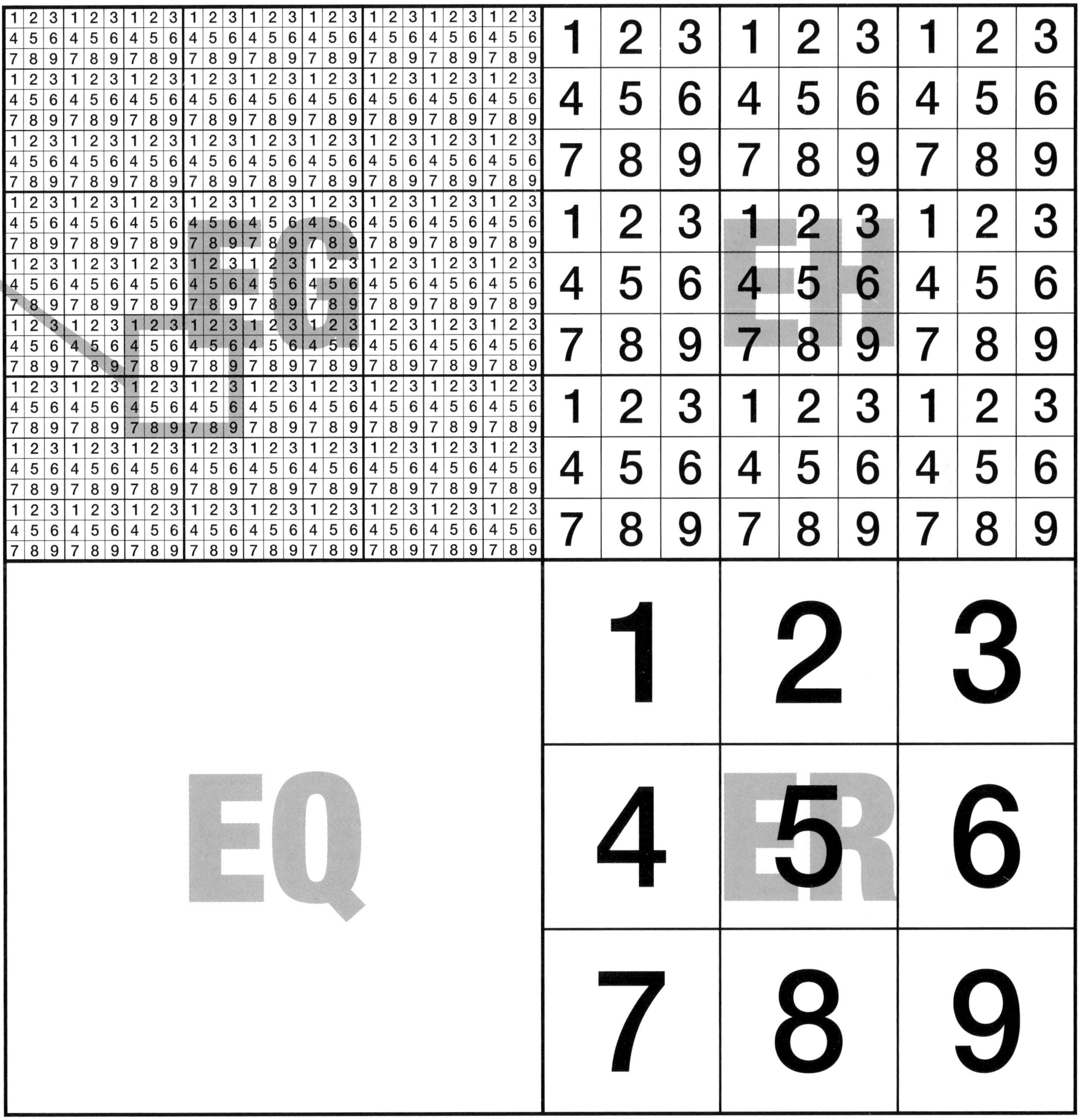

as shown in 'ER'. The numbers given in 'ER' were featured as the first digit in 'EH', and each smaller square was numbered by adding another digit. The four squares numbered 49, 57, 73 and 81, which are part of 'EG', are also shown enlarged: each of these squares was subdivided into 9 smaller squares, which were further subdivided as shown in square 49. As practical examples, the positions on the diagrams can be written as follows:

A: EG 8137
E: EG 7364

B: EG 8165
F: EG 7345
C: EG 8176
G: EG 7322
D: EG 8199
H: EG 7376

GLOSSARY

AA Anti-aircraft.

Abt/Abteilung Department, detachment, unit.

Abzeichen Badge.

aD/ausser Dienst Retired, withdrawn from service.

Adam An experimental midget submarine which went into production as Type Biber.

Adjutant Aide de camp, adjutant; name of whale-hunter captured by auxiliary cruiser *Pinguin*, placed under command of Lt.z.S. Hans-Karl Hemmer and finally scuttled near auxiliary cruiser *Komet*.

Admiral Nordmeer Admiral Polar Seas.

Admiralität Admiralty. Used until August 1920 when it was replaced by Marineleitung and later re-named Oberkommando der Marine (OKM).

Admiralstabsoffizier Admiralty Staff Officer.

AF/AFP–Artilleriefährprahm Artillery Barge.

AGRU Front Ausbildungsgruppe – Front A technical branch for training men and testing newly-built U-boats before they entered operational service.

Akku/Akkumulator Accumulator – battery.

Alberich Skin A rubber mat-like covering glued onto U-boats to help absorb asdic impulses. It didn't work terribly well.

Allgemeines Marine(haupt)amt Later known as Seekriegsleitung – Naval War Staff.

Aphrodite Code name for radar foxer used mainly by U-boats. A hydrogen-filled balloon was anchored to a floating weight by a 60m long cable holding several aluminium strips which reflected radar impulses.

Artilleriemechaniker Ordnance Mechanic.

Asdic From Allied Submarine Detection Investigation Committee – a device which sent out 'ping'-like noises for detecting submerged submarines.

Athos Code name for a German radar detection device.

Auerhahn Code name for a railway train used briefly towards the end of the war as headquarters for the Naval High Command.

Äusserste Kraft This order was not used in the British Navy, but equates to 'Full Speed (ahead or reverse) – Emergency'.

Automedon A British freighter captured by the raider *Atlantis*. Large quantities of secret materials were taken from her and some of this led directly to the Japanese attack on Pearl Harbor. A vitally important episode of the Second World War.

Auxiliary cruiser A merchant ship with heavier than normal armament. See Hilfskreuzer

Aviso Originally a small, fast warship. Later could also mean Yacht or Armed Yacht.

AVK/Artillerieversuchskommando Experimental Artillery Command.

Bachstelze (Wagtail) A gliding helicopter towed by U-boats as reconnaissance platform. Used mainly in the Indian Ocean and South Atlantic.

Back Forecastle.

Backbord/Bb Port side of a ship or boat.

Baltic Ostsee.

Battlecruiser Slightly smaller and faster than a battleship. The Germans classed *Scharnhorst* and *Gneisenau* as battleships, although foreign navies tended to refer to them as battlecruisers.

Bauwerft Ship building yard.

BBC/Brown Boveri & Co. A firm of partly French origin that built electrical equipment. The initials can often be seen on photographs of U-boat interiors.

BdA/Befehlshaber der Aufklärungsstreitkräfte C-in-C of Reconnaissance Forces.

B-Dienst Radio Monitoring Service – Funk-Beobachtungsdienst.

BdK/Befehlshaber der Kreuzer or der Kampfgruppe meaning C-in-C for Cruisers or Task Force.

BdL/Befehlshaber der Linienschiffe An early, First World War term which was later replaced by Bd Schlachtschiffe or C-in-C for battleships.

BdP/Befehlshaber der Panzerschiffe C-in-C for Pocket Battleships.

BdS/Befehlshaber der Schlachtschiffe C-in-C for Battleships.

BdSich/Befehlshaber der Sicherungsstreitkräfte C-in-C for Security Forces.

BdU/Befehlshaber der Unterseeboote C-in-C for U-boats.

Beamter Official/Civil Servant. A Beamter would usually retire with a good pension, but the costs for any mishaps due to his negligence while in service would have to be paid for by the official.

Bee German slang for an aircraft.

Befehlshaber Commander-in-Chief

Begleitschiff Escort ship.

Beiboot Ship's boat; long boat.

Beischiff Tender.

Betasom Name for the Italian U-boat Command based in Bordeaux. Beta=base, Sommergibili=submarine in Italian.

Biber A one-man submarine developed from the prototype Adam, which was designed by Hans Bartels, who never served in submarines.

Biscay Cross A U-boat-made wooden cross with wires strung around the outside to serve as aerial for a radar detector. This makeshift device was quickly replaced by a purpose built aerial.

Bismarck Code name for Naval Headquarters at Eberswalde near Berlin.

Blitz Lightning.

Blitzmädchen Could mean 'flasher' – a girl who shows off her private parts – a term for female assistants who helped with communications.

Blockadebrecher Blockade breaker – merchant ships which attempted to break the Allied blockade by running mainly into French ports. Some, such as *Rio Grande*, made several voyages.

Bluse Pullover shirt.

Bold An asdic foxer which was ejected through a small tube in the rear torpedo compartment of U-boats. After ejection it produced a mass of bubbles which reflected asdic impulses or at least made it difficult for the operator to get a true bearing on the submarine.

Bootsmann Boatswain – A warrant officer (with Portepee) rank.

Bootsmannmaat Petty Officer (without Portepee) or boatswain's assistant.

Borkum An island in the approaches to Emden and code name for a radar detector.

BRT/Brutto Register Tonnen Gross Registered Tonnage (GRT).

BSN/Befehlshaber der Sicherung der Nordsee C-in-C for the Security of the North Sea.

BSO/Befehlshaber der Sicherung der Ostsee C-in-C for the Security of the Baltic.

BSW/Befehlshaber der Sicherung West C-in-C for the Security of the West.

Bug Bows.

Bundesmarine The name for the German Navy between 1848 and 1852 and used again by the Federal Republic after 1956 until the re-unification of Germany.

C-in-C Commander-in-Chief.

Crew Class – the year when officers joined the navy.

Curly Torpedo See FAT.

Deadlight, Operation Codename for the sinking of U-boats the end of the war by the Allies.

Dekan Dean.

Delphin A midget submarine of which only a few were built before the end of the war.

DeTe/DT/Gerät Dezimeter-Telephonie-Gerät called Drehturm Gerät by many people who were not fully acquainted with the project. An early type of German radar, which worked well, but was not developed. It was used more as a rangefinder after targets had been sighted visually, rather than as a search device.

Deutsche Bucht German Bight.

Deutsche Minenräumleitung German Minesweeping Administration (GMSA) founded in August 1945.

Deutsches Kreuz German Cross; medal introduced in 1941.

Dienst Duty.

Dienstgrad Rank.

Dienstjacke Uniform jacket.

DMLR See Deutsche Minenräumleitung.

Dog Tag Slang for a metal identification tag worn around the neck. Men had their military number engraved on it while officers were identified by their name. There were two parts to the disc so that one could be handed-in by the person who buried the corpse while the other was attached to the grave.

Drifter A fishing boat; used to lay long nets in the path of approaching fish (mainly herrings), the nets and boat then drifted for many hours before being hauled in again.

E-Boat A British term derived from 'Enemy boat'. Called Schnellboot (S-boot) in Germany. A fast motor torpedo boat.

Eel German slang for torpedo.

Ehrentafel der Kriegsmarine Roll of Honour of the German Navy.

Ehrentafelspange der Kriegsmarine Clasp for the Roll of Honour of the Navy.

EK1/EK2/Eisernes Kreuz Iron Cross – First and Second Class.

EKK/Erprobungskommando für Kriegsschiffneubauten Command for experimenting with new warships.

Elefant Elephant Code name for an experimental midget submarine with tank tracks. Also known as Seeteufel (Seadevil).

EMA, EMB, EMC, EMD Einheitsmine (Standard Mine Types A, B, C, D) developed during the First World War.

E-MAA/Ersatz-Marineartillerieabteilung Naval Reserve Artillery Division.

Emden A family name ending with the name 'Emden' was a late honour bestowed by the Kaiser on men who served in the light cruiser of that name during the First World War.

EMG/Entmagnetisierungsgruppe Demagnetising Group.

EMS Code name for a periscope attached to a mine. The idea was to induce the Royal Navy to ram it, but the project was probably never used operationally.

Engelmannboot Engelmann's Boat: see VS5.

Enigma The generic name for a German coding machine. The Navy's version was usually known as Schlüsselmaschine M.

Ersatz Replacement or reserve – a term often applied to wartime substitute material.

Fähnrich zur See Cadet/Midshipman.

Falke Forerunner for the acoustic torpedo of Type Zaunkönig.

FAT (torpedo)/Federapperat-torpedo Incorrectly also called Flächenabsuchender-torpedo by people who saw it in action but were not fully acquainted with its technology. Called 'Curly' by the Royal Navy. It was aimed at a target like earlier torpedoes, but it would start running in loops after a pre-set distance, if it missed. The idea was that it might collide with another ship in the convoy rather than carry on beyond it.

Fd –/Führer der – Flag Officer, Commander for –

Feindfahrt Operational war cruise.

Feldwebel Warrant officers with Portepee.

Fernschreib – Telegrapher – followed by the person's rank.

Festungskommandant Fortress Commander.

Flächenabsuchendertorpedo See FAT.

Flak/Flug(zeug)abwehrkanone AA – anti-aircraft gun.

Flak/Fliegerabwehrkanone Anti-aircraft gun.

Fliege Code name for a German radar detector.

Flotte Fleet.

Flottille Flotilla.

Flottillentrosschiff Fleet Supply Ship.

Flugmelder Aircraft spotter.

FMB, FMC Flussmine Type B and C Mines specially developed for dropping into rivers.

Fregatte Frigate.

Fregkpt/Fregattenkapitän Junior Captain rank.

Froschschwimmer/Froschmann Frogmen, the official term was Kampfschwimmer.

Führer Flag Officer, Commander.

FuMB/Funkmessbeobachtung Device for detecting radar signals.

FuME/Funkmesserkennung Radar recognition. This device, fitted to some German ships picked up radar signals and then sent them back slightly magnified on a different wavelength to make it possible for the sender to distinguish between friend and foe.

FuMG/Funkmessgerät Radio rangefinder, radar apparatus.

FuMO/Funkmessortung Radar.

Funk Radio telegraphy.

Funkbeobachtungsdienst Radio Monitoring Service – B-Dienst.

Funker Radio Operator.

Funkpeilgerät Radio direction finder; could be used to determine the direction from which radio signals were coming.

G7a The German torpedo which was propelled by a four cylinder internal combustion engine.

G7e The German torpedo which was propelled by an electric motor. The letter 'G' comes from the old fashioned code word of 'Geradelaufapperat' meaning 'Running in a Straight Line Apparatus'.

G7v An early experimental version of the above torpedoes, which could not be ejected from submarines.

Geheimrat Not secret adviser but Privy Councillor.

Geisterschiffe Ghost ships – tend to refer to several sailing yachts used to land agents in Ireland, South America and South Africa. One was at sea as late as 1944 without being discovered by the Allies.

Geleit Convoy.

Geleitboot Escort boat.

Geleitflottille Escort flotilla.

Generaladmiral A rank (not used in the Royal Navy) for the head of the German Navy before it was large enough to warrant having a Grand Admiral.

Gerock Old fashioned term for Rock or Frock coat.

Glückauf A Bureau founded in 1943 to develop new U-boat designs.

GMSA German Minesweeping Administration founded in August 1945 (Deutsche Minenräumleitung).

Goldbutt An experimental torpedo.

Goldfisch An experimental torpedo.

Goliath Codename for a large radio transmitter at Milbe near Magdeburg. This could reach submerged U-boats off America.

Gorch Fock A North-German seaman and poet who was killed during the Battle of Jutland of the First World War. His real name was Johann Kinau. A sail training ship was named after him.

Graf Zeppelin Aircraft carrier; not completed – named after the 'father' of airships.

Grossadmiral Grand Admiral/Admiral of the Fleet.

Grosse Fahrt voraus Full speed ahead. The order 'Grosse Fahrt zurück' did not exist.

GRT/Gross Registered Tonnage BRT/Brutto-register-tonnen.

Grundausbildung Initial Training.

Grundhai A deep-diving submarine, designed as rescue craft for sunken submarines. None of these were ever built.

Hafenkapitän/Hafenkommandant Port Commander.

Hafenschutz Port protection.

Hai A midget submarine similar to Type Marder.

Halbe Fahrt Half speed – forwards or reverse.

Handelsschutzkreuzer/HSK (Trade Protection Cruiser) An early term for auxiliary cruiser, which was later replaced by Handelsstörkreuzer (Trade Harassing Cruiser).

hc/honaris causa Honorary title.

Head Naval term for lavatory. Officers on old sailing ships lived near the stern and the lavatories for the crew were at the front or head of the ships.

Hecht A midget submarine which was developed as Type Seehund.

Heizer Stoker or Ordinary Seaman; an old fashioned term which remained in colloquial use.

Hilfskreuzer (HK) Auxiliary cruiser, raider, ghost cruiser – a merchant ship with hidden armament.

Hochseeflotte High Seas Fleet; an early term left over from the Kaiser era.

Hoheitsabzeichen National Emblem.

Hohentwiel Radar equipment cum radar detector. The aerial looked something like a metal bed frame.

Hohenzollern The Kaiser's family name and also the name of the Royal Yacht.

HSK Could have meant Handelsschutzkreuzer or Handelsstörkreuzer.

Hüttenwerk Steel or iron works.

Hydra A small speed boat developed towards the end of the war. One flotilla became operational in Holland.

iD/in Dienststellung Commissioned, commissioning.

Ing/Ingenieur Engineer.

Ingolin Code word for hydrogen peroxide when used as fuel in high speed U-boats and torpedoes.

Initial training An induction course given to all soldiers, no matter what force they joined.

IO/1.Offizier First Officer.

IvS/Ingenieurskantoor voor Scheepsbouw A German submarine construction bureau established in Holland at a time when the building of submarines was still prohibited by the Dictate of Versailles.

IWO/1.Wachoffizier First Watch Officer; pronounced (in German) as 'One Double U, O' – usually a commissioned officer.

IIWO/2.Wachoffizier Second Watch Officer.

Kaiser Emperor.

Kaiserliche Marine Imperial Navy – a name used between 1871 and 1919.

Kampfabzeichen War badge.

Kampfgruppe Task Force.

Kapitän zur See/Kpt z S/KS Captain.

Kapitänleutnant/Kptlt/KL Lieutenant Commander.

Kleinkampfmittel Midget weapons.

Kleinkampfverband Midget Weapons Unit.

KM/Kriegsmarine The German Navy from 1935 – 1945.

KMA A mine developed especially for use in shallow water and on beaches where invasion forces might land.

KM-Boot/Küstenminenboot A small, fast minelayer developed towards the end of the war.

KMD/Kriegsmarine Dienststelle Naval Headquarters.

Knight's Cross See Ritterkreuz – The Knight's Cross of the Iron Cross.

Kommandant Commanding officer of a sea-going unit.

Kommandeur Commanding officer of a land-based unit.

Kommandierender Admiral The chiefs of the Baltic and North Sea Naval Stations were known by this title. The titles were later also used for the heads of Coastal Defence Regions.

Kommando Command.

Kommandoturm Conning-tower on U-boats or the bridge structure of some larger warships.

Kommodore Commodore. This was a position in the German Navy, not a rank. The title was often given to a captain who was holding an admiral's position.

Konteradmiral Rear-Admiral.

Korvettenkapitän/Korvkpt/KK Commander.

Kraftfahrer Driver (road vehicles) – followed by the person's rank.

Kriegsmarinewerft Naval ship yard, earlier Reichsmarinewerft and before that Kaiserlichewerft.

Kriegsmetal War metal – refers to inferior wartime quality.

Kriegsverdienstkreuz/KVK Distinguished Service Cross.

KS/Küstenschnellboot Fast, coastal patrol boat.

KSV/Küstensicherungsverband Coastal Security Unit/Defence Unit.

Küstenartillerie Coastal artillery.

Küstenbefehlshaber Coastal Commander.

Küstenschutz Coastal defence.

KVK/Kriegsverdienstkreuz Distinguished Service Cross.

Landungsflottille Landing flotilla.

Langsame Fahrt Slow (ahead or reverse).

LAT/Leichter Artillerieträger Light artillery barge.

Laufbahn Naval trade.

Laufbahnabzeichen Trade badge(s).

Lazaret Hospital.

Leiter Ladder or Leader, director.

Lerche Code name for a fast torpedo developed towards the end of the war. It was guided by trailing a wire.

Leutnant zur See/Lt z S/LS Lieutenant (Junior).

LI/Leitender Ingenieur Engineer Officer.

Linienschiff An early, First World War, term for battleship. Replaced by Schlachtschiff.

Linse A small speedboat packed with explosives.

Lord Man of lowest rank.

Lorientschild Lorientshield An award probably invented after the end of the war to satisfy the increasing collector market.

LS/LS Boot/Leichtes Schnellboot Light motor torpedo boat armed with smaller (aerial) torpedoes and used mainly by auxiliary cruisers and by some units in the Mediterranean.

LUT/Lagenunabhängiger Torpedo A further development of the FAT torpedo.

M/Marine Navy – the German navy tended to call itself 'Marine' rather than 'Kriegsmarine'. 'M' was often embossed or engraved on naval property.

M Fl /Minensuch flottille Minesweeper flotilla.

M Fla A/Marineflakabteilung Naval AA Division.

M Fla R/Marineflakregiment Naval AA Regiment.

MA/Marineartillerie Naval artillery.

MAA/Marineartillerieabteilung Naval artillery department/division.

Maat Petty Officer. Confused by many with Warrant Officer.

Mantel Coat, greatcoat.

Marder A type of midget submarine.

Marineausrüstungsstelle Fitting-out base or quarter master's stores.

Marinebeamter Naval administration official.

Marinedekan Naval dean.

Marineersatz – Naval Reserve –.

Marinegruppenkommando Naval Group Command, see page 68.

Marine-Hitlerjugend Naval Hitler Youth.

Marineinspektion Naval Inspectorate.

Marinekommandoamt Naval Command Office.

Marinekonstruktionsabteilung Naval Construction Department.

Marinekraftfahrerabteilung Naval Motor Transport Division (Road Transport).

Marineküstenpolizei Naval Coastal Police.

Marinelehrabteilung Training Division for warrant officers. Also known as Marineunteroffizierslehrabteilung.

Marineleitung Supreme Naval Command – a name used after the end of the First World War and before it was officially known as Oberkommando der Marine (OKM).

Marinenachrichtenabteilung Naval Intelligence Division.

Marinenachrichtenhelferinnenausbildungsabteilung Training division for female staff who helped with communications.

Marineoberkommando This should not be confused with the Supreme Naval Command – Oberkommando der Marine. Three MOKs were created in February 1943 when the names of the Naval Stations Baltic and North Sea and the Commanding Admiral for Norway were changed to this name. Later, two more MOKs were added. Also see Marinestation der Ostsee/Nordsee.

Marinepfarrer Naval chaplain.

Marineschule Mürwik The Naval Officers' School. This establishment was originally located in Kiel, in the building which now houses the provincial administration for Schleswig-Holstein. It moved to this purpose-built location near Flensburg in 1910.

Marinesonderdienst Naval Special Service. A military organisation established before the Second World War to procure essential raw materials from neutral countries and to stockpile them in safe locations. In many cases this essential work was done by naval attaches, but there was also a dedicated staff, especially in Japan. The Marinesonderdienst made it possible to operate both surface raiders and later U-boats in far-off waters.

Marinestation der Ostsee/Nordsee later re-named Marineoberkommando. Two major divisions within the Navy. They were responsible for a wide variety of services from coastal protection, maintaining ports and training new recruits.

Marinestosstruppabteilung Naval Assault Detachment.

Marineunteroffizierslehrabteilung Warrant Officer Training Division – see also Marinelehrabteilung. These divisions were created after the First World War, although several historians have stated falsely that warrant officers were abolished in 1919.

Marineverwaltungsamt Naval Administration Office.

Marinewaffenamt Naval Weapons Office.

Marinewehramt Naval Defence Department.

Marinezahnarzt Naval Dentist.

Maschinist Machinist.

Matrose Ordinary Seaman.

Matrosengefreiter Able Seaman.

Matrosenhauptgefreiter Leading Seaman – after 4½ years service.

Matrosenobergefreiter Leading Seaman.

Matrosenstabsgefreiter Leading Seaman, a more senior rank introduced towards the end of the war.

Matrosenstabsobergefreiter Leading Seaman, a more senior rank introduced towards the end of the war.

M-Boot Minesweeper.

Mechaniker Mechanic.

Meister Master (of a trade) – a name used for many warrant officer ranks after a prefix with the trade; such as Funkmeister.

MES/Magnetischer Eigenschutz De-Magnetising Unit.

Metox Name of a radar detecting device, named after the French firm which developed it.

Minenschiff/Minenleger Minelayer.

Molch Midget U-boat.

Monsoon Group Long range U-boats which operated in the South Atlantic and the Far East.

Mordsee Slang for North Sea.

MRS/Minenräumschiff The posh term for a minesweeper. They were mostly referred to as just plain Minensucher or Minensuchboot.

MTB/Motor Torpedo Boat – Schnellboot in German.

Musik – Musician – followed by the person's rank.

Nachrichtenoffizier Intelligence/information officer.

Narvik Shield An award instituted in 1940 for men involved in the heavy fighting around the Norwegian iron ore port.

Neger Midget U-boat.

Netzsperrflottille Boom Defence Flotilla.

NO/Nachrichtenoffizier or Navigationsoffizier Intelligence Officer but more often Navigation Officer. The navigation Officer was one of the senior and key staff members aboard large warships.

NSDAP/Nationalsozialistische-Deutsche-Arbeiterpartei National Socialistic German Workers Party.

Ob d M/Oberbefehlshaber der Marine Supreme Commander-in-Chief of the Navy.

Oberbootsmann Chief Boatswain – a warrant officer with Portepee.

Obersteuermann Navigator aboard small ships. – warrant officer with Portepee.

Oberfähnrich zur See Sub-Lieutenant.

Oberkommando der Marine/OKM Supreme Naval Command.

Oberleutnant zur See/Oblt.z.S./OL Lieutenant (Senior).

Obermaat Chief Petty Officer (always without Portepee).

Opium Opium tablets were carried by many naval units; not as a painkiller but to prevent men from having to go to the lavatory. In many emergencies key officers, such as commanders and engineer officers, could not leave their post for an instant, not even to go to the head.

Ostsee Baltic.

Panzerschiff Pocket battleship.

Patrol Line A U-boat formation established on the high seas to locate enemy convoys.

Portepee Sword/Dagger Knot This award distinguished warrant officers from the lower ranks.

Pour le Mérite The highest award for bravery during the Kaiser's era.

Prussia The largest of the Germanic kingdoms, of which the German Kaiser was King.

R-Boot/Räumboot Motor minesweepers – small vessels.

Reich Empire, nation.

Reichsmarine The name of the German Navy between 1920 and 1935. Earlier, it was known as Kaiserliche Marine (Imperial Navy) and afterwards re-named Kriegsmarine. The navy itself tended to use the simpler term of 'Marine'.

Ritterkreuz Knight's Cross of the Iron Cross, although there was also a Knight's Cross of the Distinguished Service Cross.

Rock Frock coat.

Rudergänger Helmsman (Not a rank but a position).

Saltzwedel Salt is translated as Salz, but the flotilla was named after a First World War U-boat Commander, who had a 't' in his name.

Sanitäts – Medical –.

SAT/Schwerer Artillerieträger Heavy artillery barge.

S-boot/Schnellboot Motor torpedo boat, speed boat.

Schiffchen A small ship – a name for a forage cap worn by officers and men; favoured because it folded flat.

Schiffsartillerieschule Ship artillery school.

Schiffsstammabteilung Training detachment for new recruits. There was one for the Baltic and another for the North Sea, specialising in initial training programmes.

Schildbutt Code name for a long-range (14–20 nautical miles) torpedo fuelled with hydrogen peroxide. Not put into production.

Schirmmütze Peaked cap.

Schlachtschiff Battleship.

Schlachtkreuzer Battlecruiser.

Schlepper Tug.

Schlitten Sledge – A midget speedboat developed towards the end of the war.

Schlüsselmaschine 'M' The naval version of the Enigma decoding machine.

Schnorchel Schnorkel in English and snorkel or snort in the United States.

Schreiber Yeoman.

Schütze Marksman, gunner.

Schulschiff (Fleet) Training Ship.

Schwein A midget submarine which was not built.

Schwertwal A fast, fighter-like, midget submarine developed towards the end of the war. Only a few experimental craft were built.

Seehund A two-man midget submarine.

Seelöwe Code name for planned invasion of England.

Sicherungsflottille Picket Boat Flotilla.

SKL/Seekriegsleitung Naval War Staff – Directorate of the War at Sea.

Smadding Non-official, colloquial term for the most senior boatswain.

SMS/Seine Majestäts Schiff HMS His/Her Majesty's Ship used until the end of the First World War.

Smut/Smutje Ship's cook.

Soldbuch Paybook, which also served as military identity card and contained a photo as well as a multitude of personal details, including details of awards.

Sonder— Special—.

Sonderdienst An organisation created in foreign ports to help acquire goods and provisions for German ships: see Marinesonderdienst.

Spange Clasp.

Spanier/Umhang Cloak.

Sperrbrecher Barrier breaking ship or auxiliary mine detonator. Merchant ships filled with flotation material and special accommodation for the men so that they could withstand mine detonations without sinking or hurting the crew.

Sperre Barrier, embargo, blockade.

Sperrmechaniker Mine engineer.

Stab Staff.

Stabs— A more senior form of rank introduced probably during the summer of 1943.

Stamm— Personnel. This gave rise to terms such as Stalag meaning a prisoner-of-war camp for men (Stamm–Lager) as opposed to Oflag for Offizier – Lager).

Stationskommando der Ostee/Nordsee Naval Command for the Baltic/North Sea. This name was used after the First World War until it was changed to Marinestation der Ostsee/Nordsee.

Steinbutt Experimental torpedo powered by hydrogen peroxide; a further development of Project Steinfisch.

Steinfisch Code name for a high-speed torpedo running on hydrogen peroxide.

Steuerbord Starboard side of ship.

Steuermann Navigator usually of warrant officer (with Portepee) rank – when the unit was too small to have a navigation officer. Not to be confused with

helmsman, which was called Rudergänger.

Streitkäfte Armed Forces.

T5 Acoustic Torpedo of Type Zaunkönig.

Thetis (boje) A radar foxer consisting of a three dimensional cross with wire strung between the supports. The end of each cross had a float to keep it above the surface of the water. The idea was to reflect radar impulses.

Tintenfischverband Octopus Division, created with small motorised sailing boats in the Adriatic towards the end of the war with a view of hunting traps set by saboteurs.

TMA, TMB, TMC Torpedo Mine Type A, B and C. Specially developed mines for ejection through submarine torpedo tubes. Boats required a special modification and not all commanders were trained to lay mines.

Tombakbronze Bronze alloy.

Torpedoerprobungskommando Torpedo Trials Command.

Torpedoinspektion/TI Torpedo Inspectorate; founded in 1886 as autonomous body to deal with all torpedoes issued to naval units. The leaders were responsible to the Supreme Naval Command in Berlin, although the personnel were administered by the Baltic and North Sea Naval Commands.

Torpedokommando Torpedo Command. Also under the jurisdiction of the TI these commands were part of the Torpedo Arsenals and responsible for torpedoes issued to operational units.

Torpedomechaniker Torpedo mechanic. Aboard the larger U-boats he was the only warrant officer with Portepee to sleep with the men in the bow compartment, but he was not responsible for discipline in that area.

Torpedoversuchsanstalt Torpedo Experiments/Trials Institute. Operational as a sub-department of the TI. Its function was to build, test and evaluate new torpedoes for the navy.

Trosschiff (Tross Schiff) Supply ship.

TSV/Trosschiffverband Supply Ship Arm.

Tunis Code name for a radar detection device which was used in U-boats towards the end if the war.

UAK/U-bootabnahmekommando U-boat Acceptance Command.

UB Originally small attack submarines built during the First World War and after 1939 UB was used to identify HMS *Seal*, after it had been captured by the Germans.

Überzieher Pea jacket.

U-boot was later, in 1972, changed to Uboot

U-boot/U-boat from Unterseeboot. In Britain the term 'U-boat' was originally taken to mean a German submarine, while boats from other navies were referred to as 'submarine'.

U-bootabwehrschule Anti-submarine school. Code name for the early submariners school in Kiel, which was founded at a time when Germany was not allowed to own submarines.

U-boots(kriegs)abzeichen U-boat Badge.

U-bootsfrontspange U-boat Clasp, introduced in May 1944.

U-bootsführung U-boat Command.

U-bootversorger U-boat supply ship also known as Z-Ship.

UC Originally a minelaying type of U-boat from the First World War and after 1939 used as identification for

submarines captured in Norway and commissioned into the German Navy.

UD Dutch submarines serving in the German Navy.

UF French submarines serving in the German Navy.

UIT Italian submarines serving in the German Navy.

UJ/Unterseebootsjäger Submarine hunter.

Umhang/Spanier Cloak.

Unterseeboot Submarine.

Ursel project A device for firing rockets from U-boats at pursuing destroyers, but not made anywhere near operational.

VA/Vizeadmiral Vice-Admiral.

Verband Unit.

Verpflegungsamt Wilhelmshaven Süd Supply Office Wilhelmshaven South – a code name for the refrigerated ship *Duquesa*, which was captured by *Admiral Scheer* and used to supply German units in the South Atlantic.

Versuch Experiment/trial.

Versuchskommando 456 Experimental Command 456 – founded by Admiral Hellmuth Heye to explore a variety of midget weapons.

Verwaltung Administration.

Verwaltungsbeamter Administration official.

Volksmarine The navy of the German Democratic Republic during the Cold War era.

von A title of nobility.

Vorläufig Provisional.

Vorläufige Reichsmarine Provisional Navy. A name given to the Reichsmarine's first few months.

Vorposten Coastal Defence.

Vorpostenboot Coastal Defence Boat.

VS5 An experimental submarine for testing new high-speed engines.

Wabos Slang for Wasserbomben – Depth charges.

Wachoffizier Watch Officer.

Wal A midget submarine which was not operational.

Walterboot A high-speed submarine developed by Hellmuth Walter.

W-anz/Wellenanzeiger/Wanze A radar detector which automatically searched through a variety of wavebands.

Welle Wave or propeller shaft.

Werftleistungsabzeichen Ship Yard Worker's Achievement Badge.

Weserübung Code name for the invasion of Norway and Denmark.

Wetterbeobachtungsschiff Weather ship.

Wik Old Germanic term for sandy bay, which has remained in some place names.

Wohnschiff Accommodation ship. Passenger ships were moored in major ports to accommodate people who were not permanently stationed in the town.

Wolf Pack Dramatic name for U-boat patrol line. Several different types operated throughout the Second World War.

Zaunbutt Experimental submarine powered with hydrogen peroxide but not put into production.

Zaunkönig T5, acoustic torpedo.

Zentrale Central control room.

Zerstörer Destroyer.

Zimmermann Carpenter.

Z-Schiff Destroyers were prefixed with the letter 'Z' followed by a number. 'Z' Ship is short for Zufuhrschiff meaning supply ship. These were converted merchant ships and usually had a traditional name. They were also known as U-bootversorger.

BIBLIOGRAPHY

Almann, K.; *Ritter der sieben Meere*; Erich Papel, Rastatt, 1963. (Deals with some men who were awarded the Knight's Cross of the Iron Cross.)

Andrews, Terry; *Report on U570 – HMS Graph*; Military Press, Milton Keynes, 2005. (Re-printed from official Royal Navy records.)

Angolia, J. R.; *For Führer & Fatherland*; R. J. Bender, San José, 1976. (Includes naval war badges with citations.)

——; and Schlicht, Adolf; *Die Kriegsmarine*; Volume 1 and 2; R. J. Bender, San Rose, 1991. (An eExcellent and well well-illustrated volumes dealing with German naval uniforms.)

Anti-Submarine Warfare Division of the British Naval Staff; 'Monthly Anti-Submarine Reports'. (Not published but a vitally important source for anyone studying the war at sea.)

Baasch, H.; *Handelsschiffe im Kriegseinsatz*; Gerhard Stalling, Oldenburg and Hamburg, 1975. (An interesting, pictorial work.)

Beaver, Paul; *German Capital Ships*; Patrick Stephens, Cambridge, 1980.

——; *E-Boats and Coastal Craft*; Patrick Stephens, Cambridge, 1980. (Books of this series, World War Two Photo Album, are worth looking for in second-hand shops because they contain some excellent photographs from the German State Archives.)

Beesly, P.; *Very Special Intelligence*; Hamish Hamilton, London, 1977; Doubleday, New York, 1978. Re-printed as revised edition by Greenhill, London, 2000. (This is the story of the British Admiralty's Operational Intelligence Centre from 1939 to 1945. A most interesting volume and essential for anyone studying the history of the Second World War.)

Bekker, C.; *The German Navy 1939–1945*; Hamlyn, London, 1974; Dial, New York, 1975. (The photographs are interesting and supported by an easy-to-follow text. Specific ship types as well as various actions are covered. The book is well worth looking at for the photographs alone.)

——; *Flucht übers Meer*; Stalling, Oldenburg, 1959. (The story of the evacuation of German people from the eastern Baltic during the last few months of the war.)

——; *Hitler's Naval War*; Macdonald and Jane's, London, 1974; Doubleday, New York, 1974. Translated from *Verdammte See*, Stalling, Oldenburg, 1971. (A most interesting book covering the main aspects of the war at sea.)

Bensel, R.; *Die deutsche Flottenpolitik von 1933–1939*; Mittler, Berlin, 1958. (A study of ship construction in the light of Hitler's foreign policy.)

Blocksdorf, Helmut; *Das Kommando der Kleinkampfverbände der Kriegsmarine*; Motorbuch Verlag, Stuttgart, 2003.

Blundel, W. D. G.; *German Navy Warships 1939–45*; Almark, London, 1972. (A small, well-illustrated paperback giving essential details of the ships. Of very good quality and one of the best on the subject.)

Bonatz, Heinz; *Der Seekrieg im Äther*; E. S. Mittler, Herford, 1981. (The author was C-in-C of the German Radio Monitoring Service and has written this account about of the role played by radio during the war. Contains a wealth of interesting material but most difficult to read due to masses of abbreviations.)

Bracke, Gerhard; *Einzelkämpfer der Kriegsmarine*; Motorbuch, Stuttgart 1981. (An interesting account about midget weapons.)

Bredemeier, H.; *Schlachtschjff Scharnhorst*; Koehlers, Jugenheim, 1962. (Written by one of *Scharnhorst*'s officers with help from one of the ship's commanders and navigation officer.)

Braeuer, Luc; *U-Boote! Saint-Nazaire*; grand-blockhaus@wanadoo.fr, 2006. (Written in French, but worth looking at even for non-French readers because the photos are most interesting and of excellent quality. The author runs a museum, Le grand Blockhaus, at Batz-sur-Mer near St. Nazaire.)

Brennecke, H. J.; *The Hunters and the Hunted*; Burke, 1958. Translated from *Jäger-Gejagte*; Koehlers, Jugenheim, 1956. (A good book, which has become a recognized classic about the U-boat war. The author outlines the events of the war at the start of each chapter and then describes specific U-boat operations in detail.)

——; *Die deutschen Hilfskreuzer im zweiten Weltkrieg*; Koehlers, Herford, 1976. (The story of German auxiliary cruisers.)

——; *Ghost Cruiser HK 33*; William Kimber, London, 1954; US title: *Cruise of the Raider HK-33*; Crowell, New York, 1955. Translated from *Gespenster-Kreuzer HK 33*,

Koehlers, Herford, 1968. (The story of auxiliary cruiser *Pinguin*, written with the co-operation of seven crew members.)

——; *Schlachtschiff Bismarck*; Koehlers, Jugenheim, 1960.

——; *Schlachtschiff Tirpitz*; Koehlers, Herford, 1975.

——; *Schwarze Schiffe, weite See*; Gerhard Stalling; Oldenburg, 1958. (One of the few books about blockade breakers.)

——; and Krancke, T.; *Battleship Scheer*; Kimber, London, 1956. Translated from *Schwerer Kreuzer Admiral Scheer*; Koehlers, Jugenheim. (Admiral Krancke was commander of *Admiral Scheer*.)

Breyer, Siegfried and Koop, Gerhard; *Von der Emden bis zur Tirpitz*; Bernard & Graefe, Bonn, 1997. (A most interesting work with fascinating photographs.)

Brice; Martin; *Axis Blockade Runners*; Batsford, London 1981.

Brown, D.; *Tirpitz: The Floating Fortress*; Arms and Armour Press, London, 1977. Naval Institute Press, Annapolis, 1977. (Contains a forty-page introduction, outlining the life of the battleship. Three-quarters of the book is devoted to an excellent collection of photographs.)

Brustat-Naval, F.; *Ali Cremer – U333*; Ullstein, Frankfurt, 1983.

——; *Unternehmung Rettung*; Koehlers, Herford, 1970. (Deals with the rescue of Germans from the eastern Baltic region towards the end the war.)

——; and Suhren, Teddy; *Nasses Eichenlaub*; Koehlers, Herford, 1983.

——; *Ali Cremer – U333*; Ullstein, Frankfurt, 1983.

Buchheim, L-G.; *U-Boat War*; Collins, London 1978; Knopf, New York, 1978. (Translated from *U-Boot-Krieg*; Piper, Zurich, 1976. (This is an excellent pictorial account of the U-boat war. The photographs were taken by the author, who served as a war correspondent. Buried towards the end of the war, they were dug up again to form the backbone of this magnificent collection.)

Busch, E. O.; *Konteradmiral Robert Eyssen*; Pabel, Rastatt.

——; *Kosaren des Seekrieges*; Pabel, Rastatt. (A chatty account of the second voyages of auxiliary cruisers *Thor* and *Michel*.)

Busch, H.; *U-boats at War*; Hamilton, London 1954; Putnam, New York, 1954. (An excellent account of life in U-boats. Busch served in the German Navy and came into contact with many U-boat men. This has become one of the essential classics.)

Busch, Rainer and Roll, Hans-Joachim; *Der U-BootKrieg 1939 bis 1945; Vol 1, Die deutschen U-Boot-Kommandanten*; Koehler/Mittler, Hamburg, Berlin, Bonn 1996. (Brief biographies produced from the records of the German U-boat Archive.)

Bussler, Peter and Schumann, Nik; *Militär und Marinegeschichte Cuxhavens*; Aug. Rauschenplat, Cuxhaven, 2000. (A most interesting book about this little little-known naval base on the Elbe estuary.)

Chapman, John W. M.; *The Price of Admiralty*; University of Sussex Printing Press, Lewes, 1982. (A three three-volume work with an annotated translation of the war diary of the German Naval Attaché in Japan from 1939 to 1943.)

Chesneau, Roger; *German Pocket Battleships*; Chatham Publishing, London, 2004. (Aimed at model makers with good photographs, diagrams and plans. An interesting volume.)

Childers, Erskine; *The Riddle of the Sands*; Sidgwick and Jackson, London, 1972. (A novel set in German coastal waters before the First World War. There probably is no better description of those waters. Sadly, the film made from the novel leaves much to be desired.)

Cooper, Alan; *Beyond the Dams to the Tirpitz*; William Kimber, London, 1983. (A fascinating story about the attacks by RAF Sqn 617 (Dam Busters) on battleship *Tirpitz*. Well written.)

Creveld, Martin van; *Fighting Power (German and US Army Performance, 1939–45)*; Greenwood Press, Connecticut, 1982. (Deals with armies rather than navies, but most interesting, especially as the author works at the Hebrew University in Jerusalem.)

Dau, Heinrich; *Unentdeckt über die Meere*; Berlin, 1940. (The story of the blockade breaker and supply ship *Altmark* written by her commander.)

Davis, B. L.; *Flags and Standards of the Third Reich*; Macdonald and Jane's, London, 1975; Arco, New York, 1975. (Naval flags are included and there are some good colour plates.)

——; *Badges and Insignia of the Third Reich 1933–1945*; Blandford, Poole, 1983.

——; *German Uniforms of the Third Reich*; Blandford, Poole, 1980.

Dechow, F. L.; *Geisterschiff 28*; Ernst Gerdes, Preest/Holstein, 1962. (The story of auxiliary cruiser *Michel*.)

Detmers, T. and Brennecke, J.; *Hilfskreuzer Kormoran*; Koehlers, Herford, 1959. (The story of the auxiliary cruiser by her commander. Translated from the original English language edition: *The Raider Kormoran*, William Kimber, London, 1959.)

Deutsches Marineinstitut; *Marineschule Mürwik*; E. S. Mittler & Sohn, Herford.

Dobson, Miller and Payne; *The Cruellest Night*; Hodder and Stoughton, London, 1979. (A most readable and interesting book about the evacuation of people from the eastern German provinces towards the end of the war.)

Dollinger, H.; *The Decline and Fall of Nazi Germany and Imperial Japan*; Odhams, London, 1965. (This volume is packed with photographs of which only a few relate to the Navy. However, the work gives a good impression of the conditions under which Germans were living towards the end of the war, and helps to put naval minds into national perspective.)

Dönitz, Karl; *Deutsche Strategie zur See im 2. Weltkrieg*; Bernard & Graefe, Frankfurt, 1972. (The Grand Admiral answers forty questions. An interesting and essential volume.)

——; *Mein wechselvolles Leben*; Muster-Schmidt, Göttingen, 1968. (An interesting autobiography, dealing with those years not covered by *Ten Years and Twenty Days*.)

——; *Ten Years and Twenty Days*; Weidenfeld & Nicolson, London, 1959: ; World Pub. Co., 1959. Translated from *Zehn Jahre und Zwanzig Tage*, Athenäum, Frankfurt, 1958. (Grand Admiral Dönitz's account of the U-boat war.)

Elfrath, U. & and Herzog B.; *Schlachtschiff Bismarck*; Podzun, Dorheim, 1975. (A collection of interesting photographs depicting the life of the battleship.)

Elfrath, Ulrich; *Die Deutsche Kriegsmarine; 1935–1945*; Podzun Pallas, Friedberg, 1985. (With extensive photo captions in English and hardly any main text; originally published in five volumes. Very good and most interesting photographs.)

Ellenbeck, Major Dr Hans; *Die Verantwortung des deutschen Offiziers*; Tornisterschrift des Oberkommando der Wehrmacht, 1941.

Enders, Gerd; *Auch kleine Igel haben Stacheln*; Koehlers, Herford, 1987. (Interesting account of U-boats in the Black Sea.)

Eyssen, Robert; *Hilfskreuzer Komet*; Koehlers, Herford, 1960. (An edited version of auxiliary cruiser *Komet*'s log-book by her commander.)

——; *Hilfskreuzer Komet*; Oberkommando der Kriegsmarine, 1942. (A souvenir album of *Komet*'s voyage with interesting photographs, most of them taken by Gerhard Julius, though the captions are poor for security reasons. Limited distribution and now very rare.)

Fock, Harald; *Kampfschiffe – Marineschiffbau auf deutschen Werften – 1870 bis heute*; Koehler, Hamburg, 1995. (A good book, well illustrated with plans and photos.)

——; *Schnellboote*; 3 vols. 1973. (The first volume deals with the development of motor torpedo-boats until shortly before the Second World War. Volume Two covers the war years, and Three the post-war period.)

Frank, Hans; *German S-boats in Action in the Second World War*; Seaforth Publishing, Barnsley, 2007.

Frank, W.; *Sea Wolves: The Story of the German U-boats at War*; Weidenfeld, London, 1955; Rinehart, New York, 1955. Translated from *Die Wölfe und der Admiral*; Stalling, Oldenburg, 1953. (An interesting account of the U-boat war by an ex-war correspondent.)

Franks, Norman L. R.; *Search, Find and Kill*; Aston Publications, Bourne End, 1990. (A record of Coastal Command U-boat successes.)

Frere-Cook, O.; *The Attacks on the Tirpitz*; Ian Allan, London, 1974.

FTU; *Das Archiv*; U-boat Archive, Cuxhaven. (A German German-language journal published once a year for members of FTU, U-Boot-Archiv, D-27478 CuxhavenAltenbruch. Please enclose two Iinternational Postal postal Reply reply Coupons coupons if asking for details.)

Gabler, U.; *Unterseebootsbau*; Wehr und Wissen, Bonn, 1964. (Professor Gabler, an experienced U-boat engineer officer, worked with Professor Walter on the new submarine designs during the war. This volume details German submarine construction before 1945.)

Gander, Terry and Chamberlain, Peter; *Small Arms, Artillery and Special Weapons of the Third Reich*; Macdonald and Jane's, London, 1978. (Although this does not deal directly with the Navy, the book is good for reference. It is well illustrated and filled with useful data)

Garrett, Richard; *Scharnhorst and Gneisenau*; David & Charles, Newton Abbot, 1978. (An interesting account of the two elusive sisters.)

Gasaway, E. B.; *Grey Wolf, Grey Sea*; Arthur Barker, London, 1972. (The story of *U124*.)

Gellermann, Günther W.; *Geheime Wege zum Frieden mit England*; Bernard & Graefe Verlag, Bonn 1995. (An interesting volume dealing with various peace initiatives, most of which are hardly known.)

General Communications Headquarters (British); 'The War at Sea'. (Not published but a vitally important source for anyone studying the war at sea.)

Gibson, Charles; *Das Schiff mit fünf Namen*; Wilhelm Heyne, Munich, 1966. (The story of Speybank/Doggerbank.)

Giese, F.; *Die deutsche Marine 1920–1945*; Bernard & Graefe, Frankfurt, 1956. (An interesting account of the German Navy.)

Giese, Otto and Wise, James; *Shooting the War*; Naval Institute Press, Annapolis, 1994. (Otto Giese was an officer aboard the liner *Columbus*, which was scuttled in December 1939. Following this, he ran the blockade to Europe aboard *Anneliese Essberger* and then went on to become a U-boat officer. An interesting account with good photos.)

Giessler, H.; *Der Marine-Nachrichten und Ortungsdienst*; J. F. Lehmanns, Munich, 1971. (This is a most interesting account of German radio and radar development.)

Görlitz, W.; *Karl Dönitz*; Muster-Schmidt; Göttingen, 1972. (This small, inexpensive volume is part of a series called 'History and Personalities', and gives a good general introduction to Dönitz.)

Gretton, Sir P. W.; *Crisis Convoy: The Story of HX231*; P. Davies, London, 1974. (The story of the first convoy to cross the Atlantic during the Second World War and fend off almost all attacking U-boats. The author was escort commander.)

Gröner, E.; *Die deutschen Kriegsschiffe 1815–1945*; J. F. Lehmanns, Munich, 1968. (This is still the standard work on German warships. Most of the information is of a technical nature and illustrated with line drawings.)

——; *Die Handlsflotten der Welt, 1942*; J. F. Lehmanns, Munich, reprinted 1976. (Includes details of ships sunk up to 1942. This valuable publication was originally a confidential document and contains a complete list of ships; in similar style to Lloyd's Register. There is also a lengthy section containing Gröner's line drawings.)

——; and Mickel, Peter; *German Warships 1815–1945; Vol. II, 'U-boats and Mine Warfare Vessels'*; Conway, London, 1991. (Some of the information about U-boat losses is terribly out of date and needs revision.)

Groos, Otto; *Seekriegslehren*; E. S. Mittler, Berlin, 1929. (An account of the lessons learned during the First World War, written by a captain in the Imperial Navy.)

Güth, Rolf; *Die Marine des Deutschen Reiches 1919–1939*; Bernard & Graefe, Frankfurt, 1972. (A most interesting account of naval developments between the wars, written by a naval captain.)

Haarr, Geirr H.; *The German Invasion of Norway*; Seaforth Publishing, Barnsley, 2009. (A hugely detailed account with stress on the naval dimension.)

Hadley, Michael; *Count not the Dead*; McGill-Queen's University Press, Montreal, Kingston and London, 1995.

——; *U-boats against Canada*; McGill-Queen's University Press, Kingston and Montreal, 1985.

Hahn, F.; *Guidebook to the Military Historical Training Centre Exhibition of the Marineschule Mürwik*; Marineschule Press, Flensburg, 1978.

Hansen, H. J.; *The Ships of the German Fleets, 1848–1945*; Hamlyn, London, 1975. Translated from *Die Schiffe der deutschen Flotten 1848–1945*; Stalling, Oldenburg, 1973. (This is a pictorial work providing an introduction to some of the more interesting warships.)

Harlinghausen, C. Harald; *Ein Junge geht zur Kriegsmarine*; Wilhelm Köhler, Minden, 1942.

Harnack, W.; *Die deutschen Zerstörer von 1934 bis 1945*; Koehlers, Herford, 1977. (German destroyers from 1934 to 1945.)

——; *Zerstörer unter deutscher Fagge*; Koehler, Herford, 1978.

Has, Ludwig and Evers, August-Ludwig; *Wilhelmshaven 1853–1945*; Lohse-Eissing, Wilhelmshaven, 1961. (A collection of most interesting and good quality photographs.)

Hering, Robert; 'Chronik der Crew 37A 1937–1987'; produced for limited distribution by the author. (An excellent account of how naval officers were trained.)

Herlin, Hans; *Der letzte Mann von der Doggerbank*; Wilhelm Heyne, Munich, 1979. (About Fritz Kuert, the only survivor of Doggerbank/Speybank). He joined the ship in mid-ocean from the *Charlotte Schliemann*, after the mine laying operation off South Africa. Most of the book deals with his survival, rather than with Doggerbank's role in the cruiser war.)

Herzog, B.; *Die deutschen U-boote 1906–1945*; J. F. Lehmanns, Munich, 1959. (A well-illustrated work about German submarines.)

——; *60 Jahre deutsche U-boote 1906–1966*; J. F. Lehmanns, Munich, 1968. (A well-illustrated book with a vast variety of interesting information – most of it tabulated and easily understood by non-German readers.).

——; *U-boats in Action*; Ian Allan, Shepperton, German edition: *U-Boote im Einsatz 1939–45*; Podzun, Dorbeim, 1970. (This is a most interesting collection of photographs, with captions written in English and German.)

Hessler, G. and others; *The U-boat War in the Atlantic*; HMSO, London, 1989. (Günter Hessler was Dönitz's son-in-law, Shortly after the war he was invited to lead the writing of this three three-volume work for the British Ministry of Defence. It remained confidential until HMSO published it. The work is a wonderful key to understanding the Log of the German U-boat Command and contains some superb charts, all of which is vital for studying the war at sea.)

Hildebrand, Hans; Röhr, Albert and Steinmetz, Hans-Otto; *Die deutschen Kriegsschiffe*; Koehlers Verlagsgesellschaft, Hamburg. (Ten volumes dealing with the period from 1815 to the present day.)

Hirschfeld, Wolfgang; *Das Letzte Boot – Atlantik Farewell*, Universitas, Munich, 1989. (The last journey of *U234*, surrender in the United States and life in prisoner of war camps.)

——; *Feindfahrten*; Neff, Vienna, 1982. (The secret diary of a U-boat radio operator compiled in the radio rooms of operational submarines. A most invaluable insight into the war and probably one of the most significant accounts of the war at sea.)

——; and Brooks, Geoffrey; *Hirschfeld – The Story of a U-boat NCO 1940–1946*; Leo Cooper, London, 1996. (A fascinating English-language edition of Hirschfeld's life in U-boats.)

Hoffmann, Rudolf; *50 Jahre Olympia-Crew*; Hoffmann, Hamburg, 1986. (An excellent history of Crew 1936. Well illustrated.)

Högel, Georg; *Embleme Wappen Malings Deutscher Uboote 1939–1945*; Koehlers, Hamburg, Berlin, and Bonn, 1997. (An excellent work dealing with U-boat emblems, especially those painted on conning towers. Very well illustrated with drawings by the author, who served in U-boats during the war.)

Hümmelchen, G.; *Die deutschen Seeflieger*; J. F. Lehmanns, Munich, 1976. (An account of the Naval Air Arm.)

Hümmelchen, Gerhard; *Handesstörer*; Mercator, Munich, 1960. (Although rather old, this is still the standard reference work on cruiser warfare. It has never been bettered and is invaluable, covering a wide aspect of the raiders' operations.)

Humble, R.; *Hitler's High Seas Fleet*; Ballantine, New York, 1972. (An account of battles fought by German surface ships.)

Hurd, Sir Archibald; *Britain's Merchant Navy*; Odhams, London. (Written during the war, it contains a fair volume of propaganda and wartime inaccuracies, but it provides an excellent insight into the British Merchant Navy.)

Janssen, Jens; *Die Einsamen der Weltmeere*; Pabel, Rastatt. (An account of the last voyage of the blockade-breaker *Ermland* and of *Passat*'s mine laying operations. Janssen is a pen name of Jochen Brennecke.)

Jones, G.; *The Month of the Lost U-boats*; William Kimber, London, 1977. (An account of U-boat losses during May 1943.)

——; *Under Three Flags*; William Kimber, London, 1973. (The story of Nordmark and the armed supply ships of the German Navy. The author served in one after the war.)

Jones, W. A.; *Prisoner of the Kormoran*; Australian Publishing Co., Sydney, 1944. (Cruiser warfare from a prisoner's point of view.)

Jung, Dieter; Abendroth, Arno and Kelling, Norbert; *Anstriche und Tarnanstriche der deutschen Kriegsmarine*; Bernard & Graefe, Munich, 1977. (With English captions.)

Jung, D., Maass, M. and Wenzel, B.; *Tanker und Versorger der deutschen Flotte 1900–1980*; Motorbuch, Stuttgart, 1981. (This excellent book is the standard reference work on the German supply system. Well illustrated with interesting photographs.)

Kähler, Wolfgang; *Schlachtschiff Gneisenau*; Koehlers, Herford, 1979. (A detailed account by the ship's First Gunnery Officer.)

Kahn, David; *Seizing the Enigma: The Race to Break the German U-boat Codes, 1939–45*; Houghton Mifflin, Boston, 1991. (A good comprehensive account.)

Kannapin, N.; *Die Feldpostnummern der deutschen Kriegsmarine 1939–1945*; published privately by the author, October 1974. (There are two volumes dealing with land forces and seagoing units. A list of postal numbers of the German Forces Post Office, published privately by the author in October 1974.)

Keatts, Henry and Farr, George; *Dive into History*; American Merchant Marine Museum Press, New York, 1986. (Well researched with excellent illustrations giving a deep insight into U-boat activity on America's eastern seaboard.)

Kemp, Paul; *The Admiralty Regrets*; Sutton Publishing, Stroud, 1998. (British warship losses of the twentieth century.)

——; *U-boats Destroyed*; Arms and Armour Press, London, 1997. (German submarine losses in both World Wars; well laid out and contains interesting anecdotes, but some of the information has been superseded by research by Axel Niestlé.)

Kennedy, L.; *Pursuit: The Chase and Sinking of the Bismarck*; Collins, London, 1974; Pinnacle, 1975.

Kern, Erich; *Verbrechen am deutschen Volk*; K. W. Schütz; Oldendorf, 1964. (Dealing with war crimes against Germany including several naval incidents.)

Klietmann, Kurt-G.; *Auszeichnungen des deutsches Reiches 1936–1945*; Motorbuch, Stuttgart, 1982. (A well-illustrated account of awards and medals.)

Köhl, Fritz and Rössler, Eberhard; *The Type XXI U-boat*; Conway Maritime Press, London, 1991.

Konstam, Angus and Showell, Jak P. Mallmann; *7th U-boat Flotilla – Dönitz's Atlantic Wolves*; Ian Allan, Hersham, 2003. (Contains many photographs from the German U-boat Museum.)

Koop, Gerhard and Mulitze, Erich; *Die Marine in Wilhelmshaven*; Bernard & Graefe, Koblenz 1987. (Contains a large number of interesting photographs.)

Koop, Gerhard and Schmolke, Klaus-Peter; *Battleships of the Bismarck Class*; Greenhill, London, 1998.

Krancke, Theodor and Brennecke, Jochen; *RRR Das glückhafte Schiff*; Koehlers, Biberach, 1955. (The story of Admiral Scheer written by the ship's commander.)

Kroschel, Günther and Evers, August-Ludwig; *Die deutsche Flotte 1848–1945*; Lohse-Eissing, Wilhelmshaven, 1974. (A collection of interesting photographs from Foto-Drüppel – now WZ Bilddienst. Most useful when identifying ships in old pictures.)

Kühn, Volkmar; *Schnellboote im Einsatz 1939–1945*; Motorbuch, Stuttgart, 1986.

——; *Torpedoboote und Zerstörer im Einsatz 1939–1945*; Motorbuch, Stuttgart, 1983.

Kutzleben, K. von, Schröder, W. and Brennecke, J.; *Minenschiffe 1939–1945*; Koehler, Herford, 1974.

Lakowski, Richard; *Deutsche U-Boote Geheim 1939–1945*; Brandenburgisches Verlagshaus Berlin, 1991. (Contains many interesting photographs.)

Ledebur, Gerhard, Freiherr von; *Die Seemine*; J. F. Lehmanns, Munich, 1977.

Lewin, R.; *Ultra Goes to War*; Hutchinson, London, 1978; McGraw, New York, 1978.

Littlejohn, D. and Dodkins, C. M.; *Orders, Decorations, Medals and Badges of the 3rd Reich*; R. J. Bender, San José, 1967. (Covers virtually all awards of the Third Reich, including naval awards.)

Lohmann, W. and Hildebrand, H. H.; *Die deutsche Kriegsmarine 1939–1945*; Podzun, Dorheim, 1956–64. (This multi-volume work is the standard reference document on the German Navy. There are three volumes: 1 deals mainly with the Naval High Command, Naval Group Commands, the entire High Seas Fleet, the Security Forces and U-boats. 2 has details of important naval operations, Naval Stations for Baltic and North Sea and Naval Forces in occupied countries. There are also other interesting lists. 3 is a brief outline of the careers of the men mentioned in the other two volumes.)

Lüdde-Neurath, W.; *Regierung Dönitz*; MusterSchmidt, Göttingen, 1964. (This book does not deal directly with the German Navy. The author was Dönitz's last adjutant and he describes the last days of the German High Command.)

Lumsden, R. A.; *Collector's Guide to Third Reich Militaria*; Ian Allan, London, 1987.

Lund, P. and Ludham, Harry; *Night of the U-boats*; W. Foulsham, Slough, 1973. (A personal account of convoy SC7, as seen through the eyes of some survivors.)

Macintyre, D.; *U-boat Killer*; Weidenfeld & Nicolson, London, 1956; Norton, New York, 1956.

Mattes, Klaus; *Die Seehunde*; Koehler/Mittler, Hamburg, Berlin, and Bonn, 1997. (A most interesting books dealing with many aspects of these two-man midget submarines.)

McCartney, Innes; *Lost Patrols – Submarine Wrecks of the English Channel*; Periscope Publishing, Penzance, 2003. (The author visited many of the wrecks and has shown that considerable amounts of what historians have written cannot be reliable because the wrecks are not where people have claimed them to be. An essential volume for anyone studying the war at sea.)

Meiser, Hans; *Gescheiterte Friedens-Initiativen 1939–1945*; Grabert, Tübingen, 2004. (Dealing with failed German peace initiatives, most of which are hardly known.)

Meister, Jürg; *Der Seekrieg in den osteuropäischen Gewässern 1941–1945*; J. F. Lehmanns, Munich, 1958. (Includes details of cruiser warfare in Arctic waters.)

Mewissen, P.; *Blockadebrecher*; Pabel, Rastatt.

Middlebrook, M.; *Convoy*; Allen Lane, London, 1977; Morrow, New York, 1977. (A personal account of the battle for convoys SC122 and HX229, as seen through the eyes of some survivors.)

Millington Drake, Sir Eugene; *The Drama of the Graf Spee and the Battle of the Plate*; Peter Davis, London, 1964.

Mohr, Ulrich; *Atlantis*; Oberkommando der Kriegsmarine, 1942. (Souvenir photograph album of *Atlantis*'s cruise produced for private distribution and now very rare.)

Mohr, Ulrich and Sellwood, A. V.; *Atlantis*; Werner Laurie, London, 1955. (Dr. Mohr was the commander's adjutant.)

Mollo, A.; *German Uniforms of World War Two*; Macdonald and Jane's, London, 1976; Hippocrene, New York, 1976. (Deals with German uniforms and insignia in chronological order of introduction.)

——; *Naval, Marine and Air Force Uniforms of WW2*; Blandford Press, London, 1975. (Covers the basic naval uniforms of most countries. Includes only a few Kriegsmarine uniforms, but there are some variations which are not described in other books. Colour illustrations.)

Moore, Captain Arthur R.; *A Careless Word… A Needless Sinking*; American Merchant Marine Museum, Maine, 1983. (A detailed and well illustrated account of ships lost during the war.)

Morison, Samuel Eliot; *History of United States Naval Operations in World War II*; Little, Brown and Company, Boston. (A multi-volume official history of the war at sea. Some of the information is rather one-sided and parts are also somewhat dubious.)

Muggenthaler, August Karl; *German Raiders of World War Two*; Robert Hale, London, 1978; Prentice Hall, New York, 1978. (A detailed account dealing with auxiliary cruisers.)

Müllenheim-Rechberg, Baron Burkhard von; *Battleship Bismarck*; Bodley Head, London, 1981; and The United States Naval Institute, 1980. (A most detailed account by *Bismarck*'s senior surviving officer.)

Mulligan, Timothy P.; *Lone Wolf; The Life and Death of U-boat Ace Werner Henke*; Praeger, Connecticut and London, 1993. (A well-researched book.)

——; *Neither Sharks nor Wolves*; Naval Institute Press, Annapolis, 1999. (A book about the men of the Germany's U-boat arm. Much of the book is based on a questionnaire sent out by the author to veterans through the German U-boat Museum.)

Neitzel, Sönke; *Die deutschen Ubootbunker und Bunkerwerften*; Bernard Graefe, Koblenz, 1991. (A most worthwhile book about U-boat bunkers packed with information and well illustrated.)

Nesbit, Roy Conyers; *The Battle of the Atlantic*; Sutton Publishing, Stroud, 2002. (An interesting and well-written volume with many good illustrations.)

——; *Coastal Command in Action 1939–1945*; Sutton Publishing, Stroud, 1997. (A well well-illustrated and useful volume.)

Niestlé, Axel; *German U-boat Losses during World War II*, Greenhill Books, London, 1998. (Although already slightly out of date as a result of more research done by the author, this book still contains the most current information regarding U-boat losses.)

Nöldeke, Hartmut and Hartmann, Volker; *Der Sanitätsdienst in der deutschen Flotte im Zweiten Weltkrieg*; Mittler, Hamburg, 1999.

OKM (Supreme Naval Command); *Bekleidungs und Anzugsbestimmungen für die Kriegsmarine*; Berlin, 1935; reprinted Showell, Jak P. Mallmann, 1979. (The official dress regulations of the German Navy.)

OKM; *Rangliste der Deutschen Kriegsmarine*; Mittler & Sohn, published annually, Berlin.

Ostertag, Reinhard; *Deutsche Minensucher 80Jahre Seeminenabwehr*; Koehlers, Herford, 1987.

Pargeter, C. J.; *'Hipper' Class Heavy Cruisers*; Ian Allan, London, 1982. (An excellent and well well-illustrated book.)

Paterson, Lawrence; *U-boat War Patrol*; Greenhill Books, London and Stackpole Books, Pennsylvania, 2004. (Based on photographs found in Brest and the war log of *U564* under Teddy Suhren.)

——; *U-boat Combat Missions*; Barnes and Noble, New York, 2007. (Contains first-hand accounts and many photographs from the German U-boat Museum.)

——; *Dönitz's Last Gamble*; Seaforth Publishing, Barnsley, 2008. (U-boats in coastal European waters in the latter stages of the war.)

Peillard, L.; *U-boats to the Rescue*; Jonathan Cape, London, 1963; published in the USA as *The Laconia Affair*; Putnam, New York, 1963. (The story of the *Laconia* rescue.)

Peter, K.; *Der Untergang der Niobe. Was geschah im Fehmarn Belt?*; Koehlers, Herford, 1976. (The sinking of the sail training ship *Niobe*.)

Pfefferle, Ernst (Editor.); *Kammeraden zur See*; Ernst Pfefferle, Altmannstein, from 1985. (At least fifteen volumes have been published since 1985. A most interesting series with many personal recollections.)

Philpott, Bryan; *German Marine Aircraft*; Patrick Stephens, Cambridge, 1981. (An album of Bundesarchiv photographs.)

Plottke, Herbert; *Fächer Loos*; Podzun-Pallas, Wölfersheim-Berstadt. (The story of *U172*.)

Pope, Dudley; *73 North*; Weidenfeld & Nicolson, London, 1958. (About the Battle of the Barents Sea.)

Porten, E. P. von der; *The German Navy in World War II*; Arthur Barker, London, 1970. (An interesting outline of the German Navy's activities during the war. The author lives in America and his book follows the classical Allied viewpoint.)

——; *Pictorial History of the German Navy in World War II*; Thomas Y. Crowell, New York, 1976. (An excellent book spoilt by poor reproduction of photographs.)

Potter, J. P.; *Fiasco*; Heinemann, London, 1970; Stein & Day, New York, 1970. (The story of the 'Channel Dash', when German battleships left the French bases and sailed through the English Channel to Germany and Norway.)

Powell, Michael; *Die Schicksalsfahrt der Graf Spee*; Heyne, Munich, 1976.

Prager, Hans-Georg; *Panzerschiff Deutschland/Schwerer Kreuzer Lützow*; Koehlers, Herford, 1981. (A detailed account of the ship, her operations and her crew. Well illustrated with many interesting photographs, diagrams and maps. The author served aboard her.)

Preston, Anthony; *U-boats*; Arms and Armour Press, London, 1978. (Excellent photographs.)

Price, A.; *Aircraft versus Submarines*; William Kimber, London, 1973; Naval Institute Press, Annapolis, 1974. (This is an excellent and most interesting volume dealing with the war against submarines.)

Prochnow, O.; *Deutsche Kriegsschiffe in zwei Jahrhunderten*; Ernst Gerdes, Preetz/Holstein, 1966. (This is a good series of small, pocket pocket-size books providing the basic mechanical details and the fate of German warships.) The following volumes are available: I: *Schlachtschiffe, Schlachtkreuzer, Flugzeugtrager*. II: *Leichte und Schwere Kreuzer*. III: *Torpedoboote und Zerstörer*. IV: *Unterseeboote*.

Profile Publications, Windsor, England. (This publisher has produced several small, inexpensive, but excellent books including *U107*, *Prinz Eugen* and *Admiral Graf Spee*.)

Raeder, E.; *My Life*; US Naval Institute, 1960. Translated from *Mein Leben*. Schild, Munich, 1956.

——; *Struggle for the Sea*; William Kimber, London, 1959. (Raeder's account of the war at sea.)

Range, C.; *Die Ritterkreuzträger der Marine*; Motorbuch, Stuttgart, 1974. (There is a brief history of the Iron Cross, followed by a photograph of almost every recipient of the Knight's Cross, together with brief biographical details.)

Rasenack, F. W.; *Panzerschiff Admiral Graf Spee*; Wilhelm Heyne, Munich, 1981.

Richter, Hanns J. and Holz, Wolf-Dieter; *Deckname Koralle*; Heinrich Jung, Meiningen, 2002. (An interesting book, but with only a few illustrations, about the U-boat cum naval headquarters near Berlin.)

Robertson, T.; *The Golden Horseshoe*; Evans, London, 1966. (The story of Otto Kretschmer written shortly after the war when the finding of information was still most difficult.)

Rogge, B. and Frank, W.; *Under Ten Flags*; Weidenfeld & Nicolson, London, 1957. Translated from *Schiff 16*, Heyne. (The story of the auxiliary cruiser *Atlantis* as told by her commander to Wolfgang Frank.)

Röhr, A.; *Deutsche Marinechronik*; Stalling, Oldenburg, 1974. (An interesting volume, which lists naval historical events in chronological order.)

Rohwer, J. and Hümmelchen, G.; *Chronology of the War at Sea*; Ian Allan, Shepperton, 1974; Arco, New York, 1975. Translated from *Chronik des Seekrieges 1939–45*; Stalling, Oldenburg, 1968. Re-printed as fully revised edition in 2005 by Chatham Publishing, London.

Rohwer, J. and Jacobsen, H. A.; *Decisive Battles of World War II*; Andre Deutsch, London, 1965. Translated from *Entscheidungsschachten des 2. Weltkrieges*; Bernard & Graefe, Frankfurt, 1960. (An account, from the German viewpoint, of decisive battles during the Second World War.)

Rohwer, J.; *Die U-Boot-Erfolge der Achsenmächte*; J. F. Lehmanns, Munich, 1968. Revised and re-printed in English as *Axis Submarine Successes of World War Two*; revised edition in 1999 by Greenhill Books, London, under the new title of *Axis Submarine Successes of World War Two*. (This excellent book consists of a table that lists the successes of Axis Powers' submarines in chronological order. The table also lists interesting additional material such as times, positions, how sunk, ship types, etc. There are also good indexes.)

——; *Eine Chronik in Bildern*; Stalling, Oldenburg, 1962. (There are numerous pages of explanatory text and an interesting collection of photographs.)

——; *The Critical Convoy Battles of 1943*; Ian Allan, Shepperton, 1977. Translated from *Geleitzugschlachten im März 1943*; Motorbuch, Stuttgart, 1975. (This is an excellent, detailed account of the battle for convoys SC122 and HX229. There is a good bibliography and the text is supported by photos, maps and tables. The author also provides an interesting introduction to the U-boat war, covering important aspects from the beginning of the war until 1943. These are not eye-witness accounts, instead, the author has consulted many British, American and German documents and he has described what went on during these battles.)

Rosignoli, Guido; *Naval and Marine Badges and Insignia*; Blandford, Poole, 1980.

Roskill, Captain S. W.; *The Secret Capture*; Collins, London, 1959; Collins, New York, 1959. (The story of how *U110* was captured.)

——; *The War at Sea*; 4 vols, HMSO, London, 1954, reprinted 1976. (The official history of the war at sea, 1939 to 1945. Somewhat one-sided and parts of it appear to be rather questionable.)

Rössler, E.; *Die deutschen Uboote und ihre Werften*; Bernard & Graefe, Koblenz, 1979.

——; *Geschichte des deutschen Ubootbaus*; J. F. Lehmanns, Munich, 1975. (An excellent history of German submarine development from the first U-boat built in 1850 to the boats of the present day. The book is illustrated with photos and with many excellent plans, many drawn by Fritz Köhl.)

——; *U-Bootstyp XXI; U-boostyp XXIII*; J. F. Lehmanns, Munich, 1967. (These two books provide an interesting study of the early electro-submarines.)

Ruge, Friedrich; *Sea Warfare 1939–45, A German Viewpoint*; Cassell, London, 1957; translation of *Der Seekrieg 1939–1945*, Koehler, Stuttgart, 1962 and published in the United States as *Der Seekrieg (The German Navy's Story, 1939–45)*, Naval Institute Press, Annapolis, 1957. (Ruge was an officer in the Kriegsmarine.)

Rust, Eric; *Naval Officers under Hitler*; Praeger, 1991. (An interesting volume.)

Saint-Loup; *Die Geisterschiffe Hitlers*; Delius Verlag and Bastei Lübbe, 1978. (The story of sailing ships which were used by the Abwehr rather than the Navy to land agents in enemy controlled territory.)

Salewski, M.; *Die deutsche Seekriegsleitung 1939–1945*; Bernard & Graefe, Frankfurt, 1970.

Savas, Theodore (ed.); *Hunt and Kill*; Savas Beatie, New York, 2004. (Essays by a variety of authors about the history of *U505* – the U-boat in the Science and Industry Museum in USA.)

Schaeffer, H.; *U-boat 977*; William Kimber, London, 1952. (The career of *U977* told by her commander, including her escape to Argentina after the war. Some of the information is questionable.)

Schmalenbach, Paul; *Die deutschen Hilfskreuzer*; Stalling, Oldenburg and Hamburg, 1977. (This is a pictorial record of German auxiliary cruisers from 1895 to 1945, the best photographs being from the two world wars.)

——; *Kreuzer Prinz Eugen unter drei Flaggen*; Koehlers, Herford, 1978.

Schmeelke, Michael; *Alarm Küste*; Podzun-Pallas, Wölfersheim-Berstadt.

Schmelzkopf, Reinhard; *Die deutsche Handelsschiffahrt 1919 – 1939*; Stalling, Oldenburg and Hamburg. (A two-volume chronology about the development of the German merchant navy between the two wars.)

Schmoeckel, Helmut; *Menchlichkeit im Seekrieg?*; Mittler und Sohn, Herford, 1987.

Schoenfeld, Max; *Stalking the U-boat*; Smithsonian Institution Press, Washington and London, 1995. (Deals with the USAAF offensive anti-submarine operations of the Second World War Two.)

Schofield, B. B.; *Loss of the Bismarck*; Ian Allan, Shepperton, 1977.

Schultz, Willy; *Kreuzer Leipzig*; Motorbuch Verlag, Stuttgart.

Schultze-Rhonhof, Gerd; *Der Krieg der viele Väter hatte*; Olzog, 2003. (The author retired as Generalmajor in the German Army before writing this startling book about significant events which led up to the beginning of the Second World War.)

Schwandtke, Karl-Heinz; *Deutschland Handelsschiffe*; Stalling, Oldenburg and Hamburg. (Details of German merchant ships at the start of the war with information about ships captured during the conflict. Also included are vessels that were not completed, and detailed line drawings.)

Seki, Eiji; *Mrs. Ferguson's Tea-Set*; Global Oriental, Folkestone, 2007. (This deals with one of the major events of the Second World War – when men from auxiliary cruiser *Atlantis* boarded the SS *Automedon* and captured vitally important secret documents which led directly to the Japanese attack on Pearl Harbor.)

Showell, Jak P. Mallmann; *Enigma U-boats – Breaking the Code*; Ian Allan, Shepperton, 2000. (Deals with U-boats and some surface ships which that were boarded by the Allies with a view of capturing radio code secrets.)

——; *German Naval Code Breakers*; Ian Allan, Hersham, 2003. (The story of the German Radio Monitoring Service under Heinz Bonatz.)

——; *The German Navy Handbook*; Sutton Publishing, Stroud, 1999. Published in Germany as *Kriegsmarine 1939–1945*; Motorbuch Verlag, Stuttgart, 2000. (Deals with the German Navy, rather than the war.)

——; *Germania International*; journal of the German Navy Study Group. Now out of print.

——; *Hitler's U-boat Bases*; Sutton Publishing, Stroud, 2002 and 2007. Published in Germany as *Deutsche U-Boot-Stützpunkte und Bunkeranlagen*; Motorbuch Verlag, Stuttgart, 2002. (Written as a book about U-boat bunkers rather than bases.)

——; *The U-boat Archive Series*; Military Press, Milton Keynes, see www.militarypress.co.uk. (Reprints of wartime secret documents essential for studying the war at sea. Produced by the German U-boat Museum – formerly U-boat Archive – in conjunction with other institutions. The following volumes have been published, vols 1–4 have been reprinted from the British Secret Anti-Submarine Reports originally compiled the Anti-Submarine Division of the Naval Staff: *What Britain Knew and Wanted to Know About U-boats*; *Weapons Used Against U-boats*; *The British Monthly Countermeasures Reviews*; *The British Monthly U-boat Offensive Reviews*; *Extracts from the US Strategic Bombing Survey of the German U-boat Industry*; '*The U-boat Archive' Early Journals Reprinted* (1998–2000); *Report on U570* see Andrews, Terry; *Operation 'Cabal': The Delivery of German U-boats to Russia 1945–46*; *U-boat Ports in Germany* (Reprinted from Naval Intelligence Geographical Handbook Series); *Unknown, Hidden and Forgotten History of Germany 1918–1948*.

——; *The U-boat Century*; Chatham, London, 2006. (German submarine warfare 1906–2006, illustrated with many photographs.)

——; *U-boat Command and the Battle of the Atlantic*; Conway Maritime Press, London, 1989; Vanwell, Ontario, 1989. (A detailed history based on the U-boat Command's war diary.)

——; *U-boat Commanders and their Crews*; Crowood Press, Marlborough, 1998. Published in Germany as *Die U-Boot-Waffe – Kommandanten und Besatzungen*; Motorbuch Verlag, Stuttgart, 2001. (Includes an alphabetical list of U-boat commanders, a chart of when U-boats were in service and a list of boats and their commanders. Well illustrated.)

——; *U-boat Warfare – The Evolution of the Wolf Pack*; Ian Allan, Hersham, 2002.

——; *U-boats in Camera*; Sutton Publishing, Stroud, 1999. (A pictorial work dealing with U-boats during the training period. Many of the photos had not been published before.)

——; *U-boats under the Swastika*; Ian Allan, Shepperton, 1973; Arco, New York, 1974. (An introduction to German submarines, 1935 to 1945, illustrated with maps, plans and well over 150 photos, many of which have not been published elsewhere. The work deals with a brief history up to the start of the war, with radar, boat types, administration of the U-boat arm, captured U-boats, the men, and there is a table of technical data plus other sections.)

——; *U-boats under the Swastika*; Ian Allan, London 1987. (A second edition with different photos and new text of the above-mentioned title.)

——; *U-boats at War – Landings on Hostile Shores*; Ian Allan, London and US Institute Press, Annapolis, 2000. Published in Germany as *Deutsche U-Boote an feindlichen Küsten 1939–1945*; Motorbuch Verlag, Stuttgart, 2002. (Deals with U-boats which that came close to coasts as well as some landings from surface ships.) Published in Germany as *Deutsche U-Boote an feindlichen Küsten 1939–1945*, Motorbuch Verlag, Stuttgart, 2002.

——; *Wolfpacks at War*; Produced by Compendium Publishing for Ian Allan, London, 2002. (Contains many photos and first-hand accounts.)

——; *Germania International*; Journal of the German Navy Study Group. Now out of print.

Smith, Constance Babington; *Evidence in Camera*; David & Charles, Newton Abbot, 1974. (The story of the Royal Air Force's Photographic Reconnaissance Unit, with an interesting insight into how the major German warships were tracked and consequently attacked.)

Sorge, Siegfried; *Der Marineoffizier als Führer und Erzieher*; ES. Mittler, Berlin, 1937.

Stahl, Peter; *Kriegsmarine Uniforms, Insignia, Daggers & Medals of the German Navy 1935–1945*; Die Wehrmacht, Stanford, (California), 1972. (A well-illustrated book.)

Stark, Hans; *Marineunteroffizierschule*; Naval Officers' School; Plön, 1974.

Sudholt, Gerd; *UN-Gesühnt*; Druffel Verlag, Berg, 1998. (Dealing with Anglo-American war crimes committed against Germans.)

Syrett, David; *The Defeat of the Wolf Packs*; South Carolina Press, Columbia, 1994.

——; *The Battle of the Atlantic and Signals Intelligence: U-boat Situations and Trends, 1941 – 1945*; The Naval Records Society/Ashgate, Aldershot and Vermont, 1998.

Taylor, J. C.; *German Warships of World War II*; Ian Allan, Shepperton, 1966; Doubleday, New York, 1968.

Terraine, John; *Business in Great Waters*; Leo Cooper, London, 1989.

Thomas, David A.; *The Atlantic Star 1939–45*; W. H. Allen, London, 1990.

Tischer, Heinz; *Die Abendteuer des letzten Kapers*; Published privately in Hamburg, 1983. (Contains some 200 photos taken aboard auxiliary cruiser *Thor*.)

Topp, Erich; *Fackeln über dem Atlantik*; Ullstein, Berlin, 1993. (An interesting book by one of the top U-boat commanders, although he seems to use different measuring sticks when describing similar activities in Germany and in Allied countries. So far it has been impossible to find documentary evidence for some of the actions the author has described.)

Trevor-Roper, H.; *Hitler's War Directives 1939–1945*; Sidgwick & Jackson, London, 1964. (One would think that the name 'Hitler' in the title would not require the years at the end! But still a good book, giving an insight into the higher command.)

Urbanke, Axel; *U-Boot im Focus*; Luftfahrtverlag, Bad Zwischenahn, 2007. (Axel-Urbanke@Luftfahrtverlag-Start.de; (The text for this series is in German and English and each volume contains a collection of interesting and high-quality photographs.)

US Naval Intelligence; *German Naval Vessels of World War Two*; Greenhill, London, 1993. (An excellent book for identifying warships. It was originally carried on board ships at sea for identifying vessels they might meet.)

Verband Deutscher Ubootsfahrer; *Schaltung Küste*; (Journal of the German Submariners' Association).

Waddington, C. H.; *OR in WW2*; Paul Hick, London, 1973. (Operational Research against the U-boat during the Second World War. This is a most interesting, but also highly technical account.)

Wagner, Gerbard (ed.); *Lagevorträge des Oberbefehlshabers der Kriegsmarine vor Hitler*; J. F. Lehmanns, Munich, 1972. (Translated as *Fuehrer Conferences on Naval Affairs*; Greenhill, London, reprinted with new introduction 1990, but originally the English English-language edition was published before the German version.)

Waters, J. M.; *Bloody Winter*; Van Nostrand Reinhold, London and New York, 1967. (An interesting account of the battles in the Atlantic during the winter of 1942/43.)

Watson-Watt, Sir R.; *Three Steps to Victory*; Odhams, London, 1957. (The development of British radar and 'similar' inventions.)

Watts, A. J.; *Axis Submarines*; Macdonald and Jane's, London, 1977; Argo, New York, 1977. (Technical data, losses and some brief comments make up this small, inexpensive volume. It is illustrated with an excellent collection of interesting photographs.)

——; *The Loss of the Scharnhorst*; Ian Allan, Shepperton, 1970; Naval Institute Press, Annapolis, 1971. (A detailed account, together with information of the ship's movements, dealing with the sinking of the famous battlecruiser. Compiled from action reports and from contemporary documents, it covers convoy JW55B, technical data, etc.)

——; *The U-boat Hunters*; Macdonald and Jane's, London, 1976. (An excellent account of the weapons used to combat U-boats, including ships, aeroplanes and small items such as depth charges. The author describes the various phases of the war as well as the techniques used to fight U-boats.)

Weiham, Michael; *Kampfschwimmer*; Motorbuch Stuttgart, 1997.

Werner, H. A.; *Iron Coffins*; Arthur Barker, London, 1970; Holt, New York, 1969. German edition as: *Die eisernen Särge*; Hoffmann und Campe, Hamburg, 1970. (A personal account of the German U-boat battles of the Second World War. It has been impossible to find documentary evidence for some of the things described in the book, but it still provides an interesting, atmospheric picture.)

Weyher, Kurt and Ehrlich, Hans-Jürgen; *Vagabunden auf See*; Katzmann, Tübingen, 1953. (The story of the auxiliary cruiser *Orion* by her commander.)

Whitley, M. J.; *Destroyer! German Destroyers in World War II*; Arms and Armour Press, London, 1983.

——; *German Cruisers of World War Two*; Arms and Armour Press, London, 1985. (An excellent account, well-illustrated with plans and photographs.)

——; *German Capital Ships of World War Two*; Arms and Armour, London, 1989; and Cassell, London, 2000. (A well well-illustrated, well well-researched and well-written book.)

——; *German Coastal Forces of World War Two*; Arms and Armour Press, London, 1992. Published in Germany as *Deutsche Seestreitkräfte 1939–1945*; Motorbuch Verlag, Stuttgart, 1995. (An interesting book dealing with coastal activities in European waters.)

Will, H. Peter; *Von der Befehlsstelle Nord zur Admiral-Armin-Zimmermann-Kaserne*; H.Peter Will and Heiber Druck & Verlag, Schortens. (This privately published study is most useful to anyone studying the Navy in Wilhelmshaven because it includes details of the U-boat Command headquarters towards the beginning of the war.)

Williamson, Gordon; *The Iron Cross*; Blandford, Poole, 1984. (An excellent and well-illustrated account.)

——; *Knights of the Iron Cross*; Blandford, Poole 1987. (An excellent follow-on from the title written with Paviovik, below.)

——; *Torpedoes Los – The fascinating world of U-boat Collectibles*; Bender Publishing, San José, 2006. (Well illustrated with colour photographs as well as war-time action pictures, covering the entire spectrum likely to be of interest to collectors or people wanting to identify items in old photos.)

——; *Wolf Pack – The Story of the U-boat in World War II*; Osprey, Oxford, 2005.

——; and Paviovik, Darko; *U-boat Crews 1914–1945*: Osprey, London, 1995. (A most interesting book with excellent illustrations.)

Winterbotham, F. W.; *The Ultra Secret*; Weidenfeld and Nicolson, London, 1974; Harper Row, New York, 1974. (The story of breaking German secret codes at Bletchley Park by the Chief of the Air Department of the Secret Intelligence Service 1930–1945.)

Winton, John; *Ultra at Sea*; Leo Cooper, London, 1988. (About breaking the U-boat radio codes.)

Wise, James E.; *U505 – The Final Journey*; Naval Institute Press, Annapolis, 2005. (An interesting volume about the capture and setting up the boat in the Science and Industry Museum in Chicago.)

Witthöft, H. J.; *Lexikon zur deutschen Marinegeschichte*; 2 vols, Koehlers, Herford, 1977. Volume 1: A to M. Volume 2: N to Z. (This is an excellent encyclopaedia of German naval history.)

Woodward, David; *The Secret Raiders*; William Kimber, London, 1955. (An account of German auxiliary cruisers.)

Zienert, J.; *Unsere Marineuniform*; Helmuth Gerhard Schulz, Hamburg, 1970. (An interesting account of the history of German naval uniforms from the beginning to the present day. Well illustrated.)

218

INDEX

secret vote, 204
Seeluftstreitktäfte, 18
selection to join navy, 14
shipbuilding commission, 45
Shoeburyness, 31, 202
shoot survivors, 203
short-range attacks, 35
Siberian Sea Passage, 129
sonar, see asdic
Spitzbergen, 115
Stalingrad, Battle of, 49
stamp, with U-boat from Hela, 54
Submarine Defence School, 35
Submarine Development Bureau, 14, 19
submarine tracking room (London), 206
Supreme Naval Command, 36, 67
surface attacks, 35
surrender, machine, 203
swearing-in ceremony, 71

T5, see Zaunkönig,
Task Forces, 93
Thiele, Task Force, 120
three front war programme, 68, 105
Tirpitz's dream, 35
TMA, TMB, TMC, see torpedo mines
torpedo, British acoustic first kill, 53, 204
torpedo, acoustic, see also Zaunkönig (T5), 46, 52
torpedo aimer, 41
torpedo contact pistol, 34
torpedo firing, 34
torpedo G5ut, 53
torpedo G7a, 31, 34
torpedo G7e, 31, 52
torpedo G7v, 34
torpedo G7ut, 53
Torpedoerprobungskommando (TEK), 34
torpedo, Ingolin propelled, 53
torpedo mines, 31
torpedo safety mechanisms, 33, 34
Torpedoversuchsanstalt (TVA), 34

U-Bootsamt, 36
U-cruisers, 36

Varel, 68
Versailles, Treaty of, 11
Versuchskommando, 204
vote, secret, 204

Weddigen, U-Flotilla, 21
Weserübung, Operation, 89
Westerplatte, 126
Wilhelmshaven, 8, 10, 22, 63, 68, 72, 106
wolf-pack tactics, 36, 150

X-craft, 108, 204
X-Plan, 25

Y-Plan, 25
Yalta Conference, 44

Z-Plan, 25
Zaunkönig (T5), 41
zwerge, small minesweepers, 30

INDEX OF PERSONS

Adalbert of Prussia, Prince, 8
Ambrosius, KL Wilhelm, 67, 89
Arnauld de la Periére, VA Lother von, 83
Asmus, KS Joachim, 99

Bachmann, KL Günther, 110
Backenköhler, Adm, Otto, 59, 196
Bartels, KK Hans, 30, 193, 196
Barten, KL Wolfgang, 67
Bassenge, KK Fritz, 58, 67, 127
Bastian, Adm Max, 57, 196
Bätge, KK Niels, 110
Bauer, KL Ernst, 129
Bauer, Hermann, 66
Bauer, KL Max-Hermann, 36
Bauer, Wilhelm, 8
Beatty, Adm Sir David, Earl of, 17
Bechtolsheim (Mauchenheim), KS Theodor, Freiherr von, 95
Beduhn, KL Heinz, 89
Behncke, Adm Paul, 56, 196
Behrens, Udo, 66, 89
Berger, KS Fritz, 67, 94, 95, 110, 196
Berger, von, 95
Berger, KS Walter, 89
Betzendahl, FK Rudolf, 97
Beucke, KL Heins-Ehler, 60, 106
Bey, KA Erich, 58, 93, 94, 95, 110, 196
Bieling, KL Axel, 110
Biesterfeld, Horst, 117
Bigalk, KK Gerhard, 203
Birnbacher, KL Heinz, 89
Bleichrodt, Heinrich 'Ajax', 134, 202
Blessingh, KL, Axel von, 58
Blöse, KL Hans, 110
Bock, Adolf, 189
Boehm, Adm Hermann, 27, 57, 64, 81, 92, 196
Bogen, KL Eberhard von, 60
Böhme, KK Friedrich, 89
Böhmig, KS Gerhardt, 59, 67, 89, 117
Bonatz, OL Heinz, 58
Bonte, KS Friedrich, 93, 94, 96, 127, 196
Brandi, FK Albrecht, 195, 196
BriII, KK Karl, 89
Brinkmann, VA Helmuth, 110, 122, 196
Brockerhoff, LS, 185
Brocksien, KS Ulrich, 91, 97, 130
Bromme (Brommy), Adm Rudolf; 8
Bucholz, FK Dr Walter, 107
Bütow, KL Hans, 57, 96
Burchardi, Adm Theodor, 65, 196
Burkart, KL Franz, 110
Bürkner, KK Leopold, 58
Busse, KL Bernhard, 60

Canaris, Adm Wilhelm, 57, 196
Carls, GA Rolf, 48, 49, 57, 58, 68, 196
Casberg, Paul, 187
Chamberlain, Neville, 201
Chatterton, John, 53
Ciliax, Adm Otto, 81, 93, 108, 110, 112, 196
Cohausz, KL Hans, 89, 105
Conrady, KL Heinz-Dietrich von, 58
Cornelius, Prof B A, 32
Cremer, KL Peter, 106, 197

Dau, KL RoIf, 67
Davidson, KL Hans von, 59
Deecke, KL Jürgen, 66, 89
Densch, Adm Hermann, 27, 64, 197
Detmers,FK Theodor, 59, 67, 97, 130
Dobratz, KS Kurt, 106
Dönitz, Grosssdm Karl, 21, 27, 32, 36, 39, 41, 42, 45, 46, 49, 54, 61, 64, 67, 105, 123, 170, 184, 187, 197, 203, 204
Dommes, KL Wilhelm, 159
Dresky, KL Hans-Wilhelm von, 66
DuIm, Commodore J. F. van, 51
Duppel, OL Martin, 54
Düvelius, KL Hellmuth, 110

Eckermann, OL Hans, 58
Eckhardt, Werner, 122
Ehrich, OL Heinz, 190
Eichain, KL Karl Daublesky von, 66, 106
Engelhardt, KL Conrad, 60
Erdmann, FK Heinrich, 110
Erdmenger, KS Hans, 59, 67, 89, 95
Ewerth, KK Klaus, 21, 108
Eyssen, VA Robert, 97, 130 , 197

Fanger, KS Paul, 58
Fein, KS Otto, 110, 112
Feldt, KK Klaus, 110
Fischel, Adm Hermann von, 64, 91, 197
Fischer, KL Heinz, 61
Flister, KL Siegfried, 60
Fock, Gorch, 134
Foerster, KL Kurt, 89
Foerster, VA Richard, 58
Förschner, FK Jak, 89
Förste, KS Erich, 111
Förster, KL Hugo, 59
Forstmann, KL Gustav, 89
Forstmann, Walter, 89
Frahm, KL Peter, 66
Franken, KL Wilhelm, 107
Franz, KK Hans, 32
Franz, KL Johannes, 66, 89
Frauenheim,, KL Fritz, 66
Freiwald, KL Kurt, 21, 61, 197
Frerichs, KL Franz, 59
Freymadl, KL Max, 58
Fricke, KS Kurt, 57
Friedeburg, GA Hans-Georg von, 24, 50, 105, 106, 198
Friedrichs, KK Herbert, 58, 67, 89
Fröhlich, KL Wilhelm, 66
Fuchs, Adm Werner, 25
Fuhrke, KL Manfred, 58, 60

Gabler, Prof Ulrich, 43, 52
Gadow, FK Hans-Joachim, 94
Gagern, Ernst Freiherr von, 56
Gartzen, KL Wirich von, 110
Geisse, KL Hans, 57
Geissler, Generalmajor, 18
Gelhaar, KL Alexander, 67
Gerlach, KS Heinrich, 95
Gerlach, KS Horst, 99
Gerstung, KL Lutz, 67
Giessler, KS Hans-Henrich, 53, 126
Gilardone, KL Hans, 36
Gladisch, Adm Walter, 57

INDEX OF SHIPS

FOLLOWING PAGE The torpedo-boat *Möwe* or *Kondor* follows the wake.